WITHDRAWN FROM
THE LIBRARY

UNIVERSITY OF
WINCHESTER

0
0

AUTH
TITL
ACCE

D0321720

ADDISON

THE FREEHOLDER

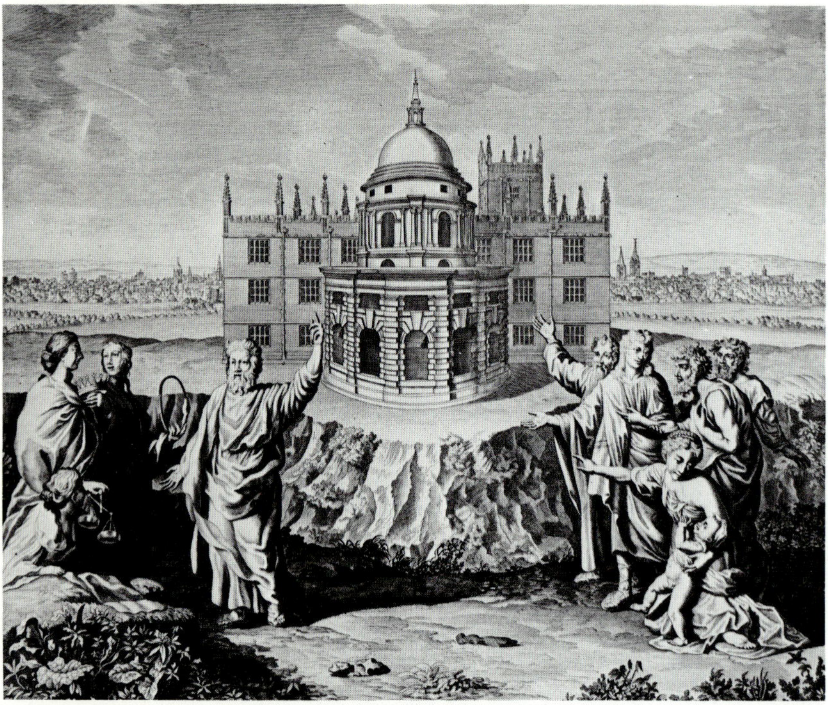

The Oxford University Almanack for 1716

JOSEPH ADDISON

THE FREEHOLDER

Edited with an Introduction and Notes by

JAMES LEHENY

CLARENDON PRESS · OXFORD

1979

Oxford University Press, Walton Street, Oxford OX2 6DP

OXFORD LONDON GLASGOW
NEW YORK TORONTO MELBOURNE WELLINGTON
KUALA LUMPUR SINGAPORE JAKARTA HONG KONG TOKYO
DELHI BOMBAY CALCUTTA MADRAS KARACHI
NAIROBI DAR ES SALAM CAPE TOWN

Published in the United States by
Oxford University Press, New York

© *Oxford University Press* 1979

All rights reserved. No part of this publication may be reproduced, stored in a retrieval system, or transmitted, in any form or by any means, electronic, mechanical, photocopying, recording, or otherwise, without the prior permission of Oxford University Press

British Library Cataloguing in Publication Data

Addison, Joseph
Addison, 'The freeholder'.
1. Great Britain—Politics and government—1714–1727
I. Leheny, James II. 'Freeholder, The'
320.9'42'071 DA498 78–41130

ISBN 0–19–812494–5

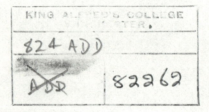

KING ALFRED'S COLLEGE
WINCHESTER.
824 ADD
~~ADD~~ 82262

Printed in Great Britain by
William Clowes & Sons Limited, Beccles and London

PREFACE

THE best description of Addison's *Freeholder* essays was his own: 'They are indeed most of them Essays upon Government, but with a View to the present Situation of Affairs in Great Britain . . . if they have the good Fortune to live longer than Works of this Nature generally do, future Readers may see, in them, the Complexion of the Times in which they were written' (*F.* 55). These essays have survived partly because they are the minor work of a major essayist and partly because Addison played a more substantial role in the politics of his time than most English authors. A shrewd observer and experienced politician, Addison describes 'the Complexion of the Times' in interesting ways, combining his perceptions, prejudices, and wit to create some essays as fine as any he wrote. Yet no one would argue that the whole periodical deserves a new edition solely for its literary merits. Because these essays concern significant events in an important stage of party politics in British history, they are a good resource for students of early Georgian society and politics. Like the political work of Swift, Steele, and Defoe, Addison's *Freeholder* essays offer students texts which are usually more lively, more involved, and more interesting than arid histories. In preparing this edition I have attempted to present the essays as fairly as possible, to point out Addison's intentions, his more flagrant distortions, and to explain his more elliptical allusions to contemporary or recent events. In glossing these essays I have tried whenever possible to use sources which were contemporary with Addison and which give us some idea of what the public knew, what the Jacobites were writing to one another, and what some of George I's ministers were thinking and doing.

As in any project of this kind there are many people who have generously offered their assistance. My first debt is to Sir Peter Smithers, who encouraged me to undertake this edition, and my largest debt is to W. A. Speck whom I asked for assistance because, although trained in literary scholarship, I was a novice to historical research. Dr. Speck responded with spontaneous generosity and enthusiasm, suggesting methods and prescribing standards which I hope this edition approaches. Other scholars—especially Donald Bond, Robert Shackleton, Frank Ellis, John Harold Wilson, Robert Schmitz, Eric Lindquist, and Hildred Crill—have assisted me in various ways, and I gratefully acknowledge their help. The British Library, the Bodleian Library, and the Beinecke Library have been predictably hospitable to me as they have been to so many before me. I am especially grateful to the staff of the Frost Library, Amherst College, and the staff of the University of Massachusetts Library for offering frequent and sensible suggestions. Finally I am indebted to Washington University, St. Louis, which helped send me to the libraries and archives of Britain to undertake my research. Although never involved in my work, my wife and daughters gave me personal support which was both unconstrained and abundant; to them I dedicate my labours.

J. L.

University of Massachusetts,
Amherst

CONTENTS

A CHRONOLOGY OF RELEVANT EVENTS

All dates are given in Old Style except that the new year begins on 1 January rather than 25 March.

1714

1 August	Queen Anne dies.
18 September	Elector of Hanover arrives at Greenwich.
20 October	Coronation of George I.

1715

5 January	Parliament dissolved.
11 January	Rewards offered for the author and printer of *English Advice to the Freeholders of England*.
15 January	Writs for a new Parliament issued.
17 March	First session of George I's first Parliament begins.
25 March	Bolingbroke flees England.
9 April	The House of Commons forms the Committee of Secrecy to examine Queen Anne's last ministry.
9 June	Walpole presents the report of the Committee of Secrecy to the House of Commons.
10 June	The Commons resolves to impeach Bolingbroke and Oxford.
21 June	The Commons resolves to impeach Ormonde.
20 July	The King addresses Parliament, asks for assistance in suppressing the 'Spirit of Rebellion'.
23 July	Suspension of habeas corpus receives royal assent.
6 August	Walpole delivers the articles of impeachment against Bolingbroke in the House of Lords.
8 August	Stanhope delivers articles of impeachment against Ormonde in the House of Lords. Ormonde flees to France.
21 August	Louis XIV dies.
6 September	Mar raises the Pretender's standard at Braemar.
8 September	Jacobite attack on Edinburgh Castle foiled.
6 October	Parliament adjourned.
9 October	Thomas Forster proclaims the Pretender in Northumberland.
22 October	English and Scottish rebels join forces at Kelso.
1 November	Rebel army enters England.
4 November	Barrier Treaty signed at Antwerp.
9 November	*A Declaration of the Archbishop of Canterbury* published.
10 November	Rebels occupy Preston.

13 November	Rebels surrender at Preston. Indecisive battle fought at Sheriffmuir.
3 December	Treaty of Commerce with Spain signed in Madrid.
4 December	Dutch troops begin to arrive in Scotland.
9 December	Prisoners taken at Preston arrive in London.
20 December	Addison's appointment to the Commission for Trade and Plantations announced.
22 December	The Pretender lands in Scotland.
23 December	*Freeholder* 1 published.

1716

9 January	Parliament reconvenes. The King addresses both houses, announces that the Pretender is in Scotland. Articles of impeachment against the seven rebel Lords captured at Preston presented.
11 January	An act to continue the suspension of habeas corpus for another six months is introduced in the Commons.
19 January	Six rebel Lords plead guilty to the articles of impeachment.
21 January	The House of Lords passes the Act to continue the suspension of habeas corpus but registers Abingdon's protest against it.
4 February	The Pretender flees for France from Montrose.
9 February	Six rebel Lords sentenced to execution.
17 February	King addresses Parliament, announces the Pretender has fled from Scotland.
22 February	The House of Commons avoids debate over petitions for mercy for the rebel Lords by adjourning until 1 March. The House of Lords receives petitions and addresses the King to reprieve those Lords who 'appear . . . to deserve' his mercy.
23 February	The King orders the execution of three rebel Lords (Nithsdale, Kenmure, Derwentwater) and grants respite until 7 March to the others. Nithsdale escapes from the Tower.
24 February	Kenmure and Derwentwater executed.
28 February	Nottingham dismissed from Lord Presidency of the Council.
1 March	*An Argument to Prove the Affections of the People of England to Be the Best Security* published.
10 April	Septennial Bill introduced in the House of Lords.
11 April	Thomas Forster escapes from Newgate.
18 April	The House of Lords passes the Septennial Bill.
19 April	Septennial Bill introduced in the House of Commons.
26 April	Death of Lord Somers. The House of Commons passes the Septennial Bill.
7 May	Septennial Bill receives royal assent.
28 May	George I's birthday.

7 June	Day of Public Thanksgiving proclaimed 'for the Suppression of the late unnatural Rebellion'.
10 June	The Pretender's birthday.
19 June	House of Commons asks the House of Lords' concurrence to repeal the clause in the Act of Settlement which required Parliament's consent for the King to leave the country.
26 June	Parliament prorogued.
29 June	*Freeholder* 55 published.

INTRODUCTION

'It is agreed, that the truest Way of judging the Dispositions of the People in the Choice of their Representatives, is by computing the County Elections.'[1] Writing this in 1711, Swift attempted to show that the Tory victory in the previous election accurately reflected responsible public opinion throughout the nation. His readers might have agreed with him since the county electorates, composed of forty-shilling freeholders, were responsible for sending Knights of the Shire to the House of Commons, and these voters were so numerous and geographically scattered that it was difficult for either party or for the Court to buy votes or to use coercive measures which were certain to persuade voters.[2] The property qualification for the county voter had been fixed at property which yielded forty shillings per annum in 1429, and inflation, particularly during the sixteenth century, had enlarged these electorates considerably. By 1621, when an unsuccessful attempt was made to raise the property qualification to eighty shillings, the forty-shilling minimum had almost become sacrosanct.[3] Lord Ilay complained in 1716 that it contributed to electoral corruption because 'the dregs of the people' were now eligible to vote.[4] In the 1715 election thirty-four of the forty English counties had more than 2,000 eligible voters; Yorkshire had about 10,000.[5] These voters, principally but not exclusively landowners, were the freeholders to whom an increasing number of pamphlets were directed during election campaigns of the early eighteenth century. During those years, when the Tories proclaimed themselves defenders of the landed interest, Swift could

[1] Swift, *Prose Works* iii. 66.

[2] This is not to say they never tried or succeeded.The Court could influence voters by bestowing offices, such as the Lord Lieutenancy of a county, upon prominent members of a party or by insinuating royal favour towards one party in proclamations dissolving Parliament. In 1714 George I made it clear that in the 1715 election he wanted those persons elected who 'shewed a Firmness to the Protestant Succession, When it was most in Danger'. However, during the first fifteen years of the century, there was a sizeable floating vote; see Speck, *Tory and Whig*, pp. 76–97.

[3] J. H. Plumb, 'The Growth of the Electorate in England from 1600 to 1715', *Past and Present*, 45 (1969), p. 93.

[4] *Parl. Hist.* vii. 302. He also estimated that a forty-shilling freehold in the fifteenth century was equivalent to a forty-pound freehold in 1716.

[5] *History of Parliament* i. 116, 20; Speck, *Tory and Whig*, pp. 126–31. There is some variation between the two estimated totals of eligible county voters in 1715 because one work examines the period up to 1715 and the other begins with 1715; both present estimated averages for the periods covered. The number of persons voting in 1715 was about 284,000 of which nearly 160,000 voted for county members.

boast with some accuracy that 'the *Whigs* themselves have always confessed, that the bulk of Landed Men in *England* was generally of *Tories*.'[6] Unlike those persons whose incomes came from trade, these landed men were considered responsible subjects because they had a 'fixed' interest in the nation which they could not easily shift into foreign banks or investments.[7] They even enjoyed a reputation for respectability in the popular slang of the period: a freeholder was a man 'whose Wife goes with him to the Ale-house'.[8]

While only relatively accurate, the belief that the county voter reflected national public opinion was a popular one, and both parties appealed to the independent voter, assuring him that if he voted for their principles—either Tory love for the Church or Whig passion for liberty—the nation would be secure. In the weeks preceding the 1715 election at least ten pamphlets appealed to freeholders, substantial evidence that politicians assumed there was a significant number of independent voters who might be persuaded.[9] Because the county voters were men for whom land taxes were usually more important than international trade, public credit, or foreign wars, they usually elected Tories. The Whigs, even in good election years like 1708, generally did poorly in the counties. In 1715 some contemporaries predicted that the Whigs would lose there again, but the Whigs won more county members than usual: Kent, Norfolk, Hampshire, Staffordshire, and Sussex all elected two Whigs to replace two Tories. In twelve other counties they gained one seat which meant that both Knights of the Shire from Gloucestershire, Monmouthshire, and Shropshire were Whigs. In Wales, where each county elected only one Knight, the Whigs won in Anglesey, Carmarthonshire, Pembrokeshire, and Radnorshire.[10] In terms of the total majority the Whigs held in the House of Commons after the 1715 election, these gains were not crucial, but their value as propaganda should not be dismissed. By calling his periodical the *Freeholder* and adopting the mask of the county voter in various essays, Addison could pretend to speak as the average, independent voter and could suggest, with recent election results as evidence, that the Tory party was not necessarily the party of the small landowner any longer.

[6] *Prose Works* iii. 66.

[7] *Prose Works* vi. 59; see also *F.* 42, n. 5.

[8] *Dictionary of the Canting Crew* (1699). Giles Jacob gives a detailed legal definition of freeholders in his *Law Dictionary* (1729).

[9] *Monthly Catalogue*, February 1716; W. A. Speck, 'The General Election of 1715', *English Historical Review*, xc (1975), 507–22.

[10] Boyer, *Pol. State* ix. 160. The party affiliations of members elected in 1715 and those who preceded them in the previous Parliament are cited in 'The Worsley List', *History of Parliament*, i. 162–87.

Appealing to his readers as an ordinary man of property also offered Addison other possibilities. John Locke's *Second Treatise of Civil Government* (1689) was for most Whigs the intellectual base for many of their policies, and Locke had argued that sovereignty was derived from the consent of property owners.[11] Addison proposes, as Locke had, that civil liberties are 'the natural Rights of Mankind',[12] that there should be 'a mixt Government consisting ... of the Regal, the Noble, and the Popular',[13] and that men of property, by actively exerting their voice in government, could eliminate arbitrary rule and strengthen the state against those who might attempt to restrict their liberties. This contractual theory of government, mutually obliging the monarch to rule with the consent of Parliament and the subject to obey all legally enacted laws, predates Locke's *Second Treatise* and was the most important intellectual defence for the Glorious Revolution. At that time leading Whigs argued that James II had violated the political contract and therefore his subjects were no longer obliged to obey him.[14] In 1716, when James's son was in Scotland, the prospect of a Stuart restoration and the abolition of this contractual theory of state was quite real. With the contract denied and a Stuart monarch governing arbitrarily, the political power of property owners could be reduced or effectively eliminated. Such fears, coupled with the possibility of a Catholic Stuart tampering with the Anglican establishment, were sufficient to dissuade most Englishmen from the Jacobite cause. One brief comment, written by Countess Cowper in her diary on George I's coronation day, sums up a combination of concerns which many people must have felt in 1716: 'I hope I shall never forget the blessing of seeing our Holy Religion thus preserv'd, as well as our Libertys & Propertys.'[15]

The Protestant succession, the preservation of the Church as well as the civil liberties and the properties which many English subjects enjoyed: these were the blessings which the Jacobites threatened and which the Whigs were eager to defend. As the party regularly defamed for endorsing revolution, republicanism, and atheism, and for rarely showing much concern for the welfare of small landowners, the Whigs could in 1716 proclaim themselves defenders of monarchy, the Church and the traditional liberties of all Englishmen. With the defection of Bolingbroke and Ormonde to France, many Tories, particularly High Church Tories, were suspected as Jacobite sympathizers, so that fears of Jacobitism bolstered support for the Whigs. To exploit these circumstances for propaganda, the ministry chose Joseph Addison, who published his *Freeholder* essays twice

[11] *Two Treatises*, pp. 110–20. [12] *F.* 2. [13] *F.* 51.
[14] Grey's *Debates* ix. 19–20. [15] Cowper Diary, 20 Oct. 1714.

weekly from 23 December 1715, the day after the Pretender landed in Scotland, to 29 June 1716, three days after Parliament rose.[16]

There is substantial evidence that George I and his ministers were unafraid of the prospect of the Jacobite rebellion: in August 1715 Daniel Dering wrote of the Court, 'The French continue their resolution of sending the Pretender to Scotland ... notwithstanding they cant send an Army with him. However I am pleased to find our Friends not frightned, for they think it will quickly be over',[17] and less than a month later George Berkeley wrote, 'The best on't is that the vigilant measures taken at Court ... gives hopes that any impious designe to imbroil the nation may be soon defeated and turned on the heads of the contrivers.'[18] Both men were writing before any fighting began, but both suggest that the ministry was ready for the Jacobite attempt and that such an attempt would revive fears which generated support for the Whigs in the election of 1715. Eighteen months after Queen Anne's death, when the popularity of the German Court had deteriorated, the rebellion offered the Whig ministry the chance to revive support for the Hanoverians and to consolidate the gains which the 1715 election had given to their party. Stanhope wrote to Lord Stair, the English ambassador at Paris, that 'it would be by no means a misfortune' for the Pretender to land in Scotland, because his presence was so unappealing that it would inspire few rebels to continue their struggles after their defeat at Preston in November 1715.[19] For turning the rebellion 'on the heads of the contrivers' and reviving confidence in the Hanoverians, Addison was a successful Whig propagandist although, like many partisan writers, he repeatedly insisted that he was only concerned with the welfare of the whole nation, not just his party.

The issues which Addison discusses in the *Freeholder* naturally overlap, yet they are generally related to the most important institutions in early eighteenth-century government—the monarchy, the Church, and Parliament. Those essays in which Addison discusses George I are perhaps his least enthusiastic and certainly his least convincing. During his first year on the throne, the King had done little to endear himself to his new

[16] John Oldmixon claims that Addison demanded and received a place on the Commission for Trade and Plantations in return for writing the *Freeholder* (*History of England*, 1735, p. 683). A previous request Addison had made for a place on the Commission had been ignored in 1714 (Smithers, *Addison*, pp. 313–15).

[17] Percival Letterbook, 18 Aug. 1715.

[18] Ibid., 8 Sept. 1715. Sir John Percival also wrote on 3 Jan. 1716, 'The Affair of Scotland gives no uneasyness to our Court.'

[19] P.R.O. State Papers 90/14, January 1716. The government's preparations for the rebellion were supervised by Stanhope and are described in detail in Basil Williams's *Stanhope* (Oxford, 1932), pp. 169–99.

subjects; ignorant of their language and unfamiliar with English customs, he frequently offended them unintentionally. He rarely appeared in public and not until June 1715 did he review his troops in Hyde Park and allow the common people to kiss his hand. He never visited the provinces.[20] The Prussian Resident in London, Friedrich Bonet, wrote that Jacobitism had made more progress in the eight months following the King's coronation than in the preceding four years of Tory administration.[21] For Addison to repair the tarnished image of the King was no easy task and one which, after being treated somewhat ungenerously by the monarch in 1714, he may not have tackled wholeheartedly. He praises the Hanoverians for their Protestantism and their progeny, two virtues they shared with most adults in Great Britain, and flatters the King with compliments which rightly belonged to Parliament, as when he asserts that the King was merciful in his treatment of the rebel Lords. The mercy granted to them was forced by the House of Lords, which had made a public address for clemency; unwilling to arouse any more hostility among his subjects, the King reprieved three of the six rebel Lords.[22] Distortions like Addison's were common practice among political writers and it seems unlikely that anyone who read other newspapers carefully would be swayed by them. However he may have included his fulsome adulation of George I to emphasize that, although a staunch Whig, he was no republican. There were also those gullible subjects, however small in number, who would believe anything they read or heard, and those in Court who might enjoy anything which flattered them.

Because the King's Protestantism was his basic claim to the throne, the religion of the Hanoverians was a subject of considerable speculation. In 1714 Francis Atterbury had described it as both too Popish and too Calvinistic:

> How Religious soever the King is, it cannot be imagined he hath any extraordinary Veneration for a Religion, which he came into but the other Day, and to which he was an absolute Stranger before. The *Lutheran*, wherein he was Educated, and which he professed to the very Hour of his Landing, is entirely different, both in Doctrine and Discipline, from ours ... There are some Ceremonies and Tenets which border too near upon Popery ... Nor are we to expect greater Favour from the *Prince* and *Princess* of *Wales* ... she is so rigid a *Calvinist*, that is, so rigid a *Presbyterian*, that hitherto she hath not been prevailed upon to receive the Sacrament according to ... the *Church* of *England.*[23]

[20] Wolfgang Michael, *Beginnings of the Hanoverian Dynasty* (1936), p. 88.
[21] Michael, p. 130.
[22] These manoeuvres are described in the notes to *F.* 31.
[23] *English Advice*, p. 20.

In fact the King and the Prince were neither Popish nor Calvinistic in their religious habits; they were simply desultory. At Christmas in 1714 neither of them attended Chapel to receive Communion, and news of their negligence was spread widely by disaffected clergymen. They did not repeat their neglect the following Easter. The King usually did attend an Anglican service every Sunday, but he understood no English, did not pray silently when he entered the Chapel, did not attempt to follow the service with a prayer book, and did not kneel with the congregation.[24]

Because 'Danger to the Church' had been a potent Tory appeal during the reign of Queen Anne, Addison takes particular care during the run of the *Freeholder* to destroy possibilities for exploiting this concern, and he attacks the problem in various ways. First he reminds his readers frequently about the dangers of Popery, thus suggesting to those familiar with the King's religious habits that his Anglicanism, although perfunctory, was preferable to 'that Religion which is most repugnant to it'.[25] He also assures his readers that the King is a friend to the Church and cites the building of the new churches in London and Westminster as evidence. The new churches he mentions were commissioned by Parliament in 1711, three years before the King came to England, and the Tories had claimed credit, not inaccurately, for initiating and passing the legislation involved.[26] A third method Addison uses to attack the critics of the King's religious habits is more ingenious, and a device he uses repeatedly in various contexts. He discredits his opponents by using their own weapon: in this instance, a concern for religion in England. He argues that the opposition's zeal 'instills into their Minds the utmost Virulence and Bitterness, instead of that Charity, which is the Perfection and Ornament of Religion, and the most indispensable and necessary Means for attaining the End of it. In a word, among these mistaken Zealots, it sanctifies Cruelty and Injustice, Riots and Treason.'[27] Concern for the Church was traditionally the political property of the Tories; with almost equal ethusiasm they had, at least in Anne's reign, proclaimed their loyalty to monarchy. By capitalizing on the reversals which the Jacobite rebellion created, Addison takes these concerns and flings them back at Jacobites and their Tory sympathizers. Fully aware of their vulnerability, he writes

[24] Michael, pp. 88–9, 375. [25] *F.* 14.

[26] Esther de Waal, 'New Churches in East London in the Early Eighteenth Century', *Renaissance and Modern Studies*, ix (1965), 98–114. Of the fifty churches planned to serve the thousands of Anglicans in the metropolis who had no parish church, only twelve were eventually built, although the expensive plans of the commissioners in charge were more instrumental in the plan's failure than the King's indifference.

[27] *F.* 37.

more essays attacking the King's critics than essays praising the Hanoverians. He may well have considered royal flattery dull reading, but he surely knew that the most attractive Hanoverian features were policies rather than personalities. Both the rebellion and Addison's propaganda were useful for the Court. In May 1716 Stanhope could write, 'His Majesty's affairs are, thanks be to God, at present in a more setled and prosperous condition than his most sanguine servants could ever have expected.'[28]

Apart from the current propaganda published by such High Church critics as Francis Atterbury, one must also look to the Sacheverell affair of 1709–10 to appreciate the context in which Addison discusses the Church. Dudley Ryder, writing less than a week before Addison published his first essay, claimed that the Whigs' failure to silence inflammatory and reactionary clergymen in their prosecution of Henry Sacheverell in 1710 had 'encouraged the clergy to do anything though never so vile ... that nobody would for the future dare to prosecute a clergyman again. It is certain the clergy in the country have been the greatest instrument in raising this spirit of rebellion through the nation.'[29] Although Addison never discusses his differences with the politics of High Churchmen in any detail, he often alludes to them obliquely: he usually writes satirically, parodying the rhetoric of highfliers like Sacheverell in *F.* 3 or mocking the hypocrisy of laymen like the innkeeper in *F.* 22. He does all this with the obvious intention of showing moderate Anglicans that such sophistry and bigotry were unchristian, a criticism which had been used by the Whigs at the Sacheverell trial.[30] High Church intolerance towards dissenters was commonplace, although most High Churchmen, clergy and laity alike, seldom proclaimed their prejudices as vehemently or as publicly as Sacheverell had in his sermon, *The Perils of False Brethren, both in Church and State*, which he preached at St. Paul's on 5 November 1709. In Addison's repeated references to Passive Obedience, Non-resistance, and 'Danger to the Church', major themes in Sacheverell's tirade which were examined in detail at his trial, he is reminding his readers of the fear and hatred which such men could arouse and thrive upon.

These religious issues were not unrelated to the threat which the rebellion posed to the contractual theory of state. The hereditary right of monarchs, the antithesis of the political contract and a principal claim for the Stuart Pretender, was associated in the mind of Addison's readers with Passive Obedience. One writer argued in the *Englishman* on 11 February

[28] P.R.O. State Papers 104/136, 17 May 1716.
[29] Ryder, *Diary*, 19 Dec. 1715.
[30] *The Tryal of Dr. Henry Sacheverell* (8vo, 1710), pp. 167–8.

1714 that Passive Obedience and hereditary right were 'empty Words, and Distinctions without Difference . . . they mean the same thing.'[31] Writing thirty years earlier, George Hickes defined Passive Obedience to royal authority and explained why it was required of subjects:

In all perfect Governments, and particularly in the *English*, all these Rights legally belong to the Soveraign, who is King, especially to be accountable to none but God, to *have the sole Power and Disposal of the Sword, and to be free from all Coercive, and Vindictive Power, and from Resistance by Force.* It is by these Common Laws of Soveraignty, that the Gospell requires Passive Obedience, which is but another name for *Non-resistance*; These Laws are in Eternal Force against the Subjects in defence of the Soveraign, be he good, or evil, just, or unjust, Christian, or Pagan; be what he will, no Subject, or number of Subjects can lift up his Hand against his *Soveraign*, & be Guiltless by these Laws.[32]

For Hickes the English government is perfect, and the subject owes total obedience to the divine and hereditary power of the crown, whether justly or unjustly exercised, since that was '*the Doctrine of the Cross*'.[33] Such assertions did not go undisputed, and the events of 1688–9 later denied or modified most of them. Nevertheless this kind of rhetoric flourished in the last years of Charles II's reign, and the political history of those years is more important for understanding it than the medieval heritage on which such rhetoric was based.[34]

[31] Steele, *Englishman*, pp. 224–6.

[32] *Jovian* (1683), p. 203. The most logical arguments in defence of absolutism are found in the secular tracts of the period; see, e.g. George Mackenzie, *Jus Regium* (1684), pp. 130 ff., and Robert Brady, *Introduction to the Old English History* (1684), pp. 130–54.

[33] *Jovian*, p. 208.

[34] In the period 1681–5, the Tory revenge which followed the Exclusion Crisis, Charles II employed almost every legal means to suppress civil liberties, presumably to prevent the exclusion of his Catholic brother, the Duke of York, from the throne. Prompted by this opportunity to diminish the power of those who threatened the authority enjoyed by Church and crown, many Anglican pulpits resounded with appeals for strict obedience to lawful superiors, particularly priests, bishops, and kings. The University of Oxford passed a decree in Convocation on 21 July 1683 which condemned 'Damnable Doctrines' such as 'All Civil Authority is derived Originally from the People' and 'There is a mutual Compact, Tacit or Express, between a Prince and his Subjects; and that if He performs not His Duty, they are discharg'd from Theirs.' That so many conservative clergymen fell silent about submission after James II issued his Declarations of Indulgence suggests that their motives were at least as political as religious. After the Glorious Revolution some clergymen, like Hickes, became non-jurors while others, like William Sherlock, accommodated their arguments to adapt to new political realities. David Ogg, *England in the Reign of Charles II* (Oxford, 1955), pp. 634–9; R. A. Beddard, 'The Commission for Ecclesiastical Promotions, 1681–84', *Historical Journal*, x (1967), 11–40; White Kennett, *History of England* (1706), iii. 419–21; Keith Feiling, *History of the Tory Party* (Oxford, 1950), pp. 203–44; G. M. Straka, 'The Final Phase of Divine Right Theory in England, 1688–1702', *English Historical Review*, lxxvii (1962), 638–58.

One would expect that twenty-eight years after the Glorious Revolution divine hereditary right and Passive Obedience would mean relatively little to most English subjects except Jacobites, and they were not the most important audience Addison addressed in the *Freeholder*. Such terms as Passive Obedience and Non-resistance might awaken memories of arbitrary government in the reigns of Charles II and James II, but they could also appeal to a deep moral commitment to obedience which continued to influence English conduct in spite of political changes inherent in the Glorious Revolution. *The Whole Duty of Man*, the most popular devotional manual of the period, discouraged resistance to authority, arguing that a ruler's unlawful commands were 'a season for the Passive Obedience; we must patiently suffer what he inflicts on us for such refusal, and not, to secure ourselves, rise up against him: *For who can stretch his hand against the Lord's Anointed, and be guiltless*?'[35] The disparity between such devotional sentiments and political events captured the nation's attention in 1710 when Sacheverell was accused of inciting sedition and rebellion for proclaiming among other things that 'the *Grand Security* of our *Government* and the very *Pillar* upon which it *stands*, is founded upon the *steady Belief* of the *Subject*'s *Obligation* to an *Absolute*, and *Unconditional Obedience* to the *Supream Power*.'[36] Some churchmen like Sacheverell found it easy in 1709 to ignore the Revolution, overlook the exiled Stuarts in France, and assume that Queen Anne was monarch by hereditary right to whom unlimited obedience was due.[37]

For various reasons, but principally to procure '*an Eternal and Indelible Brand of Infamy to be fix'd in a Parliamentary way on all those who maintain the Doctrine of Non-resistance*',[38] the leading Whigs chose to impeach Sacheverell in Parliament, the most public forum possible, thus opening the way for the most famous trial since 1649. By the time the débâcle was over, an estimated 100,000 copies of Sacheverell's sermon were published, making it the largest short-term best seller in the early eighteenth century.[39] The Whigs prosecuted this minor clergyman for a sermon which amounted to little more than illogical rant in order to silence political preaching by disaffected clergymen, a kind of preaching which Arthur Mainwaring claimed was intended to subvert the Revolution

[35] Richard Allestree, *The Whole Duty of Man* (1715), p. 290.

[36] *The Perils of False Brethren* (1709), p. 12.

[37] Defoe responded to such sloppy thinking by informing his readers of the *Review* that, in terms of divine hereditary right, 'the Queen has no more Title to the Crown than my Lord Mayor's Horse' (6 Sept. 1705).

[38] *The Tryal of Sacheverell*, p. 334.

[39] Geoffrey Holmes, *The Trial of Doctor Sacheverell* (1973), pp. 75, 117.

Settlement.[40] Ironically, one of the best Tory defences for Sacheverell came from the Whig camp. After Sir Simon Harcourt willingly agreed with the Whigs that subjects may resist authority in cases of necessity, Sir John Hawles, a Whig, opened the door for an equivocation when he said, 'perhaps the Doctor and I differ in the Persons in whom the Supreme Power is lodg'd ... I think it is lodg'd in the Queen's Majesty, the Lords Spiritual and Temporal and the Commons in Parliament assembled.'[41] Harcourt eagerly took up the point and claimed that Hawles and Sacheverell did in fact agree about supreme authority. Although the sermon and Sacheverell's defence did not support Harcourt's claim, the Tories adopted this broader definition of supreme authority, which Swift publicized for them in the *Examiner*: 'Wherever is entrusted the Power of making Laws, that Power is without all Bounds ... and justly demands Universal Obedience and Non-Resistance ... Among us, as every Body knows, this Power is lodged in the King or Queen, together with the Lords and Commons of the Kingdom.'[42] Once the rallying cry of loyalists in the Civil War, Passive Obedience became, as Swift wrote in 1710, obedience to the crown 'together with the ... Commons'.[43] Sacheverell was found guilty, but popular sympathy for the man and his defenders helped to give the Tories a clear victory at the polls in 1710.

The political disputes between 1679 and 1716 led eventually to political stability, but nearly every major event in those years—the Exclusion Crisis, the Convention Parliament, the Hanoverian succession—became an occasion for airing old arguments, and the rage of party was frequently intensified by the bellows of clergymen. Dudley Ryder's indictment of the country clergy in 1716 is substantiated by both contemporary accounts and events. Robert Patten, the Anglican chaplain to the Jacobite leader, Thomas Forster, wrote in the Preface to his *History of the Late Rebellion* (1717): 'nothing contributed more to raise the People of this Nation to a Spirit of Rebellion, then the licentious Freedom of some ... to cry up the old Doctrines of Passive Obedience, and to give Hints and Arguments to prove Hereditary Right.' While the Sacheverell affair may have encouraged some lower clergymen to inveigh against the more moderate bishops and liberal politicians in Westminster, the Church hierarchy and the ministry

[40] *Four Letters to a Friend in North-Britain* (1710), p. 5.

[41] *The Tryal of Sacheverell*, p. 97.

[42] *Prose Works* iii. 113. Sacheverell had attacked the Act of Toleration (1689) which had been passed by Parliament and had received royal assent; see Holmes, *Trial of Sacheverell*, pp. 144–5, 193–5.

[43] The earliest use of the term cited in the *O.E.D.* is in Dudley Digges, *The Unlawfulness of Taking Up Arms* (1643), p. 50.

did their best to silence the rhetoric of disaffected priests. Less than a month before the 1715 election, George I published directions to the Church for 'preserving the Peace and Quiet of the State' in which one article read, 'none of the Clergy, in their Sermons or Lectures' should 'presume to intermeddle in any Affairs of State or Government, or the Constitution' and a contemporary remarked that his directions 'were very ill relish'd by the *High-flying Clergy*.'[44] On 9 November 1715, when the most intense fighting of the rebellion was about to start, *A Declaration of the Archbishop of Canterbury and the Bishops in and near London* was published and widely reprinted. It began, 'We have thought it Incumbent upon Us ... in this Publick Manner to Declare Our Abhorrence of [the Rebellion], and to Warn both the Clergy and People under our Charge' not to assist the rebels either by joining them, by inciting others to join them, or 'even by their Silence at this Juncture ... give Hopes to the Pretender and his Friends ... Is this a Time to stand Neuters when all lies at Stake?' It reminded Anglicans of the obligation of their oaths abjuring the Pretender and called upon soldiers for battle, magistrates for exercising their authority, and 'Ministers, by their Prayers, by their Preaching' to help suppress the rebellion.[45] Such directions and declarations must have forced Anglicans mildly sympathetic to the Jacobites to question their conceptions of allegiance and obedience to bishops and monarchs. While the ministry and bishops could press the clergy to encourage loyalty to the Hanoverians, they could not police every sermon preached in England. Thus it became one of Addison's purposes, especially in the early *Freeholder* essays, to expand upon the themes in the Archbishop's *Declaration*. These essays are secular sermons—using texts drawn from classical authors rather than the Bible—and they were clearly aimed at countering the rhetoric of disaffected clergymen.

The sources for the complaint of 'Danger to the Church' were more definite, more numerous, and more substantial than Sacheverell's rant might suggest. The Toleration Act (1689), originally intended to be more limited and short-term than it became, brought relief to dissenters but generated considerable anxiety among Anglican clergymen. Dissenting academies were opened and by 1716 there were about 1,100 dissenting congregations in England.[46] Occasional conformity was fairly widespread and the first three Parliamentary attempts to eliminate it were unsuccessful.

[44] *Annals* i. 321–2.

[45] pp. 3–5. In 1715 some disaffected clergymen prayed only for 'the King' and, by not naming him, could suggest that the congregation prayed for the Pretender rather than George I (*The Immorality of the Priesthood*, 1715, p. 51).

[46] E. D. Bebb, *Nonconformity and Social and Economic Life, 1660–1800* (1935), p. 175.

The lapsing of the Licensing Act (1695) gave new freedom to the press, thus allowing anti-clerical and even heretical books to be published. Most Anglican clergymen were extremely poor and the structures of many churches badly needed repair. Not unreasonably, some clergymen sensed the Church's declining influence and envisioned a society devoid of religion and morality. Nor was their pessimism allayed by the rise of Societies for the Reformation of Manners, since many perceived them as encroaching upon the Church's religious domain: these secular groups were reporting persons for immoral conduct to civil magistrates rather than to archdeacons of the Church. The rise of secularism was, of course, the source of many of their fears and, however much the clergy complained about specific political issues, an increasing indifference towards the clergy and the Church by English subjects was a gloomy reality. Because the Whigs, for both practical and philosophical reasons, defended freedom for dissenters and the press, High Churchmen turned to the Tory party for assistance, and there they were usually greeted with eagerness and promises of change.[47]

Francis Atterbury's *Letter to a Convocation Man* (1697) was an opening shot in a battle which was to continue for over a decade. He deplored the 'open looseness in men's principles and practices and . . . settled contempt of religion and the priesthood'.[48] As a remedy for these conditions, his tactic was to use Convocation to create an effective organization for restoring the Church authority and introducing reforms; with the help of the Earl of Rochester, the nation's leading High Church Tory at the time, the stormy Convocation of 1701 was held; the lower house, composed mostly of parish priests, began inquiries into heretical books, attacked the former Whig ministry, complained of the lassitude of moderate bishops, and finally ended by defying the Archbishop of Canterbury, their spiritual leader. In the end the Convocation only deepened divisions between High Church priests and their moderate or latitudinarian colleagues; it solved nothing. But any moderate clergymen or politicians tempted to discount the political effectiveness of the lower clergy would have been mistaken to underestimate the influence of frustrated parish clergymen at election times. It happened that many clergymen proclaimed 'Danger to the Church' from their pulpits on the eve of elections, and the intensity and frequency of their cries increased when the Whigs were either in power or likely to increase their power.[49] In December 1705, after the Tories had

[47] Holmes, *Trial of Sacheverell*, pp. 27–8; J. Ecton, *A State of the Bounty of Queen Anne* (1725), p. 103; G. V. Bennett, *The Tory Crisis in Church and State* (Oxford, 1975), pp. 55–60.

[48] p. 2.

[49] Speck, *Tory and Whig*, pp. 24–5; Holmes, *Trial of Sacheverell*, pp. 44–5.

used 'Danger to the Church' as an election issue, Lord Halifax moved that the House of Lords 'might enquire into these dangers, about which so many tragical stories have been published of late.' The Earl of Rochester responded with a resolution that the Church was in danger and gave his reasons for thinking so.[50] The resolution was defeated by both houses, and on 17 December they agreed to an address to the Queen which concluded, 'Whoever goes about to suggest and insinuate, that the Church is in Danger, under her Majesty's Administration, is an Enemy to the Queen, the Church, and the Kingdom.'[51]

This address was later resurrected for the Sacheverell impeachment because Sacheverell had claimed in his sermon that priests had been '*Calumniated, Misrepresented*, and *Ridicul'd*' and that the Church's '*Altars*, and *Sacraments*' had been '*Prostituted* to *Hypocrites, Deists, Socinians*, and *Atheists*; and this done ... not only by *Our Profess'd Enemies*, but which is worse, by Our *Pretended Friends*, and *False Brethren*.'[52] Hoping to label Sacheverell an enemy to Queen and country, the Whigs argued at his impeachment that he 'doth falsely and seditiously suggest and assert, that the Church of *England* is in a Condition of great Peril and Adversity under her Majesty's Administration' and in opposition to the 'Resolution of both Houses of Parliament, approved by her Majesty ... he ... doth suggest, the Church to be in danger.'[53] In his answer to this accusation, which was perused if not actually written by Atterbury, Sacheverell said, 'I hope I may say without Offence, that the *Church* may be in Peril from *other Causes*, without any Reflection upon Her Majesty's Government, or any *Contradiction* ... to the *Resolution* of *both Houses of Parliament*, four Years ago.'[54] Although Sacheverell was banned from preaching for three years and his sermon was burned by the public hangman, the Whigs' attempt to silence pulpit politicians failed. Like any paranoia with a grain of truth, 'Danger to the Church' was easily spread and almost impossible to stamp out. The impeachment actually increased fears some Anglicans harboured about Whig policies toward the Church and the wave of enthusiasm for 'High Church and Sacheverell' only increased support for the Tories. To justify their use of this issue, Swift argued in the *Examiner*,

> I have heard it often objected as a great Piece of Insolence in the Clergy and others, to say or hint that the *Church was in Danger*, when it was voted otherwise in Parliament ... But, that the Church and State may be both in Danger under the

[50] *Parl. Hist.* vi. 479–81. [51] *L.J.* xviii. 54.
[52] *The Perils of False Brethren*, pp. 7–8.
[53] *C.J.* xvi. 258. [54] *Tryal of Sacheverell*, p. 339.

best Princes that ever reigned, and without the least Guilt of theirs, is such a Truth, as a Man must be a great Stranger to History or common sense, to doubt.[55]

In the campaign for the 1715 election, the most recent for Addison's readers, the issue was raised again in Atterbury's prediction that a Whig victory would lead to a 'general and unlimited comprehension without Common prayer or Bishops', a prohibition against defending the Church, and a toleration which would 'enable Freethinkers to Write against God and the Christian Religion'.[56] But such appeals to fear require continuing and, if possible, increasing threats to remain persuasive whereas, in the years since the Sacheverell trial, the Tories, at times with the complicity of the Whigs, had passed legislation which served as palliatives for beleaguered clergymen: the Occasional Conformity Act (1711), the Act for the Building of Fifty New Churches (1711), the Toleration Act for Scottish Episcopalians (1712), and the Schism Act (1714). When Addison began the *Freeholder*, the Whigs had controlled the ministry for over a year and had been careful not to generate new fears about the Church, although their unwillingness to implement Tory legislation against occasional conformity and dissenting academies, the target of the Schism Act, showed that they felt no obligation to enforce such legislation with any rigour. During the Jacobite rebellion, when dissenters' meeting houses were in considerably more danger than Anglican churches, the appeal of 'Danger to the Church' was ironically inappropriate. The High Church dream of uniting the episcopacy and crown in a strong authoritarian partnership which would oversee the moral welfare of the nation was only possible with a Stuart restoration. Memories of the ill-treatment the Church received from James II and the Pretender's omission of any explicit promises for the security of the Church of England in his public declarations were sufficient to extinguish that dream.

Although most points involving the Church cannot be separated from those involving the crown or Parliament, there were several crucial issues in the rebellion which were distinctly religious. Unfortunately for the Pretender, the success of his cause depended heavily upon the support of High Church Tories, potentially his largest group of supporters in England, and the failure of Ormonde's plans for an uprising in the West of England lost the Pretender much of that potential assistance.[57] To some extent the Pretender himself undermined the support of these Anglicans by hedging in his declarations. When Bolingbroke encouraged him to

[55] *Prose Works* iii. 16. [56] *English Advice*, p. 30.

[57] H.M.C. *Stuart MSS.* i. 434, 440–52 *passim*, 532–3; *Memoirs of the Mareschal de Berwick* (1779), ii. 199–205.

make 'a direct promise of securing the churches of England and Ireland', the Pretender responded 'that he could not in conscience make such a promise: and, the debate being kept up a little while, he asked me with some warmth, why the tories were so desirous to have him, if they expected those things from him which his religion did not allow?'[58] High Church support was crucial to the rebels in the North because they were the one group which both the Catholics and the Presbyterians were willing to trust. Patten wrote that Anglicans and Catholics among the rebels attended separate religious services without any difficulty and that the Scots rebels were so encouraged by a High Church service at Appleby in November 1715 that they decided such men 'were entirely Theirs, and wou'd join in a little time.'[59] With a distrust for Papists and a reluctance to fight so far from home, a diminished number of Scots, generally considered the best soldiers in the rebel force, joined the English rebels in the march to Lancashire, where they mistakenly believed 20,000 people would join them. Those who did join them there numbered fewer than that and most of them were not High Churchmen. Patten describes their meeting:

a great many *Lancashire* Gentlemen joined us, with their Servants and Friends. It's true, they were most of them Papists, which made the *Scots* Gentlemen and Highlanders mighty uneasy, very much suspecting the Cause; for they expected all the High-Church Party to have joined them. Indeed, that Party, who never are right hearty for the Cause, 'till they are Mellow, as they call it, over a Bottle or two, began now to shew us their Blind-side; and that it is their just Character, that they do not care for venturing their Carcasses any farther than the Tavern ... I have heard Mr. *Forster* say he was Blustered into this Business by such People as these, but that for the time to come he would never again believe a Drunken Tory.[60]

Most Lancashire rebels were Catholics, but most Catholics in the North of England did not actively participate in the rebellion because, although excluded from public office and subjected to double taxation, they were generally tolerated.[61] Anti-recusant statutes were usually ignored except in times of crisis. Defoe described Durham as 'full of Roman Catholicks, who live peaceably and disturb no Body, and no Body them; for we being there on a Holiday, saw them going as publickly to Mass as the Dissenters did on other Days to their Meeting-house.'[62] In the Archbishop's *Declaration* of 1715, the Anglican bishops wrote, 'We are not surprized, that Papists should rise up against a Government which they would never

[58] *Letter to Windham*, pp. 276–7.
[59] Patten, *Late Rebellion*, pp. 70, 89.
[60] Patten, *Late Rebellion*, pp. 67–9, 72, 100.
[61] J. H. Plumb, *The Growth of Political Stability in England* (1967), p. 169.
[62] *Tour Thro' Great Britain*, ii. 658.

yet own . . . tho' Rebellion is but an ill Return for the Quiet they have enjoy'd.'[63] For most English subjects Catholicism was an unappealing religion but, more importantly, it was associated with arbitrary government, an association which Louis XIV had only reinforced. For most of Addison's readers Catholic monarchy rather than Catholic dogma was the primary source for anti-Catholic sentiment, and Addison's politically motivated attacks on Catholics in the *Freeholder*, unlike his criticism of High Churchmen, are neither muted nor oblique. On several occasions he marshals the popular prejudices which equated Popery with tyranny, but he also goes beyond that to mock Catholic rituals and beliefs since Catholics, whether loyal or not, were the one religious group in England which he made no attempt to win over to support the Protestant succession. His mockery of Catholicism, unusually petty in Addison's works, originates from his firm belief that British civil liberties were lost without the Revolution Settlement and the Hanoverian succession.

Addison devotes more complete essays to Parliamentary issues than to any other subject, clear evidence that his periodical was party propaganda, not simply a war piece or a defence of the Hanoverians. Five essays defend specific measures supported by the Whigs, of which three relate directly to the Jacobite rebellion. His sixteenth essay, published on 13 February, is a rather elegant argument for suspending habeas corpus, a measure which facilitated the arrests of Jacobite suspects and which no doubt led to the arrests of some innocent Tories. Addison has been criticized for compromising his Whig principles in this essay because he ignores the flight of the Pretender from Scotland on 4 February and the ensuing disintegration of the Jacobite forces, in his support for a suspension of civil liberties.[64] But substantial contemporary evidence suggests that the scattered Jacobite forces in Scotland were by no means defeated. On 19 April General Cadogan was still pursuing the Earl of Seaforth's forces and fears about the troubles rekindling were common in the early weeks of March. Dudley Ryder reports widespread rumours that war with France was imminent because the Regent was expected to declare openly for the Pretender upon his retreat from Scotland to Paris. Various Jacobite sources report shiploads of arms being sent to north-west Scotland in March to reinforce the rebels' resistance there.[65] But even in places controlled by loyalist forces, such as Cambridge, there was considerable discontent and in Aberdeen the oath of abjuration was being administered to thousands of

[63] p. 4. [64] Bloom, *Sociable Animal*, pp. 127–9.

[65] *Post Man*, 24–6 Apr. 1716; Ryder, *Diary*, 3, 4 Mar. 1716; H.M.C. *Stuart MSS.* ii. 24–8.

Scots in mid-March.[66] With hindsight one can argue that the continued suspension of habeas corpus was probably unnecessary, but contemporary complaints focused more on its misuse than on its necessity.

Addison's twentieth essay defends an increase in the land tax, a necessary measure for meeting the expenses of the rebellion quickly and efficiently, and the thirty-first essay defends the Parliamentary impeachments of the rebel Lords. Both deal with issues raised by the rebellion, and both are relatively direct and self-explanatory. The two essays Addison devotes to the Septennial Act (*F.* 25, *F.* 37), the most important new legislation debated during the period he published the *Freeholder*, are less direct and deserve attention. Like the legislation to ensure habeas corpus (1679), the Triennial Act of 1694 was a measure supported by the Whigs, and Addison is in the difficult position of arguing against the frequent elections of Parliament which his party had previously supported.[67] Both parties had considered suspending triennial elections in the decade preceding 1716, and Francis Atterbury had predicted that a Whig victory in 1715 would lead to such a measure, so it came as no surprise when the Whigs used their large majority in the Commons and the occasion of the rebellion to argue for extending Commoners' terms of office from three to seven years in order to secure the nation's stability.[68] That the extension was self-serving was obvious to all, but other accusations, such as those concerning its legality, were unfounded: the Parliament of 1716 had as much legal right to extend the term of office as the Parliament of 1694 had to curtail it.[69] Although the opposition was doomed to lose in its struggle against the Septennial Bill, the arguments presented by the Tory and Country Whig minority were brilliant and richly ironic.

One Jacobite described the reversals in traditional party stances during the second reading of the Bill in the House of Lords: 'The most remarkable thing was that the Tories talked like Old Whigs and Republicans, against monarchy and ministers, &c., and the Whigs magnified the advantages of unlimited absolute power and prerogative, vilified the mob, ridiculed the people, and exalted the Crown.'[70] It was not quite so simple as that, but there were Whigs who complained about the 'caprice of the multitude' and reputedly described the electorate as the 'meanest and lowest of the people', hardly the rhetoric which won the Whigs support for the 1694 Triennial

[66] Ryder, *Diary*, 24 Feb. 1716; *Post Man*, 15–17 Mar. 1716.

[67] Burnet, *History* iv. 239.

[68] The Whigs were rumoured to be considering its suspension in 1708 (H.M.C. *Portland MSS.* iv. 480) and the Tories contemplated a similar move in 1713 (B.L. Add. MS. 17677 GGG, fo. 41). Atterbury made his prediction in *English Advice*, p. 30.

[69] Betty Kemp, *King and Commons, 1660–1832* (1957), pp. 39–41.

[70] H.M.C. *Stuart MSS.* ii. 122.

Act.[71] Some Tories, like Shippen, agreed that 'the radical power of the people hath been extended to a degree of extravagance and absurdity lately', but still opposed septennial elections.[72] While there is no evidence in the published debates that any Whig 'magnified the advantages of unlimited absolute power and prerogative', one does find Nottingham arguing against the Bill because it would enlarge royal prerogative, a popular Whig bugbear, and his argument is characteristic of the way Tories used traditional Whig rhetoric to oppose Whig support for the measure.[73] Snell quoted Locke to them and Bromley cited Molesworth's *History of Denmark*, the popular Whig history which described how the Danes abandoned constitutional monarchy.[74] Archibald Hutcheson, a Country Whig opposed to the Bill, may have had *Freeholder* 1 in mind when he argued that Britons 'are bred up from their cradles with deep impressions of liberty and have their properties fenced in and secured by law; and by their representatives in parliament, they have the honour to share, even in the legislative authority; and it is this gives our people the spirit and resolution of the ancient Romans, by which our nation has obtained and preserved its great character in the world.'[75]

Addison's response to the opposition's arguments was simply to ignore them. His first essay on the Septennial Bill appeared before the Bill was introduced and his second after it was assured of passage. Since he never spoke during the debates, one can only speculate about all his reasons for supporting it. The earlier essay (*F.* 25) argued that frequent elections resulted in abrupt changes in the ministry and consequently in damaging reversals in foreign policy. Steele reacted violently to the essay and proposed counter-propaganda, concluding that 'I wish as Heartily as the Freeholder that they would follow his Advice, but cannot agree with Him that *one Change more* should extend to what we all fear his discourse aims at, the suspension of the Trienniall Act.'[76] His most recent biographer suggests that Steele abandoned his opposition to the measure because Addison met with him and convinced him to do so.[77] If such was the case, Steele's arguments for supporting the Bill, presented on 24 April, may be arguments Addison had used to persuade him. Steele claimed that with triennial elections the first year was spent in 'vindictive decisions and animosities' over election petitions, the second year was spent in business but usually with a 'spirit of contradiction to what the prevailing set of men

[71] *Parl. Hist.* vii. 297, 358. [72] *Parl. Hist.* vii. 317.
[73] *Parl. Hist.* vii 303–4. [74] *Parl. Hist.* vii. 329, 334.
[75] *Parl. Hist.* vii. 358. [76] *Periodical Journalism*, p. 332.
[77] Calhoun Winton, *Sir Richard Steele, M.P.* (Baltimore, 1970), pp. 82–4.

in former parliaments brought to pass' rather than for disinterested zeal for the common good, and the third year continued the second year's business until approaching elections terrified members into 'servile management' to those principals who controlled their constituencies.[78] While there is certainly rhetorical exaggeration here, one also senses a sincere belief that longer terms would permit members of the Commons more opportunity to pursue measures which their own notions of 'the common good' dictated. Addison's second essay, published on 30 April, presents moral arguments for supporting septennial elections, and he appears to be not arguing about the Bill so much as preparing the public to accept it, since, as one contemporary explained, 'it will be so odious to the people.'[79]

Aside from the Septennial Act, the Jacobite rebellion offered the Whigs several other important opportunities for their party. First it was a crisis in which circumstances concurred to make their party's traditional policies obviously attractive to the nation. They could proclaim the blessings of the Revolution Settlement and Protestant succession, reaffirm the contractual nature of government, and even restate their distrust for the French. The rebellion also offered them the opportunity to contrast George I and his ministers with the Pretender and his followers, of whom the Regent reportedly said, 'Je trouve que lui et ses jacobites sont tous des fous.'[80] Compared to the Pretender and his Court, George I and his ministers appeared more intelligent and united than they actually were. Similarly, they could contrast Whig foreign policy with the policies of the previous Tory administration and insinuate that Harley's administration had pursued policies which were detrimental to the nation.[81] A third opportunity for propaganda which the rebellion offered was the reversal of traditional roles. The Whigs had been branded by the Tories as revolutionaries, and the rebellion gave Addison the chance to gloat: 'A Disaffection to Kings and Kingly Government, with a Proneness to Rebellion, have been often very unjustly charged on that Party which goes by the Name of *Whigs*. Our steady and continued Adherence to His Majesty and the present happy Settlement, will the most effectually confute this Calumny.'[82]

In several essays Addison admits that not all Tories are Jacobites, but in many others and usually at greater length he either says or implies that they are. In his earlier essays, those written before the rebellion was

[78] *Parl. Hist.* vii. 326. [79] H.M.C. *Stuart MSS.* ii. 123.
[80] Percival Letterbook, 8 Jan. 1716. [81] *F.* 41.
[82] *F.* 29.

suppressed, he uses the words Tory, rebel, and malcontent interchangeably.[83] His definition of Tory is usually more objective when he is serious, but then he almost defines it out of existence: 'Under the Name of *Tories*, I do not here comprehend Multitudes of well-designing Men, who were formerly included under that Denomination, but are now in the Interest of His Majesty and the present Government.'[84] The present government was, of course, overwhelmingly Whig, and most of the leaders of the Hanoverian Tories, those men who had supported the Whig opposition in the last years of Queen Anne's reign, were either withdrawing their support for the government or were being dismissed from it. The Earl of Abingdon led the opposition in the House of Lords when the continued suspension of habeas corpus was debated, an opposition which was interpreted in Court circles as a ploy to frustrate the government.[85] The Earl of Nottingham, Lord President of the Council, was dismissed in February 1716 after successfully opposing the Court concerning mercy for the convicted rebel Lords.[86] The Earl of Anglesey left Dublin to avoid signing a loyal association to George I, and the Irish Parliament branded him 'an enemy to the King and Kingdom... This was followed with an address for the Earl's being removed from the King's Council and Service; which was complied with.'[87] Sir Thomas Hanmer, who had been the leading Hanoverian Tory in the House of Commons in 1713–14, was frequently absent from the House in January 1716, and Sir John Percival wrote, 'Sr Thomas Hanmer ... and the chief of the torys come now seldom to the House of Commons, as if they would have no hand in supporting the King, since their Party is not strong enough to carry their own designs.'[88] In the midst of these dismissals, retreats, and shifting allegiances, Addison capitalizes on the confusion and offers an appealing but oversimplified explanation: 'The Contest is not in Reality between *Whigs* and *Tories*, but between *Loyalists* and *Rebels* ... In such a Case, an avow'd Indifference is Treachery ... and a Luke-warm Allegiance may prove as pernicious in its Consequences as Treason.'[89] Tories are either loyal, active supporters of the Whig ministry or else they are no better than rebels.

Addison is not consistent in his attacks on the Tories, nor is he consistent in his attitude towards party struggles in general. In the early weeks of 1716 he stokes the fires of party rage, knowing well that the Whigs had little to lose and much to gain. When the news of the Pretender's flight

[83] e.g. *F.* 7. [84] *F.* 14.
[85] *L.J.* xx. 269; Percival Letterbook, 3 Jan. 1716.
[86] Cowper Diary, 23, 26 Feb. 1716.
[87] Tindal, pp. 479–80. Anglesey was replaced by Sunderland as Vice-Treasurer of Ireland.
[88] Percival Letterbook, 28 Jan. 1716. [89] *F.* 13.

from Scotland reached London in mid-February, he begins to dampen those fires. Opponents to the government are malcontents rather than Tories or rebels. By mid-March, when a Jacobite agent wrote, 'No print nor pen can express the desolation of Scotland, and of the Jacobites and their cause in this island', Addison becomes more conciliatory towards the Tories.[90] In his Good Friday essay (*F.* 29) he even criticizes his own party, although rather mildly. His conciliation is relative, of course, and the more moderate tone of the middle essays (*F.* 23–38) remains completely Whig, persistently attacking the French, the Pretender, and the more extravagant absurdities of High Church Tories. He is moderate in that he acknowledges a loyal Tory opposition, does not exaggerate Tory complicity in treason or sedition, and consistently denounces party squabbling. At the end of April, when the Septennial Bill was passed and the Whigs were assured of another five years in office, Addison, while still critical of the Tories, focuses more frequently on previous Tory administrations than on his contemporaries. His eulogy of Somers, his essays on the Hanoverian successes in international affairs, even his sometimes comical distortions of seventeenth-century political history (*F.* 43, *F.* 54), are all reminders of Tory blunders or Whig triumphs. Some essays are coloured by revenge, others by nostalgia. Among contemporary political groups Addison deals more energetically with Court and Country factions in his final essays: he denounces both the London mob and rural politicians—two very different groups whose political behaviour was surprisingly similar in their distrust of the government—and he celebrates the vitality and strength of the ministry and their supporters.

Branding Tories as Jacobites was nothing new in 1716 although the rebellion gave some truth to the old lie. More importantly for the Whigs, the political reversals of the rebellion allowed them to go beyond name-calling, to adapt for themselves the patriotic conservatism usually associated with Tories: loyalty to the crown, concern for the Church, abhorrence of rebellion. Such a complete reversal also caused Addison some difficulty: his essay on rebellion (*F.* 12) required him to explain at some length that the Glorious Revolution was justified by necessity whereas the Jacobite rebellion was not, and in *F.* 16 he must argue for suspending habeas corpus, which the Exclusionist Whigs struggled to pass in 1679. But in spite of these difficulties there was much more profit than loss for the Whigs. Besides adopting Tory arguments for their party, they could also assume the rhetoric of a conservative establishment. And they were in fact conservative to their own principles; many of Addison's essays

[90] H.M.C. *Stuart MSS.* ii. 40 (12 Mar. 1716).

simply elaborate such old slogans of the Exclusion Crisis as 'No Popery' and 'No Arbitrary Power'. The issues of the rebellion were the issues of the Exclusion, the claims of a Catholic Stuart to the throne, but the difference between Shaftesbury's shouting mobs and Addison's quiet eloquence is evidence of the dramatic changes in circumstances between 1679 and 1716. The radical politics and mob force of Shaftesbury's followers are simply forgotten, and any mob opposed to the Hanoverian Court is dismissed as 'the Scum and Refuse of the People'.[91] On behalf of the party which had been excluded from Court during Queen Anne's last years and which was almost monopolizing St. James's by late spring in 1716, Addison cultivates a courtly sneer: 'The *Whig* Ladies ... as they daily do Duty at Court, are much more expert in the Use of their Airs and Graces than their female Antagonists, who are most of them bred in the Country: So that the Sisterhood of Loyalists ... are like an Army of regular Forces, compared with a raw undisciplin'd Militia.'[92] Addison's rhetoric in the *Freeholder*—his arguments, his tone, even his elegant language and style—is the voice of a Whig conservatism which was founded on the King's favour, a monopoly of power, and the pleasing prospect of an extended tenure for their majority in Parliament.

An examination of Addison's position on party struggles must include some remarks on his attitude toward Court and Country factions within the Whig and Tory ranks. John Toland, writing at the end of 1716, said, 'Court and Country parties, tho in themselves words significant enough, yet they are become very equivocal, as men are apt to apply them: whereas Whig and Tory ... cannot be mistaken; for men may change, and words may change, but principles never ...'[93] His remarks are only relatively true—Tory principles, for example, were modified considerably between 1685 and 1715—but his point about changing allegiances of politicians from Court to Country groups within each party is important, and such shifts could be as abrupt as a dismissal from a Court appointment. Country factions in both parties were defined primarily by their suspicion of Court ministers and intrigues, as well as their suspicion of placemen in Parliament. During Anne's reign the Country Tory members were the largest single group in the Commons, many of them rural squires whose election to Parliament meant additional social prestige in their communities.[94] They were often dilatory in their attendance and uneager to remain in Westminster: one such member, Sir Edmund Bacon, wrote, 'I

[91] *F.* 50. [92] *F.* 11. [93] *State Anatomy*, p. 18.

[94] Geoffrey Holmes describes the political behaviour of Country Tories in *British Politics in the Age of Anne* (1967), pp. 249–52.

hope I shall be excused for not coming up. It is very good hunting weather and I make the best of it I can.'[95] Aside from their number, Country Tories were characterized by their extreme, often reactionary politics and their unwillingness, at least before 1711, to organize their powerful political potential in the Commons, largely because of their suspicions about the ministers who wanted them organized. Except for their support for bills to exclude placemen from Parliament, their assistance was unpredictable and their distrust of political organization prevented moderate Tory ministers such as Harley from fully capitalizing on the broad support such men had in their constituencies.

In his depiction of the Tory fox-hunter in *F.* 22, the most frequently reprinted essay in the *Freeholder*, Addison humorously and succinctly sums up the prejudices, contradictions, and absurdities of those constituents who elected Country Tories to Parliament. His motto for the essay is well chosen for the caricature he draws: they were sloppily educated, hasty to form opinions, boisterous, and eager to pick a fight. The fox-hunter is also superstitious, xenophobic, and uninformed. Such men were, as Addison claimed, 'the greatest Enemies to the King's Honour and the Government's Safety', and his choice of the superlative is not just rhetorical; loyalty to the Hanoverian government among rural Tories was essential to political stability. That the majority of them did not join the rebellion as the Jacobites had hoped meant that the Pretender could not duplicate William III's success of 1688. Most malcontents like the fox-hunter and his innkeeper friend were unable to rouse their neighbours or even themselves to any action except against unarmed dissenters. Dr. Johnson praised Addison's generosity for having the fox-hunter eventually converted to Hanoverian loyalty, and the two later essays on the fox-hunter (*F.* 44, *F.* 47) are conciliatory, although neither essay erases the vivid image we remember from *F.* 22. Those later essays are as much a celebration of the flourishing social and economic conditions of London and the mild treatment of the rebel commoners by the government as any reconciliation of Court and Country opinions.

The most convincing evidence of Addison's disdain for Country factions in Parliament is his attack on Country members in his own party (*F.* 48). There he seems to have Whigs such as Lechmere in mind, men who were unwilling to assist the ministry in measures Addison considered important for securing the Hanoverian government. In criticizing an opponent to the ministry, Addison may have simply been the tool of the administration from which he hoped to gain favour and advancement. But such a

[95] Winterton Letters, 879 (29 Jan. 1705).

speculation is questionable for several reasons. He certainly owed no favours to either the King or his principal ministers, Walpole and Townshend. Nor is there evidence that his allegiance to them would necessarily lead to any future office, since his fate was clearly tied to the future of Sunderland, their chief competitor for royal favour. Rather, he opposed Country Whigs because he believed party unity was essential to its effectiveness and to the security of the whole nation. Moreover, in his final essay attacking Country critics of the government (*F.* 53), he argues that the unity of the whole nation is essential to prevent anarchy; given the tenor of his arguments here and elsewhere, it would appear that the fears he expressed about anarchy were not insincere.

Addison's reasons for focusing on the politics of Country Tories are obvious, but why he wrote so much about the 'Passions of our States-women' deserves some attention. Among the many lessons the Sacheverell trial taught the Whigs, one was not to underestimate the influence women could and did exert in politics. Writing during the aftermath of that affair, Alexander Cunningham complained that women's opinions were too vulnerable to political clergymen and, with Abigail Masham advising the widowed Queen and the Electress Sophia next heir to the throne, he said, 'lest . . . any thing in the conduct of the present administration should be interpreted to the prejudice of the queen, or the princess Sophia, it was thought proper rather to conceal the many failings of women, than to divulge them to no purpose . . . one thing however is certain, that all Britain was now quite disgusted at female government.'[96] Such disgust may have been ill founded, but it is based on a fear about the political influence of women which seems genuine.[97] In a humorous essay, not unlike those Addison addresses to women in the *Freeholder*, Defoe claimed that traditional sex roles had been reversed by the Sacheverell affair: men, he wrote, are learning to knit and sew while 'all manner of Discourse among the Women, runs now upon State Affairs, War, and Government; Tattling Nonsense and Slander is Transposed to the Males, and adjourned from the *Toilet*, to the Coffe-Houses.' Defoe's tone belies his genuine concern that the lack of education for British women deprived them of good judgement; this deprivation led to 'the Sympathetic Influence of the

[96] *History of Great Britain* (1787), ii. 296.

[97] Various contemporary remarks suggest that women could and did influence their husbands' or fathers' involvement in politics. Lord Ilay's comments on triennial elections assume that the whole family discussed how the father of the house would vote (*Parl. Hist.* vii. 302), and Steele describes a hen-pecked husband as 'only his Wife's Proxy' (*Englishman*, p. 11). Ann Clavering relates a humorous anecdote about the Duchess of Cleveland locking her husband in a room to prevent him from voting against Sacheverell (*Clavering Correspondence*, p. 75).

Clergy upon the Sex, and the near Affinity between the Gown, and the Petticoat . . . As soon as you pinch the Parson, he holds out his Hands to the Ladies for their Assistance—and they appear as one Woman in his Defence.'[98] His description of women's reactions is oversimplified, as the letters of Ann Clavering testify. Annoyed by the light sentence Sacheverell had received, she wrote to her brother,

> Happy are those who were a black robe, when the doctrine they preach is to be disavow'd and yet not sufferd to be punisht. I should advice all house breakers, &c., to were that habbit . . . 'Tis true the English never know when they are well. A Church Ministry we now want and shall have . . . May those who love to be priest-govern'd have enough and obey passively there superiors. I abhor that doctrine and am resolve to espouse that of resistance, when 'tis lawfull, but *in that I'll be my own judge*.[99]

Bolingbroke complained bitterly about the role women played in Jacobite intrigues in Paris. 'No sex was excluded from this ministry. *Fanny Oglethorpe*, whom you must have seen in England kept her corner in it, and *Olive Trant* was the great wheel of our machine.'[1] By bringing a beautiful young English woman to the French Court, Olive Trant was able to make contact with the Regent and, using this tenuous connection, she thought she was keeping the Jacobites informed about the Regent's opinions. Bolingbroke, after failing on several occasions to make contact with the Regent, realized that he would have to trust 'these female managers'.[2] The trust, however, was not mutual, although both Ormonde and the Pretender were informed about whatever intelligence the women obtained. Given the nature of the connections, the Jacobites were certainly less well informed than the English ambassador, who had a large and efficient network of spies. After returning to France from Scotland, the Pretender ignored Bolingbroke but spent several days with his female associates. Later Bolingbroke was to conclude that 'The regent never intended from the first, to do any thing, even indirectly, in favor of the jacobite cause. His interest was plainly on the other side, and he saw it.'[3] Whatever information or assistance Olive Trant was able to obtain was of little use when the Pretender sailed for Scotland in December 1715.

Except for their part in obtaining clemency for the rebel Lords, there is little evidence that women played significant roles in the rebellion in Britain, considerably less evidence than one finds for their involvement in the Sacheverell affair; it may be that Addison was responding to a fear that

[98] *Review* (9 May 1710).
[99] *Clavering Correspondence*, pp. 74–5 (my italics).
[1] *Letter to Windham*, p. 124.
[2] *Letter to Windham*, p. 174.
[3] *Letter to Windham*, pp. 184–5.

the Pretender and his followers could elicit as much sympathy from British women as Sacheverell had. Whatever his motive, Addison has been criticized for his 'playful condescension towards women' and his *Freeholder* essays on women will appear to offer little evidence to acquit him of such a charge.[4] There are some mitigating facts however. He was considerably less patronizing toward women than the majority of his male contemporaries. James Stanhope, for example, exclaimed at Sacheverell's trial that the sermon was 'fit only for silly Deluded Women' and an anonymous diarist, noting the remark, wrote in his margin, 'the Q---n was there'.[5] Like Defoe, Addison had, in more serious essays, clearly stated his opinion about the education of women. He wrote in *Guardian* 155 that 'Since they have the same improveable Minds as the Male part of the Species, why should they not be cultivated by the same Methods? why should Reason be left to Itself in one of the Sexes, and be disciplined with so much Care in the other?' Virginia Woolf, who was more sensitive to the issues here than most modern critics of Addison, felt that 'Addison was on the side of sense and taste and civilisation' in mocking the particular follies of particular women in an 'age ... rich in follies'. For her Addison was 'watching, discriminating, denouncing and delighting ... distinguished and strangely contemporary with ourselves'.[6] The 'Passions of our Stateswomen' are linked with the absurdities of Country Tories because, as the motto of *F.* 22 suggests, they were *studiis rudis*, poorly educated, but through no fault of their own.

The best *Freeholder* essays are characterized by an urbanity which, according to Dr. Johnson, prompted Steele to complain that 'the ministry made use of a lute, when they should have called for a trumpet.'[7] Steele's idea of a trumpet was perhaps something like his own periodical, the *Englishman*, and the burden of his complaint is that Addison did not model the *Freeholder* on his political essays or on the *Examiner*, the most successful political periodical published before 1716. Addison preferred to model his work on the *Spectator*, a less political but more successful periodical than the *Examiner*.[8] For example, the essays in which he examines questions of

[4] C. S. Lewis, *Selected Literary Essays* (Cambridge, 1969), p. 167.

[5] 'Account of the Trial of Dr. Sacheverell', Osborn MSS. 21/22, fo. 5 (Beinecke Library).

[6] *The Common Reader* (1933), p. 139.

[7] *Lives of the Poets*, ed. G. Birkbeck Hill (Oxford, 1905), ii. 110. There is no source earlier than Johnson for this remark.

[8] Of course the *Spectator* was not the only model Addison could have used. His essays in periodicals such as the *Tatler* and the *Guardian* were also important, but the *Spectator*, his most successful periodical, is the most likely model. In spite of his protests to the contrary, there are some similarities between the *Freeholder* and the *Examiner*. Cf. e.g. essays on party credulity (*F.* 14 and *Examiner*, 2–5 Jan. 1713), political women (*F.* 8 and *Examiner*, 19–23 Jan. 1713), and royal flattery (*F.* 2 and *Examiner*, 2–6 Feb. 1713). Considering the large number

loyalty, rebellion or political indifference resemble his Saturday essays in the *Spectator* more closely than essays on those subjects which appeared occasionally in political periodicals such as the *Examiner* or the *Englishman*. These Saturday essays in the *Spectator* usually instructed the readers in some general point of morality or aesthetics and, for the *Freeholder*, Addison exploits the political potential of such moral or philosophical stances. Relatively abstract essays on political issues like loyalty appealed to the rationality of his readers, flattered their intelligence, and, by ignoring petty squabbles, created at least an illusion of magnanimity. And if the Whigs wanted to assure the nation that the Church was not in danger, there was good reason to appeal to the women of the nation, since their participation in religion was more frequent and more overt than in politics. For such an appeal Addison's experience with the *Spectator*, informing and manipulating the opinions of both men and women, was no doubt valuable.

One contemporary compared Addison's essays on political women to *The Rape of the Lock*.[9] The comparison is extravagant but it points towards Pope's gentle satire as Addison's model rather than Swift's more vitriolic political satires. Addison satirizes women sympathetic to the rebels: 'If the Name of a Traitor be mentioned, they are very particular in describing his Person; and when they are not able to extenuate his Treason, commend his Shape.'[10] Public image was obviously important and, in many ways, the rebels had considerable advantage over the King: they were British, many were relatively young, and they were underdogs. Ignoring their appeal was no help to the government; attacking them viciously might simply arouse more sympathy. It was easier to reduce the rebels' appeal to a matter of physique and then laugh at anyone foolish enough to be persuaded by that. But not all of Addison's satire is so gentle. When he turns his sight on the Pretender, the French, or the Catholics, his tone is quite different: 'The Pretender ... got together vast Stores of Ammunition, consisting of Reliques, Gun-Powder and Cannon-Ball. He received from the Pope a very large Contribution, one Moiety in Money and the other in Indulgences.'[11]

The Tory fox-hunter and the anonymous Freeholder are both more political than the *Spectator* characters, Sir Roger de Coverley and Sir Andrew Freeport. The Freeholder is simply a mask which Addison uses infrequently but with some effect, as in the answer to the Pretender's proclamation (*F.* 9). The way Addison shaped this mask is interesting: he

of essays published in the *Examiner*, these few similarities do not contradict Addision's claim in *F.* 19 that his periodical was not like the *Examiner*.

[9] *Weekly Remarks*, 18 Feb. 1716. [10] *F.* 32. [11] *F.* 36.

is a small property owner who discusses political issues with unbookish common sense and, unlike Sir Andrew Freeport, he is not specifically a merchant. By making him a person with no specific profession, Addison avoids the traditional association of the Whigs with the London merchant class. In spite of its obvious advantages, the mask of the small property owner was too inconsistent and inflexible for his purposes. Since most of Addison's essays are written from the perspective of the Court, the opportunities for exploiting the opinion of the ordinary voter were limited and, at times, even contradictory to his courtly rhetoric. Addison also wanted to appeal to his audience with more than unbookish common sense, since he is eager to use any appealing arguments which his Oxford education and years of political experience might offer.

The character of the Tory fox-hunter is, in a sense, an acidic reworking of Sir Roger de Coverley, an example of the simple and appealing country gentleman revised into an aggressively stupid man with less social status than Sir Roger. This transformation is only one part of a sustained attack on provincial life and attitudes, an attack which is essentially political. Unflattering remarks about country life in the *Spectator* were usually softened by compliments about its pleasures or balanced by equally unflattering remarks about the excesses of town life. In the *Freeholder* there is no such balance. Rural life is depicted as crude and violent, dominated by religious bigots and reactionary politicians. Life in London, particularly life in Court, is described as polite, fashionable, and even devout; occasionally there are disturbances from the London mob, but they are dismissed as the 'Scum . . . of the People' who have been misled by Popish agents.

Judging from his comments about political writing, Addison may have learned as much from the shortcomings of the *Examiner* as he learned from the success of the *Spectator*. In various places he accuses the Tories of using calumny for political profit and, when defending wit, he claims that such a technique is shallow and easy; the slanderous writer, he says, 'might be sure of pleasing a great Part of his Readers, but must be a very ill Man, if by such a Proceeding he could please himself.'[12] Addison was certainly capable of calumny, as his parody of the Pretender's history (*F.* 36) shows, but perhaps for the sake of conciliating the opposition he never openly or viciously attacks such an easy target as Bolingbroke. Such an attack might easily reap little more reward than some satisfaction for the Whigs who had suffered during Harley's administration. Aside from these political

[12] *F.* 45.

considerations, Addison was a more generous person than Pope's Atticus portrait would have us believe. As one commentator remarked,

> During the reign of the Queen, polemick writings were not only sharp, but bitter, and their authors studied rather to make their adversaries feel the quickness of their reproaches, than to persuade them by sound arguments, much less to invite them, by moderate and gentle applications, to their different humours and ways of thinking. The *Freeholder* hath avoided . . . these faults.[13]

When discussing his own essays in *F.* 45, Addison apologizes for his humorous essays, claiming that politics 'will not go down with the Publick without frequent Seasonings of this Kind', but in spite of such excuses he was adept enough in politics to know that a well directed joke would easily reach more ears than the most appropriate platitude.

Writing at the end of 1716, Paul Rapin contrasted the behaviour of the two political parties in England: 'Far from going about to carry Things with a high Hand, as the *Tories* do', the Whigs 'make their Point by slow Steps, without Passion and without Violence.'[14] In choosing Addison as their spokesman during the Jacobite rebellion, the Whig ministry could hardly have found anyone in England more able, either in talent or temperament, to argue 'without Passion and without Violence'. Steele's remark about the *Freeholder*, the only contemporary comment which suggests that it was not an unqualified success, was perhaps prompted by professional jealousy, since two other contemporaries—Bolingbroke being one of them—claimed that Addison's appointment as Secretary of State in 1717 was a reward for his *Freeholder* essays.[15] The complexity of political advancements makes it doubtful that an appointment to such high ministerial office would be made that simply, but his appointment also suggests that the ministry was not displeased with its lute.

SOURCES, PUBLICATION, AND TEXT

Discussing philosophical sources for writing which is essentially party propaganda is occasionally impossible and usually inconclusive. There are tenuous connections in various directions, but even a mild sceptic will have difficulty finding sources which are both specific and certain. An obvious source for the *Freeholder* was Locke's *Second Treatise*, yet even this source can be questioned and should be qualified.[16] Addison and Locke both

[13] *Biographia Britannica*, i. 36. [14] *Dissertation*, p. 88.

[15] *Biographia Britannica*, i. 36; *Occasional Writer*, no. 1.

[16] James Harrington's *Oceana* (1656) describes an ideal commonwealth based on the political consent of property owners. Addison owned a copy of the work but was generally unsympathetic toward republicanism (see *F.* 51). Judging from the number of his references to Locke in his earlier periodical essays, it would appear that Locke was the most influential modern philosopher for Addison.

agree that civil liberties are derived from natural law and both argue for 'mixt Government', but no lesser authors than Cicero, Hooker, Grotius, and Pufendorf all discuss one or both of these issues, and Addison was familiar with their work, as well as the work of contemporaries like Benjamin Hoadly who helped to popularize such ideas. In their study of Addison's political thinking, Edward and Lillian Bloom argue that 'his sources, from Cicero to the Latitudinarians, saw the law of nature as the antecedent and basis of civil institutions, and as universal in its application. . . . All agreed that natural law was the measure of human activity, whose common denominator was reason' and they conclude that 'Addison was concerned with a complex liberalism. It originated in the law of nature and extended to the . . . contractual partnership between the governed and the governing.'[17] In spite of the number and complexity of political ideas which influenced Addison's thinking, his principal debt in the *Freeholder* is to John Locke because Locke had argued that sovereignty was derived from the consent of property owners, an assumption which other natural-law philosophers did not share. This became Addison's most obvious borrowing: he named his periodical after the property owner and he asserted the necessity of eliminating arbitrary government by actively using property owners' consent in government.

Examining the political philosophies which influenced Addison's thinking would be easier if his political ideas were not complicated by the everyday politics which created profound reversals in 1716. Without such reversals, one could point to Locke and the other natural-law philosophers of the seventeenth century who shaped so much of eighteenth-century liberalism and be done. While it is clear that Addison was a resolute Whig, that he wholeheartedly subscribed to the Revolution Settlement and advocated toleration for dissenters, that his position was essentially no different from arguments presented and defended by Whig apologists such as Hoadly, Steele, or Fleetwood, there are limits to the value of examining the history of his ideas without reference to the specific political conditions at the time he expressed them. To understand all the sources for Addison's *Freeholder* essays, one must acknowledge the reversals of 1716, then look at the traditional Tory arguments which these reversals gave the Whigs in order to appreciate how conservative some of this liberal thinker's essays are.

For intellectual bases to their arguments, Tory apologists frequently

[17] *Sociable Animal*, pp. 114, 117. This study also examines the *Freeholder* essays in the context of contemporary political philosophies and Addison's other political writing (pp. 87–148).

relied on the political theology of the Reformation, especially the work of Richard Hooker, and upon historical precedents.[18] Locke had been careful to include arguments from Hooker in his *Second Treatise*, presumably to win favour among his opponents.[19] Locke borrowed most heavily from Hooker when he discussed natural law and least when he discussed revolution. The two authors do not contradict one another about revolution, but they emphasize the subject differently: Hooker dwells on unjust rebellion and its evil consequences while Locke expounds upon the circumstances for a just rebellion. Addison's remarks on rebellion, particularly those in *F.* 12, are closer to Hooker and the Tudor *Homilies* than to anything Locke wrote. This was partly because Addison considered the Jacobite uprising an unjust rebellion, but it was also because Hooker's *Ecclesiastical Polity* and the *Homilies* were popular touchstones for Tory thinking and writing. Similarly, Addison differs from Locke by emphasizing historical examples as evidence in his essays. In this he may have been influenced by Grotius and Pufendorf, natural-law philosophers who did use historical examples, but he may also have wanted to beat the Tories with historical precedents, yet another of their own cudgels. History, particularly English and Roman history, is a subject Addison occasionally discussed in his earlier periodicals but which he frequently introduces into the *Freeholder*.[20]

Addison's literary sources are more numerous and more easily defined than his philosophical sources, but they are often less integral to his arguments. He draws almost equally from ancient and modern authors and, among the ancients, he most frequently quotes or alludes to Cicero, Sallust, and Virgil. Both Cicero and Sallust described the Catiline conspiracy, which loyalist pamphleteers in 1716 compared to the Jacobite rebellion. Cicero was also the most important ancient political theorist for exponents of natural law and, because Addison reiterates Cicero's

[18] In their defence of Sacheverell, for example, the Tory managers relied upon religious-political works such as the Homilies on Obedience, the 'King's Book' of 1543, Bishop Overall's *Convocation Book* and, of course, Hooker's *Lawes of Ecclesiastical Polity* (*Tryal of Dr. Sacheverell*, pp. 226–35). As for history, they challenged the Whigs to specify exactly when the contractual theory of monarchy became a part of the British constitution (ibid., p. 214). Robert Brady had earlier attacked the Whigs' version of Parliamentary history in his *Introduction to the Old English History* (1684), pp. 130–54.

[19] J. W. Gough, *John Locke's Political Philosophy* (Oxford, 1950), p. 44; *Two Treatises*, p. 109.

[20] *F.* 35 discusses the problems of writing history, *F.* 36 is a satiric history of the Pretender, *F.* 41 complains that economic history is ignored too much, and *F.* 54 is a capsule history of seventeenth-century British politics. Addison draws upon historical precedents to refute Atterbury in *F.* 31, when he argues for suspending habeas corpus in *F.* 16, and in various essays in which he argues that Catholics cannot rule Protestant nations or in which he discusses the problems of establishing a new family on the throne.

arguments, he alludes to Cicero more often than to Sallust and Virgil combined.[21] For his modern sources Addison uses English and French works almost exclusively. He refers to Francis Bacon and Pierre Bayle most often; John Milton, William Camden, Gilbert Burnet, and William Temple are also cited authoritatively once or twice. He draws upon travel literature and various satiric writers occasionally. His allusions are usually only illustrations, but on several occasions, such as his accounts of George I (*F.* 2) and of Mulai Ismail (*F.* 10), he draws a good deal of substantive material from contemporary works. He also expands upon themes in such contemporary publications as the Archbishop's *Declaration* (*F.* 6, *F.* 13) and uses his experience as a Commissioner for Trade and Plantations for material on British trade (*F.* 41, *F.* 42). In *F.* 40 he commends Pope's *Homer*, Rowe's translation of Lucan's *Pharsalia*, and Dryden's *Aeneid.* In other essays he attacks the *Examiner* (*F.* 19), Atterbury's *Argument to Prove the Affections* (*F.* 31), Blackmore's *Essays* (*F.* 45), and Collins's *Discourse of Freethinking* (*F.* 51). Francis Atterbury and the *Examiner* were obvious targets since both opposed Whig policies and, because Blackmore questioned the moral value of wit and used the *Spectator* as an example, Addison's motive for answering him is also clear. However, Anthony Collins was a Whig, and Addison's attack on his work was motivated by a desire to dissociate Court Whigs from Collins's heterodox sentiments and republican sympathies.

The *Freeholder* was printed and sold by S. Gray, the publisher of the *Daily Courant.* Like the *Spectator*, the *Freeholder* was printed on both sides of a folio half-sheet with two columns to the page. But the *Freeholder* sold for a half-penny less than the *Spectator*, it published only one advertisement, and the first three issues were distributed gratis; all evidence that the government was underwriting the venture. The first three essays were almost immediately reprinted on a sheet and a half, and on 27 February *F.* 20 announced that 'The Impressions of most of the first Numbers of this Paper being sold off, and great demand being made for them, the first Twelve Numbers are Reprinted and now published by S. Gray.'[22] Occasionally other London newspapers included selections from the *Freeholder* in their columns, and between 5 April and 26 June the *Freeholder*

[21] His other Roman sources include Terence, Horace, Seneca, Tacitus, and Macrobius; from literature in Greek he draws upon works by Homer, Diodorus, Plutarch, Aelian, Aesop, and Pythagoras.

[22] An announcement in *F.* 5 reads: 'The Three First Numbers of this Paper (which were separately distributed Gratis) are now printed together on a Sheet and a half, to be sold for 2d . . .' A copy of this reprint is in the Bodleian Library. A copy of the reprint of the first twelve essays is in the Rothschild Collection, Merton Hall, Cambridge.

was published in quarto at Edinburgh along with the *Weekly-Packet*.[23] In Dublin the ninth *Freeholder* was published as a folio broadside by George Greirson, and in London *F.* 31 was reissued as a duodecimo pamphlet with the title, *An Answer to a Pamphlet entituled An Argument to Prove the Affections*.[24] While the government underwrote Addison's paper, its popularity suggests that it would not have cost them very much.

One puzzling question about the publication of the *Freeholder* is why Addison continued it after the rebellion was over and the King had assented to the Septennial Act (7 May 1716). A letter written by Lord Townshend, Secretary of State, on 19 May may suggest a reason: the rebellion, he argued, was 'rather smothered ... than totally extinguished' and 'a constant, steady and uniform ... working out the inmost causes of this distemper' was essential.[25] Townshend's motive there was to postpone the King's departure for Hanover but, since Addison was writing for the ministry, he may have been obliged to continue until that issue was settled and Parliament prorogued. His farewell to women readers (*F.* 38), coupled with rumours that Parliament would rise around 10 May,[26] suggest that perhaps Addison planned to conclude his paper earlier than he did. In *F.* 40 he turns away from politics for the first time and complains that 'Authors, who have thus drawn off the spirit of their thoughts, should lie still for some time, until their minds have gathered fresh strength ...' Although discussing other kinds of writing there, Addison may well have felt that he had exhausted his own thoughts on contemporary affairs. With only a few outstanding exceptions, such as *F.* 48, Addison's vigour in the last fifteen essays is obviously diminished. The events of May and June—the King's birthday, the Day of Thanksgiving, the riots on the Pretender's birthday—provided him with material to write about, but he digresses into literary subjects (*F.* 40, *F.* 45), resurrects the Tory fox-hunter (*F.* 44, *F.* 47), and introduces such old news as the trade agreements (*F.* 41, *F.* 42) to fill out his paper. His political themes in the last essays—his criticism of the previous Tory administration and Country politicians—were not urgent issues, and the only major legislative action, the repeal of the clause in the Act of Settlement which required Parliament's consent for the monarch to leave the country, caused little stir outside the ministry. It

[23] For other newspapers using selections from the *Freeholder*, see the Nichols' Newspaper Collection (Bodleian Library), January–June 1716 *passim*. Incomplete sets of the Edinburgh quartos are in the Bodleian and the National Library of Scotland.

[24] A copy of the Dublin broadside, entitled *The Freeholder's Answer to the Pretender's Declaration*, is in the Beinecke Library and a copy of the duodecimo issue of *F.* 31 (in which the type of the original folio sheets was broken into short single columns but not reset) is in the British Library.

[25] Coxe, *Walpole* ii. 52.

[26] H.M.C. *Portland MSS.* v. 522.

would appear that Addison was simply marking time, watching the political scene in the event that his full energies might again be needed.

In half of the first thirty essays, Addison signed his essays with a variety of initials—D, W, U, B, F—none of which had ever been used as signature initials in the *Spectator*. No doubt his purpose was to make his readers think several people were writing the essays since, when revising his work for the collected octavo edition later in 1716, he changed 'The Conduct of those who are engaged in this Work . . .' to 'The Conduct of this Work. . .'[27] For a while the ploy succeeded. Dudley Ryder wrote in his diary on 16 February,

> When we sat down to conversation we talked about the manner of writing which was brought so much into fashion by the *Tatlers* and *Spectators* and which the town has by this means got a relish of. The *Freeholder* is writ now in the same manner, in which they say Addison and the Bishop of St. Asaph [William Fleetwood] and Hoadly and some of the greatest pens in England are engaged.

At the end of March, the time when Addison stopped using initial signatures, a Jacobite agent reported, 'The *Freeholder* is writ by Mr. Addison . . . as is generally believed.'[28] Most of Addison's essays on literary subjects appeared after 1 April, and obviously many readers knew who was writing about Blackmore's *Essays* or Pope's *Homer*. Nevertheless, Addison's name never appeared on the original issues or any of the three collected editions of the *Freeholder* which appeared during his life.

Of these three collected editions, one is a 1716 duodecimo edition published in Dublin which contains a great many errors, few of which are even plausible.[29] The two London editions, an octavo and duodecimo, were both published by Tonson and Midwinter. The octavo was first advertised in the *Post Boy* of 6–9 October and its title was expanded to *The Freeholder, or Political Essays*, perhaps to suggest that these essays were more philosophical and less topical than they actually were. Authorial revisions were numerous, sometimes as many as ten in an essay, and almost all of them were made between the printing of the folio sheets and the octavo edition. The duodecimo usually follows the octavo and presumably was published after it. The Errata which appeared most frequently in the first twenty essays usually only corrected typographical errors and these corrections have been incorporated silently into this text. Following Donald Bond's edition of the *Spectator*, I have used the original

[27] *F.* 19, note a. [28] H.M.C. *Stuart MSS.* ii. 62 (26 Mar. 1716).

[29] All three collected editions are in the British Library. The Dublin edition has not been used in preparing this edition.

sheets of the periodical as a copy text for this edition of the *Freeholder*.[30] The spelling, punctuation, and capitalization of the folio sheets have been retained, and authorial revisions have been introduced into this fabric. The lettered footnotes indicate an emended reading of the text and, unless indicated otherwise, the emended reading occurs in both the octavo and duodecimo editions. For example,

[a] profess / maintain *Fol.*

indicates that 'profess' is the reading in the octavo and duodecimo editions and replaces 'maintain' which appeared in the original folio text. By 1762 the *Freeholder* had been published in ten individual editions as well as in editions of Addison's complete works and miscellaneous works. For passages which seemed unclear, I have occasionally referred to them but have not found any satisfactory emendations.

[30] The Bodleian Library has the original folio half-sheets for all but the first three *Freeholders* and the British Library has a copy of the original sheet for *F.* 3. For *F.* 1 and 2 I have used the Bodleian reprint of *F.* 1–3 (see above, p. 32, n. 22); a comparison of the original sheet for *F.* 3 and the Bodleian reprint indicates that no revisions were made between the original and the reprint.

ABBREVIATED TITLES

All published works cited in this edition were published in London unless specified otherwise.

Addison, *Miscellaneous Works: The Miscellaneous Works of Joseph Addison*, ed. A. Guthkelch, 2 vols., 1914.

Annals: The Annals of King George I, 6 vols., 1716–21.

Atterbury, *Argument to Prove the Affections*: Francis Atterbury, *An Argument to Prove the Affections of the People of England to Be the Best Security of the Government*, 1716.

Atterbury, *English Advice*: Francis Atterbury, *English Advice to the Freeholders of England*, 1714.

Bacon, *Works: The Works of Francis Bacon*, ed. J. Spedding, 14 vols., 1857–74.

Bayle, *Historical Dictionary*: Pierre Bayle, *An Historical and Critical Dictionary*, 4 vols., 1710.

Bloom, *Sociable Animal*: Edward and Lillian Bloom, *Joseph Addison's Sociable Animal*, Providence, 1971.

Bolingbroke, *Letter to Windham*: Henry St. John, Viscount Bolingbroke, *A Letter to Sir William Windham*, 1753.

Boyer, *Queen Anne*: Abel Boyer, *The History of Queen Anne*, 1735.

Burnet, *History*: Gilbert Burnet, *History of His Own Time*, 6 vols., Oxford, 1833.

C.J.: Journals of the House of Commons.

Chandler: *The History and Proceedings of the House of Commons*, printed for Richard Chandler, 13 vols., 1742–43.

Clarendon, *History*: Edward Hyde, Earl of Clarendon, *The History of the Rebellion and Civil Wars in England*, ed. W. Macray, 6 vols., Oxford, 1888.

Clavering Correspondence: The Correspondence of Sir James Clavering, ed. H. Dickinson, *Publications of the Surtees Society*, Gateshead, 1967.

Cowper Diary: The Diary of Mary, Countess Cowper, Panshanger MSS., Hertfordshire Record Office.

Cowper, 'Impartial History': William, Lord Cowper, 'An Impartial History of Parties,' reprinted in John Campbell, *Lives of the Lord Chancellors*, Philadelphia, 1851.

Coxe, *Marlborough*: William Coxe, *Memoirs of John, Duke of Marlborough*, 6 vols., 1820.

Coxe, *Walpole*: William Coxe, *Memoirs of the Life and Administration of Sir Robert Walpole*, 3 vols., 1798.

Defoe, *Tour Thro' Great Britain*: Daniel Defoe, *A Tour Thro' the whole Island of Great Britain*, ed. G. Cole, 2 vols., 1927.

F.: Freeholder.

Grey's *Debates: Debates of the House of Commons from 1667 to 1694*, collected by Anchitell Grey, 10 vols., 1763.

H.M.C.: Historical Manuscripts Commission.

Hervey, *Memoirs*: John Hervey, *Some Materials toward Memoirs of the Reign of King George II*, ed. R. Sedgwick, 3 vols., 1931.

History of Parliament: Romney Sedgwick, *The History of Parliament: The House of Commons 1715–1754*, 2 vols., 1970.

L.J.: *Journals of the House of Lords.*

Lamberty, *Mémoires*: Guilliaume de Lamberty, *Mémoires pour servir à l'Histoire du XVIII Siècle*, 14 vols., Amsterdam, 1734–40.

Locke, *Two Treatises*: John Locke, *Two Treatises of Government*, ed. P. Laslett, Cambridge, 1967.

Lockhart Papers: George Lockhart, *The Lockhart Papers: Memoirs and Commentaries upon the Affairs of Scotland*, 2 vols., 1817.

Loftis, *Politics of Drama*: John Loftis, *The Politics of Drama in Augustan England*, Oxford, 1963.

London Stage: *The London Stage, 1660–1800*, ed. W. Van Lennep, 5 vols., Carbondale, 1960–68.

Macaulay: Thomas Macaulay, *The History of England*, ed. C. Firth, 6 vols., 1913–15.

Marchmont Papers: *A Selection from the Papers of the Earls of Marchmont*, ed. G. Rose, 3 vols., 1831.

Marlborough, *Private Correspondence*: *The Private Correspondence of Sarah, Duchess of Marlborough*, 2 vols., 1838.

Michael: Wolfgang Michael, *England under George I: The Beginnings of the Hanoverian Dynasty*, 1936.

Misc. State Papers: *Miscellaneous State Papers from 1501 to 1725*, ed. P. Yorke, 2 vols., 1778.

P.O.A.S.: *Poems on Affairs of State*, ed. G. Lord, 7 vols., New Haven, 1963–75.

Parl. Hist.: *The Parliamentary History of England, 1066–1803*, ed. W. Cobbett, 36 vols., 1806–20.

Patten, *Late Rebellion*: Robert Patten, *The History of the Late Rebellion*, 1717.

Percival Letterbook: The Letterbook of Sir John Percival (January 1715–December 1718), British Library, Additional Manuscript 47028.

Pol. State: *The Political State of Great Britain*, 60 vols., 1711–40.

Pope, *Correspondence*: *The Correspondence of Alexander Pope*, ed. G. Sherburn, 5 vols., Oxford, 1956.

Rapin, *Dissertation*: Paul de Rapin-Thoyras, *Dissertation sur les Whigs et les Torys*, trans. Ozell, 1717.

Ryder, *Diary*: *The Diary of Dudley Ryder, 1715–16*, ed. W. Matthews, 1939.

S.: *Spectator.*

Smithers, *Addison*: Peter Smithers, *The Life of Joseph Addison*, Oxford, 1968.

Somers Tracts: *A Collection of Scarce and Valuable Tracts*, ed. W. Scott, 13 vols., 1809–15.

Speck, *Tory and Whig*: W. A. Speck, *Tory and Whig: The Struggle in the Constituencies 1701–1715*, 1970.

Spectator: *The Spectator*, ed. D. Bond, 5 vols., Oxford, 1965.

State Trials: *A Complete Collection of State Trials*, compiled by T. Howell, 33 vols., 1811–26.

Statutes: *Statutes of the Realm*, 9 vols., 1810–22.

Steele, *Englishman*: Richard Steele, *The Englishman*, ed. R. Blanchard, Oxford, 1955.

Steele, *Periodical Journalism*: Richard Steele, *Steele's Periodical Journalism, 1714–16*, ed. R. Blanchard, Oxford, 1959.

Steele, *Tracts and Pamphlets*: Richard Steele, *Tracts and Pamphlets*, ed. R. Blanchard, Baltimore, 1944.

Swift, *Prose Works*: Jonathan Swift, *The Prose Works of Jonathan Swift*, ed. H. Davis, 14 vols., Oxford, 1939–62.

T.: *Tatler*.

Tindal: Nicholas Tindal, *The History of England by Mr. Rapin de Thoyras. Continued from the Revolution to the Accession of King George II*, 4 vols., 1732–47. All references are to volume 4 unless specified otherwise.

Toland, *State Anatomy*: John Toland, *A State Anatomy of Great Britain*, 1717.

Vernon Letters: *Letters Illustrative of the Reign of William III . . . by James Vernon*, ed. G. James, 3 vols., 1841.

Walpole, *Reminiscences*: Horace Walpole, *Reminiscences*, ed. P. Toynbee, Oxford, 1924.

Wentworth Papers: *The Wentworth Papers, 1705–1739*, ed. J. Cartwright, 1883.

Wortley Montagu, *Account*: 'An Account of the Court of George I,' *Letters and Works of Lady Mary Wortley Montagu*, ed. Lord Wharncliffe, 3 vols., 1837.

Wortley Montagu, *Complete Letters*: *The Complete Letters of Lady Mary Wortley Montagu*, ed. R. Halsband, 3 vols., Oxford, 1965–67.

The FREEHOLDER

Numb. 1 *Friday, December 23, 1715*[a]

Rara temporum felicitas, ubi sentire
quae velis, et quae sentias dicere licet.
Tacit.

THE Arguments of an Author lose a great deal of their Weight, when we are perswaded that he only writes for Argument's sake, and has no real Concern in the Cause which he espouses. This is the Case of one, who draws his Pen in the Defence of Property, without having any; except, perhaps, in the Copy of a Libel, or a Ballad. One is apt to suspect, that the Passion for Liberty which appears in a Grub-street Patriot, arises only from his Apprehensions of a Gaol; and that, whatever he may pretend, he does not write to secure, but to get something of his own: Should the Government be overturn'd, he has nothing to lose but an old Standish.

I question not but the Reader will conceive a Respect for the Author of this Paper from the Title of it; since, he may be sure, I am so considerable a Man, that I cannot have less than Forty Shillings a Year.[2]

I have rather chosen this Title than any other, because it is what I most glory in, and what most effectually calls to my Mind the Happiness of that Government under which I live. As a *British* Free-holder, I should not scruple taking place of a *French* Marquis; and when I see one of my Countrymen amusing himself in his little Cabbage-Garden, I naturally look upon him as a greater Person than the Owner of the richest Vineyard in *Champagne*.

The House of Commons is the Representative of men in my Condition.

[a] 'To be Continued every *Monday* and *Friday*' appeared after the date in the folio edition of the first eleven issues.

Motto. Tacitus, *Histories*, i. 1: It is a rare blessing of the times when you can think what you like and can say what you think.

[2] Freeholders whose income was at least 40*s.* per annum were eligible to vote in county elections and elect Knights of the Shire to represent them in the House of Commons (*Statutes*, ii. 243–4). The significance of Addison's choice of this title is discussed in the Introduction to this edition.

I consider myself as one who give my Consent to every law which passes: A Free-holder in our Government being of the Nature of a Citizen of *Rome* in that famous Commonwealth, who, by the Election of a Tribune, had a kind of remote Voice in every Law that was enacted.[3] So that a Free-holder is but one Remove from a Legislator, and for that Reason ought to stand up in the Defence of those Laws, which are in some degree of his own making. For such is the Nature of our happy Constitution, that the Bulk of the People virtually give their Approbation[b] to every thing they are bound to obey, and prescribe to themselves those Rules by which they are to walk.[4]

At the same time that I declare I am a Free-holder, I do not exclude myself from any other Title. A Free-holder may be either a Voter, or a Knight of the Shire; a Wit, or a Fox-hunter; a Scholar, or a Soldier; an Alderman, or a Courtier; a Patriot, or a Stock-Jobber.[5] But I chuse to be distinguish'd by this Denomination, as the Free-holder is the Basis of all other Titles. Dignities may be grafted upon it; but this is the substantial Stock, that conveys to them their Life, Taste and Beauty; and without which they are no more than Blossoms, that would fall away with every Shake of Wind.

And here I cannot but take occasion to congratulate my Country upon the Increase of this happy Tribe of Men, since, by the Wisdom of the present Parliament, I find the Race of Free-holders spreading into the remotest Corners of the Island. I mean that Act which pass'd in the late Session for the Encouragement of Loyalty in *Scotland*: By which it is provided, *That all and every Vassal and Vassals in* Scotland *who shall continue peaceable, and in dutiful Allegiance to His Majesty, His Heirs and Successors, holding Lands or Tenements of any Offender* [guilty of High-Treason] *who*

[b] Approbation / Consent *Fol.*

[3] At their height of power during the Roman Republic, ten Tribunes, elected by the Plebians for a term of one year, could summon and preside over meetings of Plebians, veto Senate resolutions, and prosecute anyone who threatened the common people. Polybius described the constitution of the Republic: 'The people can approve or reject laws, they have the final decision in questions of peace and war, and they can likewise ratify or reject alliances, peace terms and treaties ... One could easily say the people have the greatest share in government' (*Histories*, vi. 14).

[4] Recent studies of the electorate in 1715 indicate that about 250,000 persons voted, or about 4·3 per cent of the estimated total population of England and Wales (5·8 million). However, the number of persons eligible to vote was greater than the turn-out, so that about 300,000, or over 20 per cent of the adult male population, were eligible voters in 1715 (J. H. Plumb, 'The Growth of the Electorate in England from 1660 to 1715', *Past and Present*, 45 (1969), 109; Speck, *Tory and Whig*, pp. 16–17).

[5] Addison is using *Patriot* in its pejorative sense, 'a factious disturber of the government' (Johnson's *Dictionary*); John Toland described the nation in 1716 as divided into 'Patriots and Loyalists' (*State Anatomy*, p. 18).

holds such Lands or Tenements immediately of the Crown, shall be vested and seized, and are hereby enacted and ordained to hold the said Lands or Tenements of His Majesty, His Heirs and Successors, in Fee and Heritage for ever, by such manner of Holding, as any such Offender held such Lands or Tenements of the Crown, &c.[6]

By this means it will be in the Power of a Highlander to be at all Times a good Tenant, without being a Rebel; and to deserve the Character of a faithful Servant, without thinking himself obliged to follow his Master to the Gallows.

How can we sufficiently extol the Goodness of His present Majesty, who is not willing to have a single Slave in His Dominions! Or enough rejoyce in the Exercise of that Loyalty, which, instead of betraying a Man into the most ignominious Servitude, (as it does in some of our neighbouring Kingdoms) entitles him to the highest Privileges of Freedom and Property! It is now to be hoped, that we shall have few Vassals, but to the Laws of our Country.

When these Men have a taste of Property, they will naturally love that Constitution from which they derive so great a Blessing. There is an unspeakable Pleasure in calling any thing one's own. A Free-hold, tho' it be but in Ice and Snow, will make the Owner pleased in the Possession, and stout in the Defence of it; and is a very proper Reward of our Allegiance to our present King, who (by an unparallel'd Instance of Goodness in a Sovereign, and Infatuation in Subjects) contends for the Freedom of His People against Themselves; and will not suffer many of them to fall into a State of Slavery, which they are bent upon with so much Eagerness and Obstinacy.

A Free-holder of *Great Britain*, is bred with an Aversion to every Thing that tends to bring him under a Subjection to the arbitrary Will of another. Of this we find frequent Instances in all our Histories; where the Persons, whose Characters are the most amiable, and strike us with the highest Veneration, are those who stood up manfully against the Invasions of Civil Liberty, and the complicated Tyranny which Popery imposes upon our Bodies, our Fortunes, and our Minds. What a despicable Figure then must the present Mock-Patriots make in the Eyes of Posterity, who venture to

[6] 'An Act for encouraging all Superiors, Vassals, Landlords and Tenants, in *Scotland*, who do and shall continue in their Duty and Loyalty to his Majesty King *George*' was presented to the Commons by James Stanhope on 10 Aug. 1715 and received royal assent on 30 Aug. (*C.J.* xviii. 262; *L.J.* xx. 189). The Act empowered the government to take security from Scottish property owners whose loyalty they suspected; the government could also give loyal lessees the freehold of tenements they rented from rebel lairds. While the Act did not produce loyalty, it assisted the government in discovering which landlords were joining or helping the rebels in Scotland.

be hang'd, drawn and quartered, for the Ruin of those Civil Rights which their Ancestors rather than part with, chose to be cut to Pieces in the Field of Battle. And what an Opinion will after Ages entertain of their Religion, who bid fair for a Gibbet, by endeavouring to bring in a Superstition, which their Forefathers perished in Flames to keep out.

But how Instructive soever the Folly of these Men may prove to future Times, it will be my Business more immediately to consult the Happiness of the Age in which I live. And since so many profligate Writers have endeavoured to varnish over a bad Cause, I shall do all in my Power to recommend a good One, which indeed requires no more than barely to explain what it is. While many of my gallant Countrymen are employed in pursuing Rebels half discomfited through the Consciousness of their Guilt, I shall labour to improve those Victories to the Good of my Fellow-Subjects; by carrying on our Successes over the Minds of Men, and by reconciling them to the Cause of their King, their Country, and their Religion.

To this End, I shall in the Course of this Paper, (to be published every *Monday* and *Friday*) endeavor to open the Eyes of my Countrymen to their own Interests, to shew them the Privileges of an *English* Free-holder which they enjoy in common with my self, and to make them sensible how these Blessings are secured to us by his Majesty's Title, his Administration, and his Personal Character.

I have only one Request to make to my Readers, that they will peruse these Papers with the same[c] Candour and Impartiality in which they are written; and shall hope for[d] no other Prepossession in favour of them, than what one would think should be natural to every Man, a Desire to be happy, and a good Will towards those, who are the Instruments of making them so.

[c] the same / that *Fol.* [d] hope for / desire *Fol.*

Numb. II *Monday, December* 26, 1715

Non de Domino, sed de Parente loquimur. Intelligamus ergo bona nostra, dignosque nos illius usu probemus; atque identidem cogitemus, si majus principibus praestemus obsequium, qui servitute civium, quam qui libertate laetantur. Plin.

HAVING in my first Paper set forth the Happiness of my Station as a Freeholder of *Great Britain*, and the Nature of that Property which is secured to me by the Laws of my Country; I cannot forbear considering in the next Place, that Person who is entrusted with the Guardianship and Execution of those Laws. I have lived in one Reign, when the Prince, instead of invigorating the Laws of our Country, or giving them their proper Course, assum'd a Power of dispensing with them:[2] And in another, when the Soveraign was flattered by a Set of Men into a Persuasion, that the Regal Authority was unlimited and uncircumscribed.[3] In either of these Cases, good Laws are at best but a dead Letter; and by shewing the People how Happy they ought to be, only serve to aggravate the Sense of their Oppressions.

We have the Pleasure at this Time to see a King upon the Throne, who hath too much Goodness to wish for any Power, that does not enable him to promote the Welfare of His Subjects; and too much Wisdom to look upon those as His Friends, who would make their Court to Him by the Profession of an Obedience, which they never practised, and which has always proved fatal to those Princes who have put it to the Trial. His Majesty gave a Proof of His soveraign Vertues before He came to the Exercise of them in this Kingdom.[a] His natural Inclination to Justice led

[a] Kingdom / Nation *Fol.*

Motto. Pliny, *Panegyric*, 2: We are not speaking of a lord, but of a parent. . . . Therefore let us understand our own good and prove ourselves worthy of him; and let us repeatedly consider which prince we would rather serve, one who enjoys the slavery or one who enjoys the liberty of his subjects.

[2] James II's Declarations of Indulgence (1687, 1688) suspended penal laws in ecclesiastical matters; neither the Test Acts nor the oaths of supremacy and allegiance were to be required of office holders as a consequence of these declarations.

[3] Queen Anne. The 'Set of men' were her Tory ministers, Oxford and Bolingbroke, who used royal prerogative to justify their negotiating the terms for the Treaty of Utrecht (1713), the treaty which the Whigs vigorously opposed (Tindal, p. 435).

Him to rule His *German* Subjects in the same Manner, that our Constitution directs Him to govern the *English.* He regarded those, which are our civil Liberties, as the natural Rights of Mankind; and therefore indulged them to a People, who pleaded no other Claim to them than from His known Goodness and Humanity. This Experience of a good Prince, before we had the Happiness to enjoy Him, must give great Satisfaction to every thinking Man, who considers how apt Soveraignty is to deprave human Nature; and how many of our own Princes made very ill Figures upon the Throne, who, before they ascended it, were the Favourites of the People.

What gives us the greatest Security in the Conduct of so excellent a Prince is, that Consistency of Behaviour, whereby He inflexibly pursues those Measures which appear the most Just and Equitable. As He hath the Character of being the most Prudent in laying proper Schemes; He is no less remarkable for being steady in accomplishing what He has once concerted. Indeed, if[b] we look into the History of His present Majesty, and reflect upon that wonderful Series of Successes which have attended Him, I think they cannot be ascribed to any thing so much as to this Uniformity and Firmness of Mind, which has always discovered it-self in His proceedings. It was by This that He surmounted those many Difficulties, which lay in the Way to His Succession; and by which, we have reason to hope, He will daily make all Opposition fall before Him. The fickle and unsteady Politicks of our late *British* Monarchs, have been the perpetual Source of those Dissentions and Animosities which have made the Nation unhappy: Whereas the constant and unshaken Temper of His present Majesty, must have a natural Tendency to the Peace of His Government, and the Unanimity of His People.

Whilst I am enumerating the publick Vertues of our Soveraign, which are so conducive to the Advantage of those who are to obey Him, I cannot but take Notice, that His Majesty was bred up from His Infancy with a Love to this our Nation, under a Princess, who was the most accomplished Woman of her Age, and particularly famous for her Affection to the *English.*[4] Our Countrymen were dear to Him, before there was any Prospect of their being His Subjects; and every one knows, that nothing recommended a Man so much to the distinguishing Civilities of His Court, as the being born in *Great Britain.*

To the Fame of his Majesty's Civil Vertues, we may add the Reputation He has acquired by His Martial Atchievements. It is observed by Sir

[b] Indeed, if / If *Fol.*

[4] The Electress Sophia, granddaughter of James I and mother of George I. Addison met her at Hanover in 1706 (Smithers, *Addison*, pp. 108–9).

William Temple, that the *English* are particularly fond of a King, who is Valiant:[5] Upon which Account His Majesty has a Title to all the Esteem, that can be paid the most Warlike Prince; tho' at the same Time, for the Good of His Subjects, He studies to decline all Occasions of Military Glory; and chuses rather to be distinguished as the Father, than as the Captain of His People.[6] I am glad His rebellious Subjects are too inconsiderable to put him upon exerting that Courage and Conduct, which raised him so great a Reputation in *Hungary* and the *Morea*, when he fought against the Enemies of Christianity; and in *Germany* and *Flanders*, where he commanded against the great Disturber of the Peace of *Europe*.[7] One would think there was Reason for the Opinion of those, who make Personal Courage to be an Hereditary Vertue, when we see so many Instances of it in the Line of *Brunswick*. To go no farther back than the Time of our present King, where can we find, among the Soveraign Houses of *Europe*, any other Family, that has furnished so many Persons of distinguished Fortitude? Three of His Majesty's Brothers have fallen gloriously in the Field, fighting against the Enemies of their Native Country:[8] And the Bravery of his Royal Highness the Prince of *Wales*, is still fresh in our Memory, who fought, with the Spirit of his Father, at the Battle of *Audenarde*, when the Children of *France*, and the Pretender, fled before him.[9]

I might here take Notice of His Majesty's more private Virtues, but have rather chosen to remind my Countrymen of the publick Parts of his Character, which are supported by such incontestable Facts as are universally known and acknowledged.

Having thus far consider'd our Happiness in His Majesty's Civil and Military Character, I cannot forbear pleasing my self with regarding him in the View of One, who has been always Fortunate. *Cicero* recommends *Pompey* under this particular Head to the *Romans*,[10] with whom the Character of being Fortunate was so popular, that several of their Emperors

[5] Temple claimed that valour was one of the three sources of authority in his 'Essay upon the Original and Nature of Government', *Miscellanea* (1697), i. 56.

[6] George's military abilities were substantial enough to encourage Marlborough's opponents in England to consider him a possible replacement for Marlborough as the Allies' Commander in 1710 (Coxe, *Marlborough* v. 305).

[7] John Toland's portrait of George I in his *Account of the Courts of Prussia and Hanover* (1705), p. 70, is similar to Addison's and may have been a source for this essay.

[8] Frederick Augustus (b. 1661) was killed in Hungary, Maximilian William (b. 1666) died in Greece leading a Venetian army, and Charles Philip (b. 1669) was killed fighting the Turks in Bulgaria; see *Historical Account of our present Sovereign* (1714), pp. 13–14.

[9] The Prince fought with his father's troops at the battle of Oudenarde (1708) under the command of Lieutenant-General Bulau (*Historical Account*, p. 106).

[10] *Oratio de Imperio Cn. Pompei*, 47–9.

gave it a Place among their Titles. Good Fortune is often the Reward of Vertue, and as often the Effect of Prudence. And whether it proceeds from either of these, or from both together, or whatever may be the Cause of it, every one is naturally pleased to see his Interests conducted by a Person who is used to good Success. The Establishment of the Electoral Dignity in His Majesty's Family, was a Work reserv'd for him finally to accomplish.[11] A large Accession of Dominion fell to Him, by His succeeding to the Dukedom of *Zell*, whereby He became one of the Greatest Princes of *Germany*; and one of the most powerful Persons,[c] that ever stood next Heir to the Throne of *Great Britain*.[12] The Dutchy of *Bremen*, and the Bishoprick of *Osnaburg*, have considerably strengthned his Interests in the Empire, and given a great additional Weight to the Protestant Cause.[13] But the most remarkable Interpositions of Providence, in favour of him, have appeared in removing those seemingly invincible Obstacles to his Succession; in taking away at so critical a Juncture, the Person, who might have proved a dangerous Enemy; in confounding the secret and open Attempts of His traiterous Subjects;[14] and in giving him the delightful Prospect of transmitting his Power through a numerous and still increasing Progeny.

Upon the Whole, it is not to be doubted, but every wise and honest Subject will concur with Providence in promoting the Glory and Happiness of his present Majesty, who is endowed with all those Royal Vertues, that will naturally secure to us the National Blessings, which ought to be dear and valuable to a free People.

B

[c] one of the most powerful Persons,/by far the most powerful Person, *Fol.*

---

[11] After sixteen years of debate the three Colleges of the Empire resolved to admit Hanover to the Federal College of Electors in 1708 (*Historical Account*, pp. 101–2).

[12] The scheme for enlarging the dominions of the Brunswicks and thus forcing the Emperor to create Hanover the ninth electorate was set afoot before George I gained the dukedom of Celle. George's uncle, the Duke of Celle, had agreed many years earlier to leave his dukedom to the Hanoverians at his death which occurred in 1712 (Toland, *Account of the Courts of Prussia and Hanover*, pp. 50–1).

[13] As Elector of Hanover George purchased Bremen from Frederick IV of Denmark in 1715. Osnaburg was, by the terms of the Treaty of Westphalia, ruled alternately by a Protestant and a Catholic family; the Protestant ruler was always a Hanoverian and in December 1715 it devolved to George I at the death of the Elector of Trier (Toland, p. 51; *St. James's Evening Post*, 3–6 Dec. 1715).

[14] At this point in the margin of his *Freeholder*, Swift wrote, 'Was the Person the Queen?' (*Prose Works* v. 251). Some Whigs suspected that Queen Anne and her Tory ministers were plotting to block the Hanoverian succession during the last years of her reign (Rapin, *Dissertation*, p. 85). While her Tory ministers are certainly the 'traiterous Subjects' Addison has in mind, 'the Person who might have proved a dangerous Enemy' could also refer to Louis XIV whose death just before the rebellion began in 1715 contributed to its failure (Bolingbroke, *Letter to Windham*, p. 135).

Numb. III *Friday, December* 30, 1715

Quibus otio vel magnifice, vel molliter vivere copia erat, incerta pro certis, bellum quam pacem, malebant. Sall.

EVERY one knows, that it is usual for a *French* Officer, who can Write and Read, to set down all the Occurrences of a Campaign, in which he pretends to have been personally concern'd; and to publish them under the Title of his Memoirs, when most of his Fellow-Soldiers are dead, that might have contradicted any of his Matters of Fact. Many a gallant young Fellow has been killed in Battle, before he came to the third Page of his secret History; when several, who have taken more care of their Persons, have lived to fill a whole Volume with their military Performances, and to astonish the World with such Instances of their Bravery, as had escaped the Notice of every Body else. One of our late Preston Heroes had, it seems, resolved upon this Method of doing himself Justice: And, had he not been nipp'd in the Bud, might have made a very formidable Figure in his own Works among Posterity. A Friend of mine, who had the Pillage of his Pockets, has made me a Present of the following Memoirs, which he desires me to accept as a Part of the Spoils of the Rebels. I have omitted the Introduction, as more proper for the Inspection of a Secretary of State; and shall only set down so much of the Memoirs, as seem to be a faithful Narrative of that wonderful Expedition, which drew upon it the Eyes of all *Europe*.

'Having thus concerted Measures for a Rising, we had a general Meeting over a Bowl of Punch. It was here proposed by one of the Wisest among us to draw up a Manifesto, setting forth the Grounds and Motives of our taking Arms: For, as he observed, there had never yet been an Insurrection in *England*, where the Leaders had not thought themselves obliged to give some Reasons for it. To this End we laid our Heads together to consider what Grievances the Nation had suffered under the Reign of King *George*. After having spent some Hours upon this Subject, without being able to discover any, we unanimously agreed to rebel first, and to find out Reasons for it afterwards. It was indeed easy to guess at several Grievances of a private Nature, which influence particular Persons. One of us had spent his Fortune: Another was a younger Brother: A third had the Incumbrance

Motto. Sallust, *De Catilinae Coniuratione*, 17: Although at leisure they had the means to live in splendour and at their ease, they preferred uncertainty to certainty, war to peace.

of a Father upon his Estate. But that which principally disposed us in favour of the Chevalier was, that most of the Company had been obliged to take the Abjuration Oath against their Will.[2] Being at length thoroughly enflamed with Zeal and Punch, we resolved to take Horse the next Morning; which we did accordingly, having been joined by a considerable Reinforcement of *Roman Catholicks*, whom we could rely upon, as knowing them to be the best *Tories* in the Nation, and avow'd Enemies to *Presbyterianism*. We were likewise joined by a very useful Associate, who was a Fidler by Profession, and brought in with him a Body of lusty young Fellows, whom he had tweedled into the Service. About the third Day of our March, I was made a Colonel; tho' I must needs say I gained my Commission by my Horse's Vertues, not my own; having leapt over a six-bar Gate at the Head of the Cavalry. My General, who is a discerning Man, hereupon gave me a Regiment, telling me, He did not question but I would do the like, when I came to the Enemies Palisades.[3] We pursued our March with much Intrepidity through two or three open Towns, to the great Terror of the Market-People, and the Miscarriage of half a Dozen big-belly'd Women. Notwithstanding the Magistracy was generally against us, we could discover many Friends among our Spectators; particularly in two or three Balconies, which were filled with several tawdry Females, who are known in that Country by the ancient Name of *Harlots*. This Sort of Ladies received us every where with great Demonstrations of Joy, and promised to assist us with their Prayers.[4] After these signal Successes in the *North* of *England*, it was thought advisable by our General to proceed

[2] Judging from contemporary accounts, Addison's description of rebels' motives and behaviour is not very exaggerated. Robert Patten claimed that High Churchmen were never 'right Hearty for the Cause, 'till they are Mellow . . . over a Bottle or two' (Patten, *Late Rebellion*, p. 100). Countess Cowper wrote that the Jacobites admitted their followers were 'not many of y^{m} friends out of Principle but many were so in hopes to redress some grievances' (Diary, 23 Feb. 1716). The oath abjuring the Pretender, who became Chevalier de St. George in 1708, was for many Jacobites a bitter pill (H.M.C. *Stuart MSS*. ii. 71).

[3] Commissions were conferred so liberally in the Jacobite army that 'to each Troop they assigned Two Captains, being the only way they had to oblige so many Gentlemen' (Patten, *Late Rebellion*, p. 38). When the English rebels joined the Scots at Kelso, they 'were most of them Horse, and made, indeed, a fine Appearance; but having only Hunting Horses, with Swords on their Sides, and Whips in their Hands', one seasoned Scots general 'shook his head, and said, *This would never do*' (*Pol. State* x. 483). Thomas Forster, the leader of the English rebels, was a cousin of Countess Cowper whom she claimed 'had never seen an Army in his life' (Diary, Nov. 1715).

[4] Prostitutes were commonly depicted as ardent High Church Tories: Hogarth included a picture of Sacheverell on Moll Hackabout's wall in his *Harlot's Progress*, Defoe claimed that nineteen out of every twenty prostitutes were for the Doctor (*Review*, 11 May 1710), and the anonymous *Officers' Address to the Ladies* (1710) claimed that 'the Doctors Name is a Ticket which admits you into the best Favours of all the *Phyllises* in Drury-Lane' (p. 2). Addison assumes the Pretender has replaced Sacheverell in their political affections.

towards our *Scotch* Confederates. During our first Day's March, I amused myself with considering what Post I should accept of under *James* the Third, when we had put him in Possession of the *British* Dominions. Being a great Lover of Country-Sports, I absolutely determined not to be a Minister of State, nor to be fobb'd off with a Garter; till at length passing by a noble Country-Seat, which belongs to a *Whig*, I resolved to beg it; and pleased myself the Remainder of the Day with several Alterations I intended to make in it. For tho' the Situation was very delightful, I neither liked the Front of the House, nor the Avenues that led to it. We were indeed so confident of Success, that I found most of my Fellow-Soldiers were taken up with Imaginations of the same Nature. There had like to have been a Duel between two of our Subalterns, upon a dispute which[a] of 'em should be Governour of *Portsmouth*.[5] A *Popish* Priest about the same time gave great Offence to a *Northumberland* Squire, whom he threatned to Excommunicate, if he did not give up to him the Church-Lands, which his Family had usurped ever since the Reformation.[6] In short, every Man had cut out a Place for himself in his own Thoughts; so that I could reckon up, in our little Army, two or three Lord-Treasurers, half a Dozen Secretaries of State, and at least a Score of Lords Justices in Eyre for each side of *Trent*.[7] We pursu'd our March through several Villages, which we drank dry, making Proclamation at our Entrance, in the Name of *James* the Third, against all Concealments of Ale or Brandy. Being very much fatigu'd with the Action of a whole Week, it was agreed to rest on Sunday, when we heard a most excellent Sermon. Our Chaplain insisted principally upon two Heads. Under the First, he proved to us, that the Breach of publick Oaths is no Perjury; and under the Second expounded to us the Nature of Non-resistance, which might be interpreted, from the *Hebrew*, to signify either Loyalty or Rebellion, according as the Sovereign bestow'd his Favours and Preferments. He concluded with exhorting us, in a most

[a] Subalterns, upon a dispute which / Subalterns, which *Fol.*

[5] In 1714 Lord North and Grey, a Jacobite sympathizer, was removed from the Governership of Portsmouth and he was replaced by a Whig, General Thomas Erle, who supervised the defences at Portsmouth in 1715.

[6] Fears that a Catholic monarch would return lands to the Church which had been appropriated by the crown during the Reformation were strong enough so that James II was obliged to deny any intention to do so in his 1687 Declaration of Indulgence. As late as 1727 the Whigs were still using this scare tactic (*Craftsman*, 4 Nov. 1727).

[7] The Chief Justice in Eyre was a sinecure appointment held by such political figures as the Earl of Wharton (1706–10); in November 1715 the Tory Earl of Abingdon was replaced as Chief Justice South of Trent by the Earl of Tankerville (*St. James's Evening Post*, 10–12 Nov. 1715). Concerning the origin and function of this post, see Blackstone's *Commentaries* (1767), iii. 6.

pathetick Manner, to Purge the Land by wholsome Severities, and to propagate sound Principles by Fire and Sword.[8] We set forward the next Day towards our Friends at *Kelso*;[9] but by the way had like to have lost our General, and some of our most Active Officers. For a Fox, unluckily crossing the Road, drew off a considerable Detachment, who clapp'd Spurs to their Horses, and pursued him with Whoops and Hollows till we had lost Sight of them. A Covey of Partridges, springing in our front, put our Infantry in disorder on the same Day. It was not long after this, that we were joined by our Friends from the other Side of the *Firth*. Upon the junction of the two Corps, our Spies brought us Word, that they discover'd a great Cloud of Dust at some distance; upon which we sent out a Party to Reconnoitre. They return'd to us with Intelligence, that the Dust was raised by a great Drove of black Cattle.[10] This News was not a little welcome to us, the Army of both Nations being very Hungry. We quickly formed our selves, and received Orders for the Attack, with positive Instructions to give no Quarter. Every thing was executed with so much good Order, that we made a very plentiful Supper. We had, Three Days after, the same Success against a Flock of Sheep; which we were forced to eat with great Precipitation, having received Advice of General *Carpenter*'s March, as we were at Dinner.[11] Upon this Alarm we made incredible Stretches towards the *South*, with a Design to gain the Fastnesses of *Preston*. We did little remarkable in our Way, except setting[b] Fire to a few Houses, and frighting an old Woman into Fits. We had now got a long Day's March of the Enemy; and meeting with a considerable Refreshment of *October*, all the Officers assembled over it, among whom were several *Popish* Lords and Gentlemen, who toasted many Loyal Healths and

[b] except setting / except the setting *Fol.*

[8] Addison is parodying the sermons of Tory highfliers, particularly Henry Sacheverell who praised Queen Elizabeth for suppressing toleration for Calvinism by using '*Wholsome Severities*' (*Perils of False Brethren*, p. 19). Ann Clavering wrote, 'Wholesome severitys the Torys will allow, because 'tis Sacheverell's doctrine' (*Clavering Correspondence*, p. 102); see also Defoe's *Review*, 24 Aug. 1710. Addison discusses political perjury more seriously in *F.* 6 and the background to Non-resistance is discussed in the Introduction (pp. 7–11).

[9] The English and Scottish rebels joined forces at Kelso and proclaimed the Pretender James VIII on 24 Oct. 1715 (Patten, *Late Rebellion*, pp. 40–65).

[10] Except perhaps for linen no export from Scotland to England earned more for the Scots than the thriving cattle trade. By referring to it here, Addison is reminding his readers of the economic interdependence of the two nations. Concerning the cattle trade, see T. C. Smout, *Scottish Trade on the Eve of Union* (1963), pp. 213–15.

[11] At Kelso the rebels had about 600 horse and 1,400 foot soldiers. They were pursued by General George Carpenter whose army had only about 500 tired soldiers (Patten, *Late Rebellion*, pp. 65–6).

Confusions, and wept very plentifully for the Danger of the Church.[12] We sat till Midnight, and at our parting resolved to give the Enemy Battle; but the next Morning changed our Resolutions, and prosecuted our March with indefatigable Speed. We were no sooner arrived upon the Frontiers of *Cumberland*, but we saw a great Body of Militia drawn up in Array against us. Orders were given to Halt; and a Council of War was immediately called, wherein we agreed with that great Unanimity, which was so remarkable among us on these Occasions, to make a Retreat.[13] But before we cou'd give the Word, the Train-bands, taking Advantage of our delay, fled first. We arrived at *Preston* without any memorable Adventure; where, after having form'd many Barricades, and prepared for a vigorous Resistance; upon the Approach of the King's Troops under General *Wills*, who was used to the Out-landish Way of making War, we thought it high Time to put in Practice that Passive-Obedience, in which our Party so much Glories, and which I wou'd advise them to stick to for the future.'[14]

Such was the End of this Rebellion; which, in all Probability, will not only tend to the Safety of our Constitution, but the Preservation of the Game.

W

Numb. IV *Monday, January* 2, 1716

> *Ne se mulier extra virtutum cogitationes, extraque bellorum casus putet, ipsis incipientis matrimonii auspiciis admonetur, venire se laborum periculorumque sociam, idem in pace, idem in prœlio passuram ausuramque. Sic vivendum, sic pereundum.* Tacit.

[12] October ale was associated with country Tories who formed the October Club, a powerful Parliamentary block which met at the Bell tavern. In 1711 Jean Robethon wrote 'Le Party des Octobriens . . . sont des gentilshommes de la campagne qu'on nomme ainsy a cause de leur chaleur, et parce que la bière forte se brasse au mois d'octobre . . . De ces Octobriens la pluspart sont Jacobites' (O. Klopp, *Der Fall des Hauses Stuart* (Vienna, 1888) xiv. 673). For the background of 'Danger to the Church', see Introduction, pp. 5–7, 11–14.

[13] Although the militia was a popular joke among many of Addison's contemporaries (see *F.* 11), Patten claims that the militia were helpful to the loyalist forces both in Scotland and England (*Late Rebellion*, pp. 11, 30). On their own, however, citizen armies like the one in Penrith, Cumbria, behaved with almost comical cowardice in 1715 (*Pol. State* x. 486).

[14] Sir Charles Wills was commander of the first loyalist forces to arrive at Preston. The background of Passive Obedience is discussed in the Introduction (pp. 7–11).

Motto. Tacitus, *Germania*, xviii: So that the woman may not think herself excused from thoughts of bravery and the calamities of war, she is warned in the very marriage ceremony that she is her husband's partner in hard work and in danger, that she must suffer with him in peace and war . . . Thus she must live and thus she must die.

It is with great Satisfaction I observe, that the Women of our Island, who are the most eminent for Virtue and good Sense, are in the Interest of the present Government. As the fair Sex very much recommend the Cause they are engaged in, it would be no small Misfortune to a Soveraign, though he had all the male Part of the Nation on his Side, if he did not find himself King of the most beautiful Half of his Subjects. Ladies are always of great use to the Party they espouse, and never fail to win over Numbers to it. Lovers, according to Sir *William Petty's* Computation, make at least the Third Part of the fencible Men of the British Nation;[2] and it has been an uncontroverted Maxim in all Ages, that, though a Husband is sometimes a stubborn Sort of a Creature, a Lover is always at the Devotion of his Mistress. By this means it lies in the Power of every fine Woman, to secure at least half a Dozen able-bodied Men to his Majesty's Service. The Female World are likewise indispensably necessary in the best Causes to manage the Controversial Part of them, in which no Man of tolerable Breeding is ever able to refute them. Arguments out of a pretty Mouth are unanswerable.

It is indeed remarkable that the Inferiour Tribe of common Women, who are a Dishonour to their Sex, have in most Reigns, been the profest Sticklers for such as have acted in Opposition to the true Interest of the Nation.[3] The most numerous Converts in King *James*'s Reign, were particularly noted to be of this kind. I can give no other Reason for such a Behaviour, unless it be, that it is not for the Advantage of these Female Adventurers the Laws of the Land should take Place, and that they know *Bridewell* is a Part of our Constitution.

There are many Reasons why the Women of *Great Britain* shou'd be on the Side of the Free-holder, and Enemies to the Person who would bring in Arbitrary Government and Popery. As there are several of our Ladies who amuse themselves in the reading of Travels, they cannot but take Notice what uncomfortable Lives those of their own Sex lead, where Passive Obedience is professed and practised in its utmost Perfection. In those Countries the Men have no Property but in their Wives, who are the Slaves to Slaves; every married Woman being subject to a domestick Tyrant, that requires from her the same Vassalage which he pays to his Sultan. If the Ladies wou'd seriously consider the evil Consequences of

[2] John Graunt's *Observations upon the Bills of Mortality* (1662), sometimes attributed to Petty, claimed that 34 per cent of the male population was between the ages of sixteen and fifty-six and could be classified as 'fighting Men' (Sir William Petty, *Economic Writings*, Cambridge, 1899, ii. 387).

[3] Prostitutes were frequently depicted as High Church supporters and, by association, Jacobite sympathizers (see *F.* 3, n. 4).

arbitrary Power, they would find, that it spoils the Shape of the Foot in *China*, where the barbarous Politicks of the Men so diminish the Basis of the Female Figure, as to unqualify a Woman for an Evening Walk or a Country Dance. In the *East Indies* a Widow, who has any Regard to her Character, throws her self into the Flames of her Husband's Funeral Pile, to shew, forsooth, that she is faithful and loyal to the Memory of her deceased Lord. In *Persia* the Daughters of *Eve*, as they call 'em, are reckoned in the Inventory of their Goods and Chattels; it is a usual Thing when a Man sells a Bale of Silk, or a Drove of Camels, to toss half a dozen Women into the Bargain. Through all the Dominions of the Great Turk, a Woman thinks her self happy if she can get but the twelfth Share in a Husband, and is thought of no manner of use in the Creation, but to keep up a proper Number of Slaves for the Commander of the Faithful. I need not set forth the ill Usage, which the fair Ones meet with in those despotick Governments that lie nearer us. Every one hath heard of the several Ways of locking up Women in *Spain* and *Italy*; where, if there is any Power lodged in any of the Sex, it is not among the young and the beautiful, whom Nature seems to have formed for it, but among the old and wither'd Matrons, known by the frightful Name of *Gouvernantes* and *Duegna's*. If any should alledge the Freedoms indulged to the French Ladies, he must own that these are owing to the natural Gallantry of the People, not to their Form of Government, which excludes by its very Constitution every Female from Power, as naturally unfit to hold the Sceptre of that Kingdom.

Women ought in reason to be no less averse to Popery than to arbitrary Power. Some merry Authors have pretended to demonstrate, that the *Roman Catholick* Religion could never spread in a Nation, where Women wou'd have more Modesty than to expose their innocent Liberties to a Confessor. Others of the same Turn, have assured us, that the fine British Complection, which is so peculiar to our Ladies, would suffer very much from a Fish Diet: And that a whole *Lent* would give such a Sallowness to the celebrated Beauties of this Island, as would scarce make them distinguishable from those of *France*. I shall only leave to the serious Consideration of my Country-Women the Danger any of them might have been in, (had Popery been our National Religion) of being forced by their Relations to a State of perpetual Virginity. The most blooming Toast in the Island might have been a Nun; and many a Lady, who is now a Mother of fine Children, condemn'd to a Condition of Life, disagreeable to herself, and unprofitable to the World. To this I might add the melancholy Objects, they would be daily entertained with, of several sightly Men delivered over to an inviolable Celibacy. Let a young Lady imagine to herself the brisk embroidered Officer, who now makes Love to her with so agreeable an Air, converted into a Monk; or the Beau, who now addresses himself to her in a full bottom'd Wig, distinguish'd by a little bald Pate covered with a black Leather Skull Cap. I forbear to mention many other Objections, which the Ladies, who are no Strangers to the Doctrines of Popery, will easily recollect: Tho' I do not in the least doubt, but those I have already suggested, will be sufficient to persuade my fair Readers to be zealous in the Protestant Cause.

The Freedom and Happiness of our *British* Ladies is so singular, that it is a common Saying in foreign Countries, *If a Bridge were built cross the Seas, all the Women in* Europe *would flock into* England. It has been observed, that the Laws relating to them are so favourable, that one would think they themselves had given Votes in enacting them. All the Honours and Indulgences of Society are due to them by our Customs; and, by our Constitution, they have all the Privileges of *English*-born Subjects, without the Burdens. I need not acquaint my fair Fellow-Free-holders, that every Man who is anxious for our sacred and civil Rights, is a Champion in their Cause; since we enjoy in common a Religion agreeable to that reasonable Nature, of which we equally partake; and since, in Point of Property, our Law makes no Distinction of Sexes.[4]

We may therefore justly expect from them, that they will act in concert with us for the Preservation of our Laws and Religion, which cannot subsist, but under the Government of His present Majesty; and would necessarily be subverted, under that of a Person bred up in the most violent Principles of Popery and arbitrary Power. Thus may the Fair Sex contribute to fix the Peace of a brave and generous People, who, for many Ages, have disdained to bear any Tyranny but Theirs; and be as famous in History, as those illustrious Matrons, who, in the Infancy of *Rome*, reconciled the *Romans* and the *Sabines*, and united the two contending Parties under their new King.[5]

W

[4] Not according to Giles Jacob's *Law Dictionary* (1729): 'By *Marriage* with a Woman, the Husband is intitled to all her Estate Real and Personal; and the Effects of *Marriage* are, that the Husband and Wife are accounted one Person, and he hath Power over her Person as well as Estate, &c.' (art. Marriage); 'After *Marriage* the Will of the *Wife* in Judgment of Law is subject to the Will of the Husband . . . A *Wife* cannot contract for any Thing; or bring Actions &c. without her Husband' (art. Wife).

[5] Livy, *Ab Urbe Condita*, i. 13: 'Having dared to go into the middle of the flying missiles . . . the Sabine matrons appealed to their fathers in one army and their husbands in the other . . . 'We would rather die than . . . live as widows or orphans.' Both the armies and the leaders were moved by their appeal . . . Then the generals came forward to make a treaty. It was not simply peace that was made, but one state was formed out of two.'

Numb. V *Friday, January* 6, 1716

Omnium Societatum nulla est gravior, nulla carior, quam ea quæ cum republica est unicuique nostrum: Cari sunt parentes, cari liberi, propinqui, familiares: Sed omnes omnium caritates patria una complexa est: Pro qua quis bonus dubitet mortem oppetere, si ei sit profuturis? Cic.

THERE is no greater Sign of a general Decay of Vertue in a Nation, than a Want of Zeal in its Inhabitants for the Good of their Country. This generous and publick-Spirited Passion has been observ'd of late Years to languish and grow cold in this our Island; where a Party of Men have made it their Business to represent it as chimerical and romantick, to destroy in the Minds of the People the Sense of national Glory, and to turn into Ridicule our natural and antient Allies, who are united to us by the common Interests both of Religion and Policy.[2] It may not therefore be unseasonable to recommend to this present Generation the Practice of that Vertue, for which their Ancestors were particularly Famous, and which is call'd *The Love of one's Country*. This Love to our Country, as a moral Vertue, is a fix'd Disposition of Mind to promote the Safety, Welfare, and Reputation of the Community in which we are born, and of the Constitution under which we are protected. Our Obligations to this great Duty may appear to us from several Considerations.

In the first Place we may observe, that we are directed to it by one of those secret Suggestions of Nature, which go under the Name of *Instinct*, and which are never given in vain. As Self-love is an Instinct planted in us

Motto. Cicero, *De Officiis*, i. 17: Of all the ties of friendship there is none more serious, none more dear than that which unites each of us with the state. Parents are dear; children, relatives, friends are dear. However, one native land has encompassed the loves of us all. What good man would hesitate to meet death for his country if he could be of use to her?

[2] Addison is alluding to the propaganda which gained popular support for the Tory peace negotiations with France in 1711 and he appears to have Swift's *Conduct of the Allies*, their most influential attack on Whig foreign policies, particularly in mind. Swift argued that landed Englishmen were burdened with unnecessary taxation because the Allies—Holland, Austria, and Portugal—had not contributed their fair share of war expenses. He claimed that a 'Romantick Disposition' prompted supporters of the war to allow such disadvantageous alliances to continue and he accused London bankers and tradesmen of 'betraying the Interest of their Native Country' because they profited from government loans and war supplies (*Prose Works* v. 9, 44). With some distortion (Austria and Portugal were not Protestant), and with the memory that Hanover was one of the allies criticized, Addison returns Swift's fire by accusing Jacobites and their Tory sympathizers of 'betraying ... their Native Country'.

for the Good and Safety of each particular Person, the Love of our Country is impress'd on our Minds for the Happiness and Preservation of the Community. This Instinct is so remarkable, that we find Examples of it in those who are born in the most uncomfortable Climates, or the worst of Governments. We read of an Inhabitant of *Nova Zembla*, who, after having liv'd some Time in *Denmark*, where he was cloath'd and treated with the utmost Indulgence, took the first Opportunity of making his Escape, tho' with the Hazard of his Life, into his native Regions of Cold, Poverty and Nakedness.[3] We have an Instance of the same Nature among the very *Hottentots*. One of these Savages was brought into *England*, taught our Language, and in a great Measure polish'd out of his natural Barbarity: But upon being carry'd back to the Cape of *Good Hope* (where it was thought he might have been of Advantage to our *English* Traders) he mix'd in a kind of Transport with his Country-men, brutaliz'd with 'em in their Habit and Manners, and wou'd never agen return to his foreign Acquaintance. I need not mention the common Opinion of the *Negroes* in our Plantations, who have no other Notion of a future State of Happiness, than that, after Death, they shall be convey'd back to their native country. The *Swiss* are so remarkable for this Passion, that it often turns to a Disease among them; for which there is a particular Name in the *German* Language, and which the *French* call *The Distemper of the Country*:[4] For nothing is more usual than for several of their common Soldiers, who are listed in a foreign Service, to have such violent Hankerings after their Home, as to pine away even to Death, unless they have a Permission to return; which, on such an Occasion, is generally granted them. I shall only add under this Head, that since the Love of one's Country is natural to every Man, any particular Nation who, by false Politicks shall endeavour to stifle or restrain it, will not be upon a Level with others.[a]

As this Love of our Country is *natural* to every Man, so is it likewise very *reasonable*; and that in the first Place, because it inclines us to be Beneficial to those, who are and ought to be dearer to us than any others. It takes in our Families, Relations, Friends and Acquaintance, and, in short, all whose Welfare and Security we are oblig'd to consult, more than that of those

[a] others / *Fol.*, *12mo*; ours *8vo*.

[3] Pierre Martin de la Martinière visited Novaya Zemlya, two islands off the northern coast of Russia, in 1671 and brought two inhabitants back to Denmark with him (*A New Voyage to the North*, 1706, pp. 214–33, 247).

[4] The German word is *Heimweh* and in 1756 John Keysler wrote that the Swiss were especially vulnerable to it because of 'the fineness and subtility of the air in *Switzerland*' which made them 'feel a kind of anxiety and uneasy longing' whenever they left their country (*Travels*, i. 141).

who are Strangers to us. For this Reason it is the most sublime and extensive of all social Vertues: Especially if we consider that it does not only promote the Well-being of These who are our Contemporaries, but likewise of their Children and their Posterity. Hence it is that all Casuists are unanimous in determining, that when the Good of the Country interferes even with the Life of the most beloved Relation, dearest Friend, or greatest Benefactor, it is to be preferr'd without Exception.

Further,[b] tho' there is a Benevolence due to all Mankind, none can question but a superior Degree of it is to be paid to a Father, a Wife, or a Child. In the same Manner, tho' our Love should reach to the whole Species, a greater Proportion of it shou'd exert itself towards that Community in which Providence has plac'd us. This is our proper Sphere of Action, the Province allotted to us for the Exercise of all our civil Vertues, and in which alone we have Opportunities of expressing our Good-Will to Mankind. I cou'd not but be pleas'd in the Accounts of the late *Persian* Embassy into *France*, with a particular Ceremony of the Ambassador; who every Morning, before he went abroad, religiously saluted a Turf of Earth dug out of his own native Soil, to remind him, that in all the Transactions of the Day he was to think of his Country, and pursue its Advantages.[5] If, in the several Districts and Divisions of the World, Men would thus study the Welfare of those respective Communities, to which their Power of doing Good is limited, the whole Race of reasonable Creatures would be happy, as far as the Benefits of Society can make them so. At least, we find so many Blessings naturally flowing from this noble Principle, that in Proportion, as it prevails, every Nation becomes a prosperous and flourishing People.

It may be yet a farther Recommendation of this particular Vertue, if we consider, that no Nation was ever famous for its Morals, which was not at the same Time remarkable for its publick Spirit: Patriots naturally rise out of a *Spartan* or *Roman* Vertue: And there is no Remark more common among the antient Historians, than that when the State was corrupted with Avarice and Luxury, it was in danger of being Betray'd, or Sold.

To the foregoing Reasons for the Love which every good Man owes to his Country, we may add, that the Actions, which are most celebrated in History, and which are read with the greatest Admiration, are such as

[b] Further / *Fol.*; Farther *8vo*, *12mo*.

---

[5] Muhammed Riza Beg, the first Persian ambassador to a Western court, was in France from October 1714 until September 1715. Le Fèvre de Fontenay describes his visit and the commercial treaty he signed with Louis XIV in *Journal historique du voyage de l'ambassadeur de Perse* (Paris, 1715), but he does not include the anecdote Addison tells here.

proceed from this Principle. The establishing of good Laws, the detecting of Conspiracies, the crushing of Seditions and Rebellions, the falling in Battle, or the devoting of a Man's self to certain Death for the Safety of Fellow Citizens, are Actions that always warm the Reader, and endear to him Persons of the remotest Ages, and the most distant Countries.

And as Actions, that proceed from the Love of one's Country, are more illustrious than any other in the Records of Time; so we find that those Persons, who have been eminent in other Vertues, have been particularly distinguished by this. It would be endless to produce Examples of this Kind, out of *Greek* and *Roman* Authors. To confine my self therefore in so wide and beaten a Field, I shall chuse some Instances from Holy Writ, which abounds in Accounts of this Nature, as much as any other History whatsoever. And this I do the more willingly, because in some Books lately written, I find it objected against revealed Religion, that it does not inspire the Love of one's Country.[6] Here I must premise, that as the Sacred Author of our Religion chiefly inculcated to the *Jews* those Parts of their Duty wherein they were most defective, so there was no need of insisting upon this: The *Jews* being remarkable for an Attachment to their own Country, even to the Exclusion of all common Humanity to Strangers. We see in the Behaviour of this Divine Person, the Practice of this Vertue in Conjunction with all others. He defer'd working a Miracle in the Behalf of a *Syrophoenician* Woman, till he had declar'd his Superiour Good-will to his own Nation;[7] and was prevail'd upon to heal the Daughter of a *Roman* Centurion, by hearing from the *Jews*, that he was one who lov'd their Nation, and had built them a Synagogue.[8] But, to look out for no other Instance, what was ever more moving, than his Lamentation over *Jerusalem*, at his first approach to it, notwithstanding he had foretold the cruel and unjust Treatment, he was to meet with in that City![9] For he foresaw the Destruction which in a few Years was to fall upon that People; a Destruction not to be parallel'd in any Nation from the Beginning of the World to this Day; and in the View of it melted into Tears. His Followers

[6] In his 'Essay on the Freedom of Wit and Humour', Shaftesbury speculated 'that the true Reason why some of the most Heroick Virtues have so little notice taken of 'em in our Holy Religion, is, because there wou'd have been no room left for *Disinterestedness*, had they been intitled to a share of that infinite Reward, which Providence has by Revelation assign'd to other Dutys. *Private Friendship* and *Zeal for the Publick, and our Country* are Virtues purely voluntary in a Christian. They are no essential Parts of *Charity*.' *Characteristicks* (1714), i. 98–9.

[7] Mark 7:24–30.

[8] Luke 7:1–10. It was the Centurion's servant, not his daughter. Addison has confused this allusion with the previous one.

[9] Luke 19:41–4.

have in many Places expressed the like Sentiments of Affection for their Countrymen, among which none is more extraordinary than that of the great Convert, who wish'd he himself might be made a Curse, provided it might turn to the Happiness of his Nation; or as he words it, *Of his Brethren and Kinsmen, who are* Israelites.[10] This Instance naturally brings to mind the same heroick Temper of Soul in the great *Jewish* Law-giver, who would have devoted himself in the same manner, rather than see his People perish. It would indeed be difficult to find out any Man of extraordinary Piety in the Sacred Writings, in whom this Vertue is not highly conspicuous. The Reader however will excuse me, if I take Notice of one Passage, because it is a very fine One, and wants only a Place in some polite Author of *Greece* or *Rome*, to have been admired and celebrated. The King of *Syria* lying sick upon his Bed, sent *Hasael* one of his Great Officers, to the Prophet *Elisha*, to enquire of him whether he should recover. The Prophet look'd so attentively on this Messenger, that it put him into some Confusion; or to quote this beautiful Circumstance, and the whole Narrative, in the pathetick Language of the Scripture, Elisha *settled his Countenance steadfastly upon him, until he was ashamed: And*[c] Hasael *said, why weepeth my Lord? And he said, because I know the Evil that thou wilt do unto the Children of* Israel: *Their strong Holds wilt thou set on Fire, and their Men*[d] *wilt thou slay with the Sword, and wilt dash their Children, and rip up their Women with Child. And* Hasael *said, But what is thy Servant a Dog, that he should do this great Thing? And* Elisha *answered, The Lord hath shewed me that thou shalt be King over* Syria.[11]

I might enforce these Reasons for the Love of our Country, by Considerations adapted to my Readers as they are *Englishmen*, and as by that Means they enjoy a purer Religion, and a more excellent Form of Government, than any other Nation under Heaven. But being persuaded that every one must look upon himself as indispensably obliged to the Practice of a Duty, which is recommended to him by so many Arguments and Examples, I shall only desire the honest, well-meaning Reader, when he turns his Thoughts towards the Publick, rather to consider what Opportunities he has of doing Good to his Native Country, than to throw away his Time in deciding the Rights of Princes, or the like Speculations, which are so far beyond his Reach. Let us leave these great Points to the Wisdom of our Legislature, and to the Determination[e] of those, who are the proper Judges of our Constitution. We shall otherwise be liable to the

[c] *ashamed: And* / *ashamed: And the Man of God wept. And* *Fol.* [d] *their Men* / *their young Men* *Fol.* [e] Determination / Determinations *Fol.*

[10] Romans 9:3–4. [11] 2 Kgs. 8:11–13.

just Reproach, which is cast upon such Christians, as waste their Lives in the subtle and intricate Disputes of Religion, when they should be practising the Doctrines which it teaches. If there be any Right upon Earth, any relying on the Judgment of our most eminent Lawyers and Divines, or indeed any Certainty in Humane Reason, our present Soveraign has an undoubted Title to our Duty and Obedience. But supposing for Argument's sake, that this Right were doubtful, and that an *Englishman* could be divided in his Opinion, as to the Person to whom he should pay his Allegiance. In this Case, there is no question, but the Love of his Country ought to cast the Ballance, and to determine him on that Side, which is most conducive to the Welfare of his Community. To bring this to our present Case. A Man must be destitute of common Sense, who is capable of imagining that the Protestant Religion could flourish under the Government of a bigotted *Roman-Catholick*, or that our Civil Rights could be protected by One, who has been trained up in the Politicks of the most Arbitrary Prince in *Europe*, and who could not acknowledge his Gratitude to his Benefactor,[f] by any remarkable Instance, which would not be detrimental to the *British* Nation. And are these such desirable Blessings, that an honest Man would endeavour to arrive at 'em, through the Confusions of a Civil War, and the Blood of many Thousands of his Fellow-Subjects? On the contrary, the Arguments for our steady, loyal, and affectionate Adherence to King *George*, are so evident from this single Topick, that if every *Briton*, instead of aspiring after private Wealth or Power, would sincerely desire to make his Country happy, His present Majesty would not have a single Malecontent in his whole Dominions.

D

Numb. VI — *Monday, January* 9, 1716

Fraus enim astringit, non dissolvit Perjurium.

Cic.

AT a Time when so many of the King's Subjects present themselves before their respective Magistrates to take the Oaths required by Law, it may not be improper to awaken in the Minds of my Readers a due Sense of that

[f] Benefactor / Benefactors *Fol.*

Motto. Cicero, *De Officiis*, iii. 32: Deceit does not loosen the bonds of perjury, it only tightens them.

Engagement under which they lay themselves.[2] It is a melancholly Consideration, that there should be several among us so hardned and deluded, as to think an Oath a proper Subject for a Jest; and to make this, which is one of the most solemn Acts of Religion, an occasion of Mirth. Yet such is the Depravation of our Manners at present, that nothing is more frequent, than to hear profligate Men ridiculing, to the best of their Abilities, these sacred Pledges of their Duty and Allegiance; and endeavouring to be witty upon themselves, for daring to prevaricate with God and Man. A poor Conceit of their own, or a Quotation out of *Hudibras*, shall make 'em treat with Levity an Obligation wherein their Safety and Welfare are concern'd both as to this World and the next. Raillery of this Nature, is enough to make the Hearer tremble. As these Miscreants seem to glory in the Profession of their Impiety, there is no Man, who has any regard to his Duty, or even to his Reputation, that can appear in their Defence.[3] But if there are others of a more serious Turn, who join with us deliberately in these Religious Professions of Loyalty to our Soveraign, with any private Salvo's or Evasions, they would do well to consider those Maxims, in which all Casuists are agreed, who have gained any Esteem for their Learning, Judgment, or Morality. These have unanimously

[2] In ordinary circumstances, clergymen and office-holders were obliged to take the oaths of allegiance, supremacy, and abjuration, but on 5 Dec. 1715 the King ordered the oaths administered to anyone suspected of being dangerous or disaffected, and two weeks later the oaths were administered to all inhabitants of London and Westminster because 'Secret Abettors of the Conspiracy' were encouraging 'the Spirits of the disaffected Populace, in the very Heart of the Metropolis' (*Pol. State* x. 572, 579; Ryder, *Diary*, 21 Dec. 1715). Addison's purpose in this essay is to make the gesture more effective by impressing readers with the seriousness of oaths, a point which the Archbishop emphasized in his *Declaration* in November 1715: 'that profess'd Members of the Church of *England* should... out of Private Discontents, Attempt to set up a Person whom they have so often and so lately Abjured, is so vile and detestable a thing, as may justly make them Odious both to God and Man' (p. 4). The oath of abjuration which Addison quotes at the end of his essay was considered the most unpopular oath required (H.M.C. *Stuart MSS.* ii. 72).

[3] Addison's moral theme in this essay rehearses the traditional Anglican argument which *The Whole Duty of Man* presented: 'In all oaths you know, God is solemnly called to witness the truth of that which is spoken: Now, if the thing be false, it is the basest affront and dishonour that can possibly be done to God' (1715, p. 102). However, as early as 1689, some members of both parties took political oaths rather lightly. Lord Wharton, the former Parliamentarian and father of Addison's contemporary, confessed that 'he was a very old man, and had taken a multitude of oaths in his time, and hoped God would forgive him if he had not kept them all ... The earl of Macclesfield, who had been an old cavalier, ... said he was much in the same case as Lord Wharton, though they had not always taken the same oaths' (Burnet, *History* iv. 79). In 1716 a Jacobite agent reported that the Earl of Nottingham, a scrupulous Churchman who had opposed the legislation requiring the oath of abjuration in 1702, gloried in his opposition 'to all State oaths, which he thinks serve only to debauch the conscience' (H.M.C. *Stuart MSS.* ii. 122–23). For many Jacobites the issue of oaths was very serious and Charles Cox complained in 1705 that 'ye Jacks were milksops for kicking at oaths. ... they should ... take all oaths y^t could be imposed' (Blenheim MS. D. 1–32).

determined, that an Oath is always to be taken in the Sense of that Authority which imposes it: And that those, whose Hearts do not concur with their Lips in the Form of these publick Protestations; or who have any mental Reserves, or who take an Oath against their Consciences, upon any Motive whatsoever; or with a design to break it, or repent of it, are guilty of Perjury.[4] Any of these, or the like Circumstances, instead of alleviating the Crime, make it more heinous, as they are premeditated Frauds (which it is the chief Design of an Oath to prevent) and the most flagrant Instances of Insincerity to Men, and Irreverence to their Maker. For this Reason, the Perjury of a Man, who takes an Oath, with an Intention to keep it, and is afterwards seduced to the Violation of it, (tho' a Crime not to be thought of, without the greatest Horrour) is yet, in some Respects, not quite so black as the Perjury above-mentioned. It is indeed a very unhappy Token of the great Corruption of our Manners, that there should be any so inconsiderate among us, as to sacrifice the standing and essential Duties of Morality, to the Views of Politicks; and that, as in my last Paper, it was not unseasonable to prove the Love of our Country to be a Virtue, so in this there should be any Occasion to shew that Perjury is a Sin. But it is our Misfortune to live in an Age when such wild and unnatural Doctrines have prevailed among some of our Fellow-Subjects, that if one looks into their Schemes of Government, they seem according as they are in the Humour, to believe that a Soveraign is not to be restrained by his Coronation-Oath, or his People by their Oaths of Allegiance: Or to represent them in a plainer Light, in some Reigns they are both for a Power and an Obedience that is unlimited, and in others are for retrenching within the narrowest Bounds, both the Authority of the Prince, and the Allegiance of the Subject.[5]

[4] There was less unanimity than Addison suggests. Aristotle said that any oath which is not completely voluntary cannot be morally binding (*Rhetoric* i. 1377[b]). Cicero's *De Officiis*, the work Addison mentions twice in this essay, claims that oaths made to enemies are not binding (iii. 29). Among patristic writers there is agreement about the guilt of perjury as Addison describes it, but these remarks are usually accompanied by warnings against taking oaths; see e.g. Chrysostom, *Homilies Concerning the Statues*, xiv. 3–4.

[5] William and Mary's coronation oath included a reference to Parliament which had recently been added: they swore to 'Governe the People of this Kingdome of England ... according to the Statutes in Parlyament Agreed on' (*Statutes* vi. 56). When the oath of allegiance was revised in 1702, some members of Parliament wanted subjects to swear allegiance to both crown and Parliament, but a majority defeated the new inclusion of Parliament because, as Burnet noted, it was ' a barefaced republican notion' to consider Parliament the government (*History* iv. 52). Some Tory members who opposed this inclusion in 1702 were the same people who defended Sacheverell in 1710 by arguing that the priest meant obedience to both crown and Parliament when he claimed that the security of the government was founded on an '*Absolute*, and *Unconditional Obedience* to the *Supream Power*' (Burnet, *History* iv. 552n). A more recent contradiction on this issue for Addison's readers

Now the Guilt of Perjury is so self-evident, that it was always reckoned among the greatest Crimes, by those who were only govern'd by the Light of Reason: The inviolable observing of an Oath, like the other practical Duties of Christianity, is a Part of Natural Religion. As Reason is common to all Mankind, the Dictates of it are the same through the whole Species: And since every Man's own Heart will tell him, that there can be no greater Affront to the Deity, whom he worships, than to appeal to him with an Intention to deceive; nor a greater Injustice to Men, than to betray them by false Assurances; it is no wonder that Pagans and Christians, Infidels and Believers, should concur in a Point wherein the Honour of the Supream Being, and the Welfare of Society are so highly concerned. For this Reason, *Pythagoras* to his first Precept of honouring the immortal Gods, immediately subjoins that of paying Veneration to an Oath.[6] We may see the Reverence which the Heathens shew'd to these sacred and solemn Engagements, from the Inconveniencies which they often suffered, rather than break through them. We have frequent Instances of this kind in the *Roman* Common-Wealth; which, as it has been observed by several eminent *Pagan* Writers,[a] very much excell'd all other *Pagan* Governments in the Practice of Vertue. How far they exceeded in this Particular, those great Corrupters of Christianity, and indeed of Natural Religion, the Jesuits, may appear from their Abhorrence of every Thing that looked like a fraudulent or mental Evasion. Of this I shall only produce the following Instance. Several *Romans*, who had been taken Prisoners by *Hannibal*, were released, upon their obliging themselves by an Oath to return again to his Camp. Among these there was One, who, thinking to elude the Oath, went the same Day back to the Camp, on Pretence of having forgot something. But this Prevarication was so shocking to the *Roman* Senate, that they order'd him to be apprehended, and deliver'd up to *Hannibal*.[7]

We may further[b] see the just Sense the Heathens had of the Crime of Perjury, from the Penalties which they inflicted on the Persons guilty of it.

[a] eminent *Pagan* Writers / eminent Writers *Fol.*   [b] further / *Fol.*, *8vo*; farther *12mo.*

would have been those Lords who defended Queen Anne's prerogative in negotiating the Treaty of Utrecht, but who protested George I's prerogative in arresting Jacobite suspects after the suspension of habeas corpus (*L.J.* xix. 339; *L.J.* xx. 269).

[6] First to the Gods thy humble Homage pay;
The greatest this, and first of Laws obey:
Perform thy Vows, observe thy plighted Troth,
And let Religion bind thee to thy Oath.
Golden Verses, 1–4 (trans. Rowe)

[7] Cicero relates this incident in *De Officiis* iii. 32; the motto of this essay is the conclusion he drew from the story.

Perjury among the *Sythians* was a Capital Crime; and among the *Egyptians* also was punished with Death, as *Diodorus Siculus* relates, who observes that an Offender of this kind, is guilty of those two Crimes (wherein the Malignity of Perjury truly consists,) a failing in his Respect to the Divinity, and in his Faith towards Men.[8] 'Tis unnecessary to multiply Instances of this Nature, which may be found in almost every Author who has written on this Subject.

If Men, who had no other Guide but their Reason, considered an oath to be of such a tremendous Nature, and the Violation of it to be so great a Crime; it ought to make a much deeper Impression upon Minds enlighten'd by reveal'd Religion, as they have more exalted Notions of the Divinity. A supposed Heathen Deity might be so poor in his Attributes, so stinted in his Knowledge, Goodness, or Power, that a Pagan might hope to conceal his Perjury from his Notice, or not to provoke him shou'd he be discover'd, or shou'd he provoke him, not to be punish'd by him. Nay, he might have produced Examples of Falshood and Perjury in the Gods themselves, to whom he appeal'd. But as reveal'd Religion has given us a more just and clear Idea of the Divine Nature, He, whom we appeal to, is Truth itself, the great Searcher of Hearts, who will not let Fraud and Falshood go unpunish'd, or *hold him guiltless that taketh his Name in vain.* And as with regard to the Deity, so likewise with regard to Man, the Obligation of an Oath is stronger upon Christians than upon any other Part of Mankind; and that because Charity, Truth, mutual Confidence, and all other Social Duties are carry'd to greater Heights, and enforc'd with stronger Motives by the Principles of our Religion.

Perjury, with relation to the Oaths which are at present requir'd of us, has in it all the aggravating Circumstances, which can attend that Crime. We take them before the Magistrates of publick Justice; are reminded by the Ceremony, that it is a Part of that Obedience which we learn from the Gospel; expressly disavow all Evasions and mental Reservations whatsoever; appeal to Almighty God for the Integrity of our Hearts, and only desire Him to be our Helper, as we fulfil the Oath we there take in his Presence. I mention these Circumstances, to which several other might be added, because it is a received Doctrine among those, who have treated of the Nature of an Oath, that the greater the Solemnities are which attend it, the more they aggravate the Violation of it. And here what must be the Success that a Man can hope for who turns a Rebel, after having disclaimed the Divine Assistance, but upon Condition of being a faithful and loyal Subject? He first of all desires that God may help him, as he shall keep his

[8] Herodotus, *History*, iv. 68; Diodorus Siculus, *Bibliotheca Historica*, i. 77.

Oath, and afterwards hopes to prosper in an Enterprize, which is the direct Breach of it.

Since therefore Perjury, by the common Sense of Mankind, the Reason of the Thing, and from the whole Tenor of Christianity, is a Crime of so flagitious a Nature, we cannot be too careful in avoiding every Approach towards it.

The Vertue of the ancient *Athenians* is very remarkable in the Case of *Euripides.* This great Tragick-Poet, tho' famous for the Morality of his Plays, had introduced a Person, who, being reminded of an Oath he had taken, replied, *I swore with my Mouth, but not with my Heart.* The Impiety of this Sentiment set the Audience in an Uproar; made *Socrates* (tho' an intimate Friend of the Poet) go out of the Theatre with Indignation; and gave so great Offence, that he was publickly accused, and brought upon his Trial, as one who had suggested an Evasion of what they thought the most holy and indissoluble Bond of Human Society.[9] So jealous were these vertuous Heathens of any the smallest Hint, that might open a Way to Perjury.

And here it highly imports us to consider, that we do not only break our Oath of Allegiance by actual Rebellion, but by all those other Methods which have a natural and manifest Tendency to it. The Guilt may lye upon a Man, where the Penalty cannot take hold of him. Those who speak irreverently of the Person to whom they have sworn Allegiance; who endeavour to alienate from him the Hearts of his Subjects; or to inspire the People with Disaffection to his Government, cannot be thought to be true to the Oath they have taken. And as for those, who by concerted Falshoods and Defamations endeavour to blemish his Character, or weaken his Authority; they incur the complicated Guilt both of Slander and Perjury. The moral Crime is compleated in such Offenders, and there are only accidental Circumstances wanting, to work it up for the Cognizance of the Law.

Nor is it sufficient for a Man, who has given these solemn Assurances to his Prince, to forbear the doing him any Evil, unless at the same Time he do him all the Good he can in his proper Station of Life.

Loyalty is of an active Nature, and ought to discover itself in all the Instances of Zeal and Affection to our Soveraign: And if we carefully examine the Duty of that Allegiance which we pledge to His Majesty, by the Oaths that are tendred to us, we shall find that *We do* not only *renounce*,

[9] The remark which caused the uproar is in *Hippolytos* (line 612). For Addison a contemporary account of Socrates' reaction was available in François Charpentier's *Life of Socrates*, 1712, pp. 24–5.

refuse, and abjure any Allegiance or Obedience to the Pretender, but *Swear to defend King* George *to the utmost of our Power, against all traiterous Conspiracies and Attempts whatsoever, and to disclose and make known to His Majesty, all Treasons and traiterous Conspiracies, which we shall know to be against Him.*

To conclude, as among those who have bound themselves by these sacred Obligations, the actual Traytor or Rebel is guilty of Perjury in the Eye of the Law; the secret Promoter, or well-wisher of their Cause, is so before the Tribunal of Conscience. And tho' I should be unwilling to pronounce the Man who is indolent, or indifferent in the Cause of his Prince, to be absolutely perjured; I may venture to affirm, that he falls very short of that Allegiance to which he is obliged by Oath. Upon the whole we may be assured, that in a Nation which is tyed down by such religious and solemn Engagements, the People's Loyalty will keep Pace with their Morality; and that in Proportion as they are sincere Christians, they will be faithful Subjects.

D

Numb. VII — *Friday, January* 13, 1716

> *Veritas pluribus modis infracta: primum inscitia reipublicæ, ut alienæ; mox libidine assentandi, aut rursus odio adversus dominantes. Obtrectatio et livor pronis auribus accipiuntur: quippe adulationi fœdum crimen servitutis, malignitati falsa species libertatis inest.* Tac.

THERE is no greater Sign of a bad Cause, then when the Patrons of it are reduced to the Necessity of making use of the most wicked Artifices to support it. Of this Kind are the Falshoods and Calumnies, which are invented and spread abroad by the Enemies to our King and Country. This Spirit of Malice and Slander does not discover itself in any Instances so ridiculous, as in those, by which seditious Men endeavour to depreciate His Majesty's Person and Family; without considering, that His Court at *Hanover* was always allow'd to be one of the Politest in *Europe*, and that,

Motto. Tacitus, *Histories*, i. 1: The truth was weakened in many ways: first because men were ignorant of politics, as though politics was not their concern, then because of their desire to flatter or, its opposite, their hatred for their leaders . . . Detraction and spite are heard with ready ears. Indeed the foul accusation of slavery is contained in flattery, but spite has the false appearance of liberty.

before he became our King, he was reckoned among the Greatest Princes of *Christendom.*[2]

But the most Glorious of His Majesty's Predecessors was treated after the same Manner. Upon that Prince's first Arrival, the inconsiderable Party, who then labour'd to make him odious to the People, gave out, That he brought with him Twenty thousand *Laplanders*, cloathed in the Skins of Bears, all of their own killing; and that they mutiny'd because they had not been regaled with a bloody Battle within two Days after their Landing.[3] He was no sooner on the Throne, than those, who had contributed to place him there, finding that he had made some Changes at Court which were not to their Humour, endeavour'd to render him Unpopular by Misrepresentations of his Person, his Character, and his Actions. They found that his Nose had a Resemblance to that of *Oliver Cromwel*, and clapt him on a huge Pair of Mustachoes to frighten his People with:[4] His Mercy was Fear; his Justice was Cruelty; his Temperance, Œconomy, prudent Behaviour, and Application to Business, were *Dutch* Vertues, and such as we had not been used to in our *English* Kings. He did not fight a Battle, in which the *Tories* did not slay double the Number of what he had lost in the Field; nor ever rais'd a Siege, or gain'd a Victory, which did not cost more than 'twas worth.[5] In short, he was contriving the Ruin of his Kingdom;

[2] Countess Cowper began her diary, 'The Perpetual lyes that one hears has determin'd me ... to write down all the Events that are worth remembring whilst I am at Court' (October 1714). Sir John Percival recorded some of the rumours he heard concerning the royal family: 'They say the Prince has the infirmity that he can't help bewraying [exposing] himself, and has given the Princess the pox. That he has sent £40,000 into the Country to bribe Elections. . .That the King goes into the Chocolat Houses and Cofee houses incognito to hear what is said of him. That he is frantick often times and walks about in his shirt. That he keeps two Turks for abominable uses. That he gives his hand behind his back to the English to be kissd, that they may at the same time kiss his Breech. That the Prince says he knows a Tory and a Common whore by their looks. We that are every day at Court know all these things to be lyes, but they serve to give People in the Country an ill impression' (Letterbook, 26 Jan. 1715). Robert Patten concurs that hereditary right, Passive Obedience, and 'the basest of Reflections, and the worst of lying Stories' were very important for inciting the people to rebel (*Late Rebellion*, 'Preface', 1–2). Dudley Ryder heard perhaps the most incredible story: one priest told 'his parishioners in the country that the notion of the Hanover succession was all a fiction. . .and told them that there was no such place as Hanover' (*Diary*, 19 Dec. 1715).

[3] Addison is alluding to reports of William III's army in 1688 which included a squadron of Swedish horsemen who wore fur cloaks. One contemporary described them as '200. . .Laplanders in Bear Skins taken from the Wild Beasts they had Slain, the common Habbit of that cold Climat' ('A True and Exact Relation of the Prince of Orange', reprinted in Macaulay, iii. 1137).

[4] Faithorne's emblematic portrait of Cromwell altered to represent William III is reprinted in Macaulay, iii. 1433.

[5] The Tories were not alone in slandering William III. Although he supported the Whig interest in most issues concerning religion and foreign policy, William was a strong advocate of royal prerogative which the Whigs traditionally opposed before 1714. As early as 1689 some Whigs who feared William 'would strain for a high stretch of prerogative. . .got together a great many stories, that went about the city, of his sullenness, and imperious way of dictating' (Burnet, *History* vi. 61).

and in order to it advanc'd Dr. *Tillotson* to the highest Station of the Church, my Lord *Sommers* of the Law, Mr. *Montagu* of the Treasury, and the Admiral at *la Hogue* of the Fleet.[6] Such were the Calumnies of the Party in those Times, which we see so faithfully copied out by Men of the same Principles under the Reign of His present Majesty.

As the Schemes of these Gentlemen are the most absurd and contradictory to common Sense, the Means by which they are promoted must be of the same Nature. Nothing but Weakness and Folly can dispose *Englishmen* and *Protestants*, to the Interests of a *Popish Pretender*: And the same Abilities of Mind will naturally qualify his Adherents to swallow the most palpable and notorious Falshoods. Their self-interested and designing Leaders cannot desire a more ductile and easy People to work upon. How long was it before many of this simple deluded Tribe were brought to believe, that the *Highlanders* were a Generation of Men that cou'd be Conquer'd! The Rabble of the Party were instructed to look upon 'em as so many *Giants* and *Saracens*; and were very much surprized to find, that every one of 'em had not with his broad Sword mow'd down at least a Squadron of the King's Forces. There were not only publick Rejoycings in the Camp at *Perth*, but likewise many private Congratulations nearer us, among these Well-wishers to their Country, upon the Victories of their Friends at Preston; which continued till the Rebels made their solemn Cavalcade from *Highgate*.[7] Nay there were even then some of these wise Partisans, who concluded the Government had hired two or three Hundred hale Men, who looked like Fox-hunters, to be Bound and Pinion'd, if not to be Executed, as Representatives of the pretended Captives. Their Victories in *Scotland* have been innumerable; and no longer ago than last Week, they gained a very remarkable One, in which the *Highlanders* cut off all the *Dutch* Forces to a Man;[8] and afterwards, disguising themselves in their Habits, came up as Friends to the King's Troops, and put 'em all to

[6] Some critics of the Whigs claimed that John Tillotson, Archbishop of Canterbury, was a Socinian, that John, Lord Somers, was an adulterous Lord Chancellor, that Charles Montague, Earl of Halifax, was a Lord Treasurer who tampered with the currency, and that Edward Russell, Earl of Orford, was a timid admiral (*P.O.A.S.* v. 319, 427, 505–6, 518).

[7] On 9 Dec. 1715 the Preston prisoners arrived in Highgate on the Great North Road. Countess Cowper avoided the spectacle because she had relatives among the rebels, but she gives a vivid second-hand account of their arrival in her diary (December 1715). Major General Tatton, along with 300 foot guards and 120 horse guards, received the prisoners and had them bound together to distinguish them from the crowds of spectators. There was a '*Mock* Triumph' into London which was accompanied by 'Drums beating a triumphant March. . .Heaven seem'd to smile. . .by forming the finest and brightest Winter day that was ever known' (*Pol. State* x. 542–3).

[8] By the terms of the Barrier Treaty of 1715 the Dutch promised to send military assistance to support the Hanoverians in the event of an open rebellion (*C.J.* xviii. 353–4). The first Dutch troops to arrive in Scotland landed at Leith on 4 December.

the Sword. This Story had a great Run for a Day or two; and I believe one might still find out a Whisper among their secret Intelligence, that the Duke of *Mar*[9] is actually upon the Road to *London*, if not within two Days March of the Town. I need not take Notice, that their Successes in the Battle of *Dunblain*,[10] are magnify'd among some of them to this Day; tho' a *Tory* may very well say with King *Pyrrhus*, *That such another Victory would undo them.*

But the most fruitful Source of Falshood and Calumny is that, which, one would think, should be the least apt to produce them; I mean a pretended Concern for the Safety of our Establish'd Religion. Were these People as anxious for the Doctrines, which are essential to the Church of *England*, as they are for the nominal Distinction of adhering to its Interests, they would know, that the sincere Observation of publick Oaths, Allegiance to their King, Submission to their Bishops, Zeal against Popery, and Abhorrence of Rebellion, are the great Points that adorn the Character of the Church of *England*, and in which the Authors of the Reformed Religion in this Nation have always gloried.[11] We justly reproach the Jesuits, who have adapted all Christianity to Temporal and Political Views, for maintaining a Position so repugnant to the Laws of Nature, Morality and Religion, That Evil may be committed for the sake of Good which may arise from it. But we cannot suppose even this Principle, (as bad a One as it is) should influence those Persons, who, by so many absurd and monstrous Falshoods, endeavour to delude Men into a Belief of the Danger of the Church. If there be any relying on the solemn Declarations of a Prince, fam'd for keeping his Word, constant in the publick Exercises of our Religion, and determined in the Maintenance of our Laws, we have all the Assurances[a] that can be given to us, for the Security of the Establish'd Church under his Government. When a leading Man therefore begins to grow apprehensive for the Church, you may be sure, that he is either in Danger of losing a Place, or in Despair of getting one. It is pleasant on these Occasions to see a notorious Profligate seized with a Concern for his Religion, and converting his Spleen into Zeal. These narrow and selfish

[a] Assurances/Security *Fol.*

[9] John Erskine, eleventh Earl of Mar and Jacobite commander in Scotland, was created Duke of Mar by the Pretender in October 1715 (H.M.C. *Stuart MSS.* i. 445).

[10] Usually called the battle of Sheriffmuir (13 Nov. 1715) which lies to the east of Dunblane. Both sides claimed a victory, but Boyer argued that the loyalists had the greater success because Argyll's troops, although outnumbered, prevented the rebels from crossing the Firth of Forth, thus forcing them to return to Perth (*Pol. State* x. 513–14, 521).

[11] Addison is reiterating the main points of the Archbishop's *Declaration* published in November 1715.

Views have so great an Influence in this Cry, that, among those who call themselves the Landed Interest, there are several of my Fellow Free Holders, who always fancy the Church in Danger upon the rising of Bank-Stock.[12] But the standing Absurdities, without the Belief of which no Man is reckon'd a staunch Churchman, are, that there is a Calves-Head Club, for which (by the way) some pious *Tory* has made suitable Hymns and Devotions:[13] That there is a Confederacy among the greatest Part of the Prelates, to destroy Episcopacy; and that all, who talk against Popery, are *Presbyterians* in their Hearts.[14] The Emissaries of the Party are so diligent in spreading ridiculous Fictions of this Kind, that at present, if we may credit common Report, there are several remote Parts of the Nation in which it is firmly believed, that all the Churches in *London* are shut up, and that if any Clergyman walks the Streets in his Habit, 'tis Ten to One but he is knock'd down by some sturdy Schismatick.

We may observe, upon this Occasion, that there are many particular Falshoods suited to the particular Climates and Latitudes in which they are published, according as the Situation of the Place makes them less liable to Discovery: There is many a Lye, that will not thrive within a hundred Miles of *London*: Nay, we often find a Lye born in *Southwark*, that dyes the same Day on this Side the Water: And several produced in the Loyal *Ward* of *Port-soken*, of so feeble a Make, as not to bear Carriage to the *Royal Exchange.*[15] However, as the Mints of Calumny are perpetually at Work, there are a great Number of curious Inventions issued out from Time to Time, which grow current among the Party, and circulate through the whole Kingdom.

As the Design of this Paper is not to exasperate, but to undeceive my Countrymen, let me desire them to consider the many Inconveniencies they bring upon themselves, by these mutual Intercourses of Credulity and Falshood. I shall only remind the Credulous of the strong Delusion they

[12] Because the Bank was a symbol of Whig power, a mob threatened to storm it during the Sacheverell riots in 1710 (Boyer, *Queen Anne*, p. 416).

[13] The Calves Head Club, reputedly a republican club which met on 30 January, the anniversary of Charles I's execution; instead of fasting, members feasted and sang songs (H.M.C. *Hope Johnstone MSS.*, p. 116). The 'pious Tory' was Ned Ward whose *Secret History of the Calves-Head Club* (1703) described rituals and reprinted songs which celebrated republicanism.

[14] At the Convocation in 1702 Burnet reports that 'All that treated the dissenters with temper and moderation. . .were represented as secret favourers of presbytery' (*History* v. 70–71).

[15] The residents of Portsoken ward, situated about a mile east of the Royal Exchange, were among the 4,000 persons who signed the loyal association presented to George I by the Tower Hamlets; it was the first such association since the rebellion began (*St. James's Post*, 6–9 Jan. 1716; *Pol. State* x. 456).

have by this Means been led into, the greatest part of their Lives. Their Hopes have been kept up by a Succession of Lyes for near thirty Years. How many Persons have starved in expectation of those profitable Employments, which were promised them by the Authors of these Forgeries! How many of them have died with great Regret, when they thought they were within a Month of enjoying the inestimable Blessings of a Popish and Arbitrary Reign!

I would therefore advise this blinded Set of Men, not to give Credit to those Persons, by whom they have been so often fooled and imposed upon; but on the contrary to think it an Affront to their Parts, when they hear from any of them such Accounts as they would not dare to tell them, but upon the Presumption that they are Ideots. Or if their Zeal for the Cause shall dispose them to be Credulous in any Points that are favourable to it, I would beg of them not to venture Wagers upon the Truth of them: And in this present Conjuncture, by no means to sell out of the Stocks upon any News they shall hear from their good Friends at *Perth.*[16] As these Party-fictions are the proper Subjects of Mirth and Laughter, their deluded Believers are only to be treated with Pity or Contempt. But as for those Incendiaries of Figure and Distinction, who are the Inventors and Publishers of such gross Falshoods and Calumnies, they cannot be regarded by others, but with the utmost Detestation and Abhorrence; nor one would think, by themselves, without the greatest Remorse and Compunction of Heart; when they consider that in order to give a Spirit to a desperate Cause, they have by their false and treacherous Insinuations and Reports, betrayed so many of their Friends into their own Destruction.

Numb. VIII *Monday, January* 16, 1716

Advenit qui vestra dies muliebribus armis
Verba redargueret. Virg.

I HAVE heard that several Ladies of Distinction, upon the Reading of my Fourth Paper, are studying Methods how to make themselves useful to the

[16] Fears that a Stuart restoration would result in a refusal to honour public debts incurred since 1688 prompted some owners of Bank stock to sell it during the Jacobite attempt in 1708. The Commons responded by resolving that anyone who tried to destroy public credit during an invasion was 'an Enemy to. . .the Kingdom' (*C.J.* xv. 621).

Motto. Virgil, *Aeneid*, xi. 687–8: The day has arrived to refute your words with a woman's armaments.

Publick. One has a Design of keeping an open Tea-Table, where every Man shall be welcome that is a Friend to King *George*. Another is for setting up an Assembly for Basset, where none shall be admitted to *Punt*, that have[a] not taken the Oaths.[2] A Third is upon an Invention of a Dress, which will put every *Tory* Lady out of Countenance: I am not informed of the Particulars, but am told in general, that she has contriv'd to shew her Principles by the setting of her Commode; so that it will be impossible for any Woman that is *disaffected*, to be in the Fashion. Some of 'em are of Opinion that the Fan may be made use of with good Success, against Popery, by exhibiting the Corruptions of the Church of *Rome* in various Figures; and that their Abhorrence of the superstitious Use of Beads, may be very aptly express'd in the Make of a Pearl Necklace. As for the Civil Part of our Constitution, it is unanimously agreed among the Leaders of the Sex, that there is no Glory in making a Man their Slave who has not naturally a Passion for Liberty; and to disallow of all Professions of Passive Obedience, but from a Lover to his Mistress.

It happens very luckily for the Interest of the *Whigs*, that their very Enemies acknowledge the finest Women of *Great Britain* to be of that Party. The *Tories* are forc'd to borrow their Toasts from their Antagonists; and can scarce find Beauties enough of their own Side, to supply a single Round of *October*. One may, indeed, sometimes discover among the Malignants of the Sex, a Face that seems to have been naturally designed for a *Whig* Lady: But then it is so often flush'd with Rage, or sower'd with Disappointments, that one cannot but be troubled to see it thrown away upon the Owner. Would the pretty Malecontent be perswaded to love her King and Country, it would diffuse a Chearfulness through all her Features, and give her quite another Air. I would therefore advise these, my gentle Readers, as they consult the Good of their Faces, to forbear frowning upon Loyalists, and Pouting at the Government. In the mean Time, what may we not hope from a Cause, which is recommended by the Allurement of Beauty, and the Force of Truth! It is therefore to be hoped that every fine Woman will make this laudable Use of her Charms; and that she may not want to be frequently reminded of this great Duty, I will only desire her to think of her Country every Time she looks in her Glass.

But because it is impossible to prescribe such Rules as shall be suitable to the Sex in general, I shall consider them under their several Divisions of Maids, Wives, and Widows.

[a] have/has *Fol.*

[2] Basset, a card game resembling faro, was popular among aristocrats and was often played for high stakes. The players were called punters (*Spectator*, iii. 182n).

As for Virgins, who are unexperienc'd in the Wiles of Men, they would do well to consider how little they are to rely on the Faith of Lovers, who in less than a Year have broken their Allegiance to their lawful Soveraign; and what Credit is to be given to the Vows and Protestations of such as shew themselves so little afraid of Perjury. Besides, what would an innocent young Lady think, should she marry a Man without examining his Principles, and afterwards find herself got with Child by a Rebel?

In the next Place, every Wife ought to answer for her Man. If the Husband be engag'd in a seditious Club, or drinks mysterious Healths, or be frugal of his Candles on a rejoycing Night, let her look to him, and keep him out of Harms way; or the World will be apt to say, she has a mind to be a Widow before her Time. She ought in such Cases to exert the Authority of the Curtain-Lecture;[3] and if she finds him of a rebellious Disposition, to tame him, as they do Birds of Prey, by dinning him in the Ears all Night long.

Widows may be supposed Women of too good Sense not to discountenance all Practices that have a Tendency to the Destruction of Mankind. Besides they have a greater Interest in Property than either Maids or Wives, and do not hold their Jointures by the precarious Tenure of Portions or Pin-Money: So that it is as unnatural for a Dowager as for a Free-holder to be an Enemy to our Constitution.

As nothing is more Instructive than Examples, I wou'd recommend to the Perusal of our *British* Virgins the Story of *Clelia*, a *Roman* Spinster, whose Behaviour is represented by all their Historians, as one of the chief Motives that discouraged the *Tarquins* from prosecuting their Attempt[b] to regain the Throne, from whence they had been expell'd.[4] Let the Marry'd Women reflect upon the Glory acquired by the Wife of *Coriolanus*, who, when her Husband, after long Exile, was returning into his Country with Fire and Sword, diverted him from so cruel and unnatural an Enterprize.[5] And let those who have out-lived their Husbands never forget their Countrywoman Widow *Boadicea*, who headed her Troops in Person against the Invasion of a *Roman* Army, and encouraged them with this

[b] Attempt/Attempts *Fol.*

---

[3] A reproof given by a wife to her husband in bed (Johnson's *Dictionary*).

[4] Cloelia was a hostage given by the Romans to the Etruscans by the terms of a truce. She escaped from the enemy camp and crossed the Tiber on horseback. The Romans, abiding by the truce, returned her to the Etruscan leader, Porsenna, who was so impressed by her bravery that he returned all the hostages and withdrew from Rome (Plutarch, *Lives*, 1716 edn., i. 252–3).

[5] Plutarch, *Lives*, 1716, ii. 87–92.

memorable Saying, *I who am a Woman am resolv'd upon Victory or Death: But as for you who are Men, you may, if you please, chuse Life and Slavery.*[6]

But I do not propose to our *British* Ladies, that they shou'd turn *Amazons* in the Service of their Soveraign, nor so much as let their Nails grow for the Defence of their Country.[7] The Men will take the Work of the Field off their Hands, and shew the World, that *English* Valour cannot be matched, when it is animated by *English* Beauty. I do not however disapprove the Project which is now on Foot for a *Female Association*;[8] and since I hear the fair Confederates cannot agree among themselves upon a Form, shall presume to lay before them the following rough Draught, to be corrected or improved, as they in their Wisdom[c] shall think fit.

'We the Consorts, Relicts, and Spinsters of the Isle of *Great Britain*, whose Names are under-written, being most passionately Offended at the Falshood and Perfidiousness of certain faithless Men, and at the Lukewarmth and Indifference of others, have enter'd into a voluntary Association for the Good and Safety of our Constitution. And we do hereby engage ourselves to raise and arm our[d] Vassals for the Service of His Majesty King *George*, and Him to Defend with our Tongues and Hearts, our Eyes, Eye-Lashes, Favourites, Lips, Dimples, and every other Feature, whether natural or acquired. We promise publickly and openly to avow the Loyalty of our Principles in every Word we shall utter, and every Patch we shall stick on. We do further[e] promise, to annoy the Enemy with all the Flames, Darts, and Arrows with which Nature has armed us; never to correspond with them by Sigh, Ogle, or Billet-doux; not to have any Intercourse with them either in Snuff or Tea; nor to accept the Civility of any Man's Hand, who is not ready to use it in the Defence of his Country. We are determined in so good a Cause to endure the greatest Hardships and Severities, if there shou'd be Occasion; and even to wear the Manufacture of our Country,[f] rather than appear the Friends of a foreign Interest in the richest *French* Brocade. And forgetting all private Feuds,

[c] their Wisdom / their better Wisdom *Fol.* [d] arm our / arm all our *Fol.* [e] further / *Fol.*; farther *8vo, 12mo.* [f] our Country / our own Country *Fol.*

[6] Tacitus, *Annals*, xiv. 35.

[7] The *Examiner* (19–23 Jan. 1713) accused Whig women of being political Amazons.

[8] Addison is alluding to political associations, the most famous being the Association of 1696 which began as a motion passed by Parliament after the Assassination Plot and in which members attested to their loyalty for William III. From Parliament it was carried 'over all England, and was signed by all sorts of people, a very few only excepted' (Burnet, *History* iv. 307). During January 1716 various boroughs in England drew up loyalist associations and sent them to George I; the Irish Parliament did likewise (*Daily Courant*, 12, 26, 28 January). The text of Addison's female association comically imitates the style of such declarations; for the text of the 1696 Association, see *Statutes* vii. 114–15.

Jealousies and Animosities, we do unanimously oblige ourselves, by this our Association, to stand and fall by one another, as loyal and faithful Sisters and Fellow-Subjects.'

N.B. This Association will be lodged at Mr. *Motteux*'s,[9] where Attendance will be given to the Subscribers, who are to be ranged in their respective Columns as, Maids, Wives, and Widows.

Numb. IX *Friday, January* 20, 1716

Consilia qui dant prava cautis hominibus,
Et perdunt operam, et deridentur turpiter.
Phædr.

THOUGH I have already seen, in *The Town-Talk*, a Letter from a celebrated *English* Man to the Pretender, which is indeed an excellent Answer to his Declaration;[2] the Title of this Paper obliges me to publish the following Piece, which considers it in different Lights.

The Declaration of the Free-holders of Great Britain, *in Answer to that of the Pretender.*

We, by the Mercy of God, Free-holders of *Great Britain*, to the Popish Pretender, who stiles himself King of *Scotland* and *England*, and Defender of our Faith, *Defiance*. Having seen a Libel which you have lately published against the king and People of these Realms under the Title of a *Declaration*, We, *in Justice to the Sentiments of our own Hearts*, have thought fit to return you the following Answer; wherein we shall endeavour to

[9] Peter Motteux (1663–1718), playwright and translator, described his India shop in *S.* 288 as 'known for Choice and Cheapness of China and Japan-wares, Tea, Fans, Muslins, Pictures, Arrack, and other *Indian* Goods' (*Spectator*, iii. 25–6).

Motto. Phaedrus, *Fables*, I. xxv. 1–2: Those who give bad advice to discreet people both lose their pains and are dishonourably scorned.

[2] Although dated 25 Oct. 1715, the Pretender's *Declaration* was published, posted, and read widely after he landed in Scotland on 22 Dec. (Patten, *Late Rebellion*, pt. II, p. 64). Steele published an answer to the *Declaration* in *Town Talk* on 13 Jan. 1716 and was criticized for reprinting the *Declaration* (*Periodical Journalism*, pp. 213–27; *Annals* ii. 176–7). This *Freeholder* essay appeared a few days after Steele published a second, less humorous reply to the *Declaration*. Bolingbroke was involved in drawing up the *Declaration* but later claimed that he was so opposed to the revisions the Pretender and his advisors made that he refused to allow his name on the document (*Letter to Windham*, pp. 277–88).

reduce to Method the several Particulars, which you have contrived to throw together with much Malice, and no less Confusion.

We believe you sincere in the first Part of your Declaration, where you own it wou'd be a great Satisfaction to you to be placed upon the Throne by our Endeavours: But you discourage us from making use of them, by declaring it to be your Right *both by the Laws of God and Man.*[3] As for the Laws of God, we shou'd think ourselves great Transgressors of them, shou'd we for your Sake rebel against a Prince, who, under God, is the most powerful Defender of that Religion which we think the most pleasing to Him: And as for the Laws of Man, we conceive those to be of that Kind, which have been enacted from Time to Time for near thirty Years past against you and your Pretensions, by the Legislature of this Kingdom.

You afterwards proceed to Invectives against the Royal Family: Which we do assure you is a very unpopular Topick, except to your few deluded Friends among the Rabble.[4]

You call them *Aliens to our Country*, not considering that King *George* has lived above a Year longer in *England* than ever you did. You say they are *Distant in Blood*; whereas no Body ever doubted that King *George* is Great Grandson to King *James* the First, tho' many believe that you are not son to King *James* the Second.[5] Besides all the World acknowledges he is the nearest to our Crown of the Protestant Blood; of which you cannot have one Drop in your Veins, unless you derive it from such Parents as you don't care for owning.

Your next Argument against the Royal Family, is, that they are *Strangers to our Language*: But they must be Strangers to the *British* Court who have told you so. However you must know, that we plain Men shou'd prefer a King who was a Stranger to our Language, before one who is a Stranger to our Laws and Religion: For we cou'd never endure *French* Sentiments, tho' deliver'd in our native Dialect; and shou'd abhor an arbitrary Prince, tho' he tyranniz'd over us in the finest *English* that ever was spoken. For these Reasons, Sir, we cannot bear the Thought of hearing a Man that has

[3] 'As We are firmly resolved never to omit any Opportunity of Asserting Our undoubted Title to the Imperial Crown of these Realms, and of endeavouring to put Our self into the Possession of that Right, which is devolved upon Us by the Laws of God and Man; so must We, in Justice to the Sentiments of Our own Heart, Declare, That nothing in the World can give Us so great Satisfaction, as to owe to the Endeavours of Our Loyal Subjects both Our and their Restoration to that happy Settlement, which can alone deliver this Church and Nation from the Calamities which they ly at present under, and from these future Miseries, which must be the Consequences of the present Usurpation' (Pretender's *Declaration*).

[4] 'We have beheld a foreign Family, Aliens to Our Country, distant in Blood, and Strangers even to our Language, ascend the Throne.'

[5] The best historian to question the legitimacy of the Pretender seriously was Gilbert Burnet (*History* iii. 239–46).

been bred up in the Politicks of *Louis* the Fourteenth, talk intelligibly from the *British* Throne; especially when we consider, however he may boast of his speaking *English*, he says his Prayers in an unknown Tongue.

We come now to the Grievances for which in your Opinion we ought to take up Arms against our present Soveraign. The greatest you seem to insist upon, and which is most in the Mouths of your Party, is the Union of the Two Kingdoms;[6] for which His Majesty ought most certainly to be deposed, because it was made under the Reign of Her, whom you call your *Dear Sister of Glorious Memory.*[7] Other Grievances which you hint at under His Majesty's Administration, are, the Murder of King *Charles* the First, who was Beheaded before King *George* was born; and the Sufferings of King *Charles* the Second, which perhaps His present Majesty cannot wholly clear Himself of, because He came into the World a Day before His Restoration.[8]

As on the one Side you arraign His present Majesty by this most extraordinary Retrospect, on the other Hand you condemn His Government by what we may call the Spirit of Second-Sight. You are not content to draw into His Reign those Mischiefs that were done a hundred Years ago, unless you anticipate those that may happen a hundred Years hence. So that the keenest of your Arrows either fall short of Him, or fly over His Head. We take it for a certain Sign that you are at a loss for present Grievances, when you are thus forced to have recourse to your

[6] 'We are come to take Our Part in all the Dangers and Difficulties to which any of Our Subjects, from the greatest down to the meanest, may be exposed on this important Occasion, to relieve Our Subjects of *Scotland* from the Hardships they groan under on Account of the late unhappy Union; and to restore the Kingdom to its antient, free, and independent State.'

[7] 'During the Life of our dear Sister of Glorious Memory, the Happiness which Our People enjoyed, softened in some Degree the Hardship of Our own Fate: And We must further confess, That when We reflected on the Goodness of Her Nature, and Her Inclinations to Justice, We could not but persuade Our self, That She intended to establish and perpetuate the Peace, which She had given to these Kingdoms, by destroying forever all Competition to the Succession of the Crown, and by securing to Us at last the Enjoyment of that Inheritance, out of which We had been so long kept, which her Conscience must inform Her was Our Due, and which her Principles must lead Her to desire that We might obtain.' Bolingbroke claimed that, because the Queen was so respected by Tories, 'it was in his interest to weave the honour of her name into his cause'; however, the Pretender deleted 'blessed' from the original draft which read 'sister of Glorious and Blessed Memory'. For the Pretender's revisions concerning references to Queen Anne, see Bolingbroke, *Letter to Windham*, pp. 279–81.

[8] 'We have before Our Eyes the Example of Our Royal Grandfather, who fell a Sacrifice to Rebellion; and of Our Royal Uncle, who, by a Train of Miracles, escaped the Rage of barbarous and blood-thirsty Rebels, and lived to exercise His Clemency towards those who had waged War against his Father and Himself; who had driven Him to seek Shelter in foreign Lands, and who had even set a Price upon His Head.' Bolingbroke claimed that the original draft called Charles I a blessed martyr and the Pretender deleted that passage (*Letter to Windham*, p. 282).

future Prospects, and future Miseries.[9] Now, Sir, you must know, that we Free-holders have a natural Aversion to Hanging, and don't know how to answer it to our Wives and Families, if we shou'd venture our Necks upon the Truth of your Prophecies. In our ordinary Way of Judging, we guess at the King's future Conduct by what we have seen already; and therefore beg you will excuse us if for the present we defer entring into a Rebellion, to which you so graciously invite us. When we have as bad a Prospect of our King[a] *George*'s Reign, as we shou'd have of yours, then will be your Time to date another Declaration from your Court at *Commerci*: Which, if we may be allowed to Prophecy in our Turn, cannot possibly happen before the hundred and fiftieth Year of your Reign.[10]

Having considered the past and future Grievances mentioned in your Declaration, we come now to the present; all of which are founded upon this Supposition, That whatever is done by His Majesty or His Ministers to keep you out of the *British* Throne, is a Grievance. These, Sir, may be Grievances to you, but they are none to us. On the contrary, we look upon them as the greatest Instances of His Majesty's Care and Tenderness for His People. To take them in Order: The first relates to the Ministry; who are chosen, as you observe very rightly, out of the Worst, and not the Best of *Your* Subjects.[11] Now, Sir, can you in Conscience think us to be such Fools as to rebel against the King, for having employed those who are His most eminent Friends, and were the greatest Sufferers in His Cause before He came to the Crown; and for having removed a General who is now actually in Arms against him, and two Secretaries of State, both of whom have listed themselves in your Service;[12] or because He chose to substitute in their Places such Men who had distinguish'd themselves by their Zeal against you, in the most famous Battles, Negociations, and Debates.

The second Grievance you mention, is, that the Glory of the late Queen has suffer'd, who, you insinuate, *had secured to you the Enjoyment of that Inheritance out of which you had been so long kept.*[13] This may indeed be a Reason why Her Memory should be precious with you: But you may be

[a] of our King / of King *Fol.*

[9] See above, n. 3.

[10] The Pretender concluded his *Declaration*: 'Given under Our Sign Manual and Privy Signet, at Our Court at *Commercy*, the 25th Day of *October*, in the Fifteenth Year of Our Reign.'

[11] 'We have seen the Reins of Government put into the Hands of a Faction, and that Authority, which was designed for the Protection of all, exercised by a few of the worst to the Oppression of the best and greatest Number of Our Subjects.'

[12] The General was the Duke of Ormonde and the Secretaries were Viscount Bolingbroke and the Earl of Mar (Tindal, p. 404).

[13] See above, n. 7.

sure we shall think never the better of Her, for Her having your good Word. For the same Reason it makes us stare, when we hear it objected to His present Majesty, *That he is not kind to Her faithful Servants*;[14] since, if we can believe what you yourself say, it is impossible they should be *His faithful Servants.* And by the way, many of your private Friends here wish you would forbear blabbing at this rate: For to tell you a Secret, we are very apt to suspect that any *English* Man who deserves your Praise, deserves to be Hang'd.

The next Grievance which you have a mighty Mind to redress among us, is the Parliament of *Great Britain*, against whom you bring a stale Accusation which has been used by every Minority in the Memory of Man; namely, that it was procured by unwarrantable Influences and Corruptions.[15] We cannot indeed blame you for being angry at those, who have set such a round Price upon your Head. Your Accusation of our High Court of Parliament, puts us in mind of a Story, often told among us *Freeholders*, concerning a rattle-brain'd young Fellow, who being indicted for two or three Pranks upon the High-way, told the Judge he would swear the Peace against him, for putting him in fear of his Life.

The next Grievance is such a one, that we are amazed how it could come into your Head. Your Words are as follow. *Whilst the principal Powers engaged in the late Wars do enjoy the Blessings of Peace, and are attentive to discharge their Debts, and ease their People,* Great Britain *in the midst of Peace, feels all the Load of War.* New Debts *are contracted*, new Armies *are raised at Home*, Dutch *Forces are brought into these Kingdoms.* What in the Name of Wonder do you mean? Are you in earnest, or do you design to banter us? Whom is the Nation obliged to for all this Load of War that it feels? Had you been wise enough to have slept at *Bar-le-duc* in a whole Skin, we should not have contracted new Debts, raised new Armies, or brought over *Dutch* Forces to make an Example of you.

The most pleasant Grievance is still behind, and indeed a most proper one to close up this Article. *King* George *has taken Possession of the Dutchy of* Bremen, *whereby a Door is open'd to let in an Inundation of Foreigners from Abroad, and to reduce these Nations to the State of a Province to one of the most inconsiderable Provinces of the Empire.* And do you then really believe the Mob-Story, that King *George* designs to make a Bridge of Boats from

[14] 'Our Sister has not been left at Rest in Her Grave, Her Name has been scurrilously abused, Her Glory, as far as in these People lay, insolently defaced, and Her faithful Servants inhumanely persecuted.'

[15] 'A Parliament has been procured by the most unwarrantable Influences, and by the grossest Corruption to serve the vilest Ends; And they who ought to be the guardians of the Liberties of the People, are become the Instruments of Tyranny...'

Hanover to *Wapping*? We would have you know that some of us read *Baker*'s Chronicle,[16] and don't find that *William* the Conqueror ever thought of making *England* a Province to his Native Dutchy of *Normandy*, notwithstanding it lay so much more convenient for that Purpose: Nor that King *James* the First had ever any Thoughts of reducing this Nation to the State of a Province to his ancient Kingdom of *Scotland*, though it lies upon the same Continent. But pray how comes it to pass that the Electorate of *Hanover* is become all of a sudden one of the most inconsiderable Provinces of the Empire? If you undervalue it upon the Account of its Religion, you have some Reason for what you say; tho' you should not think we are such Strangers to Maps, and live so much out of the World, as to be ignorant that it is for Power and Extent the second Protestant State in *Germany*; and whether you know it or no, the Protestant Religion in the Empire, is looked upon as a sufficient Ballance against Popery. Besides, you should have considered that in your Declaration upon the King's coming to the Throne of *Great Britain*, you endeavour'd to terrify us from receiving him, by representing him *as a powerful foreign Prince, supported by a numerous Army of his own Subjects.*[17] Be that as it will; we are no more afraid of being a Province to *Hanover*, than the *Hanoverians* are apprehensive of being a Province to *Bremen*.

We have now taken Notice of those great Evils which you are come to rescue us from: But as they are such as we neither feel nor see,[b] we desire you will put yourself to no further[c] Trouble for our sakes.

You afterwards begin a kind of *Te Deum*, before the Time, in that remarkable Sentence, *We adore the Wisdom of the Divine Providence, which has opened a Way to our Restoration, by the Success of those very Measures that were laid to disappoint us for ever.* We are at a Loss to know what[d] you mean by this devout Jargon: But by what goes before and follows, we suppose it to be this: That the coming of King *George* to the Crown, has made many Malecontents, and by that Means opened a Way to your Restoration; whereas you should consider that if he had not come to the Crown, the Way had been open of itself. In the same pious Paragraph, *You most*

[b] we neither feel nor see / *Fol.*; we have neither felt or seen *8vo, 12mo.* [c] further / *Fol.*; farther *8vo, 12mo.* [d] Loss to know what / Loss what *Fol.*

[16] Richard Baker's *Chronicle of the Kings of England*, published in many editions from 1643 to 1730, was popular with country gentlemen like Sir Roger de Coverley (*Spectator*, ii. 551).

[17] Addison is referring to the Pretender's manifesto, dated 29 Aug. 1714 at Plombières, which was mailed from France the following November to the Duke of Marlborough, the Earl of Nottingham, and other political leaders in England. He claimed in the declaration that an allied army of Hanoverians, Prussians, and Palatines was preparing to assist George I in oppressing the English (Lamberty, *Mémoires*, viii. 686; Tindal, pp. 409–10).

earnestly conjure us to pursue those Methods for your Restoration which the Finger of God seems to point out to us. Now the only Methods which we can make use of for that End, are, Civil War, Rapine, Bloodshed, Treason and Perjury; Methods, which we Protestants do humbly conceive, can never be pointed out to us by the Finger of God.

The rest of your Declaration contains the Encouragements you give us to Rebell. First, you promise to share with us *all Dangers and Difficulties* which we shall meet with in this worthy Enterprize.[18] You are very much in the Right on't: You have nothing to lose, and hope to get a Crown. We don't hope for any new Free-holds, and only desire to keep what we have. As therefore you are in the right to undergo Dangers and Difficulties to make yourself our Master, we shall think ourselves as much in the right to undergo Dangers and Difficulties to hinder you from being so.

Secondly, You promise to *refer your and our Interest to a* Scotch *Parliament*, which you are resolved to call immediately.[19] We suppose you mean if the Frost holds.[20] But Sir, we are certainly inform'd there is a Parliament now sitting at *Westminster*, that are busy at present in taking care both of the *Scotch* and *English* Interest, and have actually done every thing which you would *let* be done by our Representatives in the High-Lands.

Thirdly, *You promise that if we will Rebel for you against our present Soveraign, you will remit and discharge all Crimes of High-Treason, Misprision, and*[e] *all other Crimes and Offences whatsoever, done or committed against you, or your Father.* But will you answer in this Case that King *George* will forgive us? Otherwise we beseech you to consider, what poor Comfort it would be for a *British* Free-holder to be conveyed up *Holbourn*, with your Pardon in his Pocket. And here we cannot but remark, that the Conditions of your General Pardon are so stinted, as to shew that you are very cautious lest your good nature should carry you too far. You exclude from the Benefit of it, all those who do not *from the Time of your Landing lay hold on Mercy, and return to their Duty and Allegiance.* By this means all Neuters and Lookers on are to be executed of Course: And by the studied Ambiguity

[e] *Misprision, and | Misprision of Treason, and Fol.*

[18] See above, n. 6.

[19] 'But We hope for better Things: . . . to see Our just Rights, and those of the Church and People of *Scotland*, once more settled in a free and independent *Scots* Parliament, on their Ancient Foundation: To such a Parliament [which we Will immediately Call] shall We entirely refer both Our and their Interests; being sensible, that these Interests rightly understood are always the same . . .'

[20] The winter of 1715–16 was especially cold and the Thames was so frozen that shops of all kinds were set up on the ice (*Dawks's News-Letter*, 14 Jan.).

in which you couch the Terms of your gracious Pardon, you still leave room to gratify yourself in all the Pleasures of Tyranny and Revenge.

Upon the Whole, we have so bad an Opinion of Rebellion, as well as of your Motives to it, and Rewards for it, that you may rest satisfy'd, there are few Free-holders on this Side the *Forth* who will engage in it: And we verily believe that you will suddenly take a Resolution in your Cabinet of *Highlanders* to scamper off with your new Crown, which we are told the Ladies of those Parts have so generously Clubb'd for. And you may assure yourself that it is the only One you are like to get by this notable Expedition. And so we bid you heartily Farewel.

Dated Jan. 19, *in the*
Second Year of our
Publick Happiness.

F

Numb. x *Monday, January* 23, 1716

Potior visa est periculosa Libertas quieto Servitio.
Sall.

ONE may venture to affirm, that all honest and disinterested *Britons* of what Party soever, if they understood one another, are of the same Opinion in Points of Government: And that the Gross of the People, who are imposed upon by Terms which they do not comprehend, are *Whigs* in their Hearts. They are made to believe, that Passive-Obedience and Non-Resistance, Unlimited Power and Indefeasible Right, have something of a venerable and religious Meaning in them; whereas in Reality they only imply, that a King of *Great Britain* has a Right to be a Tyrant, and that his Subjects are obliged in Conscience to be Slaves. Were the Case truly and fairly laid before them, they would know, that when they make a Profession of such Principles, they renounce their legal Claim to Liberty and Property, and unwarily submit to what they really abhor.

It is our Happiness, under the present Reign, to hear our King from the Throne exhorting us to be *zealous Assertors of the Liberties of our Country*;[2] which exclude all Pretensions to an arbitrary, tyrannick or despotick Power. Those who have the Misfortune to live under such a Power, have

Motto. Sallust, *Fragmenta*, i. 26: Freedom with danger seemed preferable to peace with slavery.

[2] The King's speech to Parliament, 9 Jan. 1716 (*C.J.* xviii. 330).

no other Law but the Will of their Prince, and consequently no Privileges, but what are precarious. For tho' in some arbitrary Governments there may be a Body of Laws observed in the ordinary Forms of Justice, they are not sufficient to secure any Rights to the People; because they may be dispensed with, or laid aside at the Pleasure of the Soveraign.

And here it very much imports us to consider, that arbitrary Power naturally tends to make a Man a bad Soveraign, who might possibly have been a good One, had he been invested with an Authority limited and circumscribed by Laws. None can doubt of this Tendency in arbitrary Power, who consider, that it fills the Mind of Man with great and unreasonable Conceits of himself; raises him into a Belief, that he is of a superior Species to his Subjects; extinguishes in him the Principle of Fear, which is one of the greatest Motives to all Duties; and creates an Ambition of magnifying himself, by the Exertion of such a Power in all its Instances. So great is the Danger, that when a Soveraign Can do what he Will, he Will do what he Can.

One of the most arbitrary Princes in our Age was *Muley Ishmael*, Emperour of *Morocco*, who, after a long Reign, dy'd about a Twelvemonth ago.[3] This Prince was a Man of much Wit and natural Sense, of an Active Temper, undaunted Courage, and great Application. He was a Descendent of *Mahomet*;[4] and so Exemplary for his Adherence to the Law of his Prophet, that he abstained all his Life from the Taste of Wine;[5] began the annual Fast, or *Lent* of *Ramadan* two Months before his Subjects; was frequent in his Prayers; and that he might not want Opportunities of Kneeling, had fixed in all the spacious Courts of his Palace large consecrated Stones pointing towards the East, for any occasional Exercise of his Devotion. What might not have been hoped from a Prince of these Endowments, had they not all been rendered useless and ineffectual to the Good of his People by the Notion of that Power which They ascribed to him! This will appear, if we consider how he exercised it towards his Subjects in those Three great Points which are the chief Ends of

[3] Mulai Ismail (1646–1726), the second Moroccan ruler of the Filali dynasty, ascended the throne in 1672. He occasionally sent out false reports of his death, such as Addison must have seen (e.g. in the *St. James's Post*, 25 Jan. 1716), to test the fidelity of his subordinates and family (Busnot, p. 115). Sources Addison used for this essay include François Pidou de St. Olon's *Present State of Morocco* (1695), Simon Ockley's *Account of South-West Barbary* (1713), and Dominick Busnot's *History of the Reign of Muley Ismael* (1715). Whenever Addison's remarks closely resemble those of these authors, the authors and page references are cited.

[4] Ockley claims that this was only a pretension (p. 82).

[5] St. Olon says that he did drink 'a certain Hypocras that he makes himself with Brandy . . . which happens pretty often' (p. 63).

Government, the Preservation of their Lives, the Security of their Fortunes, and the Determinations of Justice between Man and Man.

Foreign Envoys, who have given an Account of their Audiences, describe this holy Man mounted on Horseback in an open Court, with several of his *Alcaydes*, or Governours of Provinces about him, standing bare-foot, trembling, bowing to the Earth, and at every Word he spoke, breaking out into passionate Exclamations of Praise, as, *Great is the Wisdom of our Lord the King*; *Our Lord the King speaks as an Angel from Heaven.* Happy was the man among them, who was so much a Favourite as to be sent on an Errand to the most remote Street in his Capital; which he perform'd with the greatest Alacrity, ran through every Puddle that lay in his Way, and took care to return out of Breath and cover'd with Dirt, that he might shew himself a diligent and faithful Minister. His Majesty at the same time, to exhibit the Greatness of his Power, and shew his Horsemanship, seldom dismiss'd the Foreigner from his Presence, till he had entertain'd him with the Slaughter of two or three of his Liege Subjects, whom he very dexterously put to Death with the Tilt of his Launce. St. *Olon*, the *French* Envoy, tells us, that when he had his last Audience of him, he receiv'd him in Robes just stain'd with an Execution; and that he was blooded up to his Elbows by a Couple of *Moors*, whom he had been butchering with his own Imperial Hands.[6] By the Calculation of that Author, and many others, who have since given an Account of his Exploits, we may reckon that by his own Arm he kill'd above Forty Thousand of his People.[7] To render himself the more Awful, he chose to wear a Garb of a particular Colour when he was bent upon Executions; so that when he appear'd in Yellow his Great Men hid themselves in Corners, and durst not pay their Court to him, till he had satiated his Thirst of Blood by the Death of some of his loyal Commoners, or of such unwary Officers of State as chanc'd to come in his Way.[8] Upon this Account we are told, that the first News enquir'd after every Morning at *Mequinez*,[9] was, Whether the Emperour were stirring, and in a good or bad Humour? As this Prince was a great Admirer of Architecture, and employ'd many Thousands in Works of that Kind, if he did not approve the Plan or the

[6] St. Olon (1640–1720) was sent by Louis XIV to Morocco in 1693 to negotiate the release of French prisoners and settle terms for a commercial treaty. He describes his final audience on pp. 170–2.

[7] Busnot, p. 47.

[8] Busnot, p. 36.

[9] Meknès. St. Olon described it as 'very populous, having above 60,000 Inhabitants, but so ill built and unpleasant in it self, that it might well pass for a pittiful Country Town, were it not for the . . . Prince's Presence and his *Alcassave* that graces it' (pp. 71–2).

Performance, it was usual for him to shew the Delicacy of his Taste by demolishing the Building, and putting to Death all that had a Hand in it.[10] I have heard but of one Instance of his Mercy; which was shewn to the Master of an *English* Vessel. This our Countryman presented him with a curious Hatchet, which he receiv'd very graciously; and asking him whether it had a good Edge, try'd it upon the Donor, who slipping aside from the Blow, escaped with the loss only of his right Ear; for old *Muley*, upon second Thoughts, considering that it was not one of his own Subjects, stopp'd his Hand, and would not send him to Paradise. I cannot quit this Article of his Tenderness for the Lives of his People, without mentioning one of his Queens, whom he was remarkably fond of; as also a Favourite Prime Minister, who was very dear to him. The first dy'd by a Kick of her Lord the King, when she was big with Child, for having gather'd a Flower as she was walking with him in his Pleasure-Garden. The other was bastinado'd to Death by his Majesty; who, repenting of the Drubs he had given him when it was too late, to manifest his Esteem for the Memory of so worthy a man, executed the Surgeon that could not cure him.

This absolute Monarch was as notable a Guardian of the Fortunes, as of the Lives of his Subjects. When any Man among his People grew rich, in order to keep him from being dangerous to the State, he used to send for all his Goods and Chattels. His Governours of Towns and Provinces, who form'd themselves upon the Example of their *Grand Monarque*, practised Rapine, Violence, Extortion, and all the Arts of despotick Government in their respective Districts, that they might be the better enabled to make him their yearly Presents. For the greatest of his Viceroys could only propose to himself a comfortable Subsistance out of the Plunder of his Province, and was in certain Danger of being recall'd or hang'd, if he did not remit the Bulk of it to his Dread Soveraign. That he might make a right Use of these prodigious Treasures, which flow'd in to him from all the Parts of his wide Empire, he took Care to bury them under Ground, by the Hands of his most trusty Slaves, and then cut their Throats, as the most effectual Method to keep them from making Discoveries.[11] These were his *Ways and Means* for raising Money, by which he weaken'd the Hands of the Factious, and in any Case of Emergency, could employ the whole Wealth of his Empire, which he had thus amassed together in his subterraneous Exchequer.

As there is no such thing as Property under an arbitrary Government, you may learn what was *Muley Ishmael*'s Notion of it from the following

[10] Ockley, p. 89.

[11] Busnot claims this was done by Ismail's minister (p. 84).

Story. Being upon the Road, amidst his Life-Guards, a little before the Time of the *Ram-Feast*, he met one of his *Alcaydes* at the Head of his Servants, who were driving a great Flock of Sheep to Market. The Emperor ask'd whose they were: The Alcayde answered with profound Submission, *They are Mine*, O Ishmael, *Son of* Elcherif, *of the Line of* Hassan. Thine! *thou Son of a Cuckold*, said this Servant of the Lord, *I thought I had been the only Proprietor in this Country*; upon which he run him through the Body with his Launce, and very piously distributed the Sheep among his Guards, for the Celebration of the Feast.[12]

His Determinations of Justice between Man and Man, were indeed very summary and decisive, and generally put an end to the Vexations of a Law-Suit, by the Ruin both of Plaintiff and Defendant.[13] Travellers have recorded some Samples of this Kind, which may give us an Idea of the Blessings of his Administration. One of his Alcaydes complaining to him of a Wife, whom he had received from His Majesty's Hands, and therefore could not divorce her, that she used to pull him by the Beard; the Emperor to redress this Grievance, order'd his Beard to be pluck'd up by the Roots, that he might not be liable to any more such Affronts.[14] A Country Farmer having accus'd some of his Negro-Guards for robbing him of a Drove of Oxen, the Emperour readily shot the Offenders: But afterwards demanding Reparation of the Accuser, for the Loss of so many brave Fellows and finding him insolvent, compounded the Matter with him by taking away his Life. There are many other Instances of the same Kind. I must observe however under this Head, that the only good Thing he is celebrated for, during his whole Reign, was the clearing the Roads and High-ways of Robbers, with which they used to be very much infested. But his method was to slay Man, Woman and Child, who liv'd within a certain Distance from the Place, where the Robbery was committed. This extraordinary Piece of Justice could not but have its Effect, by making every road in his Empire unsafe for the Profession of a Free-Booter.

I must not omit this Emperour's Reply to Sir *Cloudesly Shovel*, who had taken several of his Subjects by way of Reprizal for the *English* Captives that were detained in his Dominions. Upon the Admiral's offering to exchange them on very advantageous Terms, this good Emperor sent him Word, The Subjects he had taken were poor Men, not worth the

[12] Ockley, pp. 93–4.

[13] On 6 Mar. 1716, eleven days after the execution of the two rebel Lords, an anonymous *Freeholder Extraordinary* was published in which George I and Mulai Ismail were described as similarly harsh in the justice they demanded.

[14] Ockley, p. 94.

Ransoming, and that he might throw them over board, or destroy them otherwise as he pleased.[15]

Such was the Government of *Muley Ishmael, the Servant of God, the Emperor of the Faithful, who was Courageous in the Way of the Lord, the Noble, the Good.*

To conclude this Account, which is extracted from the best Authorities, I shall only observe that he was a great Admirer of His late Most Christian Majesty.[16] In a Letter to him, he compliments him with the Title of *Soveraign Arbiter of the Actions and Wills of his People.* And in a Book published by a *French* Man, who was sent to him as an Ambassador, is the following Passage, *He is absolute in his States, and often compares himself to the Emperour of* France, *who he says is the only Person that knows how to Reign like himself, and to make his Will the law.*[17]

This was that Emperour of *France* to whom the Person who has a great Mind to be King of these Realms owed his Education, and from whom he learn'd his Notions of Government. What should hinder one, whose Mind is so well season'd with such Prepossessions, from attempting to copy after his Patron, in[a] the Exercise of such a Power; especially considering that the Party who espouse his Interest, never fail to compliment a Prince that distributes all his Places among them, with unlimited Power on his Part, and unconditional Obedience on that of his Subjects.

Numb. XI *Friday, January* 27, 1716

Honi Soit Qui Mal Y Pense.

BY our latest Advices, both from Town and Country, it appears, that the Ladies of *Great Britain*, who are *able to bear Arms*, that is, to Smile or Frown to any Purpose, have already begun to commit Hostilities upon the Men of each opposite Party. To this End we are assured, that many of them on both Sides *Exercise* before their Glasses every Morning; that they have already cashier'd several of their Followers as Mutineers, who have

[a] his Patron, in / his Patron, and him whom he calls his Father, in *Fol.*

[15] Sir Cloudesley Shovell (1650–1707) was Commander of the British fleet when he died in a shipwreck. He had been in the Mediterranean in 1684 and Ismail's reply, later published as an appendix to Ockley's *Account*, is dated 26 Aug. 1684: 'As for the Captives you have taken, you may do with them as you please; heaving them into the Sea, or destroy them otherways' (p. 144).

[16] Louis XIV.

[17] St. Olon, p. 65.

contradicted them in some political Conversations; and that the *Whig* Ladies in particular design very soon to have a general Review of their Forces at a Play bespoken by one of their Leaders. This Sett of Ladies, indeed, as they daily do Duty at Court, are much more expert in the Use of their Airs and Graces than their female Antagonists, who are most of them bred in the Country: So that the Sisterhood of Loyalists, in respect of the fair Malecontents, are like an Army of regular Forces, compared with a raw undisciplin'd Militia.[1]

It is to this Misfortune in their Education that we may ascribe the rude and opprobrious Language with which the disaffected Part of the Sex treat the present Royal Family. A little lively Rustick, who hath been trained up in Ignorance and Prejudice, will prattle Treason a whole Winter's Evening, and string together a Parcel of silly seditious Stories, that are equally void of Decency and Truth. Nay you sometimes meet with a zealous Matron, who sets up for the Pattern of a Parish, uttering such Invectives as are highly misbecoming her, both as a Woman and a Subject. In Answer therefore to such disloyal Termagants, I shall repeat to 'em a Speech of the honest and blunt Duke *du Sully*[2] to an Assembly of *Popish* Ladies, who were railing very bitterly against *Henry* the Fourth, at his Accession to the *French* Throne; *Ladies*, said he, *you have a very good King, if you know when you are well. However set your Hearts at rest, for he is not a Man to be scolded or scratch'd out of his Kingdom.*

But as I never care to speak of the fair Sex, unless I have an Occasion to Praise them, I shall take my Leave of these ungentle Damsels; and only beg of them, not to make themselves less amiable than Nature design'd 'em, by being Rebels to the best of their Abilities, and endeavouring to bring their Country into Bloodshed and Confusion. Let me therefore recommend to them the Example of those beautiful Associates whom I mention'd in my Eighth Paper, as I have receiv'd the Particulars of their Behaviour from the Person with whom I lodg'd their Association.

This Association being written at length in a large Roll of the finest Vellum, with three distinct Columns for the Maids, Wives, and Widows, was open'd for the Subscribers near a Fortnight ago. Never was a Subscription for a *Raffling* or an *Opera* more crowded. There is scarce a celebrated Beauty about Town that you may not find in one of the three

[1] The county militias, supported and led by the local gentry, were popular with country Tories (*F.* 22, n. 14), but their military value was something of a joke; Dryden described them as 'Mouths without Hands; maintain'd at Vast Expence,/ In peace a Charge, in War a weak Defence' ('Cymon and Iphigenia', 11. 401–2). During the rebellion they never performed well on their own (see *F.* 3, n. 13).

[2] Maximilien de Béthune, duc de Sully (1560–1641), friend and adviser to Henry IV.

Lists; insomuch, that if a Man, who did not know the Design, should read only the Names of the Subscribers, he would fancy every Column to be a Catalogue of Toasts. Mr. *Motteux* has been heard to say more than once, that if he had the Portraits of all the Associates, they would make a finer Auction of Pictures, than he or any Body else had ever exhibited.

Several of the Ladies indeed criticised upon the Form of the Association. One of them after the Perusal of it, wonder'd that among the Features to be used in Defence of their Country, there was no mention made of *Teeth*; upon which she smiled very charmingly, and discovered as fine a Sett as ever Eye beheld. Another, who was a tall lovely Prude, holding up her Head in a most majestick Manner, said, with some Disdain, She thought a *good Neck* might have done His Majesty as much Service as Smiles or Dimples. A third look'd upon the Association as defective, because so necessary a Word as *Hands* was omitted; and by her Manner of taking up the Pen, it was easy to guess the Reason of her Objection.

Most of the Persons who associated, have done much more than by the Letter of the Association they were obliged to; having not only set their Names to it, but subscrib'd their several Aids and Subsidies for the carrying on so good a Cause. In the Virgin Column is one who subscribes fifteen Lovers, all of them good Men and true. There is another who subscribes five Admirers, with one tall handsome black Man fit to be a Collonel. In short, there is scarce one in this List who does not engage herself to supply a Quota of brisk young Fellows, many of 'em already equipt with Hats and Feathers. Among the rest, was a pretty sprightly Coquette, with sparkling Eyes, who subscrib'd two Quivers of Arrows.

In the Column of Wives, the first who took Pen in Hand writ her[a] own Name and one Vassal, meaning her Husband. Another subscribes her Husband and three Sons. Another her Husband and six Coach-Horses. Most in this Catalogue paired themselves with their respective Mates, answering for them as Men of honest Principles, and fit for the Service.

N. B. There were two in this Column that wore Association-Ribbons:[3] The first of 'em subscrib'd her Husband, and her Husband's Friend; the second a Husband and five Lovers; but upon Enquiry into their Characters, they are both of 'em found to be *Tories*, who hung out false Colours to be Spies upon the Association, or to insinuate to the World by their

[a] writ her / writ down her *Fol.*

[3] Party badges were not uncommon among women. In 1711 Lady Mary Wortley Montagu wrote that women of the 'low Party (of which I declare my selfe) wear . . . long ribands to their Muffs' (*Complete Letters* i. 70–1).

Subscriptions, as if a Lady of *Whig* Principles could love any Man besides her Husband.

The Widows Column is headed by a fine Woman who calls herself *Boadicea*, and subscribes six hundred Tenants. It was indeed observed that the Strength of the Assocation lay most in this Column, every Widow, in proportion to her Jointure, having a great Number of Admirers, and most of them distinguished as able Men. Those who have examined this List, compute that there may be three Regiments rais'd out of it, in which there shall not be one Man under six Foot high.

I must not conclude this Account, without taking Notice of the *Association-Ribbon*, by which these beautiful Confederates have agreed to distinguish themselves. It is indeed so very pretty an Ornament, that I wonder any *English* Woman will be without it. *A Lady of the Association*, who bears[b] this Badge of Allegiance upon her Breast, naturally produces a Desire in every Male-Beholder, of gaining a Place in a Heart which carries on it such a visible Mark of its Fidelity. When the Beauties of our Island are thus industrious to shew their Principles, as well as their Charms, they raise the Sentiments of their Country-men, and inspire 'em at the same Time both with Loyalty and Love. What Numbers of Proselytes may we not expect, when the most amiable of the *Britons* thus exhibit to their Admirers the only Terms upon which they are to hope for any Correspondence or Alliance with them. It is well known that the greatest Blow the *French* Nation ever receiv'd, was the dropping of a fine Lady's Garter, in the Reign of King *Edward* the Third.[4] The most remarkable Battles which have been since gained over that Nation, were fought under the Auspices of a blue Ribbon. As our *British* Ladies have still the same Faces, and our Men the same Hearts, why may we not hope for the same glorious Atchievements from the Influence of this beautiful Breast-Knot.

U

[b] bears / carries *Fol.*

[4] Joshua Barnes, in his *History of King Edward III* (1688), tells the following anecdote about the Order of the Garter and its motto: following Queen Philippa to her chamber, Edward 'happen'd to espy a Blew-Garter on the ground, which his Attendants slightly passing by, the King, who knew the Owner, commanded it to be taken up and given to him; at the Receipt whereof he said, "You make but small account of this Garter, but within a little while the very best of You shall be glad to Reverence the like"; And . . . the Motto of the Garter, *Honi Soit, qui mal y pense*, was the Queen's Answer, when the King asked what she thought, Men would conjecture of her, upon dropping her Garter in such a Manner' (p. 293).

Numb. XII *Monday, January* 30, 1716

Quapropter, de summa salute vestra, P.C. de vestris conjugibus ac liberis, de aris ac focis, de fanis ac templis, de totius urbis tectis ac sedibus, de imperio, de libertate, de salute Patriæ, deque universa Republica decernite diligenter, ut instituistis, ac fortiter. Cic.

THIS Day having been set apart by Publick Authority, to raise in us an Abhorrence of the *Great Rebellion*, which involv'd this Nation in so many Calamities, and ended in the Murder of their Soveraign; it may not be unseasonable to shew the Guilt of Rebellion in general, and of that Rebellion in particular which is stirr'd up against His present Majesty.[2]

That Rebellion is one of the most hainous Crimes which it is in the Power of Man to commit, may appear from several Considerations. *First*, As it destroys the End of all Government, and the Benefits of Civil Society. Government was instituted for maintaining the Peace, Safety, and Happiness of a People. These great Ends are brought about by a general Conformity and Submission to that Frame of Laws which is establish'd in every Community, for the Protection of the Innocent, and the Punishment of the Guilty. As on the one Side Men are secur'd the [a] quiet Possession of their Lives, Properties, and every Thing they have a Right to: So on the other Side, those who offer them an Injury in these Particulars, are subject to Penalties proportion'd to their respective Offences. Government

[a] secur'd the / secur'd in the *Fol.*

Motto. Cicero, *Oratio in Catilinam*, iv. 24: Therefore, Senators, decree as you have begun, assiduously and bravely, concerning your greatest safety, concerning your wives and children, your altars and hearths, holy places and shrines, the roofs and homes of the whole city, concerning political authority, concerning freedom, concerning the welfare of the country and the entire commonwealth.

[2] 30 January, the anniversary of Charles I's execution, was traditionally a day when High Church clergymen extolled Anglicanism and monarchy while attacking dissenters and revolution. Luke Milbourne, for example, angered Whigs and moderate Tories with his sermon on 30 Jan. 1708 at St. Ethelburga's in which he called Milton and Locke 'Agents of Darkness' because they taught 'Principles fit for nothing, but to *Ruin Kingdoms* and *Commonwealths*, to *overturn Churches*, to *Extirpate Christianity*' (p. 16). In 1716 Whig clergymen were able to return the fire since the Jacobites were then attempting to overthrow the monarch (Ryder, *Diary*, 30 Jan.). In this essay Addison uses a considerable amount of traditional Tory rhetoric to attack the rebels: here and in *F.* 52, for example, he refers to the civil war as 'the *Grand Rebellion*'. Swift claimed that by 1689 anyone who 'durst call it *Rebellion*' was considered a Jacobite (*Prose Works* iii. 128).

therefore mitigates the Inequality of Power among particular Persons, and makes an innocent Man, tho' of the lowest Rank, a Match for the Mightiest of his Fellow-Subjects; since he has the Force of the whole Community on his Side, which is able to controul the Insolence or Injustice of any private Oppressor. Now Rebellion disappoints all these Ends and Benefits of Government, by raising a Power in opposition to that Authority which has been establish'd among a People for their mutual Welfare and Defence. So that Rebellion is as great an Evil to Society, as Government itself is a Blessing.[3]

In the next Place, Rebellion is a Violation of all those Engagements, which every Government exacts from such Persons as live under it; and consequently, the most base and pernicious Instance of Treachery and Perfidiousness. The Guilt of Rebellion increases in Proportion as these Engagements are more Solemn and Obligatory. Thus if a Man makes his Way to Rebellion thro' Perjury, he gives additional Horrours to that Crime, which is in itself of the blackest Nature.

We may likewise consider Rebellion as a greater Complication of Wickedness than any other Crime we can commit. It is big with Rapine, Sacrilege, and Murder. It is dreadful in its mildest Effects, as it impoverishes the Publick; ruines particular Families; begets and perpetuates Hatreds among Fellow-Subjects, Friends and Relations; makes a Country the Seat of War and Desolation, and exposes it to the Attempts of its foreign Enemies. In short, as it is impossible for it to take effect, or to make the smallest Progress, but thro' a continued Course of Violence and Bloodshed; a Robber or a Murderer looks like an innocent Man, when we compare him with a Rebel.[4]

I shall only add, that as in the Subordinations of a Government the King is offended by any Insults or Oppositions to an inferior Magistrate; so the Soveraign Ruler of the Universe is affronted by a Breach of Allegiance to those whom He has set over us: Providence having delegated to the supreme Magistrate in every Country the same Power for the Good of Men, which that Supreme Magistrate transfers to those several Officers and Substitutes who act under Him, for the preserving of Order and Justice.[5]

[3] The Sources for Addison's conception of government and the individual are discussed at length by Edward and Lillian Bloom, *Sociable Animal*, pp. 113–48.

[4] Because Tory arguments relied heavily upon the political theology of the Reformation, Addison attacks the Jacobites here with the same rhetoric which Elizabethans used against rebellion; see, e.g., *An Homilie against Disobedience and Wylfull Rebellion* (1573), pp. 39–40.

[5] The argument that God was offended by breaches of allegiance to magistrates was also commonplace in Tudor political tracts. See, e.g., Hooker's *Ecclesiastical Polity*, VIII. iv. 6;

Now if we take a View of the present Rebellion which is formed against His Majesty, we shall find in it all the Guilt that is naturally inherent in this Crime, without any single Circumstance to alleviate it. Insurrections among a People to rescue themselves from the most violent and illegal Oppressions; to throw off a Tyranny that makes Property precarious, and Life painful; to preserve their Laws and their Religion to themselves and their Posterity; are excused from the Necessity of such an Undertaking, when no other Means are left for the Security of every thing that is dear and valuable to reasonable Creatures. By the Frame of our Constitution, the Duties of Protection and Allegiance are reciprocal; and as the Safety of a Community is the ultimate End and Design of Government, when this, instead of being preserved, is manifestly destroy'd, Civil Societies are excusable before God and Man, if they endeavour to recover themselves out of so miserable a Condition. For in such a Case Government becomes an Evil instead of a Blessing, and is not at all preferable to a State of Anarchy and mutual Independence. For these Reasons, we have scarce ever yet heard of an Insurrection that was not either colour'd with Grievances of the highest Kind, or countenanc'd by one or more Branches of the Legislature. But the present Rebellion is form'd against a King, whose Right has been establish'd by frequent Parliaments of all Parties, and recogniz'd by the most solemn Oaths; who has not been charged with one illegal Proceeding; who acts in perfect Concert with the Lords and Commons of the Realm; who is famed for his Equity and Goodness, and has already very much advanc'd the Reputation and Interest of our Country. The Guilt therefore of this Rebellion has in it all the most aggravating Circumstances; which will still appear more plainly, if we consider in the first Place the real Motives to it.[6]

William Tyndal, *Doctrinal Treatises*, ed. H. Walter, (Cambridge, 1848), xlii. 179; Locke's quotation of William Barclay, *Two Treatises*, p. 441. Addison's Whig contemporaries like Benjamin Hoadly argued that allegiance to civil authority was different from paternal or religious authority because civil governors derived their authority from a voluntary contract; see *Some Considerations humbly offered to the Lord Bishop of Exeter* (1708) in Hoadly's *Works* (1773), ii. 126. By referring to God's providence Addison is raising a popular conservative argument used in the reign of William III. After 1688 some writers like William Sherlock replaced their belief in divine hereditary right of monarchy with a providential right; they argued that God's providence justified the rights of monarchs who gained their thrones by hereditary claim, by election or by conquest; see Sherlock's *Case of Allegiance Due to Soveraign Powers* (1691), pp. 11–17.

[6] By arguing that the Jacobites have no alleviating circumstances for rebelling, Addison is assuming, as Locke had argued, that there are circumstances in which rebellion is justified (*Two Treatises*, pp. 443–4). His emphasis on Parliament as the guardian of the contract between monarch and subject is introduced to distinguish the Jacobite rebellion from the Revolution of 1688.

The Rebellion, which was one of the most flagitious in itself, and describ'd with the most horrour by Historians, is that of *Catiline* and his Associates. Their Motives to it are display'd at large by the *Roman* Writers, in order to inspire the Reader with the utmost Detestation of it. *Catiline* the Chief of the Rebellion, had been disappointed in his Competition for one of the first Offices in the Government, and had involv'd himself in such private Debts and Difficulties, as nothing could extricate him out of, but the Ruin of an Administration that would not entrust him with Posts of Honour or Profit. His principal Accomplices were Men of the same Character, and animated by the same Incentives. They complained that Power was lodged in the Hands of the Worst, to the Oppression of the Best; and that Places were confer'd on unworthy Men, to the Exclusion of themselves and their Friends. Many of 'em were afraid of publick Justice for past Crimes, and some of them stood actually condemn'd as Traitors to their Country. These were joined by Men of desperate Fortunes, who hoped to find their Account in the Confusions of their Country, were applauded by the meanest of the Rabble who always delighted in Change, and privately abetted by Persons of a considerable Figure, who aim'd at those Honours and Preferments which were in the Possession of their Rivals. These are the Motives with which *Catiline*'s Rebellion is branded in History, and which are expressly mentioned by *Sallust.* I shall leave it to every unprejudiced Reader to compare them with the Motives which have kindled the present Rebellion in His Majesty's Dominions.[7]

As this Rebellion is of the most criminal Nature from its Motives, so is it likewise if we consider its Consequences. Should it Succeed, (a Supposition which, God be thanked, is very extravagant) what must be the natural Effects of it upon our Religion! What could we expect from an Army, blest by the Pope, headed by a zealous *Roman-Catholick*, encourag'd by the most bigotted Princes of the Church of *Rome*, supported by Contributions not only from these several Potentates, but from the Wealthiest of their Convents, and Officer'd by *Irish* Papists and Outlaws! Can we imagine that the *Roman-Catholicks* of our own Nation would so heartily embark in an Enterprize, to the visible Hazard of their Lives and Fortunes, did they only hope to enjoy their Religion under those Laws which are now in Force? In short, the Danger to the Protestant Cause is

[7] Sallust, *De Catilina Coniuratione*, 14, 16, 18, 26, 33, 36. Addison has abridged Sallust's description of Catiline's conspiracy to emphasize its similarities with the Jacobite rebellion. In January 1716 Jacob Tonson published Cicero's *Fourth Speech on the Catilinarian Conspiracy* which included a ten-page preface comparing the two rebellions.

so manifest, that it would be an Affront to the Understanding of the Reader to endeavour further[b] to prove it.[8]

Arbitrary Power is so interwoven with Popery, and so necessary to introduce it, so agreeable to the Education of the Pretender, so conformable to the Principles of his Adherents, and so natural to the Insolence of Conquerors, that should our Invader gain the Soveraign Power by Violence, there is no doubt but he would preserve it by Tyranny. I shall leave to the Reader's own Consideration, the Change of Property in General, and the utter Extinction of it in our National Funds, the Inundation of Nobles without Estates, Prelates without Bishopricks, Officers Civil and Military without Places; and in short, the several Occasions of Rapine and Revenge, which would necessarily ensue upon such a fatal Revolution.[9] But by the Blessing of Providence, and the Wisdom of His Majesty's Administration, this melancholly Prospect is as distant as it is dreadful.

These are the Consequences which would necessarily attend the Success of the present Rebellion. But we will now suppose that the Event of it should for some Time remain Doubtful. In this Case we are to expect all the Miseries of a Civil War: Nay, the Armies of the greatest Foreign Princes would be subsisted, and all the Battels of *Europe* fought in *England.* The Rebels have already shewn us, that they want no Inclination to promote their Cause by Fire and Sword, where they have an Opportunity of practising their Barbarities. Should such a fierce and rapacious Host of Men as that which is now in the *Highlands*, fall down into our Country that is so well Peopled, adorned, and cultivated, how would their March be distinguished by Ravage and Devastation! Might not we say of them in the sublime and beautiful Words of the Prophet, describing the Progress of an enrag'd Army from the North; *Before them is as the Garden of* Eden, *and behind them as the desolate Wilderness; yea, and nothing shall escape them.*[10]

What then can we think of a Party, who would plunge their native Country into such Evils as these; when the only avow'd Motive for their Proceedings is a Point of Theory, that has been already determined by those who are the proper Judges, and in whose Determination we have so many Years acquiesced. If the Calamities of the Nation in General can make no Impression on them; let them at least, in Pity to themselves, their

[b] further/*Fol.*; farther *8vo, 12mo.*

---

[8] For the involvement of Catholics in the rebellion, see Introduction, pp. 15–16.

[9] The evils of politics and economics in Catholic countries was a persistent theme in Addison's work (see *F.* 18, 30) and, for his readers, the extinction of the national debt ('our National Funds') was a fear associated with a Stuart restoration (see *F.* 7, n. 17).

[10] Joel 2:3.

Friends and Dependants, forbear all open and secret Methods of Encouraging a Rebellion, so destructive, and so unprovok'd. All human Probabilities are against them; and they cannot expect Success but from a miraculous Interposition of the Almighty. And this we may with all Christian Humility hope, will not turn against us, who observe those Oaths which we have made in His Presence; who are Zealous for the Safety of that Religion which we think most acceptable in His Sight; and who endeavour to preserve that Constitution which is most conducive to the Happiness of our Country.

Numb. XIII *Friday, February 3, 1716*

Ignavum, fucos, pecus a præsepibus arcent.
Virg.

THE most common, and indeed the most natural Division of all Offences, is into those of Omission, and those of Commission. We may make the same Division of that particular Set of Crimes which regard Human Society. The greatest Crime which can be committed against it is Rebellion; as was shewn in my last Paper. The greatest Crime of Omission, is an Indifference in the particular Members of a Society, when a Rebellion is actually begun among them. In such a Juncture, tho' a Man may be innocent of the great Breach which is made upon Government, he is highly culpable, if he does not use all the Means that are suitable to his Station for reducing the Community into its former State of Peace and good Order.[2]

Our Obligation to be active on such an Occasion appears from the very Nature of Civil Government; which is an Institution, whereby we are all confederated together for our mutual Defence and Security. Men who profess a State of Neutrality in Times of Publick Danger, desert the Common Interest of their Fellow-Subjects; and act with Independence to

Motto. Virgil, *Georgics*, iv. 168: They prevent the drones, a sluggish horde, from approaching the hives.

[2] Although Addison mentions no names in this essay, it was widely known that many disaffected Tories had absented themselves from Parliament. Percival wrote that 'S[r] Thomas Hanmer, Bromly, Ward and the chief of the torys come now seldom to the House of Commons, as if they would have no hand in supporting the King, since their Party is not strong enough to carry their own designs. It is a most scandalous lukewarmness for which I cannot excuse them, and I fear God will neither, for in my opinion the oaths oblige us to be actively obedient in such times as these, or else we dont support, maintain and defend the King' (Letterbook, 28 Jan. 1716).

that Constitution into which they are incorporated. The Safety of the Whole requires our joint Endeavours. When this is at Stake, the Indifferent are not properly a Part of the Community; or rather are like dead Limbs, which are an Incumbrance to the Body, instead of being of Use to it. Besides that, the Protection which all receive from the same Government justly calls upon the Gratitude of All to Strengthen it, as well as upon their Self-Interest to Preserve it.[3]

But further;[a] If Men, who in their Hearts are Friends to a Government, forbear giving it their utmost Assistance against its Enemies, they put it in the Power of a few desperate Men to ruine the Welfare of those who are much superiour to them in Strength, Number, and Interest. It was a remarkable Law of *Solon*, the great Legislator of the *Athenians*, that any Person who in the Civil Tumults and Commotions of the Republick remain'd Neuter, or an indifferent Spectator of the contending Parties, should, after the Re-establishment of the publick Peace, forfeit all his Possessions, and be condemn'd to perpetual Banishment.[4] This Law made it necessary for every Citizen to take his Party, because it was highly probable the Majority would be so Wise as to espouse that Cause which was most agreeable to the publick Weal, and by that Means hinder a Sedition from making a successful Progress. At least, as every prudent and honest Man, who might otherwise favour any Indolence in his own Temper, was hereby engag'd to be active, such a one would be sure to join himself to that Side which had the Good of their Country most at Heart. For this Reason their famous Lawgiver condemn'd the Persons who sate Idle in Divisions so dangerous to the Government, as Aliens to the Community, and therefore to be cut off from it as unprofitable Members.

Further; Indifference cannot but be criminal, when it is conversant about Objects which are so far from being of an indifferent Nature, that they are of the highest Importance to ourselves and our Country. If it be indifferent to us whether we are Free Subjects or Slaves; whether our Prince be of our own Religion, or of one that obliges him to extirpate it; we are in the right to give ourselves no trouble in the present Juncture. A Man governs himself by the Dictates of Vertue and good Sense, who acts

[a] further / *Fol.*; farther *8vo, 12mo.*

---

[3] Addison is expanding upon one theme in the Archbishop's *Declaration*: 'All those must have a Share in the Guilt of the Innocent blood that shall be spilt, not only who actually joyn in the Rebellion, but who do any way promote it; or even by their Silence at this Juncture, shall give Hopes to the Pretender and his Friends, and just cause of Jealousie and Suspicion to the Government ... Is this a Time to stand Neuter when all lies at Stake?' (p. 4).

[4] Plutarch, *Lives*, 1716 edn., i. 224.

without Zeal or Passion in Points that are of no Consequence: But when the whole Community is shaken, and the Safety of the Publick endanger'd, the Appearance of a Philosophical or an affected Indolence must arise either from Stupidity, or Perfidiousness.

When in the Division of Parties among us, Men only strove for the first Place in the Prince's Favour; when all were attached to the same Form of Government, and contended only for the highest Offices in it; a prudent and an honest Man might look upon the Struggle with Indifference, and be in no great Pain for the Success of either Side. But at present the Contest is not in Reality between *Whigs* and *Tories*, but between *Loyalists* and *Rebels*. Our Country is not now divided into two Parties, who propose the same End by different Means; but into such as would preserve, and such as would destroy it. Whatever Denominations we might range our selves under in former Times, Men who have any natural Love to their Country, or Sense of their Duty, should exert their united Strength in a Cause that is common to all Parties, as they are Protestants and *Britons*. In such a Case, an avow'd Indifference is Treachery to our Fellow-Subjects; and a Luke-warm Allegiance may prove as pernicious in its Consequences as Treason.

I need not repeat here what I have proved at large in a former Paper, that we are oblig'd to an active Obedience by the solemn Oaths we have taken to His Majesty;[5] and that the neutral Kind of Indifference, which is the Subject of this Paper, falls short of that Obligation they lie under, who have taken such Oaths; as will easily appear to any one who considers the Form of those sacred and religious Engagements.

How then can any Man answer it to himself, if, for the sake of managing his Interest or Character among a Party, or out of any personal Pique to those who are the most conspicuous for their Zeal in His Majesty's Service, or from any other private and self-interested Motive, he stands as a Looker on when the Government is attack'd by an open Rebellion; especially when those engaged in it, cannot have the least Prospect of Success, but by the Assistance of the ancient and hereditary Enemies to the *British* Nation. It is strange that these Luke-warm Friends to the Government, whose Zeal for their Soveraign rises and falls with their Credit at Court, do not consider, before it be too late, that as they strengthen the Rebels by their present Indifference, they at the same time establish the Interest of those who are their Rivals and Competitors for publick Posts of Honour. When there is an End put to this Rebellion, these Gentlemen cannot pretend to

[5] *F.* 6.

have had any Merit in so good a Work: And they may well believe the Nation will never care to see those Men in the highest Offices of Trust, who when they are out of them, will not stir a finger in its Defence.

D

Numb. XIV *Monday, February* 6, 1716

Periculosum est credere, et non credere:
Utriusque exemplum breviter exponam rei.
Hippolytus obiit, quia novercæ creditum est:
Cassandræ quia non creditum, ruit Ilium.
Ergo exploranda est veritas multum prius,
Quam stulta prave judicet sententia.

Phædr.

HAVING in the Seventh Paper consider'd many of those Falshoods, by which the Cause of our Malecontents is supported; I shall here speak of that extravagant Credulity, which disposes each particular Member of their Party to believe them. This strange Alacrity in Believing Absurdity and Inconsistence may be call'd the *Political Faith* of a Tory.[2]

A Person who is thoroughly endow'd with this Political Faith, like a Man in a Dream, is entertain'd from one end of his Life to the other with Objects that have no Reality or Existence. He is daily nourish'd and kept in Humour by Fiction and Delusion; and may be compared to the old obstinate Knight in *Rabelais*, that every Morning swallowed a Chimera for his Breakfast.[3]

This Political Faith of a Malecontent is altogether founded on Hope. He does not give Credit to any thing because it is probable, but because it is pleasing. His Wishes serve him instead of Reasons, to confirm the Truth

Motto. Phaedrus, *Fables*, III. x. 1–6: It is dangerous alike to believe or to disbelieve. Of either fact I will briefly give you an instance. Hippolytus met his death because his step-mother was believed; because Cassandra was not believed, Troy fell. Therefore we ought to examine strictly the truth of a matter rather than allow a false impression to distort our judgement.

[2] Paradox was a familiar rhetorical device in political writing of the period; see, e.g., 'Articles of a *Whig-Creed*' in the *Examiner* (2–5 Jan. 1713), 'High Church Miracles' and 'The Age of Riddles' (*Somers Tracts*, xii. 320, 653–4).

[3] *Gargantua and Pantagruel* (1708), Bk. IV, Chap. xvii. Addison has confused Don Quixote who mistook windmills with Rabelais's giant, le bon Bringuenarilles, who ate them. When the supply ran out, he ate every piece of kitchenware in the town of Tohu Bohu, then choked to death on a pat of soft butter prescribed for his indigestion. Swift also used Rabelais's giant as an example of gullibility in *Examiner* 19 (*Prose Works* iii. 38).

of what he hears.[4] There is no Report so incredible or contradictory in itself which he doth not chearfully believe, if it tends to the Advancement of the Cause. In short, a Malecontent who is a good Believer has generally reason to repeat the celebrated Rant of an Ancient Father, *Credo quia impossibile est*:[5] Which is as much as to say, *It must be True, because it is Impossible.*

It has been very well observed, that the most credulous Man in the World is the Atheist, who believes the Universe to be the Production of Chance.[6] In the same Manner a Tory, who is the greatest Believer in what is improbable, is the greatest Infidel in what is certain. Let a Friend to the Government relate to him a Matter of Fact, he turns away his Ear from him, and gives him the Lye in every Look. But if one of his own Stamp should tell him that the King of *Sweden* would be suddenly at *Perth*, and that his Army is now actually marching thither upon the Ice; he hugs himself at the good News, and gets Drunk upon it before he goes to Bed.[7] This sort of People puts one in Mind of several Towns in *Europe* that are inaccessible on the one Side, while they lie open and unguarded on the other. The Minds of our Malecontents are indeed so depraved with those Falshoods which they are perpetually imbibing, that they have a natural Relish for Error, and have quite lost the Taste of Truth in political Matters. I shall therefore dismiss this Head with a Saying of King *Charles* the Second. This Monarch, when he was at *Windsor*, us'd to amuse himself with the Conversation of the famour *Vossius*, who was full of Stories relating to the Antiquity, Learning, and Manners of the *Chinese*; and at the same time a Free-thinker in Points of Religion. The King upon hearing him repeat some incredible Accounts of these Eastern People, turning to those who were about him, *This Learned Divine*, said he, *is a very strange Man*: *He believes every thing but the Bible.*[8]

Having thus far considered the political Faith of the Party as it regards Matters of Fact, let us in the next Place take a View of it with respect to those Doctrines which it embraces, and which are the Fundamental Points whereby they are distinguished from those, whom they used to represent

[4] Bolingbroke claimed that letters from Jacobites to the Pretender's supporters in France 'seemed to me to contain rather such things as the writers wished might be true, than such as they knew to be so' (*Letter to Windham*, p. 125).

[5] Tertullian, *De Carne Christi*, 210.

[6] Addison is referring to his own essay on atheists, *S.* 185.

[7] Because Hanover was allied with Denmark and Prussia against Sweden, some Jacobites hoped that a Swedish army might assist them in the rebellion (H.M.C. *Stuart MSS.* i. 527).

[8] Isaac Vossius (1618–89), Canon of Windsor and a scholar who collected one of the finest libraries in seventeenth-century Europe. The remark Addison cites appears in Bayle's *Historical Dictionary*, article 'Vossius'.

as Enemies to the Constitution in Church and State. How far their great Articles of political Faith, with respect to our Ecclesiastical and Civil Government, are consistent with themselves, and agreeable to Reason and Truth, may be seen in the following Paradoxes, which are the Essentials of a *Tory*'s Creed, with relation to political Matters. Under the Name of *Tories*, I do not here comprehend Multitudes of well-designing Men, who were formerly included under that Denomination, but are now in the Interest of His Majesty and the present Government. These have already seen the evil Tendency of such Principles, which are the *Credenda* of the Party as it is opposite to that of the *Whigs*.

Article I.

That the Church of *England* will be always in Danger, till it has a Popish King for its Defender.

II.

That, for the Safety of the Church, no Subject should be Tolerated in any Religion different from the Establish'd; but that the Head of our Church may be of that Religion which is most repugnant to it.

III.

That the Protestant Interest in this Nation, and in all *Europe*, could not but flourish under the Protection of One, who thinks himself obliged, on Pain of Damnation, to do all that lies in his Power for the Extirpation of it.

IV.

That we may safely rely upon the Promises of One, whose Religion allows him to make them and at the same Time obliges him to break them.

V.

That a good Man should have a greater Abhorrence of Presbyterianism which is Perverseness, than of Popery which is but Idolatry.

VI.

That a Person who hopes to be King of *England* by the Assistance of *France*, would naturally adhere to the *British* Interest, which is always opposite to that of the *French*.

VII.

That a Man has no Opportunities of learning how to Govern the People of *England* in any foreign Country, so well as in *France.*

VIII.

That ten Millions of People should rather chuse to fall into Slavery, than not acknowledge their Prince to be invested with an Hereditary and Indefeasible Right of Oppression.[9]

IX.

That we are obliged in Conscience to become Subjects of a Duke of *Savoy*, or of a *French* King, rather than enjoy for our Soveraign a Prince who is the First of the Royal Blood in the Protestant Line.[10]

X.

That Non-Resistance is the Duty of every Christian whilst he is in a good Place.

XI.

That we ought to profess the Doctrine of Passive-Obedience till such Time as Nature rebels against Principle, that is, till we are put to the Necessity of practising it.

XII.

That the Papists have taken up Arms to defend the Church of *England* with the utmost Hazard of their Lives and Fortunes.

XIII.

That there is an unwarrantable Faction in this Island, consisting of King, Lords, and Commons.

[9] In 1696 Gregory King estimated that the population of England and Wales was 5·5 million and J. D. Chambers, a recent historian of demography, estimates that there were about 6 million people in 1715 (*Population, Economy and Society in Pre-industrial England*, 1972, p. 108). If Addison includes Scotland and Ireland in his estimate, he is not far off, since those two countries had populations of approximately 1 and 2 million, respectively.

[10] Victor Amadeus of Savoy and Sicily (1675–1732) was married to the granddaughter of Charles I, and Bolingbroke hoped to avoid the Hanoverian succession by having the Duke's second son named to succeed Queen Anne. See Gaultier to Torcy (December 1713), Quai d'Orsay, *Aff. Etr. Angl.* MS. 247, fo. 135 (reprinted in *English Historical Review*, xxx (1915), p. 506).

XIV.

That the Legislature, when there is a Majority of *Whigs* in it, has not Power to make Laws.[11]

XV.

That an Act of Parliament to impower the King to secure suspected Persons in Times of Rebellion, is the Means to establish the Soveraign on the Throne, and consequently a great Infringement of the Liberties of the Subject.[12]

Numb. XV *Friday, February* 10, 1716

— — Auxilium, quoniam sic cogitis ipsi,
Dixit ab hoste petam: vultus avertite vestros
Si quis amicus adest: et Gorgonis extulit ora.
Ovid.

It is with great Pleasure that I see a Race of Female-Patriots springing up in this Island. The fairest among the Daughters of *Great Britain* no longer confine their Cares to a Domestick Life, but are grown anxious for the Welfare of their Country, and show themselves good Stateswomen as well as good Housewives.

Our She-Confederates keep pace with us in quashing that Rebellion which had begun to spread itself among part of the fair Sex. If the Men who are true to their King and Country have taken *Preston* and *Perth*, the Ladies have possess'd themselves of the Opera and the Playhouse, with as little Opposition or Bloodshed. The Non-resisting Women, like their Brothers in the *Highlands*, think no Post tenable against an Army that makes so fine an Appearance; and dare not look them in the Face, when they are drawn up in Battle-array.

As an Instance of the Chearfulness in our fair Fellow-Subjects to oppose the Designs of the Pretender, I did but suggest in one of my former Papers,

[11] Swift argued in *Examiner* 25 that a Whig majority in Parliament meant that the nation was ruled by the Junto and the monarch (*Prose Works* iii. 72) and in 1716 the Whigs held 391 seats in the Commons while the Tories had only 167 (*History of Parliament* i. 23).

[12] Addison is referring to the protest made in the Lords by the Earl of Abingdon on 21 Jan. 1716 concerning the continued suspension of habeas corpus (*L.J.* xx. 269). Such resistance was interpreted by the Court as an attempt to block the measure (Percival Letterbook, 3 Jan.)

Motto. Ovid, *Metamorphoses*, v. 178–80: 'Since you yourselves force me in this way,' he said, 'I shall seek aid from my enemy. Turn away your faces, if any friend be here.' Then he raised the Gorgon's head.

That the Fan might be made use of with good Success against Popery, by exhibiting the Corruptions of the Church of Rome *in various Figures*;[2] when immediately they took the Hint, and have since had frequent Consultations upon several Ways and Methods *to make the Fan useful.* They have unanimously agreed upon the following Resolutions, which are indeed very suitable to Ladies who are at the same Time the most Beautiful and the most Loyal of their Sex. To hide their Faces behind the Fan, when they observe a *Tory* gazing upon 'em. Never to peep through it, but in order to pick out Men, whose Principles make them worth the[a] Conquest. To return no other Answer to a *Tory*'s Addresses, than by counting the Sticks of it all the while he is talking to them. To avoid dropping it in the Neighbourhood of a Malecontent, that he may not have an Opportunity of taking it up. To shew their Disbelief of any *Jacobite* Story by a Flirt of it. To fall a Fanning themselves when a *Tory* comes into one of their Assemblies, as being disorder'd at the Sight of him.

These are the Uses by which every Fan may in the Hands of a fine Woman become serviceable to the Publick. But they have at present under Consideration, certain Fans of a Protestant Make, that they may[b] have a more extensive Influence, and raise an Abhorrence of Popery in a whole Crowd of Beholders: For they intend to let the World see what Party they are of, by Figures and Designs upon these Fans; as the Knights Errant used to distinguish themselves by Devices on their Shields.

There are several Sketches of Pictures which have been already presented to the Ladies for their Approbation, and out of which several have made their Choice.[3] A pretty young Lady will very soon appear with a Fan, which has on it a Nunnery of lively black-Eyed Vestals, who are endeavouring to creep out at the Grates. Another has a Fan mounted with a fine Paper, on which is represented a Groupe of People upon their Knees very devoutly worshipping an old Ten-penny Nail. A certain Lady of great Learning has chosen for her Device the Council of *Trent*; and another, who has a good Satyrical Turn, has filled her Fan with the Figure of a huge tawdry Woman, representing the Whore of *Babylon*; which she is resolved to spread full in the Face of any Sister-Disputant, whose Arguments have a Tendency to Popery. The following Designs are already executed on

[a] the/their *Fol.* [b] that they may/that may *Fol.*

[2] *F.* 8.

[3] In 1710, after Sacheverell had been sentenced and before the elections were held, some Tory supporters manufactured 'Emblematical *Fans*, with the true Effigies of the Reverend Dr *Henry Sacheverell* done to the Life, and several curious Hieroglyphicks in Honour of the Church of England' (*Supplement*, 18–21 Aug. 1710). Addison satirized the proliferation of such articles as Sacheverell handkerchiefs and snuff-boxes in *S.* 57.

several Mountings. The Ceremony of the Holy Pontiff opening the Mouth of a Cardinal in a full Consistory. An old Gentleman with a Triple Crown upon his Head, and big with Child, being the Portrait of Pope *Joan.*[4] Bishop *Bonner* purchasing great Quantities of Fagots and Brush-Wood, for the Conversion of Hereticks.[5] A Figure reaching at a Sceptre with one Hand, and holding a Chaplet of Beads in the other: With a distant View of *Smithfield.*[6]

When our Ladies make their Zeal thus visible upon their Fans, and, every time they open them, display an Errour of the Church of *Rome*, it cannot but have a good Effect, by shewing the Enemies of our present Establishment the Folly of what they are contending for. At least, every one must allow that Fans are much more innocent Engines for propagating the Protestant Religion, than Racks, Wheels, Gibbets, and the like Machines, which are made use of for the Advancement of the Roman-Catholick. Besides, as every Lady will of Course study her Fan, she will be a perfect Mistress of the Controversy at least in one Point of Popery; and as her Curiosity will put her upon the Perusal of every other Fan that is fashionable, I doubt not but in a very little Time there will scarce be a Woman of Quality in *Great Britain*, who wou'd not be an Over-match for an *Irish* Priest.

The beautiful Part of this Island, whom I am proud to number amongst the most candid of my Readers, will likewise do well to reflect, that our Dispute at present concerns our Civil as well as Religious Rights. I shall therefore only offer it to their Thoughts as a Point that highly deserves their Consideration, Whether the Fan may not also be made use of with regard to our Political Constitution. As a Free-holder, I would not have them confine their Cares for us as we are Protestants, but at the same time have an Eye to our Happiness as we are *Britons.* In this Case they wou'd give a new Turn to the Minds of their Countrymen, if they wou'd exhibit on their Fans the several Grievances of a Tyrannical Government. Why might not an Audience of *Muley Ishmael*,[7] or a *Turk* dropping his Handkerchief in his Seraglio, be proper Subjects to express their Abhorrence both of despotick Power, and of male Tyranny? Or if they

[4] A British woman supposedly became Pope John VIII in 853. By the eighteenth century, however, few historians believed that there had ever been a woman pope ('Pope John VIII', Louis Moreri's *Great Dictionary*, 1701).

[5] Edmund Bonner (1500–69), Bishop of London, led a purge of English Protestant clergymen in 1555. As many as seven clergymen were executed at one time in Smithfield Square (John Foxe, *Acts and Monuments*, ed. Pratt, vi, vii, *passim*).

[6] Probably the Pretender, since the figure is reaching at, rather than holding, the sceptre.

[7] See *F.* 10.

have a Fancy for Burlesque, what wou'd they think of a *French* Cobler cutting Shoes for several of his Fellow-Subjects out of an old Apple-Tree?[8] On the contrary, a fine Woman, who wou'd maintain the Dignity of her Sex, might bear a String of Gally-Slaves, dragging their Chains the whole Breadth of her Fan; and at the same Time, to celebrate her own Triumphs, might order every Slave to be drawn with the Face of one of her Admirers.

I only propose these as Hints to my gentle Readers, which they may alter or improve as they shall think fit: But cannot conclude without congratulating our Country upon this Disposition among the most amiable of its Inhabitants, to consider in their Ornaments the Advantage of the Publick as well as of their Persons. It was with the same Spirit, tho' not with the same Politeness, that the ancient *British* Women had the Figures of Monsters painted on their naked Bodies, in order (as our Historians tell us) to make themselves Beautiful in the Eyes of their Countrymen, and Terrible to their Enemies.[9] If this Project goes on, we may boast, that our Sister *Whigs* have the finest Fans, as well as the most Beautiful Faces, of any Ladies in the World. At least, we may venture to foretel, that the Figures in their Fans will lessen the *Tory* Interest, much more than those in the *Oxford* Almanacks will advance it.[10]

Numb. XVI *Monday, February* 13, 1716

Itaque quod plerumque in atroci negotio solet, Senatus decrevit, Darent operam consules ne quid Respublica Detrimenti caperet. Ea potestas per Senatum more Romano

[8] Wooden shoes were a symbol of the poverty and tyranny French peasants suffered and in 1715 the Earl of Clare used them as an emblem to encourage voters to elect Whigs in Yorkshire (Addison, *Miscellaneous Works* i. 427; B.L. Add. MS. 17677 iii, fo. 81). Addison is also alluding here to *The Cobler of Preston*, a topical afterpiece by Charles Johnson which mocked the rebels' defeat at Preston. During February 1716 it was produced ten times at the Drury Lane Theatre, twice with Addison's *Cato* and once with Steele's *Distrest Mother* (*London Stage*, Pt. 2, vol. i, pp. 388–91; Loftis, *Politics of Drama*, pp. 69–70).

[9] Camden claims that both Picts and Britons decorated their bodies with paints and stains (*Britannia*, 1695, p. cx) and Polydore Vergil wrote that Britons 'peincte theyr boddies in sondrie wise, in all poincts representinge the shape of beasts' (*History of England*, ed. H. Ellis, 1846, p. 87).

[10] The University Almanack for 1716 depicts a young boy held by a woman and flanked by men on each side (see Frontispiece). Various newspapers claimed that it symbolized the University's support for the Pretender and one verse explanation of the Almanack published in January 1716 is reprinted in an Appendix to this edition.

Numb. XVI *Monday, February* 13, 1716

Magistratui maxuma permittitur, exercitum parare, bellum gerere, coercere omnibus modis socios atque cives, domi militiæque imperium atque judicium summum habere. Aliter, sine populi jussu nulli earum rerum Consuli jus est.

Sall.

IT being the Design of these Papers to reconcile Men to their own Happiness, by removing those wrong Notions and Prejudices which hinder them from seeing the Advantage of themselves and their Posterity in the present Establishment, I cannot but take Notice of every thing that by the Artifice of our Enemies is made a Matter of Complaint.

Of this Nature is the Suspension of the *Habeas Corpus* Act, by which His Majesty has been enabled in these Times of Danger, to seize and detain the Persons of such who he had reason to believe were conspiring against His Person and Government.[2] The Expediency and Reasonableness of such a temporary Suspension in the present Juncture may appear to every considerate Man, who will turn his Thoughts impartially on this Subject.

I have chosen in Points of this Nature to draw my Arguments from the first Principles of Government, which, as they are of no Party, but assented to by every reasonable Man, carry the greater Weight with them, and are accommodated to the Notions of all my Readers.[3] Every one knows, who has consider'd the Nature of Government, that there must be in each particular Form of it an absolute and unlimited Power; and that this Power is lodg'd in the Hands of those who have the making of its Laws, whether by the Nature of the Constitution it be in one or more Persons, in a single Order of Men, or in a mixt Body of different Ranks and Degrees. It is an Absurdity to imagine that those, who have the Authority of making

Motto. Sallust, *De Catilinae Coniuratione*, 29: translated in the essay.

[2] In July 1715 the Habeas Corpus Act (1679) was suspended for six months and in January 1716 a bill was introduced to continue the suspension for another six months. In spite of a protest in the Lords, it was passed. The protest, presented by the Earl of Abingdon, argued that provision should be made to punish false informers, that the government should assign a reason for each arrest, and that Members of Parliament should be exempt from the King's power to arrest and detain suspects (*L.J.* xx. 269). Sir John Percival wrote that this opposition was 'the last weak Effort the Tories made in the house of Lords . . . they would have clog'd the Act and renderd it innefectuall, but on a division they were but 16 against above 60' (Letterbook, 3 Jan. 1716).

[3] Addison is retreating from party arguments because he is advocating the suspension of a law which the Whigs supported and which, according to Burnet, they passed by duping the opposition (*History* ii. 256–7). The right of habeas corpus existed in common law before 1679; the Act made habeas-corpus procedures statutory, thus increasing the subject's protection against arbitrary imprisonment. In the context of party ideologies, Addison is supporting expanded royal prerogative and limited civil liberties, policies the Whigs traditionally opposed.

Laws, cannot suspend any particular Law, when they think it expedient for the Publick. Without such a Power all Government would be defective, and not arm'd with a sufficient Force for its own Security. As Self-preservation by all honest Methods is the first Duty of every Community, as well as of every private Person, so the publick Safety is the general View of all Laws. When therefore any Law does not conduce to this great End, but on the contrary in some extraordinary and unnatural Junctures, the very Observation of it would endanger the Community, that Law ought to be laid asleep for such a Time, by the proper Authority. Thus the very Intention of our *Habeas Corpus* Act, namely, the Preservation of the Liberties of the Subject, absolutely requires that Act to be now suspended, since the Confinement of dangerous and suspected Persons, who might strengthen this Rebellion, and spread a Civil War through all Parts of this Kingdom, secures to us our Civil Rights, and every thing that can be valuable to a Free People.[4]

As every Government must in its Nature be arm'd with such an Authority, we may observe that those Governments which have been the most famous for Publick Spirit, and the most jealous of their Liberty, have never failed to exert it upon proper Occasions. There cannot be a greater Instance of this than in the old Commonwealth of *Rome*, who flatter'd themselves with an Opinion that their Government had in it a due Temper of the Regal, Noble, and Popular Power, represented by the Consuls, the Senators, and the Tribunes. The Regal Part was however in several Points notoriously defective, and particularly because[a] the Consuls had not a Negative in the passing of a Law, as the other two Branches had. Nevertheless in this Government, when the Republick was threaten'd with any great and imminent Danger, they thought it for the common Safety to appoint a temporary Dictator, invested with the whole Power of the three Branches; who, when the Danger was over, retired again into the Community, and left the Government in its natural Situation. But what is more to our Case, the Consular Power itself, tho' infinitely short of the Regal Power in *Great Britain*, was intrusted with the whole Authority which the Legislature has put into the Hands of His Majesty. We have an eminent Instance of this in the Motto of my Paper, which I shall Translate for the Benefit of the *English* Reader, after having advertised him, that the

[a] Points notoriously defective, and particularly because/*Errata, 8vo, 12mo*; Points and Particulars notoriously defective, because *Fol.*

[4] The Jacobite plans to invade the West of England in October 1715 were thwarted by arrests made possible by the suspension of habeas corpus (H.M.C. *Stuart MSS.* i. 444, 452, 535).

Power there given to the Consul, was in the Time of a Conspiracy. *The Senate therefore made a Decree, as usual when they have Matters before them of so horrid a Nature, That the Consuls should take Care the Common-Wealth did not suffer any Prejudice. By Virtue of this very great Power which the Senate allows to the Magistrate, according to the ancient customs of* Rome, *he may raise an Army, wage War, make use of all kinds of Methods to restrain the Associates and Citizens of* Rome, *and exercise the Supreme Authority both at Home and Abroad in Matters Civil and Military; whereas otherwise the Consul is not invested with any one of these Powers without the express Command of the People.*

There now only remains to shew, that His Majesty is legally possest of this Power; and that Necessity of the present Affairs requires he should be so. He is entrusted with it by the Legislature of the Nation; and in the very Notion of a Legislature is implied a Power to change, repeal, and suspend what Laws are in Being, as well as to make what new Laws they shall think fit for the Good of the People. This is so uncontroverted a Maxim, that I believe never any Body attempted to refute it.[5] Our Legislature have however had that just Regard for their Fellow-Subjects, as not to entertain a Thought of abrogating this Law, but only to hinder it from operating at a Time when it wou'd endanger the Constitution. The King is empower'd to act but for a few Months by Virtue of this Suspension; and by that Means differs from a King of *France*, or any other tyrannical Prince, who in Times of Peace and Tranquility, and upon what Occasion he pleases, sends any of his Subjects out of the Knowledge of their Friends into such Castles, Dungeons, or Imprisonments as he thinks fit. Nor did the Legislature do any thing in this that was unprecedented. The *Habeas Corpus* Act was made but about five and thirty Years ago, and since that time has[b] been suspended four Times before His present Majesty's Accession to the Throne: Twice under the Reign of King *William* and Queen *Mary*; once under the Reign of King *William*; and once under the Reign of Queen *Anne*.[6]

The Necessity of this Law at this Time arose from the Prospect of an Invasion, which has since broke out into an actual Rebellion; and from Informations of secret and dangerous Practices among Men of considerable

[b] that time has / *Fol., 8vo, 12mo*; that has *Errata*.

---

[5] The point was less uncontroverted than Addison claims. The Articles of Union with Scotland (1707), for example, secured the Church of Scotland 'without any Alteration . . . in all succeeding Generations' (*C.J.* xv. 268).

[6] The Habeas Corpus Act was suspended twice in 1689, once in February 1696 and once in March 1708 (*C.J.* x. 38–40, 143; xi. 479; xv. 590). Addison cites these examples because historical precedents were important 'Principles of Government' for Tories.

Figure, who cou'd not have been prevented from doing Mischief to their Country but by such a Suspension of this Act of Parliament.

I cannot however but observe, that notwithstanding the Lawfulness and Necessity of such a Suspension, had not the Rebellion broke out after the passing of this Act of Parliament, I do not know how those who had been the most instrumental in procuring it cou'd have escaped that popular Odium, which their malicious and artful Enemies have now in vain endeavour'd to stir up against them. Had it been possible for the Vigilance and Endeavours of a Ministry to have hinder'd even the Attempt of an Invasion, their very Endeavours might have prov'd Prejudicial to them. Their prudent and resolute Precautions wou'd have turn'd to their Disadvantage, had they not been justify'd by those Events, which they did all that was in their Power to obviate. This naturally brings to Mind the Reflection of *Tully* in the like Circumstances, *That*, amidst the Divisions of *Rome, a Man was in an unhappy Condition who had a Share in the Administration, nay even in the Preservation of the Commonwealth.* O conditionem miseram non modo administrandæ, verum etiam conservandæ Reipublicæ![7]

Besides, every unprejudiced Man will consider how mildly and equitably this Power has been used.[8] The Persons confined have been treated with all possible Humanity, and abridged of nothing but the Liberty of hurting their Country, and very probably of ruining both themselves and their Families. And as to the Numbers of those who are under this short Restraint, it is very observable, that People do not seem so much surpriz'd at the Confinement of some, as at the Liberty of many others. But we may from hence conclude, what every *Englishman* must observe with great Pleasure, that His Majesty does not in this great Point regulate himself by any private Jealousies or Suspicions, but by those Evidences and Informations which he has received.

We have already found the good Consequences of this Suspension, in that it has hinderd the Rebellion from gathering the Strength it wou'd otherwise have gained; not to mention those Numbers it has kept from engaging in so desperate an Enterprise, with the many Lives it has preserved, and the Desolations it has prevented.

For these and many other Reasons the Representatives of *Great Britain* in Parliament cou'd never have answered it to the People they represent,

[7] Cicero, *Oratio in Catilinam*, ii. 17.

[8] No 'unprejudiced Man' commented on the action, but it is obvious from Jacobite papers that the suspension contributed significantly to the failure of the rebellion. Bolingbroke wrote in January 1716, 'Every creature who might stand up . . . is imprison'd, dispers'd or dispirited' (H.M.C. *Stuart MSS.* i. 494).

who have found such great Benefits from the Suspension of the *Habeas Corpus* Act, and without it must have felt such fatal Consequences, had they not in a Case of such great Necessity made use of this customary, legal, and reasonable Method for Securing His Majesty on the Throne, and their Country from Misery or Ruine.

F

Numb. XVII *Friday, February* 17, 1716

— *Hic Niger est: hunc tu, Romane, caveto.*
Hor.

WE are told, that in *Turkey*, when any Man is the Author of notorious Falshoods, it is usual to blacken the whole Front of his House: Nay we have sometimes heard, that an Ambassador, whose *Business it is* (if I may quote his Character in Sir *Henry Wootton*'s Words) *to Lye for the Good of his Country*,[2] has sometimes had this Mark set upon his House; when he has been detected in any Piece of feign'd Intelligence, that has prejudiced the Government, and misled the Minds of the People. One cou'd almost wish that the Habitations of such of our own Countrymen as deal in Forgeries detrimental to the Publick, were distinguished in the same Manner; that their Fellow-Subjects might be cautioned not to be too easy in giving Credit to them. Were such a Method put in Practice, this Metropolis wou'd be strangely Checquer'd; some entire Parishes wou'd be in Mourning, and several Streets darkned from one End to the other.

But I have given my Thoughts in two preceding Papers, both on the Inventors and the Believers of these publick Falshoods and Calumnies,[3] and shall here speak of that Contempt with which they are and ought to be received by those in high Stations, at whom they are levell'd. Any Person, indeed, who is zealous for promoting the Interest of his Country, must conquer all that Tenderness and Delicacy which may make him afraid of being spoken ill of; or his Endeavours will often produce no less Uneasiness to himself, than Benefit to the Publick. Among a People who indulge themselves in the utmost Freedoms of Thought and Speech, a Man must either be Insignificant, or able to bear an undeserved Reproach. A true Patriot may comfort himself under the Attacks of Falshood and Obloquy, from several Motives and Reflections.

Motto, Horace, *Satires*, I. iv. 85: This man is black-hearted; Roman, beware of him.
[2] Izaak Walton, 'Life of Sir Henry Wotton', *Reliquae Wottonianiae* (1651), p. 26.
[3] *F.* 7, 14.

In the first Place he shou'd consider, that the Chief of his Antagonists are generally acted by a Spirit of Envy; which wou'd not rise against him, if it were not provoked by his Desert. A Statesman, who is possest of real Merit, shou'd look upon his political Censurers with the same Neglect, that a good Writer regards his Criticks; who are generally a Race of Men that are not able to discover the Beauties of a Work they examine, and deny that Approbation to others, which they never met with themselves. Patriots therefore shou'd rather rejoyce in the Success of their honest Designs, than be mortify'd by those who misrepresent them.

They shou'd likewise consider, that not only Envy, but Vanity has a Share in the Detraction of their Adversaries. Such Aspersions therefore do them honour at the same Time that they are intended to lessen their Reputation. They shou'd reflect, That those who endeavour to stir up the Multitude[a] against them, do it to be thought considerable; and not a little applaud themselves in a Talent that can raise Clamours out of nothing, and throw a Ferment among the People, by Murmurs or Complaints, which they know in their own Hearts are altogether groundless. There is a pleasant Instance of this Nature recorded at length in the First Book of the Annals of *Tacitus*. When a great Part of the *Roman* Legions were in a Disposition to mutiny, an impudent Varlet, who was a private Centinel, being mounted upon the Shoulders of his Fellow-Soldiers, and resolved to try the Power of his Eloquence, address'd himself to the Army, in all the Postures of an Orator, after the following Manner: *You have given Liberty to these miserable Men*; said he, (pointing to some Criminals whom they had rescued) *but which of you can restore Life to my Brother? Who can give me back my Brother? He was murder'd no longer ago than last Night, by the Hands of those Ruffians, who are entertain'd by the General to butcher the poor Soldiery. Tell me*, Blæsus, (for that was the Name of the General, who was then sitting on the Tribunal) *tell me, Where hast thou cast his dead Body? An Enemy does not grudge the Rites of Burial. When I have tired myself with kissing his cold Corps, and weeping over it, order me to be slain upon it. All I ask of my Fellow-Soldiers, since we both dye in their Cause, is that they wou'd lay me in the same Grave with my Brother.* The whole Army was in an Uproar at this moving Speech, and resolved to do the Speaker Justice; when, upon Enquiry, they found that he never had a Brother in his Life; and that he had stir'd up the Sedition only to shew his Parts.[4]

[a] Multitude/People *Fol.*

---

[4] Tacitus, *Annals*, i. 16–22. The incident occurred in A.D. 14 when, at the death of Augustus, three Pannonian legions under the command of Junius Blaesus mutinied.

Publick Ministers would likewise do well to consider, that the principal Authors of such Reproaches as are cast upon them, are those who have a mind to get their Places: And as for a Censure arising from this Motive, it is in their Power to escape it when they please, and turn it upon their Competitors. Malecontents of an inferiour Character, are acted by the same Principle; for so long as there are Employments of all Sizes, there will be Murmurers of all Degrees. I have heard of a Country Gentleman, who made a very long and melancholly Complaint to the late Duke of *Buckingham*, when he was in great Power at Court, of several publick Grievances. The Duke, after having given him a very patient Hearing, *My dear Friend*, says he, *this is but too true*; *but I have thought of an Expedient which will set all Things right, and that very soon.* His Country Friend asked him, what it was. *You must know*, says the Duke, *there's a Place of five hundred Pounds*[b] *a Year fallen this very Morning, which I intend to put you in Possession of.* The Gentleman thanked his Grace, went away satisfied, and thought the Nation the happiest under Heaven, during that whole Ministry.[5]

But further;[c] every Man in a publick Station ought to consider, that when there are two different Parties in a Nation, they will see Things in different Lights. An Action however conducive to the Good of their Country, will be represented by the Artful and appear to the Ignorant as prejudicial to it. Since I have here, according to the usual Liberty of Essay Writers, rambled into several Stories, I shall fetch one to my present Purpose out of the *Persian* History. We there read of a vertuous young Emperor, who was very much afflicted to find his Actions misconstrued and defamed by a Party among his Subjects that favour'd another Interest. As he was one Day sitting among the Ministers of his *Divan*, and amusing himself after the *Eastern* Manner, with the Solution of difficult Problems and Enigma's he proposed to them in his Turn, the following one. *What is the Tree that bears three hundred and sixty five Leaves, which are all Black on the one Side, and White on the other?* His Grand Visier immediately replied, it was the Year which consisted of three hundred and sixty five Days and Nights: *But Sir*, says he, *permit me at the same Time to take Notice, that these Leaves represent Your Actions, which carry different Faces to your Friends and Enemies, and will always appear Black to those who are resolv'd only to look upon the wrong Side of 'em.*[6]

[b] *Pounds* / *Pound Fol.* [c] further / *Fol.*; farther *8vo, 12mo.*

[5] The anecdote Addison repeats about George Villiers, second Duke of Buckingham (1628–87), is almost certainly fictitious. Places worth £500 were relatively scarce in Charles II's government, and for most places there were usually several people who were promised it when the incumbent died or retired.

[6] This story dates from the Safavid period in Persia (1501–1725) but Addison's source has not been identified.

A vertuous Man therefore who lays out his Endeavours for the Good of his Country, should never be troubled at the Reports which are made of him, so long as he is Conscious of his own Integrity. He should rather be pleased to find People descanting upon his Actions, because when they are thoroughly canvassed and examined, they are sure in the End to turn to his Honour and Advantage. The reasonable and unprejudiced Part of Mankind will be of his Side, and rejoyce to see their common Interest lodged in such honest Hands. A strict Examination of a great Man's Character, is like the Trial of a suspected Chastity which was made among the *Jews* by the Waters of Jealousy. *Moses* assures us that the Criminal burst upon the drinking of them; but if she was accused wrongfully, the *Rabbins* tell us, they heighten'd her Charms, and made her much more amiable than before: So that they destroyed the Guilty, but beautified the Innocent.[7]

Numb. XVIII — *Monday*, *February* 20, 1716

— — *Inopem me Copia fecit.*

Ovid.

EVERY *Englishman* will be a good Subject to King *George*, in Proportion as he is a good *Englishman*, and a Lover of the Constitution of his Country. In order to awaken in my Readers the Love of this their Constitution, it may be necessary to set forth its superior Excellency to that Form of Government, which many wicked and ignorant Men have of late Years endeavour'd to introduce among us. I shall not therefore think it improper to take Notice from Time to Time of any particular Act of Power, exerted by those among whom the Pretender to His Majesty's Crown has been educated; which wou'd prove fatal to this Nation, shou'd it be Conquer'd and Govern'd by a Person, who, in all Probability, wou'd put in Practice the Politicks in which he has been so long instructed.

There has been nothing more observable in the Reign of His present *Gallick* Majesty, than the Method he has taken for Supplying his Exchequer with a necessary Sum of Money. The Ways and Means for raising it has

[7] Num. 5:11–31.

Motto. Ovid, *Metamorphoses*, iii. 466: Too much plenty makes me die for want (trans. ADDISON).

been an Edict, or a Command in Writing signed by himself, to encrease the Value of *Louis d'Ors* from Fourteen to Sixteen *Livres*, by Vertue of a new Stamp which shall be struck upon them.[2] As this Method will bring all the Gold of the Kingdom into his Hands, it is provided by the same Edict that they shall be payed out again to the People at Twenty *Livres* each; so that Four *Livres* in the Score by this Means accrue to His Majesty out of all the Money in the Kingdom of *France.*

This Method of raising Money is consistent with that Form of Government, and with the repeated Practice of their late Grand Monarque; so that I shall not here consider the many evil Consequences which it must have upon their Trade, their Exchange, and Publick Credit: I shall only take Notice of the whimsical Circumstances a People must lie under, who can be thus made Poor or Rich by an Edict, which can throw an Alloy into a *Louis d'Or*, and debase it into half its former Value, or, if His Majesty pleases, raise the Price of it, not by the Accession of Metal, but of a Mark. By the present Edict many a Man in *France* will swell into a Plumb,[3] who fell several Thousand Pounds short of it the Day before its Publication. This conveys a kind of *Fairy* Treasure into their Chests, even whilst they are under Lock and Key; and is a Secret of Multiplication without Addition. It is natural enough however for the Vanity of the *French* Nation to grow Insolent upon this imaginary Wealth, not considering that their Neighbours think them no more Rich by Virtue of an Edict to make Fourteen Twenty, than they wou'd think 'em more Formidable should there be another Edict to make every Man in the Kingdom Seven Foot high.[4]

It was usual for his late Most Christian Majesty to sink the Value of their *Louis d'Ors* about the Time he was to receive the Taxes of his good People, and to raise them when he got them safe into his Coffers.[5] And there is no

[2] This edict, undertaken by the Regent in the name of Louis XV, aged 5, was registered on 8 Jan. 1716 N.S. although news of it was published in England earlier (*Post Man*, 22–4 Dec. 1715). The French government expected to gain 200 million *livres* by this transaction, but only 72 million were made in the end. One consequence was that much French gold was transported to foreign countries where individuals could earn substantial profits by bringing the gold back to France after the currency had been devalued (Pierre Lémontey, *Histoire de la régence*, Paris, 1832, i. 58–62).

[3] *Plumb*: a slang expression for a person worth £100,000 (*O.E.D.*).

[4] Such analogies were often used in debates over revaluing money. In 1695 Locke described devaluation as an attempt to 'lengthen a foot by dividing it into Fifteen parts ... and calling them Inches' (*Further Considerations Concerning Money*, p. 12); see also *Parl. Hist.* v. 968–72.

[5] There were more than forty 'mutations monétaires' during Louis XIV's reign (Germain Martin, *Histoire économique et financière*, Paris, 1927, p. 238); François Forbonnais describes a similar revaluation (1689) in detail (*Recherches et considérations sur les finances de France*, Liège, 1758, iv. 51–3).

question but the present Government in that Kingdom, will so far observe this Kind of Conduct, as to reduce the Twenty *Livres* to their old Numbers of Fourteen, when they have paid them out of their Hands; which will immediately sink the present Timpany of Wealth, and re-establish the natural Poverty of the *Gallick* Nation.

One cannot but pity the melancholly Condition of a Miser in this Country, who is perpetually telling his *Livres*, without being able to know how rich he is. He is as ridiculously puzzled and perplexed as a Man that counts the Stones on *Salisbury-Plain*, which can never be settled to any certain Number, but are more or fewer every time he reckons them.[6]

I have heard of a young *French* Lady, a Subject of *Louis* the Fourteenth, who was contracted to a Marquis upon the Foot of a Five Thousand Pound Fortune, which she had by her in Specie; but one of these unlucky Edicts coming out a Week before the intended Marriage, she lost a Thousand Pound, and her Bridegroom into the Bargain.

The Uncertainty of Riches is a Subject much discoursed of in all Countries, but may be insisted on more emphatically in *France* than any other. A Man is here under such a kind of Situation, as one who is managed by a Jugler. He fancies he has so many Pieces of Money in his Hand; but let him grasp them never so carefully, upon a Word or two of the Artist they encrease or dwindle to what Number the Doctor is pleased to Name.

This Method of lowering or advancing Money, we, who have the Happiness to be in another Form of Government, should look upon as an unwarrantable Kind of Clipping and Coining.[7] However, as it is an Expedient that is often practised, and may be justify'd in that Constitution which has been so thoroughly studied by the Pretender to His Majesty's Crown, I do not see what should have hinder'd him from making use of so expeditious a Method for raising a Supply, if he had succeeded in his late Attempt to dethrone His Majesty, and subvert our Constitution. I shall leave it to the Consideration of the Reader, if in such a Case the following Edict, or something very like it, might not have been expected.

[6] This myth about Stonehenge was, according to Defoe, '*a meer Country Fiction*, and a Ridiculous one too; the Reason why they cannot easily be told, is, that many of them lye Half, or Part buryed in the Ground . . . it cannot be known easily, which belong to one Stone, and which to another, or which are separate Stones' (*Tour thro' Great Britain*, i. 197).

[7] Addison is implying a comparison between the way the Whigs successfully overcame the coinage crisis of 1695 and the way Louis XIV manipulated French currency. The English crisis arose because silver was coined in England at a price lower than silver could be sold in Holland; hence, unmilled coins were shaved and the silver clippings exported to Holland. Between 1672 and 1696 it was estimated that English silver coins depreciated about 40 per cent and, in December 1695, a committee led by Lord Halifax proposed that the losses should be absorbed by the government and that all silver coins should be recast into milled coins (*Parl. Hist.* v. 967–72; *C.J.* xi. 358).

'Whereas these our Kingdoms have long groaned under an expensive and consuming Land-War, which has very much exhausted the Treasure of the Nation, we, being willing to increase the Wealth of our People, and not thinking it advisable for this Purpose to make use of the tedious Methods of Merchandise and Commerce, which have been always promoted by a Faction among the worst of our Subjects, and were so wisely discountenanc'd by the best of them in the late Reign,[8] do hereby Enact by our sole Will and Pleasure, that every Shilling in *Great Britain*, shall pass in all Payments for the Sum of fourteen Pence, till the first of *September* next, and that every other Piece of Money shall rise and pass in current Payment in the same Proportion. The Advantage which will accrue to these Nations by this our Royal Donative, will visibly appear to all Men of sound Principles, who are so justly famous for their Antipathy to Strangers, and would not see the Landed Interest of their Country weaken'd by the Importations of Foreign Gold and Silver. But since by reason of the great Debts which we have contracted Abroad, during our fifteen Years Reign, as well as of our present Exigencies, it will be necessary to fill our Exchequer by the most prudent and expeditious Methods, we do also hereby order every one of our Subjects to bring in these his Fourteen-penny Pieces, and all the other current Cash of this Kingdom, by what new Titles soever dignified or distinguished, to the Master of our Mint, who, after having set a Mark upon them shall deliver out to them, on or after the first of *September* aforesaid, their respective Sums, taking only Four Pence for our self for such his Mark on every Fourteen-Penny Piece, which from henceforth[a] shall pass in Payment for Eighteen Pence, and so in proportion for the rest. By this Method, the Money of this Nation will be more by one Third than it is at present; and we shall content our self with not quite one Fifth Part of the Current Cash of our loving Subjects; which will but barely suffice to clear the Interest of those Sums in which we stand indebted to our most dear Brother and ancient Ally. We are glad of this Opportunity of shewing such an Instance of our Goodness to our Subjects, by this our Royal Edict, which shall be read in every Parish Church of *Great Britain*, immediately after the Celebration of High Mass.[9] *For such is our Pleasure.*'

[a] henceforth / thenceforth *Fol.*

[8] An allusion to the Commercial Treaty with France (1713) which both Whigs and 'whimsical' Tories opposed.

[9] In May 1688 James II ordered his second Declaration of Indulgence read in all the 'churches and chapels throughout this Kingdom' (*London Gazette*, 3–7 May 1688). Reading royal declarations at religious services was a permissible but, according to Burnet, pernicious use of the Church (*History* ii. 282–83).

Numb. XIX *Friday, February* 24, 1716

Pulchrum est bene facere reipublicæ; etiam bene dicere haud absurdum est. Sall.

It has been usual these many Years for Writers, who have approved the Scheme of Government which has taken place, to Explain to the People the Reasonableness of those Principles which have prevailed, and to Justify the Conduct of those who act in Conformity to such Principles. It therefore happens well for the Party which is undermost, when a Work of this Nature falls into the Hands of those who content themselves to attack their Principles, without exposing their Persons, or singling out any particular Objects for Satyr and Ridicule. This Manner of Proceeding is no inconsiderable Piece of Merit in Writers, who are often more influenc'd by a Desire of Fame, than a Regard to the Publick Good; and who, by this Means, lose many fair Opportunities of shewing their own Wit, or of gratifying the Ill-Nature of their Readers.

When a Man thinks a Party engaged in such Measures as tend to the Ruine of his Country, it is certainly a very laudable and vertuous Action in him to make War after this Manner upon the whole Body. But as several Casuists are of Opinion, that in a Battle you shou'd discharge upon the Gross of the Enemy, without levelling your Piece at any particular Person; so in this kind of Combat also, I cannot think it fair to aim at any one Man, and make his Character the Mark of your Hostilities. There is now to be seen in the Castle of *Milan*, a Cannon-Bullet, inscribed, *This to the Mareschal de Crequi*;[2] which was the very Ball that shot him. An Author who points his Satyr at a Great Man, is to be looked upon in the same View with the Engineer who signalized himself by this ungenerous Practice.

But as the Spirit of the *Whigs* and *Tories* shews itself, upon every Occasion, to be very widely different from one another; so is it particularly visible in the Writings of this kind, which have been published by each Party. The latter may, indeed, assign one Reason to justify themselves in this Practice; That, having nothing of any manner of Weight to offer

Motto. Sallust, *De Catilinae Coniuratione*, 3: 'Tis . . . a noble Thing to act bravely for the Commonwealth: And to write or speak to the Advantage of it is . . . not without its worth' (trans. ROWE).

[2] Charles de Créquy de Blanchefort, duc de Lesdiguières (1578–1638), a brilliant soldier who commanded the French forces on the Italian frontier between 1621 and 1625. He led the victorious siege against Milan in 1625 and was killed while going to the aid of Brema in 1638.

against the Principles of their Antagonists, if they speak at all, it must be against their Persons. When they cannot refute an Adversary, the shortest Way is to libel him; and to endeavour at the making his Person odious, when they cannot represent his Notions as absurd.[3]

The *Examiner* was a Paper, in the last Reign, which was the Favourite-Work of the Party. It was usher'd into the World by a Letter from a Secretary of State, setting forth the great Genius of the Author, the Usefulness of his Design, and the mighty Consequences that were to be expected from it.[4] It is said to have been written by those among 'em whom they looked upon as their most celebrated Wits and Politicians, and was dispersed into all Quarters of the Nation with great Industry and Expence. Who would not have expected, that at least the Rules of Decency and Candour would be observed in such a Performance? But instead of this, you saw all the Great Men, who had done eminent Services to their Country but a few Years before, draughted out one by one, and baited in their Turns.[5] No Sanctity of Character, or Privilege of Sex, exempted Persons from this barbarous Usage. Several of our Prelates were the standing Marks of publick Raillery, and many Ladies of the first Quality branded by Name for Matters of Fact, which, as they were false, were not heeded, and if they had been true, were Innocent.[6] The Dead themselves were not spared.[7] And here I cannot forbear taking Notice of a kind of Wit

[3] Swift also accused the Whigs of using *ad hominem* attacks and it is true that Addison and Steele both were willing to attack the person as well as the issues (*Prose Works* iii. 68; *F.* 36; *Englishman*, pp. 253–90 *passim*). However, Swift used the device more brilliantly than any of his contemporaries; see, e.g., his *Short Character of the Earl of Wharton* (1711) and his *Examiner* essays on the Duke of Marlborough.

[4] The *Examiner* was published from 3 Aug. 1710 until 26 July 1714. It was introduced by a letter written by Henry St. John (appointed Secretary of State several weeks later) which appeared at the head of the first essay and which implied that the periodical expressed the opinions of the new Tory administration. Although the *Examiner* ran for four years, it was especially powerful during its first year when, with Swift as its editor, it attacked the principal statesmen of the previous ministry. Other editors included William King, Francis Atterbury, Matthew Prior, and Mary Manley. Swift's essays and St. John's letter are published in *Prose Works* iii (references to essays in that edition cite only page numbers); references to other *Examiners* cite the publication date.

[5] The 'Great Men' attacked in the *Examiner* were Marlborough (pp. 19–24, 80–5), Wharton (pp. 24–9), and Somers (p. 79). Less space, but no less venom, was devoted to attacking Cowper (p. 57), Sunderland (p. 20), Stanhope (14–18 June 1714), Godolphin (pp. 71, 86; 31 Aug.–7 Sept. 1710), and the whole Junto (5 June 1712).

[6] The prelates attacked were leading Whig bishops such as William Fleetwood (22–9 May 1712), Benjamin Hoadly (1 Jan. 1714), and Gilbert Burnet (14–21 Aug. 1712). Swift wrote none of these essays, preferring, as he said, to keep the 'Inclinations of the People favourable to *Episcopacy*' (p. 51). However, he attacked the Duchess of Marlborough mercilessly, describing her as haughty, dishonest, greedy, and ungentle (*Prose Works* iii, *passim*).

[7] The Earl of Godolphin was calumniated in the *Examiner* of 30 Oct.–3 Nov. 1713, and Steele responded to this posthumous attack by claiming the *Examiner* 'can find no one more readily to abuse than this Man of safe and established Honour, who is gathered to the Grave,

(*continued*)

which has lately grown into Fashion among the Versifiers, Epigrammatists, and other Authors, who think it sufficient to distinguish themselves by their Zeal for what they call the High-Church, while they sport with the most tremendous Parts of Revealed Religion. Every one has seen Epigrams upon the deceased Fathers of our Church, where the whole Thought has turned upon Hell-Fire. Patriots, who ought to be remember'd with Honour by their Posterity, have been introduced as Speakers in a State of torments.[8] There is something dreadful even in repeating these execrable Pieces of Wit, which no Man who really believes in another Life, can peruse without Fear and Trembling. It is astonishing to see Readers who call themselves Christians, applauding such Diabolical Mirth, and seeming to rejoyce in the Doom which is pronounced against their Enemies, by such abandoned Scriblers. A Wit of this Kind, may with great Truth be compared to the Fool in the *Proverbs, who plays with Arrows, Fire-brands and Death, and says, am I not in Sport?*[9]

I must, in Justice to the more sober and considerate of that Party, confess, that many of them were highly scandalised at that Personal Slander and Reflection which was flung out so freely by the Libellers of the last Reign, as well as by those profane Liberties which have been since continued. And as for those who are either the Authors or Admirers of such Compositions, I would have them consider with themselves, whether the Name of a good Churchman can attone for the want of that Charity which is the most essential Part of Christianity. They would likewise do well to reflect, how, by these Methods, the Poison has run freely into the Minds of the Weak and Ignorant; heightned their Rage against many of their Fellow-Subjects; and almost divested them of the common Sentiments of Humanity.

In the former Part of this Paper, I have hinted that the Design of it is to oppose the Principles of those who are Enemies to the present Government, and the main Body of that Party who espouse those Principles. But even in such general Attacks there are certain Measures to be kept, which may have a Tendency rather to gain, than to irritate those who differ with you

---

and secure from every thing but this diabolical Worm, that can eat into a Coffin, to tear the body of a Man who had done Good to his Country' (*Englishman*, p. 56). John Dolben, who had introduced the impeachment against Sacheverell in the House of Commons, was also posthumously attacked; see *Examiner* 28 (p. 86).

[8] *A Dialogue of the Dead between the very Eminent Signor Glbertini and Count Thomaso in the Vales of Acheron*, a prose satire which attacked Gilbert Burnet and the Earl of Wharton, was published in 1715. Addison is also referring to articles and poems in *News from the Dead*, a periodical published between November 1715 and August 1716.

[9] Prov. 26:18–19.

in their Sentiments. The *Examiner* would not allow such as were of a contrary Opinion to him, to be either Christians or Fellow Subjects. With him they were all Atheists, Deists, or Apostates, and a separate Common-Wealth among themselves, that ought either to be extirpated, or, when he was in a better Humour, only to be banished out of their Native Country.[10] They were often put in mind of some approaching Execution, and therefore all of them advised to prepare themselves for it, as Men who had then nothing to take care of, but how to die decently.[11] In short, the *Examiner* seemed to make no distinction between Conquest and Destruction.

The Conduct of this Work[a] has hitherto been regulated by different Views, and shall continue to be so; unless the Party it has to deal with, draw upon themselves another kind of Treatment. For if they shall persist in pointing their Batteries against particular Persons, there are no Laws of War that forbid the making of Reprisals. In the mean time, this Undertaking shall be managed with that generous Spirit which was so remarkable among the *Romans*, who did not subdue a Country in order to put the Inhabitants to Fire and Sword, but to incorporate them into their own Community, and make them happy in the same Government with themselves.

U

Numb. XX *Monday, February* 27, 1716

Privatus illis Census erat brevis,
Commune magnum——

Hor.

It is very unlucky for those who make it their Business to raise Popular Murmurs and Discontents against His Majesty's Government, that they

[a] of this Work / of those who are engaged in this Work *Fol.*

[10] Swift wrote, 'I remember to have asked some considerable Whigs, whether it did not bring a Disreputation upon their Body, to have the whole Herd of Presbyterians, Independents, Atheists, Anabaptist, Deists, Quakers and Socinians, openly and universally Listed under their Banners?' (p. 92) and 'We accuse them [the Whigs] as Enemies to Monarchy; as endeavouring to undermine the present Form of Government, and to build a Commonwealth . . . upon its Ruins' (p. 142).

[11] In an 'Epigram upon Tyburn' (5–12 June 1712), the *Examiner* predicted that the Junto, the Marlboroughs, and Godolphin were all about to be executed.

Motto. Horace, *Odes* II. xv. 13–14: In their day an individual's property was small, but the commonwealth's was great.

find so very few and so very improper Occasions for them. To shew how hard they are set in this Particular, there are several, who for want of other Materials, are forced to represent the Bill which was passed this Session, for laying an additional Tax of Two Shillings in the Pound upon Land, as a kind of Grievance upon the Subject.[2] If this be a Matter of Complaint, it ought in Justice to fall upon those who have made it necessary.[3] Had there been no Rebellion, there would have been no Increase of the Land-Tax; so that in Proportion as a Man declares his Aversion to the one, he ought to testify his Abhorrence of the other. But it is very remarkable that those, who would perswade the People that they are aggrieved by this additional Burthen, are the very Persons who endeavour, in their ordinary Conversation, to extenuate the Heinousness of the Rebellion, and who express the greatest Tenderness for the Persons of the Rebels. They shew a particular Indulgence for that unnatural Insurrection which has drawn this Load upon us, and are angry at the Means which were necessary for suppressing it. There needs no clearer Proof of the Spirit and Intention with which they act: I shall therefore advise my Fellow-Free-Holders to consider the Character of any Person who would possess them with the Notion of a Hardship that is put upon the Country by this Tax. If he be one of known Affection to the present Establishment, they may imagine there is some Reason for Complaint. But if on the contrary he be one who has shewn himself Indifferent, as to the Success of the present Rebellion, or is suspected as a private Abettor of it, they may take it for granted, his Complaint against the Land-Tax is either the Rage of a disappointed Man, or the Artifice of one who would alienate their Affections from the present Government.

The Expence which will arise to the Nation from this Rebellion, is already computed at near a Million. And it is a melancholly Consideration for the Free-Holders of *Great Britain*, that the Treason of their Fellow-Subjects should bring upon them as great a Charge as the War with *France*.

[2] The land tax, a basic source of government income, usually varied from 2*s*. to 4*s*. in the pound for the value of land, offices, and, in theory, other property such as cash, wares, debts due, and merchandise; in practice, however, the tax was mainly on land. Each year Parliament passed an act which set the tax rate according to the estimated expenses for the year. In 1716 the tax rate was raised from 2*s*., the most common peacetime rate, to 4*s*., the usual wartime rate (Stephen Dowell, *A History of Taxation*, 1888, iii. 81–92).

[3] The most obvious complaint was that the 4*s*. rate was excessive. Atterbury had predicted before the 1715 election that a Whig victory would result in a 6*s*. rate (*English Advice*, p. 30). There were also other complaints: the Preamble to the 1716 Land Tax Act blamed the rise in taxes on 'the fatal and pernicious councils given by some Persons in the late mal-administration' and the Lords registered a protest against the Preamble (*Parl. Hist.* vii. 287; *L.J.* xx. 291). Countess Cowper called the Preamble 'a defamatory Libel upon the late *Queen*' (Diary, 11 Feb. 1716).

At the same Time every reasonable Man among them will pay a Tax with at least as great Chearfulness for stifling a Civil War in its Birth, as for carrying on a War in a Foreign Country. Had not our first Supplies been effectual for the crushing of our Domestick Enemies, we should immediately have beheld the whole Kingdom a Scene of Slaughter and Desolation: Whereas, if we had failed in our first Attempts upon a distant Nation, we might have repaired the Losses of one Campaign by the Advantages of another, and after several Victories gained over us, might still have kept the Enemy from our Gates.

As it was thus absolutely necessary to raise a Sum that might enable the Government to put a speedy Stop to the Rebellion, so could there be no Method thought of for raising such a sum more proper, than this of laying an additional Tax of Two Shillings in the Pound upon Land.

In the first Place: This Tax has already been so often tried, that we know the exact Produce of it, which in any new Project is always very doubtful and uncertain.[4] As we are thus acquainted with the Produce of this Tax, we find it is adequate to the Services for which it is designed, and that the[a] additional Tax is proportioned to the Supernumerary Expence, which falls upon the Kingdom this Year by the unnatural Rebellion, as it has been above stated.

In the next Place: No other Tax could have been thought of, upon which so much Money would have been immediately advanced as was necessary in so critical a Juncture for pushing our Successes against the Rebels, and preventing the Attempts of their Friends and Confederates both at Home and Abroad. No Body cares to make Loans upon a new and untried Project; whereas Men never fail to bring in their Money upon a Land-Tax, when the Præmium or Interest allowed them, is suited to the Hazard they run by such Loans to the Government. And here one cannot but bewail the Misfortune of our Country, when we consider, that the House of Commons had last Year reduced this Interest to Four *per Cent.* by which Means there was a considerable Saving to the Nation; but that this Year they have been forced to give Six *per Cent.* as well knowing the fatal Consequences that might have ensued, had there not been an Interest

[a] and that the / and the *Fol.*

[4] The land tax was a pillar of government finances because its income could be very accurately predicted. For each shilling in the rate the tax would produce slightly less than one-half million pounds; hence the 2*s.* increase would have covered the additional expense of 'near a Million' occasioned by the rebellion. Other sources of government income, such as customs and excise or government loans, were less predictable. During the period 1706–8 the government collected about 98 per cent of the money the land tax was expected to yield (P.G.M. Dickson, *The Financial Revolution in England*, New York, 1967, p. 359).

allowed, which would certainly encourage the Lender to venture, in such a time of Danger, what was indispensably necessary for the Exigences of the Publick.[5]

Besides; This is a Method for raising a Sum of Money, that, with the ordinary Taxes, will in all Probability defray the whole Expence of the Year: So that there is no Burden laid upon our Posterity, who have been sufficiently loaded by other Means of raising Money; nor any Deficiency to be hereafter made up by ourselves; which has been our Case in so many other Subsidies.[6]

To this we may add; That we have no Example of any other Tax, which in its Nature would so particularly affect the Enemies to His Majesty's Government. Multitudes of *Papists* and *Nonjurors* will be obliged to furnish a double Proportion out of their Revenues towards the clearing of that Expence, which by their open and secret Practices they have been Instrumental in bringing upon their Fellow-subjects.[7]

I shall only mention one Consideration more; That no other Tax is so likely to cease as this is, when there is no farther Occasion for it. This Tax is established by a House of Commons, which, by Virtue of an Act of Parliament passed a few Years ago, must consist for the most Part of Landed Men; so that a great Share of the Weight of it must necessarily fall upon the Members of their own Body.[8] As this is an Instance of their Publick Spirit, so we may be sure they would not have exerted it, had there

[5] Once a land-tax act was passed, the government made a short-term loan for the estimated yield and thus obtained the income quickly. Since deficits in collecting this tax were usually small, it was a safe investment for lenders. The interest rate for this loan was set by Parliament when the tax was levied; in 1715 the rate had been 4 per cent, but in 1716 it was raised to 6 per cent to attract investors during the rebellion (Dickson, p. 364).

[6] Addison is referring to long-term loans which became known as the National Debt. The three privileged companies—the Bank, the East India Company, and the South Sea Company—lent the government large amounts and individuals could also lend money by buying tax-free annuities. Such long-term loans were repaid by the government from less predictable sources of income than the land tax. The government's reluctance to float such a loan was more practical than Addison suggests. In 1715 the government floated a loan for £910,000 at 4 per cent, but because of the rebellion only £451,800 had been subscribed when the loan closed on 29 September (Dickson, pp. 81–2). Fears that a Stuart restoration would result in cancellation of government debts were sufficient for the government to conceal intelligence concerning the Pretender's landing in 1715 for five days while they borrowed money (Percival Letterbook, 8 Jan. 1716).

[7] Since 1692 anyone refusing to take the oaths of supremacy and allegiance was obliged to pay double taxes. On 23 Jan. 1716 the Commons read a bill which would allow the government to seize two-thirds of the land owned by Catholics and to apply the profits from this seizure to the supply granted to the King (*C.J.* xviii. 347).

[8] The Landed Qualifications Act (1711) required county representatives to own property worth 'Six hundred Pounds above Reprizes' and borough representatives to own property worth 'Three hundred Pounds above Reprizes' (*Statutes* ix. 365). Although nominally intended to reduce the susceptibility of members to bribes, the Act was a Tory measure aimed at strengthening the influence of property owners in Parliament.

not been an absolute Necessity: Nor can we doubt, that for the same Reasons, when this Necessity ceases, they will take the first Opportunity of easing themselves in this Particular, as well as those whom they represent. It is a celebrated Notion of a Patriot, who signally distinguished himself for the Liberties of his Country, That a House of Commons should never grant such Subsidies as are easy to be raised, and give no Pain to the People, lest the Nation should acquiesce under a Burden they did not feel, and see it perpetuated without repining. Whether this Notion might not be too refined, I shall not determine; but by what has been already said, I think we may promise ourselves, that this additional Tax of Two Shillings in the Pound will not be continued another Year, because we may hope the Rebellion will be entirely ended in This.

And here, I believe, it must be obvious to every one's Reflection, that the Rebellion might not have concluded so soon, had not this Method been made use of for that End. A foreign Potentate trembles at the Thought of entering into a War with so wealthy an Enemy as the *British* Nation, when he finds the whole Landed Interest of the Kingdom engaged to oppose him with their united Force; and at all Times ready to employ against him such a Part of their Revenues, as shall be sufficient to baffle his Designs upon their Country: Especially when none can imagine, that he expects any Encouragement from those whose Fortunes are either lodged in the Funds, or employed in Trade.

The Wisdom therefore of the present House of Commons has by this Tax, not only enabled the King to subdue those of his own Subjects who have been actually in Arms against him, but to divert any of his Neighbours from the Hopes of lending them a competent Assistance.

Numb. XXI *Friday, March* 2, 1716

Qualis in Eurotæ ripis, aut per juga Cynthi,
Excercet Diana choros; quam mille secutæ
Hinc atque hinc glomerantur Oreades: illa pharetram
Fert humero, gradiensq; Deas superereminet omnes.

Virg.

Motto. Virgil, *Aeneid*, i. 498–501:

Such on *Eurotas* Banks, or *Cynthus* hight,
Diana seems; and so she charms the sight,
When in the Dance the graceful Goddess leads
The Quire of Nymphs, and overtops their Heads.
Known by her Quiver, and her lofty Meen,
She walks Majestick, and she looks their Queen. (trans. DRYDEN)

It is not easy for any one, who saw the Magnificence of Yesterday in the Court of *Great Britain*, to turn his Thoughts for some time after on any other Subject. It was a Solemnity every way suited to the Birth-Day of a Princess, who is the Delight of our Nation, and the Glory of her Sex.[2] *Homer* tells us, that when the Daughter of *Jupiter* presented herself among a Crowd of Goddesses, she was distinguished from the rest by her graceful Stature, and known by her superiour Beauty, notwithstanding they were all beautiful.[3] Such was the Appearance of the Princess of *Wales* among our *British* Ladies; or (to use a more solemn Phrase) of *the King's Daughter among her honourable Women.* Her Royal Highness in the midst of such a Circle raises in the Beholder the Idea of a fine Picture, where (notwithstanding the Diversity of pleasing Objects that fill up the Canvas) the principal Figure immediately takes the Eye, and fixes the Attention.

When this excellent Princess was yet in her Father's Court, she was so celebrated for the Beauty of her Person, and the Accomplishments of her Mind, that there was no Prince in the Empire, who had room for such an Alliance, that was not ambitious of gaining her into his Family, either as a Daughter, or as a Consort. He, who is now the Chief of the Crowned Heads in *Europe*, and was then King of *Spain*, and Heir to all the Dominions of the House of *Austria*, sought her in Marriage.[4] Could her Mind have been captivated with the Glories of this World, she had them all laid before her; but she generously declined them, because she saw the Acceptance of them was inconsistent with what she esteems more than all the Glories of this World, the Enjoyment of her Religion. Providence however kept in Store a Reward for such an exalted Vertue; and, by the secret Methods of its Wisdom, opened a Way for her to become the

[2] Caroline of Anspach, Princess of Wales, celebrated her thirty-third birthday on 1 Mar. 1716 with an elaborate ball which was described at length in the *St. James's Evening Post* (1–3 Mar.). Caroline was an attractive person, intellectually superior to her husband and his father, and the only adult woman in the royal family in England (the King's wife, Sophia Dorothea, was imprisoned for life in the Council House of Ahlden). Caroline and her husband were frequent hosts to fashionable London society, both at St. James's Palace and at Somerset House (Cowper Diary, 16 Feb. 1715; B.L. Add. MS. 17677 iii, fo. 65). John Lord Hervey claimed that Caroline 'loved reading and the conversation of men of wit and learning' (*Memoirs* i. 261). By directing attention to Caroline, Addison is presenting the Court in one of its most favourable lights.

[3] *Odyssey*, vi. 102–8.

[4] Caroline's father died in 1687 and she was an orphan by the age of twelve. She spent most of her next ten years at the Court of her guardian, the Electoral Prince of Brandenburg, where she met the Electress Sophia of Hanover. Plans for her marriage to Archduke Charles, later Emperor Charles VI, were discussed in 1704, but her conversion to Catholicism was required and the Electress Sophia made it clear at the time that she wanted Caroline at Hanover (*Die Werke von Leibniz*, ed. O. Klopp, Hanover, 1864, ix. 107). Although Caroline later claimed that she 'refusd to be Empress for ye Sake of ye Protestant Religion', Archduke Charles was not the heir apparent to the Empire when she refused him (Cowper Diary, 23 Dec. 1714).

Greatest of her Sex, among those who profess that Faith to which she adhered with so much Christian Magnanimity.

This her illustrious Conduct might, in the Eye of the World, have lost its Merit, had so accomplished a Prince as his Royal Highness declared his Passion for the same Alliance at that time: It would then have been no Wonder that all other Proposals had been rejected. But it was the Fame of this heroick Constancy that determined his Royal Highness to desire in Marriage a Princess whose personal Charms, which had before been so universally admired, were now become the least Part of her Character. We of the *British* Nation have reason to rejoice, that such a Proposal was made and accepted; and that her Royal Highness, with regard to these two successive Treaties of Marriage, shewed as much Prudence in her Compliance with the one, as Piety in her Refusal of the other.[5]

The Princess was no sooner arrived at *Hanover*, than she improved the Lustre of that Court, which was before reckoned among the Politest in *Europe*; and increased the Satisfaction of that People, who were before looked upon as the Happiest in the Empire. She immediately became the Darling of the Princess *Sophia*, who was acknowledged in all the Courts of *Europe* the most accomplished woman of the Age in which she lived, and who was not a little pleased with the Conversation of one in whom she saw so lively an Image of her own Youth.

But I shall insist no longer on that Reputation which Her Royal Highness has acquired in other Countries. We daily discover those admirable Qualities for which she is so justly famed, and rejoyce to see them exerted in our own Country, where we our selves are made happy by their Influence. We are the more pleased to behold the Throne of these Kingdoms surrounded by a numerous and beautiful Progeny, when we consider the Vertues of those from whom they descend. Not only the Features, but the Mind of the Parent is often copied out in the Offspring. But the Princess we are speaking of, takes the surest Method of making her Royal Issue like herself, by instilling early into their Minds all the Principles of Religion, Vertue and Honour, and seasoning their tender Years with all that Knowledge which they are capable of receiving.[6] What may we not hope from such an uncommon Care in the Education of the Children of *Great Britain*, who are directed by such Precepts, and will be formed by such an Example!

[5] Caroline was married to the Electoral Prince on 2 Sept. 1705 N.S.

[6] Caroline had four children at this time—Frederick (b. 1707), Anne (b. 1709), Amelia (b. 1710), and Caroline (b. 1713)—but only her daughters were with her in England. Frederick remained at Hanover where Lady Mary Wortley Montagu was favourably impressed by him in November 1716 (*Complete Letters* i. 286).

The Conjugal Vertues are so remarkable in her Royal Highness, as to deserve those just and generous Returns of Love and Tenderness, for which the Prince her Husband is so universally celebrated.[7]

But there is no Part of Her Royal Highness's Character which we observe with greater Pleasure, than that Behaviour by which she has so much endear'd herself to His Majesty; tho' indeed we have no Reason to be surprized at this mutual Intercourse of Duty and Affection, when we consider so wise and vertuous a Princess possessing, in the same sacred Person, the kindest of Fathers, and the best of Kings.[8] And here it is natural for us to congratulate our own good Fortune, who see our Soveraign blest with a numerous Issue, among whom are Heirs Male in two direct Descents, which has not happened in the Reign of any *English* King since the time of his Majesty's Great Ancestor *Edward* III, and is a Felicity not enjoyed by the Subjects of any other of the Kings of *Europe* who are his Contemporaries. We are like Men entertained with the View of a spacious Landskip, where the Eye passes over one pleasing Prospect into another, till the Sight is lost by degrees in a Succession of delightful Objects, and leaves us in the Persuasion that there remain still more behind.

But if we regard Her Royal Highness in that Light which diffuses the greatest Glory round a Humane Character, we shall find the Christian no less conspicuous than the Princess. She is as eminent for a sincere Piety in the Practice of Religion, as for an inviolable Adherence to its Principles. She is constant in her Attendance on the daily Offices of our Church, and by her serious and devout Comportment on these solemn Occasions, gives an Example that is very often too much wanted in Courts.[9]

Her Religion is equally free from the Weakness of Superstition, and the Sourness of Enthusiasm. It is not of that uncomfortable melancholy Nature

[7] When describing the Prince's virtues, Bonet emphasizes 'l'attachement qu'il a pour la princesse son épouse', although Hervey claims that by 1715 the Prince was involved with two English women, Mrs. Howard and Mrs. Bellenden (Michael, p. 376; *Memoirs* i. 40–2). In spite of his attachments to other women, the Prince remained affectionate toward Caroline and she continued to influence him (Hervey, *Memoirs* i. 44–5; iii. 909–15).

[8] Strained relations between the King and his son were evident to English observers when the Hanoverians arrived in 1714 (Wortley Montagu, *Account*, p. 119). Although the King referred to Caroline as 'Cette Diablesse Madame la Princesse', there is evidence that she played a mediating role between her husband and father-in-law for a while (Walpole, *Reminiscences*, p. 27). Bonet describes her Court as one place where the two men sometimes met, and Pope wrote in 1717 that Caroline had little to do with the division between father and son (Michael, p. 376; *Correspondence* i. 407).

[9] Both the King and Prince offended 'les rigides Anglais' by their apparent indifference to Anglicanism, but Caroline made a better impression by her daily attendance at morning prayers and frequent reception of communion (Michael, p. 375). Although the Princess was accused of Calvinism, Countess Cowper attests to Caroline's devotion to Anglicanism (*English Advice*, p. 20; Cowper Diary, 25 Dec. 1714).

which disappoints its own End, by appearing unamiable to those whom it would gain to its Interests. It discovers itself in the genuine Effects of Christianity, in Affability, Compassion, Benevolence, Eveness of Mind, and all the Offices of an active and universal Charity.

As a cheerful Temper is the necessary Result of these Virtues, so it shines out in all the Parts of her Conversation, and dissipates those Apprehensions which naturally hang on the Timorous or the Modest, when they are admitted to the Honour of her Presence. There is none who[a] does not listen with Pleasure to a Person in so high a Station, who condescends to make herself thus agreeable, by Mirth without Levity, and Wit without Ill-Nature.

Her Royal Highness is, indeed, possest of all those Talents which make Conversation either delightful or improving. As she has a fine Taste of the elegant Arts, and is skilled in several modern Languages, her Discourse is not confined to the ordinary Subjects or Forms of Conversation, but can adapt itself with an uncommon Grace to every Occasion, and entertain the politest Persons of different Nations. I need not mention, what is observed by every one, that agreeable Turn which appears in her Sentiments upon the most ordinary Affairs of Life, and which is so suitable to the Delicacy of her Sex, the Politeness of her Education, and the Splendor of her Quality.[10]

It would be vain to think of drawing into the Compass of this Paper, the many eminent Virtues which adorn the Character of this Great Princess; but as it is one chief End[b] of this Undertaking to make the People sensible of the Blessings which they enjoy under His Majesty's Reign, I could not but lay hold on[c] this Opportunity to speak of That which ought in Justice to be reckoned among the greatest of them.

[a] who/*Fol.*; that *8vo*, *12mo*. [b] one chief End/the chief Design *Fol.* [c] but lay hold on/omit taking *Fol.*

[10] Caroline had genuine intellectual interests in spite of her husband who 'used often to brag of the contempt he had for books and letters' (Hervey, *Memoirs* i. 261). She tried to speak English and was interested in English intellectual works, requesting, for example, 'all my Ld Bacons works' and conversing occasionally with Samuel Clarke and Sir Isaac Newton (Cowper Diary, 2 Nov. 1714; Burnet, *History* v. 323n). Caroline was instrumental in beginning the Leibniz–Clarke correspondence on time and space which Clarke later published with a dedication to her. Like many poets, Addison wrote flattering verses to the Princess (*Miscellaneous Works* i. 331–2). While Caroline was undeniably more intellectual than most royalty, two contemporaries, Horace Walpole and Lord Hervey, both describe her knowledge and thinking as occasionally superficial (*Reminiscences*, p. 71; *Memoirs* i. 262).

Numb. XXII *Monday, March* 5, 1716

Studiis rudis, sermone barbarus, impetu strenuus, manu promptus, cogitatione celer. Vell. Paterc.

FOR the Honour of His Majesty, and the Safety of His Government, we cannot but observe, that those who have appeared the greatest Enemies to both, are of that Rank of Men who are commonly distinguished by the Title of *Fox-hunters*.[2] As several of these have had no Part of their Education in Cities, Camps, or Courts, it is doubtful whether they are of greater Ornament or Use to the Nation in which they live. It would be an everlasting Reproach to Politicks, should such Men be able to overturn an Establishment which has been formed by the wisest Laws, and is supported by the ablest Heads. The wrong Notions and Prejudices which cleave to many of these Country-Gentlemen who have always lived out of the way of being better informed, are not easy to be conceived by a Person who has never conversed with them.

That I may give my Readers an Image of[a] these Rural Statesmen, I shall without farther Preface, set down an Account of a Discourse I chanced to have with one of them some Time ago. I was Travelling towards one of the remote Parts of *England*, when about Three a-Clock in the Afternoon, seeing a Country-Gentleman trotting before me with a Spaniel by his Horse's Side, I made up to him. Our Conversation opened, as usual, upon the Weather, in which we were very unanimous, having both agreed that

[a] Image of/Image of one of *Fol.*

Motto. Velleius Paterculus, *Historiae Romanae*, ii. 73: '. . . unpolished with Learning and barbarous in his Language; of a very audacious Temper, great Activity of Body, and Precipitation in his Resolutions' (trans. NEWCOMB).

[2] According to Oldmixon, Tory fox-hunters were synonymous with 'October Men' (see *F.* 3, n. 12) and 'had most of their Conversation with the Rural Clergy', who taught them that the best way to serve Anglicanism was to pluck the schism of Presbyterianism 'up by the Roots' (*History of England*, 1735, p. 344). The caricature Addison creates in this essay is an acidic revision of Sir Roger de Coverley; although in most respects the fox-hunter is a person of lower social standing than Sir Roger, he is 'one of the Quorum' (*F.* 44). A number of themes Addison mentions in *S.* 126, one of his de Coverley essays, are more fully developed here: the association of Tories with fox-hunting, the country habit of choosing inns according to the innkeeper's politics, the false notions country people have about their London friends, and the suspicions they held about 'fanaticks'. Addison's fox-hunter embodies nearly all the prejudices associated with the Country Tories during Queen Anne's reign (see Introduction, pp. 22–3).

it was too dry for the Season of the Year. My Fellow-Traveller upon this observed to me, that there had been no good Weather since the Revolution. I was a little startled at so extraordinary a Remark,[b] but would not interrupt him till he proceeded to tell me of the fine Weather they used to have in King *Charles* the Second's Reign. I only answered that I did not see how the Badness of the Weather could be the King's Fault; and, without waiting for his Reply, asked him whose House it[c] was we saw upon a Rising-Ground at a little Distance from us. He told me it belonged to an old Fanatical Cur, Mr. Such a one, *You must have heard of him*, says he, *He's one of the Rump*.[3] I knew the Gentleman's Character upon hearing his Name, but assured him that to my Knowledge he was a good Churchman: *Ay*, says he with a kind of Surprize, *We were told in the Country, that he spoke twice in the Queen's Time against taking off the Duties upon* French *Claret*.[4] This naturally led us into the Proceedings of late Parliaments, upon which Occasion he affirmed roundly, that there had not been one good Law passed since King *William's* Accession to the Throne, except the Act for preserving the Game.[5] I had a mind to see him out, and therefore did not care for contradicting him. *Is it not hard*, says he, *that honest Gentlemen should be taken into Custody of Messengers to prevent them from acting according to their Consciences?*[6] *But*, says he, *what can we expect when a Parcel of Factious Sons of Whores*—. He was going on in great Passion, but chanced to miss his Dog, who was amusing himself about a Bush, that grew[d] at some Distance behind us. We stood still till he had whistled him up; when he fell into a long Panegyrick upon his Spaniel, who seem'd indeed excellent in his Kind: But I found the most remarkable Adventure of his Life was, that he had once like to have worried a Dissenting-Teacher.[7] The Master could

[b] a Remark / an Observation *Fol.* [c] it / that *Fol.* [d] grew / stood *Fol.*

[3] So few Tories attended the House of Commons in 1715 that some Lancashire Jacobites referred to it as a Rump Parliament (B.L. Stowe MS. 228, fo. 61).

[4] The Commercial Treaty with France (1713), supported by Bolingbroke and the Tory ministry, contained terms so favourable to France that it endangered British trade with Portugal, an ally during the war. When the treaty was debated in the Commons during May and June, the Whigs opposed it; they were joined by some 'whimsical' Tories, and the Commercial Treaty was defeated (*C.J.* xvii. 430; *Parl. Hist.* vi. 1210–13). The fox-hunter assumes that no good Churchman could be a Whig or a 'whimsical'.

[5] One recent 'Act for the better Preservation of the Game' was passed in 1710 (*Statutes* ix. 492).

[6] A reference to the arrest of suspected Jacobites after the suspension of habeas corpus (see *F.* 16, n. 2).

[7] Many High Church Tories hated the numerous dissenting academies in England. Sacheverell had claimed in 1709 that they taught fanaticism, regicide, and anarchy (*Perils of False Brethren*, p. 15). The Schism Act, passed by a sizeable majority in the Tory Commons in 1714, required all schoolmasters to conform to the Anglican communion (*Statutes* ix. 915).

hardly sit on his Horse for laughing all the while he was giving me the Particulars of this Story, which I found had mightily endeared his Dog to him, and as he himself told me, had made him a great Favourite among all the honest Gentlemen of the Country. We were at length diverted from this Piece of Mirth by a Post-Boy, who winding his Horn at us, my Companion gave him two or three Curses, and left the Way clear for him. *I fancy* said I, *that Post brings News from* Scotland. *I shall long to see the next* Gazette. *Sir*, says he, *I make it a Rule never to believe any of your printed News. We never see, Sir, how Things go, except now and then in* Dyer's *Letter, and I read that more for the Style than the News.*[8] *The Man has a cleaver Pen it must be own'd. But is it not strange that we should be making War upon Church of* England *Men, with* Dutch *and* Swiss *Soldiers, Men of Antimonarchical Principles?*[9] *These Foreigners will never be loved in* England, *Sir; they have not that Wit and Good-breeding that we have.* I must confess I did not expect to hear my new Acquaintance value himself upon these Qualifications, but finding him such a Critick upon Foreigners, I ask'd him if he had ever Travelled; He told me, he did not know what Travelling was good for, but to teach a Man to ride the Great Horse, to jabber *French*, and to talk against Passive-Obedience: To which he added, that he scarce ever knew a Traveller in his Life who had not forsook his Principles, and lost his Hunting-Seat. *For my Part*, says he, *I and my Father before me have always been for Passive-Obedience, and shall be always for opposing a Prince who makes use of Ministers that are of another Opinion. But where do you intend to Inn to Night?* (for we were now come in Sight of the next Town) *I can help you to a very good Landlord if you will go along with me. He's a lusty jolly Fellow, that lives well, at least three Yards in the Girt, and the best Church of* England *Man upon the Road.* I had a Curiosity to see this High-Church Inn-Keeper, as well as to enjoy more of the Conversation of my Fellow-Traveller, and therefore readily consented to[e] set our Horses together for that Night. As we rode Side by Side through[f] the Town, I was let into the Characters of all the principal Inhabitants whom we met in our Way. One was a Dog, another a Whelp, another a Cur, and another the Son of a Bitch, under which several Denominations were comprehended all that Voted on the

[e] consented to / consented with him to *Fol.* [f] through / into *Fol.*

[8] The fox-hunter prefers John Dyer's *News-Letters*, a conservative version of political news which was produced in script, to the government's printed newspaper, the *London Gazette*. Addison and Steele joked about Dyer in *S.* 43, *S.* 127, and *T.* 18.

[9] Of the 6,000 soldiers sent by the Dutch to assist in suppressing the rebellion, about 4,000 were Swiss mercenaries (*C.J.* xviii. 354).

Whig Side in the last Election of Burgesses. As for those of his own Party, he distinguished them by a Nod of his Head, and asking them how they did by their Christian Names. Upon our Arrival at the Inn, my Companion fetch'd out the jolly Landlord, who knew him by his Whistle. Many Endearments, and private Whispers passed between them; tho' it was easy to see, by the Landlord's scratching his Head, that Things did not go to their Wishes. The Landlord had swell'd his Body to a prodigious Size, and work'd up his Complection to a standing Crimson by his Zeal for the Prosperity of the Church, which he expressed every Hour of the Day, as his Customers dropt in, by repeated Bumpers. He had not time to go to Church himself, but as my Friend told me in my Ear, had headed a Mob at the pulling down two or three Meeting-Houses.[10] While Supper was preparing, he enlarged upon the Happiness of the neighbouring Shire; *For*, says he, *there is scarce a Presbyterian in the whole County, except the Bishop.*[11] In short, I found by his Discourse that he had learned a great deal of Politicks, but not one Word of Religion, from the Parson of his Parish; and, indeed, that he had scarce any other Notion of Religion, but that it consisted in Hating Presbyterians. I had a remarkable Instance of his Notions in this Particular. Upon seeing a poor decrepid Old Woman pass under the Window where we sate, he desired me to take Notice of her; and afterwards informed me, that she was generally reputed a Witch by the Country People, but that for his Part he was apt to believe she was a Presbyterian.[12]

Supper was no sooner served in, than he took occasion, from a Shoulder of Mutton that lay before us, to cry up the Plenty of *England*, which would be the happiest Country in the World, provided we would live within our selves. Upon which, he expatiated on the Inconveniencies of Trade, that carried from us the Commodities of our Country, and made a Parcel of

[10] In July 1715 the Commons read a letter from Richard Ames which described the damage done to seven meeting houses by one mob from Wolverhampton. Addison served on a committee which drew up an address to the King asking him to direct magistrates to prosecute such mobs vigorously and to have kept 'an exact Account . . . of the Losses and Damages . . . that the Sufferers may have full Compensation' (*C.J.* xviii. 227–8). Edmund Calamy complained in June 1716 about delays in receiving reparations for damages 'to so many places of worship' (*My Own Life*, 1830, ii. 355).

[11] Anglican clergymen who advocated toleration for dissenters were accused by High Churchmen of secretly favouring Presbyterianism (Burnet, *History* v. 70–1). In 1705 Bishop Hough of Lichfield complained to the Lords about 'the opprobrious names the clergy gave their bishops and the calumnies they laid on them, as they were in a plot to destroy the church' (*Parl. Hist.* vi 496–7).

[12] In *S.* 131, Will Honeycomb invites Sir Roger de Coverley to return to London but warns him not to bring back any country stories of 'Spirits and Witches' (*Spectator*, ii. 21).

Upstarts as rich as Men of the most ancient Families of *England.*[13] He then declared frankly, that he had always been against all Treaties and Alliances with Foreigners; *Our Wooden Walls*, says he, *are our Security, and we may bid Defiance to the whole World, especially if they should attack us when the Militia is out.*[14] I ventured to reply, that I had as great an Opinion of the *English* Fleet as he had; but I cou'd not see how they could be pay'd and mann'd, and fitted out, unless we encouraged Trade and Navigation.[15] He replied, with some Vehemence, That he would undertake to prove, Trade would be the Ruine of the *English* Nation. I would fain have put him upon it; but he contented himself with affirming it more eagerly, to which he added two or three Curses upon the *London* Merchants, not forgetting the Directors of the Bank. After Supper he asked me if I was an Admirer of Punch; and immediately called for a Sneaker. I took this Occasion to insinuate the Advantages of Trade, by observing to him, that Water was the only Native of *England* that could be made use of on this Occasion: But that the Lemons, the Brandy, the Sugar, and the Nutmeg, were all Foreigners. This put him into some Confusion; but the Landlord, who overheard me, brought him off, by affirming, That for constant use, there was no Liquor like a Cup of *English* Water, provided it had Malt enough in it. My Squire laughed heartily at the Conceit, and made the Landlord sit down with us. We sate pretty late over our Punch; and, amidst a great deal of improving Discourse, drank the Healths of several Persons in the Country, whom I had never heard of, that, they both assur'd me, were the ablest Statesmen in the Nation: And of some *Londoners*, whom they extoll'd to the Skies for their Wit, and who, I knew, passed in Town for silly Fellows. It being now Midnight, and my Friend perceiving by his Almanack that the Moon was up, he called for his Horses, and took a sudden Resolution to go to his House, which was at three Miles distance

[13] Defoe countered this country myth by arguing that 'most, if not all' of England's 'best Families, owe their Wealth and Rise, first or last, to the Oppulence and Profits of Trade' (*Review*, 6 Mar. 1705). Addison waged his own defence of trade in various *Spectator* essays; e.g. *Spectator*, i. 296, 448–9; iii. 67–71.

[14] The fox-hunter's point is that the navy and militia made a standing army and foreign alliances unnecessary. The Tories generally preferred the navy to the army, and Defoe countered such arguments in the *Review* (3 July 1707): 'those that cry'd up these wooden Walls, as an Equivalent to a good Army abroad, would soon have seen their ridiculous Notions, of *England*'s being able to defend her self against all the World, without the Help of Confederacies and Allies, fatally confuted.' The military strength of the militia was considered a joke (see *F.* 11, n. 1).

[15] When arguing against the war Swift frequently referred to the navy debt (*Prose Works* iii. 32, 34, 136, 170) and a statement of that debt in 1711 indicates that more than half of it was 'discharged by the South Sea Stock' (*C.J.* xvii. 20–1); such long term loans were often borrowed from trading companies and repaid with income from customs and excise (see *F.* 20, n. 6).

from the Town, after having bethought himself that he never slept well out of his own Bed. He shook me very heartily by the Hand at parting, and discover'd a great Air of Satisfaction in his Looks, that he had met with an Opportunity of showing his Parts, and left[g] me a much wiser Man than he found me.

W

Numb. XXIII *Friday, March* 9, 1716

Illis ira modum supra est, et sæpe venenum
Morsibus inspirant. — —

Virg.

IN the Wars of *Europe* which were waged among our Forefathers, it was usual for the Enemy, when there was a King in the Field, to demand by a Trumpet in what Part of the Camp he resided, that they might avoid firing upon the Royal Pavilion. Our Party-Contests in *England* were heretofore managed with the same kind of Decency and Good-Breeding. The Person of the Prince was always looked upon as Sacred; and whatever severe Usage his Friends or Ministers met with, none presumed to direct their Hostilities at their Soveraign.[2] The Enemies of our present Settlement are of such a coarse kind of Make, and so equally void of Loyalty and Good Manners, that they are grown Scurrilous upon the Royal Family, and treat the most exalted Characters with the most opprobrious Language.

This Petulance in Conversation is particularly observed to prevail among some of that Sex where it appears the most unbecoming and the most unnatural. Many of these act with the greater Licentiousness, because they know they can act with the greater Impunity. This Consideration, indeed, engages the most generous and well bred even of our She[a]

[g] and left / and had left *Fol.*   [a] our She / these Female *Fol.*

Motto. Virgil, *Georgics*, iv. 236–7: They are wrathful above measure and often breathe venom in their strings. [Addison has changed *læsaque* (and, when provoked . . .) to *et sæpe* (and often . . .).]

[2] The immunity of the crown was a principle the Whigs espoused in the late seventeenth century for more political reasons than Addison suggests. By assuming the monarch could do no wrong, an assumption the regicides clearly did not share, Parliament was able to criticize royal policies by impeaching ministers for having wrongly advised the monarch. By this means the Whigs successfully removed the Earl of Danby in 1679 (*C.J.* ix. 559–62, 574–5). The Tories attempted a similar tactic against William's foreign policies by impeaching Somers, Orford, and Halifax in 1701 (see *F.* 39, n. 13). In August 1715 Oxford used the Queen's immunity to defend Tory policies during her last years (Tindal, p. 435).

Malecontents, to make no ill Use of the Indulgence of our Law-givers; and to discover in their Debates at least the Delicacy of the Woman, if not the Duty of the Subject. But it is generally remarked, that every one of them who is a Shrew in domestick Life, is now become a Scold in Politicks. And as for those of the Party who are of a superior Rank and unblemished Vertue, it must be a melancholy Reflexion for them to consider, that all the Common Women of the Town are of their Side;[3] for which Reason they ought to preserve a more than ordinary Modesty in their Satyrical Excursions, that their Characters may not be liable to Suspicion.

If there is not some Method found out for allaying these Heats and Animosities among the Fair Sex, one does not know to what Outrages they may proceed. I remember a Heroe in *Scarron*, who finding himself opposed by a mix'd Multitide of both Sexes with a great deal of virulent Language, after having brought them to a Submission, gave Order (to keep 'em from doing further[b] Mischief) that the Men should be disarmed of their Clubs, and that the Women should have their Nails pared.[4] We are not yet reduced to the Necessity of applying such violent Remedies; but as we daily receive Accounts of Ladies batteling it on both Sides, and that those who appear against the Constitution make War upon their Antagonists by many unfair Practices and unwarrantable Methods, I think it is very convenient there should be a Cartel[5] settled between them. If they have not yet agreed upon any thing of this Nature among themselves, I would propose to them the following Plan, in which I have sketched out several Rules suited to the politest Sex in one of the most civilized Nations.

That in every Political Rencounter between Woman and Woman, no Weapon shall be made use of but the Tongue.

That in the Course of the Engagement, if either of the Combatants, finding herself hard prest by her Adversary, shall proceed to personal Reflexions or Discovery of Secrets, they shall be parted by the Standers-by.

That when both Sides are drawn up in a full Assembly, it shall not be lawful for above Five of them to talk at the same Time.

[b] further / *Fol.*; farther *8vo, 12mo.*

[3] This remark prodded someone to publish *Nanny Roc—d's Letter to a Member of the B—f Stake Club* in which a prostitute complains, '... hard is our Lot indeed if we must be stigmatiz'd as *Tories*, because the Errours of our Youth, and the Complacency of our Humour, has made our Conduct resemble some *Chevrel* Ladies in a few Particulars' (p. 2).

[4] Paul Scarron (1610–60), author of the *Roman comique*, numerous burlesques and comic plays. Although there are many similar battles in his works, this specific incident has not been identified.

[5] Cartel: a written agreement between warring enemies, usually relating to the exchange or ransom of prisoners (*O.E.D.*).

That if any shall detract from a Lady's Character, (unless she be absent,) the said Detractress shall be forthwith ordered to the lowest Place of the Room.

That none presume to speak disrespectfully of His Majesty, or any of the Royal Family, on Pain of Three Hours Silence.

That none be permitted to talk spightfully of the Court, unless they can produce Vouchers that they have been there.

That the making use of News which goes about in Whisper, unless the Author be produced, or the Fact well attested, shall be deemed Fighting with White Powder,[6] and contrary to the Laws of War.

That any one who produces Libels or Lampoons, shall be regarded in the same manner as one who shoots with poisoned Bullets.

That when a Lady is throughly convinced of the Falshood of any Story she has related, she shall give her Parole not to tell it for a certain Truth that Winter.

That when any Matter of Doubt arises, which cannot otherwise be decided, Appeal shall be made to a Toast, if there be any such in the Company.

That no Coquette, notwithstanding she can do it with the good Air, shall be allowed to Sigh for the Danger of the Church, or to Shiver at the Apprehensions of Fanaticism.

That when a Woman has talked an Hour and a half, it shall be lawful to call her down to Order.

As this Civil Discord among the Sisterhood of *Great Britain* is likely to engage them in a long and lingring War, consisting altogether of Drawn Battles, it is the more necessary that there should be a Cartel settled among them. Besides, as our *English* Ladies are at present the greatest Stateswomen in *Europe*, they will be in danger of making themselves the most unamiable Part of their Sex, if they continue to give a Loose to intemperate Language, and to a low kind of Ribaldry, which is not used among the Women of Fashion in any other Country.

Discretion and good Nature have been always looked upon as the distinguishing Ornaments of Female Conversation. The Woman, *whose Price is above Rubies*, has no Particular in the Character given of her by the Wise Man, more endearing, than that *she openeth her Mouth with Wisdom, and in her Tongue is the Law of Kindness.*[7] Besides, every fierce She-Zealot should consider, that however any of the other Sex may seem to applaud

[6] Francis Bacon reported that there were rumours about a white gunpowder, 'a mixture of petre and sulphur, without coal', which could 'discharge a piece without noise; which is a dangerous experiment, if it should be true: for it may cause secret murders' (*Works*, ii. 392).

[7] Prov. 31:10, 26.

her as a Partisan, there is none of them who would not be afraid of associating himself with her in any of the more private Relations of Life.

I shall only add, that there is no Talent so pernicious as Eloquence, to those who have it not under Command: For which Reason, Women who are so liberally gifted by Nature in this Particular, ought to study with the greatest Application, the Rules of Female Oratory, delivered in that excellent Treatise, entituld *The Government of the Tongue.*[8] Had that Author foreseen the Political Ferment which is now raised among the Sex, he would probably have made his Book larger by some Chapters than it is at present: But what is wanting in that Work, may, I hope, in some Measure, be supplyed by the above written Cartel.

Numb. XXIV *Monday, March* 12, 1716

Bellum importunum, cives, cum gente deorum
Invictisque viris geritis — — Virg.

A PHYSICIAN makes use of various Methods for the Recovery of Sick Persons; and tho' some of them are painful, and all of them disagreeable, his Patients are never angry at him, because they know he has nothing in view besides the restoring of them to a good State of Health. I am forced to treat the disaffected Part of His Majesty's Subjects in the same manner, and may therefore reasonably expect the same Returns of Good-Will. I propose nothing to my self but their Happiness as the End of all my Endeavours; and am forced to adapt different Remedies to those different Constitutions, which are to be found in such a distemper'd Multitude. Some of them can see the unreasonable, and some of them the ridiculous Side of wrong Principles, and, according to the different Frame of their Minds, reject an Opinion as it carries in it either the Appearance of Wickedness, or of Danger, or of Folly.

I have endeavoured to expose in these several Lights the Notions and Practices of those who are the Enemies to our present Establishment. But there is a Set of Arguments, which I have not yet touched upon, and which often succeed, when all others fail. There are many who will not quit a

[8] A popular religious tract attributed to Richard Allestree, which was first published in 1674; by 1716 more than ten editions had been published.

Motto. Virgil, *Aeneid*, xi. 305–6: Citizens, with a nation of gods and unconquerable heroes you wage unequal war.

Project, tho' they find it pernicious, or absurd: But will readily desist from it, when they are convinced it is impracticable. An Attempt to subvert the present Government is, God be thanked, of this Nature. I shall therefore apply the Considerations of this Paper rather to the Discretion than the Vertue of our Malecontents, who should act in the present Juncture of Affairs like experienced Gamesters, that throw up their Cards when they know the Game is in the Enemy's Hand, without giving themselves an unnecessary Vexation in playing it out.

In the Reign of our two last *British* Soveraigns, those who did not favour their Interest might be Ungenerous enough to act upon the Prospect of a Change, considering the precarious Condition of their Health, and their want of Issue to succeed them. But at present we enjoy a King of a long-lived Family, who is in the Vigour of His Age, and blest with a numerous Progeny. To this we may add His remarkable Steadiness in adhering to those Schemes which he has formed upon the maturest Deliberation, and that submissive Deference of his Royal Highness both from Duty and Inclination to all the Measures of his Royal Father.[2] Nor must we omit that Personal Valour so peculiar to His Majesty and His Illustrious House, which would be sufficient to Vanquish, as we find it actually Deterrs, both His foreign and domestick Enemies.

This Great Prince is supported by the whole Protestant Interest of *Europe*, and strengthened with a long Range of Alliances that reach from one End of the Continent to the other. He has a great and powerful King for His Son-in-Law;[3] and can Himself command when He pleases the whole Strength of an Electorate in the Empire. Such a Combination of Soveraigns puts one in Mind of the Apparition of Gods which discouraged *Aeneas* from opposing the Will of Heaven. When his Eyes were cleared of that mortal Cloud which hung upon them, he saw the several Celestial Deities acting in a Confederacy against him, and immediately gave up a Cause which was excluded from all Possibility of Success.[4]

But it is the greatest Happiness, as well as the greatest Pleasure of our Soveraign, that His chief Strength lies in His own Kingdoms. Both the Branches of our Legislature espouse His Cause and Interest with a

[2] Lady Mary Wortley Montagu claimed that by 1714 the Prince of Wales had lost 'all respect for his indulgent father. He downright abused his ministers, and [had] talked impertinently to his old grandmother ... which ended in such a coldness towards all his family as left him entirely under the government of his wife. The indolent Elector [George I] contented himself with showing his resentment by his silence towards him; and this was the situation the family first appeared in when they came into England' (*Account*, p. 119).

[3] The King's daughter, Sophia Dorothy, was married to Frederick William, Electoral Prince of Brandenburg, later Frederick I of Prussia.

[4] *Aeneid*, ii. 588–623.

becoming Duty and Zeal. The most considerable and wealthy of His Subjects are convinced, that the Prosperity of our Soveraign and His People are inseparable: And we are very well satisfied, that His Majesty, if the Necessity of Affairs should require it, might find, among the most Dutiful of His Subjects, Men celebrated for their Military Characters above any of the Age in which they live. There is no question but His Majesty will be as generally valued and beloved in His *British* as He is in His *German* Dominions, when He shall have time to make His Royal Vertues equally known among us. In the mean while we have the Satisfaction to find, that His Enemies have been only able to make ill Impressions upon the low and ignorant Rabble of the Nation; and to put the Dregs of the People into a Ferment.

We have already seen how poor and contemptible a Force has been raised by those who have dared to appear openly against His Majesty, and how they were headed and encouraged by Men whose Sense of their Guilt made them desperate in forming so rash an Enterprize, and dispirited in the Execution of it. But we have not yet seen that Strength which would be exerted in the Defence of His Majesty, the Protestant Religion, and the *British* Liberties, were the Danger great enough to require it. Should the King be reduced to the Necessity of setting up the Royal Standard, how many Thousands would range themselves under it! What a Concourse would there be of Nobles and Patriots! We should see Men of another Spirit than what has appeared among the Enemies to our Country, and such as would out-shine the rebellious Part of their Fellow-Subjects as much in their Gallantry as in their Cause.

I shall not so much suspect the Understandings of our Adversaries, as to think it necessary to enforce these Considerations, by putting them in Mind of that Fidelity and Allegiance which is so visible in His Majesty's Fleet and Army, or of many other Particulars which in all human Probability, will perpetuate our present Form of Government, and which may be suggested to them by their own private Thoughts.

The Party, indeed, that is opposite to our present happy Settlement, seem to be driven out of the Hopes of all human Methods for carrying on their Cause, and are therefore reduced to the poor Comfort of Prodigies and Old Women's Fables. They begin to see Armies in the Clouds, when all upon the Earth have forsaken them.[5] Nay, I have been lately shewn a

[5] A reference to the numerous political interpretations of the aurora borealis which appeared over London on 6 Mar. 1716. Many contemporaries describe the incident and various people's reactions to it: Dudley Ryder (*Diary*, 6, 7 Mar.); Countess Cowper (Diary, 6 Mar.); Anthony Corbiere's letter to Horatio Walpole, 9 Mar. (Plumb, *Walpole*, p. 221).

written Prophecy that is handed among them with great Secresy, by which it appears their[a] chief Reliance at present is upon a *Cheshire* Miller[6] that was born with two Thumbs upon one Hand.[b]

I have adressed this whole Paper to the Despair of our Malecontents, not with a Design to aggravate the Pain of it, but to use it as a Means of making them Happy. Let them seriously consider the Vexation and Disquietude of Mind that they are treasuring up for themselves, by struggling with a Power which will be always too hard for them; and by converting His Majesty's Reign into their own Misfortune, which every impartial Man must look upon as the greatest Blessing to his Country. Let them extinguish those Passions, which can only imbitter their Lives to them, and deprive them of their Share in the happiness of the Community. They may conclude that His Majesty, in spite of any Opposition they can form against him, will maintain His just Authority over them; and whatever Uneasiness they may give themselves, they can create none in Him, excepting only because[c] they prevent Him from exerting equally His natural Goodness and Benevolence to every Subject in His Dominions.

B

Numb. XXV *Friday, March* 16, 1716[a]

Quid est Sapientiæ? semper idem velle atque idem nolle. Senec.

If we may believe the Observation which is made of us by Foreigners, there is no Nation in *Europe* so much given to Change as the *English.* There are some who ascribe this to the Fickleness of our Climate; and others to the Freedom of our Government. From one or both of these Causes their Writers derive that Variety of Humours which appears among the People

[a] appears their / appears that their *Fol.* [b] with two Thumbs upon one Hand. / with two Thumbs. *Fol.* [c] excepting only because / but from the Concern that *Fol.*

[a]All editions read '*Friday, March* 17,' but 17 March was a Saturday.

[6] Robert Nixon, the Cheshire prophet, promised that 'a Miller, nam'd *Peter*, shall be born with two Heels on one Foot, and ... shall be Instrumental in delivering the Nation. A Boy shall be born with three Thumbs, and shall hold three King's Horses, while England shall three times be Won and Lost in one Day.' The 1715 edition of *Nixon's Cheshire Prophecy* assured readers that a boy with three thumbs and two heels was born in Budworth and that the boy, now eighteen years old, was 'a Loyal Subject to King *George*, zealous for the Protestant Succession ...' (pp. 9–13).

Motto. Seneca, *Epistles*, xx. 5: What is wisdom? Always wanting the same things, always refusing the same things.

in general, and that Inconsistency of Character which is to be found in almost every particular Person. But as a Man should always be upon his Guard against the Vices to which he is most exposed, so we[b] should take a more than ordinary Care not to lie at the Mercy of the Weather in our moral Conduct, nor to make a capricious Use of that Liberty which we enjoy by the Happiness of our Civil Constitution.

This Instability of Temper ought in a particular Manner to be check'd when it shews itself in Political Affairs, and disposes Men to wander from one Scheme of Government to another: Since such a Fickleness of Behaviour in publick Measures, cannot but be attended with very fatal Effects to our Country.[2]

In the first Place; It hinders any great Undertaking, which requires length of Time for its Accomplishment, from being brought to its due Perfection. There is not any Instance in History which better confirms this Observation, than that which is still fresh in every one's Memory. We engaged in the late War with a Design to reduce an exorbitant Growth of Power in the most dangerous Enemy to *Great-Britain.* We gained a long and wonderful Series of Victories, and had scarce any thing left to do, but to reap the Fruits of them: When on a sudden our Patience failed us; we grew tired of our Undertaking; and received Terms from those, who were upon the Point of giving us whatever we could have demanded of them.[3]

[b] exposed, so we / exposed, we *Fol.*

---

[2] This essay marks the beginning of the Whig campaign for the Septennial Act which extended the maximum term for the House of Commons from three to seven years. The Bill was introduced in the Lords on 10 Apr. 1716 and, after passing its third reading on 18 April, went to the Commons where it was passed on 26 Apr. (*L.J.* xx. 325; *C.J.* xviii. 425, 429–32). In the weeks between 17 Mar. and 5 Apr. there is evidence that many Whigs were unwilling to support the Bill (Percival Letterbook, 27 Mar.; H.M.C. *Stuart MSS.* ii. 84) but the large majority with which it passed suggests that the ministry used the Easter recess (28 Mar.–9 Apr.) to quiet dissent in the Whig ranks. Addison's task here and in *F.* 37 is to explain to the public some of the more altruistic reasons for the change. An important assumption in his argument here is that Parliament and the ministry shaped foreign policy, but as Burnet pointed out, 'all foreign negotiations were trusted entirely to the crown' (*History* iv. 479).

[3] In this reference to the War of the Spanish Succession and the Treaty of Utrecht which concluded it, Addison echoes the address of the Commons to the Queen in 1702 when they pledged support for 'reducing the exorbitant Power of *France*' (*C.J.* xiii. 782). He exaggerates the Allies' victories in the war—Malplaquet (1709) was their last major victory and the campaign in Spain was marked by more failure than success—and he also exaggerates the suddenness with which the nation lost patience with the war. Although Rochester and some Tories opposed direct involvement in the war from the beginning, both parties in the Commons agreed to the Queen's declaration of war (Tindal, iii. 545; *C.J.* xiii. 870). By 1708 the inordinate expense and the Whigs' ambitious war policies prompted Harley and St. John to consider joining Rochester's opposition (H.M.C. *Bath MSS.* i. 191). After the Tories gained control in 1710 and the Allies were defeated in Spain at Brihuega, the unpopularity of the war reached a new peak and peace negotiations were begun with France, although previous negotiations at The Hague and Gertruydenberg had failed.

This Mutability of Mind in the *English*, makes the ancient Friends of our Nation very backward to engage with us in such Alliances as are necessary for our mutual Defence and Security. It is a common Notion among Foreigners, That the *English* are good Confederates in an Enterprize which may be dispatched within a short Compass of Time; but that they are not to be depended upon in a Work which cannot be finished without Constancy and Perseverance. Our late Measures have so blemished the National Credit in this Particular, that those Potentates who are entered into Treaties with His present Majesty, have been solely encouraged to it by their Confidence in His Personal Firmness and Integrity.[4]

I need not, after this, suggest to my Reader the Ignominy and Reproach that falls upon a Nation which distinguishes itself among its Neighbours by such a wavering and unsettled Conduct.

This our Inconsistency in the Pursuit of Schemes which have been thoroughly digested, has as bad an Influence on our Domestick as on our Foreign Affairs. We are told, that the famous Prince of *Conde*[5] used to ask the *English* Ambassador, upon the Arrival of a Mail, *Who was Secretary of State in* England *by that Post?* as a Piece of Raillery upon the Fickleness of our Politicks. But what has render'd this a Misfortune to our Country, is, that Publick Ministers have no sooner made themselves Masters of their Business, than they have been dismissed from their Employments; and that this Disgrace has befallen very many of them, not because they have deserved it, but because the People love to see new Faces in high Posts of Honour.

It is a double Misfortune to a Nation, which is thus given to Change, when they have a Soveraign at the Head of them, that is prone to fall in with all the Turns and Veerings of the People. *Sallust*, the Gravest of all the *Roman* Historians, who had form'd his Notions of Regal Authority from the Manner in which he saw it exerted among the Barbarous Nations, makes the following Remark: *Plerumque Regiæ Voluntates uti vehementes, sic mobiles, sæpe ipsæ sibi adversæ. The Wills of Kings, as they are generally vehement, are likewise very fickle, and at different Times opposite to themselves.*[6]

[4] The Treaty of Utrecht was negotiated without including the Empire, thus contradicting the solidarity pledged in the eighth article of the Treaty of Grand Alliance (1701), and this inconsistency was cited by advocates of septennial elections (*Pol. State* xi. 498). One example of how treaties were used in party battles was the Tory Commons' examination of the 1709 Barrier Treaty which was negotiated by the Whig Lord Townshend; in 1712 the Commons resolved that the treaty was destructive to British interests and that 'Lord Viscount *Townshend* ... and all those who advised the Ratifying of the said Treaty, are Enemies to the Queen and Kingdom' (*C.J.* xvii. 92).

[5] Louis II de Bourbon, Prince of Condé (1621–86).

[6] *Bellum Iugurthinum*, 113.

Were there any Colour for this general Observation, how much does it redound to the Honour of such Princes who are Exceptions to it!

The natural Consequence of an unsteady Government, is the Perpetuating of Strife and Faction among a divided People.[7] Whereas a King who persists in those Schemes which he has laid, and has no other View in them but the Good of his Subjects, extinguishes all Hopes of Advancement in those who would grow Great by an Opposition to His Measures, and insensibly unites the Contending Parties in their Common Interest.

Queen *Elizabeth*, who makes the greatest Figure among our *English* Soveraigns, was most eminently remarkable for that Steadiness and Uniformity which ran through all her Actions during that long and glorious Reign. She kept up to her chosen Motto in every part of her Life; and never lost Sight of those great Ends, which she proposed to herself on her Accession to the Throne, the Happiness of her People, and the Strengthening of the Protestant Interest. She often interposed her Royal Authority to break the Cabals which were forming against her First Ministers, who grew old and died in those Stations which they filled with so great Abilities. By this Means she baffled the many Attempts of her foreign and domestick Enemies, and entirely broke the whole Force and Spirit of that Party among her Subjects which was Popishly affected, and which was not a little Formidable in the Beginning of Her Reign.[8]

The frequent Changes and Alterations in publick Proceedings, the Multiplicity of Schemes introduced one upon another, with the Variety of short-lived Favourites, that prevailed in their several Turns under the Government of Her successors, have by Degrees broken us into those unhappy Distinctions and Parties which have given so much Uneasiness to our Kings, and so often endangered the Safety of their People.

I question not but every Impartial Reader hath been before-hand with me, in considering on this Occasion, the Happiness of our Country under the Government of His present Majesty; who is so deservedly Famous for an inflexible Adherence to those Counsels which have a visible Tendency to the publick Good, and to those Persons who heartily concur with him in promoting these His generous Designs.

[7] The current 'violent and lasting Heats and Animosities among the Subjects of this Realm', one major argument for less frequent elections, was included in the Act's Preamble; triennial elections were blamed for exacerbating such domestic turmoils (*Statutes at Large*, 1735, iv. 675).

[8] Elizabeth's motto was *Semper Eadem* (Always the same) and Camden describes one example of the Queen using her authority to break a Popish cabal against William Cecil in 1569 (*Annals*, 1635, p. 104).

A Prince of this Character will be dreaded by his Enemies, and served with Courage and Zeal by his Friends; and will either instruct us by his Example, to fix the Unsteadiness of our Politicks, or by his Conduct, hinder it from doing us any Prejudice.

Upon the Whole, as there is no Temper of Mind more un-manly in a private Person, nor more pernicious to the Publick in a Member of a Community, than that Changeableness with which we are too justly branded by all our Neighbours, it is to be hoped that the sound Part of the Nation will give no further[c] Occasion for this Reproach, but continue steady to that happy Establishment which has now taken place among us. And as Obstinacy in Prejudices which are detrimental to our Country, ought not to be mistaken for that vertuous Resolution and Firmness of Mind which is necessary to our Preservation, it is to be wished that the Enemies to our Constitution, would so far indulge themselves in this National Humour, as to come into one Change more, by falling in with that Plan of Government which at present they think fit to oppose.[9] At least we may expect they will be so wise as to shew a Legal Obedience to the Best of Kings, who profess the Duty of Passive Obedience to the Worst.

Numb. XXVI *Monday, March* 19, 1716

Bella Viri pacemque gerant, queis bella gerenda.
Virg.

WHEN the *Athenians* had long contended against the Power of *Philip*, he demanded of them to give up their Orators, as well knowing their Opposition would be soon at an end if it were not irritated from Time to

[c] further / *Fol.*; farther *8vo, 12mo.*

[9] Steele originally opposed the Septennial Bill and planned to answer this *Freeholder.* His essay is among the Blenheim manuscripts and was never published; it concludes, 'I wish as Heartily as the Freeholder that they would follow his Advice, but cannot agree with Him that *one Change more* should extend to what we all fear his discourse aims at, the suspension of the Trienniall Act' (the complete draft is published in *Periodical Journalism*, pp. 330–2). Steele's biographer, Calhoun Winton, suggests that Addison met with Steele and persuaded him to support the Bill (*Sir Richard Steele, M.P.*, Baltimore, 1970, pp. 82–4).

Motto. Virgil, *Aeneid*, vii. 444: Let men have the management of war and peace, for war ought to be managed by them.

Time by these Tongue-Warriors.[2] I have endeavoured for the same Reason to gain our Female Adversaries, and by that Means to disarm the Party of its principal Strength. Let them give us up their Women, and we know by Experience how inconsiderable a Resistance we are to expect from their Men.

This sharp political Humour has but lately prevailed in so great a Measure as it now does among the beautiful Part of our Species. They used to employ themselves wholly in the Scenes of a domestick Life, and provided a Woman could keep her House in Order, she never troubled herself about regulating the Commonwealth. The Eye of the Mistress was wont to make her Pewter shine, and to inspect every Part of her Household-Furniture as much as her Looking-Glass. But at present our discontented Matrons are so conversant in Matters of State, that they wholly neglect their private Affairs; for we may always observe that a Gossip in Politicks, is a Slattern in her Family.

It is indeed a melancholy Thing to see the Disorders of a Houshold that is under the Conduct of an angry Stateswoman, who lays out all her Thoughts upon the Publick, and is only attentive to find out Miscarriages in the Ministry. Several Women of this Turn are so earnest in contending for Hereditary Right, that they wholly neglect the Education of their own Sons and Heirs; and are so taken up with their Zeal for the Church, that they cannot find Time to teach their Children their Catechism. A Lady who thus intrudes into the Province of the Men, was so astonishing a Character among the old *Romans*, that when *Amœsia* presented herself to speak before the Senate, they looked upon it as a Prodigy, and sent Messengers to inquire of the Oracle what it might portend to the Commonwealth.[3]

It would be manifestly to the Disadvantage of the *British* Cause, should our pretty Loyalists profess[a] their Indifference in State-Affairs, while their disaffected Sisters are thus industrious to the Prejudice of their Country; and accordingly we have the Satisfaction to find our She-Associates are not idle upon this Occasion. It is owing to the good Principles of these His

[a] profess / maintain *Fol.*

[2] It was Philip's son, Alexander the Great, who made the demand. After he had conquered Thebes and enslaved the captives, Athens was eager to avoid the same fate. Alexander 'sent to *Athens* to demand Ten of the Orators to be deliver'd up to him, (amongst whom *Demosthenes* and *Lycurgus* were the chief), because they had stirr'd up the People against him' (Diodorus, *Bibliotheca Historica*, xvii. 1, trans. Booth).

[3] Amaesia Sentia pleaded her own defence before the Praetor Titius, a contemporary of Cicero, and was acquitted (Valerius Maximus, *Factorum ac Dictorum Memorabilia*, viii. 3; Plutarch, *Lives*, 1716 edn., i. 204).

Majesty's fair and faithful Subjects, that our Country-Women appear no less amiable in the Eyes of the Male-World, than they have done in former Ages. For where a great Number of Flowers grow, the Ground at a Distance seems entirely cover'd with them, and we must walk into it, before we can distinguish the several Weeds that spring up in such a beautiful Mass of Colours. Our great Concern is, to find that Deformity can arise among so many Charms, and that the most lovely Parts of the Creation can make themselves the most disagreeable. But it is an Observation of the Philosophers, that the best Things may be corrupted into the worst; and the Ancients did not scruple to affirm, that the Furies and the Graces were of the same Sex.

As I should do the Nation and themselves good Service, if I could draw the Ladies, who still hold out against His Majesty, into the Interest of our present Establishment, I shall propose to their serious Consideration, the several Inconveniencies which those among them undergo who have not yet surrender'd to the Government.

They should first reflect on the great Sufferings and Persecutions to which they expose themselves by the Obstinacy of their Behaviour. They lose their Elections in every Club where they are set up for Toasts. They are obliged by their Principles to stick a Patch on the most unbecoming Side of their Foreheads.[4] They forego the Advantage of Birth-Day Suits. They are insulted by the Loyalty of Claps and Hisses every Time they appear at a Play. They receive no Benefit from the Army, and are never the better for all the young Fellows that wear Hats and Feathers. They are forced to live in the Country and feed their Chicken; at the same Time that they might shew themselves at Court, and appear in Brocade, if they behaved themselves well. In short, what must go to the Heart of every fine Woman, they throw themselves quite out of the Fashion.

The above-mention'd Motive must have an Influence upon the gay Part of the Sex; and as for those who are acted by more sublime and moral Principles, they should consider, that they cannot signalize themselves as Malecontents, without breaking through all the amiable Instincts and softer Vertues, which are peculiarly Ornamental to Womankind. Their timorous, gentle, modest Behaviour; their Affability, Meekness, Good-Breeding, and many other beautiful Dispositions of Mind must be sacrificed to a blind and furious Zeal for they do not know what. A Man is startled when he sees a pretty Bosom heaving with such Party-Rage, as is disagreeable even in that Sex which is of a more coarse and rugged Make.

[4] Addison discusses party patches at greater length in *S.* 81, but he does not say which side of the face represented which party.

And yet such is our Misfortune, that we sometimes see a Pair of Stays ready to burst with Sedition; and hear the most masculine Passions exprest in the sweetest Voices. I have lately been told of a Country-Gentlewoman, pretty much famed for this Virility of Behaviour in Party-Disputes, who, upon venting her Notions very freely in a strange Place, was carry'd before an honest Justice of Peace.[b] This prudent Magistrate observing her to be a large black Woman, and finding by her Discourse that she was no better than a Rebel in a Riding-Hood, began to suspect her for my Lord *Nithisdale*;[5] till a Stranger came to her Rescue, who assur'd him, with Tears in his Eyes, that he was her Husband.

In the next Place our *British* Ladies may consider, that by interesting themselves so zealously in the Affairs of the Publick, they are engaged, without any necessity, in the Crimes which are often committed even by the Best of Parties, and which they are naturally exempted from by the Privilege of their Sex. The worst Character a Female could formerly arrive at, was of being an ill Woman; but by their present Conduct, she may likewise deserve the Character of an ill Subject. They come in for their Share of political Guilt, and have found a Way to make themselves much greater Criminals, than their Mothers before them.

I have great Hopes that these Motives, when they are assisted by their own Reflections, will incline the Fair Ones of the adverse Party to come over to the national Interest, in which their own is so highly concern'd; especially if they consider, that by these superfluous Employments which they take upon them as Partisans, they do not only dip themselves in an unnecessary Guilt, but are obnoxious to a Grief and Anguish of Mind, which doth not properly fall within their Lot. And here I would advise every one of these exasperated Ladies, who indulges that opprobrious Eloquence which is so much[c] in fashion, to reflect on *Æsop*'s Fable of the Viper. *This little Animal*, says the old Moralist, *chancing to meet with a file, began to lick it with her Tongue till the Blood came; which gave her a very silly Satisfaction, as imagining the Blood came from the File, notwithstanding all the Smart was in her own Tongue.*[6]

U

[b] of Peace / *Fol., 12mo*; of the Peace *8vo.*   [c] is so much / *Fol., 12mo*; is much *8vo.*

[5] William Maxwell, fifth Earl of Nithsdale, was taken prisoner at Preston, was impeached by Parliament and sentenced to execution on 9 Feb. 1716 (see *F.* 31, n. 4). The night before his execution was to take place he escaped from the Tower in a woman's riding hood which his wife had smuggled in with her. Lady Nithsdale's detailed account of the escape is published in Henrietta Tayler, *Lady Nithsdale*, 1939, pp. 46–58.

[6] Fable 44, Sir Roger L'Estrange's *Aesop* (1708); the moral of the tale is: 'Tis a Madness to stand Biting and Snapping at any thing to no manner of purpose, more then the Gratifying of an Impotent Rage, in the fancy of Hurting Another, when in Truth, we only Wound our selves' (pp. 57–8).

Numb. XXVII *Friday, March* 23, 1716

———*dii Visa secundant.*

Luc.

IT is an old Observation, that a Time of Peace is always a Time of Prodigies; for as our News-Writers must adorn their Papers with that which the Criticks call *The Marvellous*, they are forced in a dead calm of Affairs to[a] ransack every Element for proper Materials, and either to astonish their Readers from Time to Time with a strange and wonderful Sight, or be content to lose their Custom. The Sea is generally filled with Monsters when there are no Fleets upon it. Mount *Ætna* immediately began to rage upon the Extinction of the Rebellion: And woe to the People of *Catanea*, if the Peace continues; for they are sure to be shaken every Week with Earthquakes, till they are relieved by the Siege of some other great Town in *Europe*. The Air has likewise contributed its Quota of Prodigies. We had a blazing Star by the late Mail from *Genoa*; and in the present Dearth of Battles have been very opportunely entertained, by Persons of undoubted Credit, with a civil War in the Clouds, where[b] our sharp-sighted Malecontents discovered many Objects, invisible to an Eye that is dim'd by *Whig*-Principles.

I question not but this Paper will fall in with the present Humour, since it contains a very remarkable Vision of a *Highland* Seer, who is famous among the Mountains, and known by the Name of *Second-Sighted Sawney*.[2] Had he been able to Write, we might probably have seen this Vision sooner in Print; for it happened to him very early in the late hard Winter; and is transmitted to me by a Student of *Glasgow*, who took the whole Relation

[a] forced in a dead calm of Affairs, to / forced to *Fol.* [b] where / in which *Fol.*

Motto. Lucan, *Pharsalia*, i. 635: The gods favour what we have witnessed.

[2] John Aubrey, in 'An Accurate Account of Second-Sighted-Men', attributes this capacity for visions to the Scots, the Irish, and the Laplanders (*Miscellanies*, 1696, pp. 149–79). The most notable second-sighted person in England at this time was Duncan Campbell who was born in Lapland of a Scottish father. Although deaf and dumb, he made a profitable career in London by fortune-telling; see Defoe's *History of the Life and Adventures of Mr. Duncan Campbell* (1720). Addison also used the dream fable for political purposes in the *Spectator* (e.g. *S.* 3), a device which Smithers claims 'enabled him to make certain premises and to attach consequences to them without any logical sequence of reasoning, the simplest and most effective of all forms of political propaganda when directed to a relatively uninstructed audience' (*Addison*, p. 213).

from him, and stuck close to the Facts, though he has delivered them in his own Stile.

Sawney was descended of an ancient Family, very much renowned for their Skill in Prognosticks. Most of his Ancestors were Second-Sighted, and his Mother but narrowly escaped being burnt for a Witch. As he was going out one Morning very early to steal a Sheep, he was seized on the sudden with a Fit of Second-Sight. The Face of the whole Country about him was changed in the Twinkling of an Eye, and presented him with a wide Prospect of new Scenes and Objects, which he had never seen till that Day.

He discovered at a great Distance from him a large Fabrick, which cast such a glistering Light about it, that it looked like a huge Rock of Diamond. Upon the Top of it was planted a Standard, streaming in a strong Northern Wind, and embroidered with a Mixture of Thistles and Flower-de-luces. As he was amusing himself with this strange Sight, he heard a Bagpipe at some Distance behind him, and, turning about, saw a General, who seemed very much animated with the Sound of it, marching towards him at the Head of a numerous Army.[3] He learnt, upon Enquiry, that they were making a Procession to the Structure which stood before him, and which he found was the *Temple of Rebellion.* He immediately struck in with them; but described this March to the Temple with so much Horrour, that he shivered every Joint all[c] the while he spoke of it. They were forced to clamber over so many Rocks, and to tread upon the Brink of so many Precipices, that they were very often in danger of their Lives. *Sawney* declared, that for his own Part, he walked in fear of his Neck every Step he took. Upon their coming within a few Furlongs of the Temple, they passed through a very thick Grove, consecrated to a Deity who was known by the Name of *Treason.* They here dispersed themselves into abundance of Labyrinths and covered Walks that led to the Temple. The Path was so very slippery, the Shade so exceeding gloomy, and the whole Wood so full of Ecchoes, that they were forced to march with the greatest Wariness, Circumspection[d] and Silence. They at length arrived at a great Gate, which was the principal Avenue to that magnificent Fabrick. *Sawney* stood some Time at the Entrance to observe the Splendour of the Building, and was not a little entertained with a prodigious Number of Statues, which

[c] Joint all / Joint of him all *Fol.* [d] Wariness, Circumspection / Caution *Fol.*

[3] The banner is the Pretender's and the general is the Earl of Mar. The Jacobites used various banners and Patten describes one which was reputedly made by the wife of the rebel Lord Kenmure: one side was blue with the Scottish arms in gold, the other side had a thistle with the motto, 'No Union', below it (*Late Rebellion*, p. 34).

were planted up and down in a spacious Court that lay before it; but, upon examining it more nicely, he found the whole Fabrick, which made such a glittering Appearance, and seemed Impregnable, was composed of Ice, and that the several Statues which seemed at a distance to[e] be made of the whitest Marble, were nothing else but so many Figures in Snow. The Front of the Temple was very curiously adorned with Stars and Garters, Ducal Coronets, General's Staffs, and many other Emblems of Honour wrought in the most beautiful Frost-Work. After having stood at gaze some Time before this great Gate, he discovered on it an Inscription, signifying it to be the *Gate of Perjury*. There was erected[f] near it a great Colossus in Snow that had two Faces, and was drest like a *Jesuit*, with one of its Hands upon a Book, and the other grasping a Dagger. Upon entering into the Court, he took a particular Survey of several of the Figures. There was Sedition with a Trumpet in her Hand, and Rapine in the Garb of a Highlander: Ambition, Envy, Disgrace, Poverty, and Disappointment, were all of them represented under their proper Emblems. Among other Statues,[g] he observed that of Rumour whispering an Ideot in the Ear, who was the Representative of Credulity; and Faction embracing with her hundred Arms an old-fashioned Figure in a Steeple-Crown'd Hat, that was design'd to express a cunning old Gipsy, call'd Passive-Obedience.[4] Zeal too had a Place among the rest, with a Bandage over her Eyes, tho' one would not have expected to have seen her represented in Snow. But the most remarkable Object in this Court-Yard, was a huge Tree that grew up before the Porch of the Temple, and was of the same kind with that, which *Virgil* tells us flourished at the Entrance of the infernal Regions. For it bore nothing but Dreams, which hung in Clusters under every Leaf of it.[5] The travellers refreshed themselves in the Shade of this Tree before they entered the *Temple of Rebellion*, and after their Frights and Fatigues, received great Comfort in the Fruit which fell from it. At length the Gates of the Temple flew open; and the Crowd rushed into it. In the Centre of it was a grim Idol, with a Sword in the Right Hand, and a Firebrand[h] in the Left. The Fore-part of the Pedestal was curiously embossed with a Triumph, while the Back-part, that lay more out of Sight, was filled with Gibbets and Axes. This dreadful Idol is worshipped, like several of old,

[e] seemed at a distance to / seemed to *Fol.* [f] was erected / stood *Fol.*
[g] Statues / Figures *Fol.* [h] Firebrand / Torch *Fol.*

[4] Lady Mary Wortley Montagu wrote in 1711 that 'all the High Church Ladies affect to wear Heads in the Imitation of Steeples' (*Complete Letters* i. 70).

[5] *Aeneid*, vi. 282–4: In the middle, a huge, dark elm extends its branches and aged arms. Empty dreams are commonly said to possess that place and under every leaf they cling.

with human Sacrifices, and his Votaries were consulting among themselves, how to gratify him with Hecatombs; when, on a sudden, they were surprized with the Alarm of a great Light which appeared in the Southern Part of the heavens, and made its Progress directly towards them. This Light appeared as a great Mass of Flame, or rather Glory, like that of the Sun in its Strength. There were three Figures in the midst of it, who were known by their several Hieroglyphicks, to be Religion, Loyalty, and Valour. The last had a graceful Air, a blooming Countenance, and a Star upon its Breast, which shot forth[i] several pointed Beams of a peculiar Lustre. The Glory which encompassed them, covered the Place,[j] and darted its Rays with so much Strength, that the whole Fabrick and all its Ornaments began to melt. The several Emblems of Honour, which were wrought on the Front in the brittle Materials above-mentioned, trickled away under the first Impressions of the Heat. In short, the Thaw was so violent, that the Temple and Statues ran off in a sudden Torrent, and the whole Winter Piece was dissolved. The covered Walks were laid open by the Light which shone through every Part of them, and the Dream-Tree withered like the famous Gourd, that was smitten by the Noon-Day Sun.[6] As for the Votaries, they left the Place with the greatest Precipitation, and dispersed themselves by a Flight into a Thousand different Paths among the Mountains.

Numb. XXVIII *Monday, March* 26, 1716

— — — Incendia lumen
Præbebant, aliquisque malo fuit usus in illo.
Ov. Met.

SIR *Francis Bacon*, in the Dedication before his History of *Henry* the Seventh, observes, that peaceable Times are the best to live in, though not so proper to furnish Materials for a Writer: As hilly Countries afford the most entertaining Prospects, though a Man would chuse to travel through

[i] forth / from it *Fol.* [j] the Place / the whole Place *Fol.*

[6] The gourd which had sheltered Jonah from the sun (Jonah 4:6–10).

Motto. Ovid, *Metamorphoses*, ii. 331–2: The flames supplied the light and there was some advantage in that calamity.

a plain One.[2] To this we may add, That the Times, which are full of Disorders and Tumults, are likewise the fullest of Instruction. History, indeed, furnishes us with very distinct Accounts of Factions, Conspiracies, Civil Wars and Rebellions, with the fatal Consequences that attend them: But they do not make such deep and lasting Impressions on our Minds, as Events of the same Nature, to which we have ourselves been Witnesses, and in which we or our Friends and Acquaintance have been Sufferers. As Adversity makes a Man Wise in his private Affairs, civil Calamities give him Prudence and Circumspection in his publick Conduct.

The Miseries of the Civil War under the Reign of King *Charles* the First, and the Consequences which ensued upon them, did, for many Years, deter the Inhabitants of our Island from the Thoughts of engaging anew in such desperate Undertakings; and convinced them, by fatal Experience, that nothing could be so pernicious to the *English*, and so opposite to the Genius of the People, as the Subversion of Monarchy. In the like Manner we may hope, that the great Expences brought upon the Nation by the present Rebellion; the Sufferings of innocent People, who have lived in that Place which was the Scene of it; with that dreadful Prospect of Ruin and Confusion which must have followed its Success, will secure us from the like Attempts for the future, and fix His Majesty upon the Throne of *Great Britain*; especially when those who are prompted to such wicked Practices reflect upon the just Punishments to which the Criminals have exposed themselves, and the Miseries in which they have involved their Relations, Friends and Families.

It will be likewise worth their while to consider, how such Tumults and Riots, as have been encouraged by many, who, we may hope, did not propose to themselves such fatal Consequences, lead to a Civil War: And how naturally that seditious Kind of Conversation, which many seem to think consistent with their Religion and Morality, ends in an open Rebellion. I question not but the more vertuous and considerate Part of our Malecontents are now stung with a very just Remorse for this their Manner of Proceeding, which has so visibly tended to the Destruction of their Friends, and the Sufferings of their Country. This may, at the same Time, prove an instructive Lesson to the Boldest and Bravest among the disaffected, not to build any Hopes upon the talkative Zealots of their Party; who have shewn by their whole Behaviour, that their Hearts are equally filled with Treason and Cowardice. An Army of Trumpeters

[2] 'And it is with times as it is with ways. Some are more up-hill and down-hill, and some are more flat and plain; and the one is better for the liver, and the other for the writer' (*Works* vi. 25).

would give as great a Strength to a Cause, as this Confederacy of Tongue-Warriours; who, like those military Musicians, content themselves with animating their Friends to Battle, and run out of the Engagement upon the first Onset.

But one of the most useful Maxims we can learn from the present Rebellion, is, That nothing can be more contemptible and insignificant, than the Scum of a People, when they are instigated against a King, who is supported by the Two Branches of the Legislature. A Mob may pull down a Meeting House, but will never be able to over-turn a Government, which has a courageous[a] and wise Prince at the Head of it, and one who is[b] zealously assisted by the great Council of the Nation, who best know the Value of him. The Authority of the Lords and Commons of *Great Britain*, in Conjunction with that of their Soveraign, is not to be controul'd by a tumultuary Rabble. It is big with Fleets and Armies, can fortify itself with what Laws it shall judge proper for its own Defence, can command the Wealth of the Kingdom for the Security of the People, and engage the whole Protestant Interest of *Europe* in so good and just a Cause. A disorderly Multitude contending with the Body of the Legislature, is like a Man in a Fit under the Conduct of one in the Fullness of his Health and Strength. Such a one[c] is sure to be over-ruled in a little Time, though he deals about his Blows, and exerts himself in the most furious Convulsions while the Distemper is upon him.

We may further[d] learn from the Course of the present Rebellion, who among the foreign States in our Neighbourhood are the true and natural Friends of *Great Britain*, if we observe which of them gave us their Assistance in reducing our Country to a State of Peace and Tranquility; and which of them used their Endeavours to heighten our Confusions, and plunge us into all the Evils of a Civil War.[3] I shall only take Notice under this Head, that in former Ages it was the constant Policy[e] of *France* to raise and cherish intestine Feuds and Discords in the Isle of *Great Britain*, that

[a] courageous/valiant *Fol.* [b] and one who is/and is *Fol.* [c] Strength. Such a one/Strength; who *Fol.* [d] further/*Fol.*; farther *8vo*, *12mo*. [e] Policy/Politicks *Fol.*

[3] The 6,000 troops the Dutch sent began arriving in England on 15 November (*St. James's Evening Post*, 15–17 Nov. 1715), too late to participate in the battle of Sheriffmuir (13 Nov.) or the siege of Preston (12–13 Nov.) but in time to reinforce Argyll and Cadogan in their pursuit of Jacobites in the highlands during the early months of 1716. Because the Regent supported the claims of the Pretender less enthusiastically than Louis XIV had, the French gave the Pretender less assistance in 1715 than he had received in 1708. Similarly, the Spanish had promised to aid the Pretender but their assistance was meagre and very slow to arrive (Bolingbroke, *Letter to Windham*, 135, 184–5, 198–9).

we might either fall a Prey into their Hands, or that they might prosecute their Designs upon the Continent with less Interruption. Innumerable Instances of this Nature occur in History. The most remarkable One was that in the Reign of King *Charles* the First. Though that Prince was married to a Daughter of *France*, and was personally beloved and esteemed in the *French* Court, it is well known that they abetted both Parties in the Civil War, and always furnished Supplies to the weaker Side, least there should be an End put to those fatal Divisions.[4]

We might also observe, that this Rebellion has been a Means of discovering to His Majesty, how much he may depend upon the Professions and Principles of the several[f] Parties among his own Subjects; who are those Persons that have espoused his Interests with Zeal or Indifference, and who[g] among them are influenced to their Allegiance by Places, Duty, or Affection. But as these, and several other Considerations, are obvious to the Thoughts of every Reader, I shall conclude, with observing how naturally many of those who distinguish themselves by the Name of the *High-Church*, unite themselves to the Cause of *Popery*; since it is manifest that all the Protestants concerned in the Rebellion, were such as gloried in this Distinction.

It would be very unjust, to charge all who have ranged themselves under this New Denomination,[h] as if they had done it with a Design to favour the Interests of Popery.[5] But it is certain that many of them, who at their first setting out were most averse to the Doctrines of the Church of *Rome*, have, by the Cunning of our Adversaries, been inspired with such an unreasonable

[f] several/different *Fol.* [g] who/which *Fol.* [h] this New Denomination/*Fol.*, *12mo*; this Denomination *8vo.*

[4] According to Clarendon, Richelieu recognized the French advantage in a British civil war and sent arms and encouragement to the Scots 'to warm that people into rebellion' (*History* i. 166–7; iv. 159–60). He also undermined Charles's support in Parliament and denied Queen Henrietta, Louis XIII's sister, asylum in France (ii. 415; iii. 240; iv. 160). Mazarin later allowed Henrietta asylum, but he offered Charles only 'little and ordinary supplies', more to 'enable him to continue the struggle, than to see him victorious over his enemies' (iv. 161).

[5] Burnet claims 'this New Denomination' began at the Convocation of 1702 when 'divisions ran through the whole body of the clergy, and to fix these, new names were found out: they were distinguished by the names of *high-church* and *low-church*' (*History* v. 70). However, High Churchman (used in a religious sense) predates 1702: in 1695 William Wake described Lord Charberry as one because 'He bows at going into Chappell, & at the Name of Jesus . . . & seems to mind little in his family more than y[t] they strictly conform to the Church Service & Ceremonies' (Bodl. Ballard MS. 3, fo. 14). Less than a year after Addison's *Freeholder*, John Toland described High Churchmen as treating 'all Protestants abroad and Dissenters at home as no Christians, so farr are they from acknowledging them as their brethren' and claimed they were 'for the Pretender, if not for Popery' (*State Anatomy*, pp. 24–5).

Aversion to their Protestant Brethren, and taught to think so favourably of the *Roman-Catholick* Principles, (not to mention the Endeavours that have been used to reconcile the Doctrines of the Two Churches, which are in themselves as opposite as Light and Darkness) that they have been drawn over insensibly into its Interests.[6] It is no wonder, therefore, that so many of these deluded Zealots have been engaged in a Cause which they at first abhorr'd, and have wished or acted for the Success of an Enterprize, that might have ended in the Extirpation of the Protestant Religion in this Kingdom, and in all *Europe*. In short, they are like the *Syrians*, who were first smitten with Blindness, and unknowingly led out of their Way into the Capital of their Enemy's Country; insomuch that the Text tells us, *When they opened their Eyes, they found themselves in the midst of* Samaria.[7]

D

Numb. XXIX — *Friday, March* 30, 1716

Dis te minorem quod geris, imperas.
Hinc omne principium, huc refer exitum.
Dii multa neglecti dederunt
Hesperiæ mala luctuosæ.

Hor.

THIS being a Day in which the Thoughts of our Countrymen are, or ought to be employed on serious Subjects,[2] I shall take the Opportunity of that Disposition of Mind in my Readers, to recommend to them the Practice of those Religious and Moral Vertues, without which all Policy is vain, and the best Cause deprived of its greatest Ornament and Support.

[6] In his *Introduction to the Third Volume of the History of the Reformation* (1714), Gilbert Burnet claimed that Charles Leslie, by emphasizing the priest's necessary role in auricular confession, communion, and baptism, was arguing the 'Necessity of the Priesthood to all Sacred Functions ... further than Popery: Their Devotions are openly recommended, and a Union with the *Gallican* Church has been impudently proposed' (p. 70). Leslie had suggested that, in their resistance to 'the *Pretensions* of the *Pope* to. . .*Unlimited Supremacy*', the French episcopacy was similar to the Anglican clergy; Leslie's opponents claimed that he believed Anglicans had more in common with such French Catholics than they had with English dissenters (Charles Leslie, *A Case Stated between the Church of Rome and the Church of England*, 1713, p. 197; *Englishman*, pp. 148–51).

[7] 2 Kgs. 6:8–23.

Motto. Horace, *Odes*, III. vi. 5–8: You rule because you make yourself submissive to the gods. From them comes every beginning; to them ascribe its issue. The neglected gods have bestowed many misfortunes on unhappy Hesperia.

[2] Good Friday.

Common Sense, as well as the Experience of all Ages, teaches us, that no Government can flourish which doth not encourage and propagate Religion and Morality among all its particular Members. It was an Observation of the ancient *Romans*, that their Empire had not more increased by the Strength of their Arms, than by the Sanctity of their Manners: And *Cicero*, who seems to have been better versed than any of them, both in the Theory and the Practice of Politicks, makes it a Doubt, whether it were possible for a Community to exist that had not a prevailing Mixture of Piety in its Constitution.[3] Justice, Temperance, Humility, and almost every other Moral Vertue, do not only derive the Blessings of Providence upon those who exercise them, but are the natural Means for acquiring the publick Prosperity. Besides; Religious Motives and Instincts are so busy in the Heart of every reasonable Creature, that a Man who would hope to govern a Society without any regard to these Principles, is as much to be contemned for his Folly, as to be detested for his Impiety.

To this we may add, That the World is never sunk into such a State of Degeneracy, but they pay a natural Veneration to Men of Vertue; and rejoyce to see themselves conducted by those, who act under the Awe of a supreme Being, and think themselves accountable for all their Proceedings to the great Judge and Superintendent of human Affairs.

Those of our Fellow-Subjects, who are sensible of the Happiness they enjoy by His Majesty's Accession to the Throne, are obliged, by all the Duties of Gratitude, to adore that Providence which has so signally interposed in our Behalf, by clearing a Way to the Protestant Succession through such Difficulties as seemed insuperable; by detecting the Conspiracies which have been formed against it; and, by many wonderful Events, weakening the Hands and baffling the Attempts of all His Majesty's Enemies, both foreign and domestick.

The Party, who distinguish themselves by their Zeal for the present Establishment, should be careful, in a particular Manner, to discover in their whole Conduct such a Reverence for Religion, as may shew how groundless that Reproach is which is cast upon them by their Enemies, of being averse to our national Worship. While others engross to themselves the Name of *The Church*, and, in a Manner, excommunicate the best Part of their Fellow-Subjects; let us shew ourselves the genuine Sons of it, by practising the Doctrines which it teaches.[4] The Advantage will be visibly

[3] *Oratio de Haruspicum Responsis*, 19; *De Natura Deorum*, i. 3–4.

[4] Francis Atterbury claimed that the Whigs would destroy the Church because 'they neither like our Doctrines nor our Clergy, but would abolish Bishops, Priests and Deacons, assume the Church Lands to themselves, appoint a small Allowance to the Parsons, and (*continued*)

on our Side, if we stick to its Essentials; while they triumph in that empty Denomination which they bestow upon themselves. Too many of them are already dipt in the Guilt of Perjury and Sedition; and as we remain unblemished in these Particulars, let us endeavour to excel them in all the other Parts of Religion, and we shall quickly find, that a regular Morality is, in its own Nature, more popular, as well as more meritorious, than an intemperate Zeal.

We have likewise, in the present Times of Confusion and Disorder, an Opportunity of shewing our Abhorrence of several Principles which have been ascribed to us by the Malice of our Enemies. A Disaffection to Kings and Kingly Government, with a Proneness to Rebellion, have been often very unjustly charged on that Party which goes by the Name of *Whigs.*[5] Our steady and continued adherence to His Majesty and the present happy Settlement, will the most effectually confute this Calumny. Our Adversaries, who know very well how odious Commonwealth-Principles are to the *English* Nation, have inverted the very Sense of Words and Things, rather than not continue to brand us with this imaginary Guilt: For with some of these Men, at present, Loyalty to our King is Republicanism, and Rebellion Passive-Obedience.

It has been an old Objection to the Principles of the *Whigs*, that several of their Leaders, who have been zealous for redressing the Grievances of Government, have not behaved themselves better than the *Tories* in domestick Scenes of Life. But at the same time have been publick Patriots and private Oppressors.[6] This Objection, were it true, has no Weight in it, since the Misbehaviour of particular Persons does not at all affect their Cause, and since a Man may act laudably in some Respects, who does not so in others. However; it were to be wished, that Men would not give

---

prescribe them what Doctrines to teach from the Pulpit . . . they would introduce a general Comprehension, and blend up an Ecclesiastical *Babel* of all the Sects and Heresies upon the Face of the Earth' (*English Advice*, p. 18).

[5] Swift wrote in *Examiner* 36 that 'excepting the *Antimonarchial Principle*, and a few false Notions about *Liberty*', he could see little agreement among various Whig factions (*Prose Works* iii. 129). Atterbury predicted that a Whig victory in 1715 would lead to 'An entire and thorough Revolution' (*English Advice*, p. 30).

[6] In 1703 Charles Leslie claimed that the Whigs 'whose chief *Topick* is the *Liberty* of the *People*, and against *Arbitrary Power*, are the most *Absolute* of any other in their *Families*, and so Proportionably, as they rise *Higher*. If they Believ'd *Themselves* . . . they wou'd go *Home*, and call a *Council* of their *Wives*, *Children*, and *Servants*, and tell them that the *Master* of a *Family* was ordain'd for the *Good* of those that were put under his *Government* . . . and that they must be the best *Judges* of what was for their own *Good*; And therefore, that they shou'd *Meet* and *Consult* together, as oft as they thought fit; and set him *Rules* for the *Government* of his *Family* . . . I desire no other *Test* for these Publick *Patrons* for *Liberty*, than to look into their *Conversation* and their *Families*. Then let any Man *Believe* them, if he *Can*; and *Trust* them, if he *please*' (*The New Association*, Pt. II, Supplement, pp. 6–7).

occasion even to such Invectives; but at the same time they consult the Happiness of the Whole, that they would promote it to their utmost in all their private Dealings among those who lie more immediately within their Influence. In the mean while[a] I must observe, that this Reproach, which may be often met with both in Print and Conversation, tends in Reality to the Honour of the *Whigs*, as it supposes that a greater Regard to Justice and Humanity is to be expected from them, than from those of the opposite Party; And it is certain we cannot better recommend our Principles, than by such Actions as are their natural and genuine Fruits.

Were we thus careful to guard ourselves in a particular Manner against these groundless Imputations of our Enemies, and to rise above them as much in our Morality as in our Politicks, our Cause would be always as flourishing as it is just. It is certain that our Notions have a more natural Tendency to such a Practice, as we espouse the Protestant Interest in Opposition to that of Popery, which is so far from advancing Morality by its Doctrines, that it has weakned, or entirely subverted, many of the Duties even of [b] Natural Religion.

I shall conclude, with recommending one Vertue more to the Friends of the present Establishment, wherein the *Whigs* have been remarkably deficient; which is a general Unanimity and Concurrence in the Pursuit of such Measures as are necessary for the Well-being of their Country.[7] As it is a laudable Freedom of Thought which unshackles their Minds from the poor and narrow Prejudices of Education, and opens their Eyes to a more extensive View of the publick Good; the same Freedom of Thought disposes several of them to the embracing of particular Schemes and Maxims, and to a certain Singularity of Opinion which proves highly prejudicial to their Cause; especially when they are encouraged in them by a vain Breath of Popularity, or by the artificial Praises which are bestowed

[a] mean while / mean time *Fol.* [b] many of the Duties even of / even the Duties of *Fol.*

[7] There were at least three divisions among the Whigs at this time. The first was over the Septennial Bill (see *F.* 25, n. 2), the second concerned the issue of clemency for the captured rebel Lords (see *F.* 31, n. 4), and the third was the division between the Sunderland and Walpole factions. In the clemency debate on 22 Feb., Steele supported the petitioners for mercy and was attacked for his stance in the *St. James's Post* of 2 Mar. (*Pol. State* xi. 230–4). In reponse to accusations of 'craving Ambition' which had been leveled at him by Walpole Whigs, Steele published *A Letter to a Member* (Steele, *Tracts and Pamphlets*, pp. 405–15). A less public but more important division among the Whigs was being manoeuvred by the Earl of Sunderland who was angry that his former subordinate, Townshend, was appointed Secretary of State in 1714. Sunderland courted the Germans and gathered disaffected Whigs around him to oppose Townshend and Walpole (H.M.C. *Onslow MSS.* 508–9; Coxe, *Walpole* i. 80, 95).

on them by the opposite Party. This Temper of Mind, though the Effect of a noble Principle, very often betrays their Friends, and brings into Power the most pernicious and implacable of their Enemies. In Cases of this Nature, it is the Duty of an honest and prudent Man, to sacrifice a doubtful Opinion to the concurring Judgment of those whom he believes to be well-intentioned to their Country, and who have better Opportunities of looking into all its most complicated Interests. An honest Party of Men acting with Unanimity, are of infinitely greater Consequence than the same Party aiming at the same End by different Views: As a large Diamond is of a thousand Times greater Value whilst it remains entire, than when it is cut into a Multitude of smaller Stones, notwithstanding they may, each of them, be[c] very curiously set, and are all of the same Water.

D

Numb. XXX *Monday, April* 2, 1716

— — *I, verbis virtutem illude superbis.*

Virg.

As I was some Years ago engaged in Conversation with a Fashionable *French Abbé*, upon a Subject which the People of that Kingdom love to start in Discourse, the comparative Greatness of the two Nations; He asked me, *How many Souls I thought there might be in* London? I replied, being willing to do my Country all the Honour I fairly could, That there were several who computed them at near a Million: But not finding that Surprize I expected in his Countenance, I returned the Question upon him, How many he thought there might be in *Paris*? To which he answered, with a certain Grimace of Coldness and Indifference, *About ten or twelve Millions.*[2]

It would, indeed, be incredible to a Man who has never been in *France*, should one relate the extravagant Notion they entertain of themselves, and the mean Opinion they have of their Neighbours. There are certainly (notwithstanding the visible Decay of Learning and Taste which has appeared among them of late Years) many particular[a] Persons in that

[c] may, each of them, be / may be *Fol.*

[a] Years) many particular / Years) particular *Fol.*

Motto. Virgil, *Aeneid*, ix. 634: Go, mock valour with arrogant words.

[2] London was the largest city in Europe in 1700 with a population of about 575,000 and an annual increase of approximately 2,750; the population of Paris was slightly more than 500,000 in 1700. See E. A. Wrigley, 'A Simple Model of London's Importance in Changing English Society and Economy 1650–1750', *Past and Present*, 37 (1967), 44–70.

Country, who are eminent in the highest Degree for[b] their Good Sense, as well as for their Knowledge in all the Arts and Sciences. But I believe every one, who is acquainted with them, will allow, that the People in general fall far[c] short of those, who border upon them, in Strength and Solidity of Understanding. One would, therefore, no more wonder to see the most shallow Nation of *Europe* the most Vain, than to find the most empty Fellows in every distinct Nation more Conceited and Censorious than the rest of their Countrymen. Prejudice and Self-Sufficiency naturally proceed from Inexperience of the World, and Ignorance of Mankind. As it requires but very small Abilities to discover the Imperfections of another, we find that none are more apt to turn their Neighbours into Ridicule, than those who are the most ridiculous in their own private Conduct.[3].

Those among the *French*, who have seen nothing but their own Country, can scarce bring themselves to believe, that a Nation which lies never so little North of them is not full of *Goths* and *Vandals*. Nay those among them who travel into foreign Parts are so prejudiced in favour of their own imaginary Politeness, that they are apt to look[d] upon every thing as barbarous, in Proportion as it deviates from what they find at Home. No less a Man than an Ambassador of *France* being in Conversation with our King of glorious Memory, and willing to encourage his Majesty, told him that he talked like a *Frenchman*. The King smiled at the Encomium which was given him, and only reply'd, *Sir, I am sure You do*. An eminent Writer of the last Age was so offended at this kind of Insolence, which shewed itself very plentifully in one of their Travellers who gave an Account of *England*, that he vindicated the Honour of his Country in a Book full of just Satyr and Ingenuity. I need not acquaint my Reader, that I mean Bishop *Sprat*'s Answer to *Sorbiere*.[4]

Since I am upon this Head, I cannot forbear mentioning some profound Remarks that I have been lately shewn in a *French* Book, the Author of

[b] eminent in the highest Degree for / eminent for *Fol.* [c] fall far / fall very far *Fol.*
[d] they are apt to look / they look *Fol.*

[3] In this essay Addison attempts to discredit French influence in England by misrepresenting the opinions of various Frenchmen. Anti-French prejudice, a recurrent theme in his political writing, had been a major feature of Whig foreign policy even before the war. Poussin, a French chargé d'affaires, wrote in 1701 that both parties advocated war with France, but the Whigs 'n'y entrent que par passion' while the Tories were prompted 'par politique et en quelque sorte malgré eux mêmes' (P.R.O. *Transcripts* (France) 189, fo. 537). Anti-French sentiment was especially vehement in England during the early months of 1716, but in March the Regent complied with British demands concerning the Pretender and this helped to abate British anger (*Pol. State* xi. 298–302).

[4] Samuel Sorbière's *Relation d'un voyage en Angleterre* was published in Paris in 1664 and Thomas Sprat's *Observations* on it was published in London the following year.

which lived, it seems, some Time in *England. The* English, says this curious Traveller, *very much delight in Pudding. This is the favourite Dish not only of the Clergy, but of the People in general. Provided there be a Pudding upon the Table, no matter what are the other Dishes; they are sure to make a Feast. They think themselves so happy when they have a Pudding before them, that if any one would tell a Friend he is arrived in a lucky Juncture, the ordinary Salutation is, Sir, I am glad to see you; you are come in Pudding-Time.*[5]

One cannot have the Heart to be angry at this judicious Observer, notwithstanding he has treated us like a Race of *Hottentots*, because he only taxes us with our inordinate Love of Pudding, which, it must be confess'd, is not so elegant a Dish as Frog and Sallat. Every one who has been at *Paris*, knows that *Un gros Milord Anglois* is a frequent Jest upon the *French* Stage;[6] as if Corpulence was a proper Subject for Satyr, or a Man of Honour could help his being Fat, who Eats suitable to his Quality.

It would be endless to recount the Invectives which are to be met with among the *French* Historians, and even in *Mezeray* himself, against the Manners of our Countrymen.[7] Their Authors in other Kinds of Writing are likewise very liberal in Characters of the same Nature. I cannot forbear mentioning the learned Monsieur *Patin* in particular; who tells us, in so many Words, *That the* English *are a People whom he naturally abhors*: And in another place, *That he looks upon the* English *among the several Nations of Men, as he does upon Wolves among the several Species of Beasts.*[8] A *British* Writer would be very justly charged with want of Politeness, who, in return to this Civility, should look upon the *French* as that Part of Mankind which answers to a Species in the Brute Creation, whom we call in *English* by the Name of Monkies.

If the *French* load us with these Indignities, we may observe, for our Comfort, that they give the rest of their Borderers no better Quarter. If we

[5] Source unidentified.

[6] In Saint-Evremond's *Sir Politick Would-be* (1662), Antonio comments disparagingly about the eating habits of the British nobility to the Englishman, Mylord Tancrède (Act I, scene iv). However, such unflattering remarks were not frequent jokes in French plays; see Georges Ascoli, *La Grande Bretagne devant l'opinion française au XVIIe siècle* (Paris, 1930), i. 337–40, and H. K. Lancaster, *A History of Parisian Drama, 1701–1715* (Baltimore, 1945), p. 146.

[7] Eudes de Mézeray's *Histoire de France* (1643), a relatively unbiased history from the fifth to the seventeenth centuries, criticized Henry VIII and Elizabeth for their treatment of Catholics, but does not contain any invectives against the English. On the contrary, Mézeray was regarded as an admirer of the English (Ascoli, i. 440).

[8] Addison is again unfair. Charles Patin's *Relations historiques et curieuses de voyages* (Lyons, 1674) only praises the English. The first quotation Addison cites is taken from a Latin note to Patin's edition of Erasmus's *Moriæ Encomium* (Basel, 1676), p. 102, and the second, written by Gui Patin, was published in *Naudeana et Patiniana* (Amsterdam, 1703), Pt. II, p. 18.

are a dull, heavy, phlegmatick People, we are it seems no worse than our Neighbours. As an Instance, I shall set down at large a remarkable Passage in a famous Book intituled *Chevræana*, written many Years ago by the celebrated Monsieur *Chevreau*; after having advertised my Reader that the Dutchess of *Hanover*, and the Princess *Elizabeth* of *Bohemia*, who are mentioned in it, were the late excellent Princess *Sophia* and her Sister.

Tilenus, pour un Allemand, parle & ecrit bien François, *dit Scaliger*: Gretzer a bien de l'esprit pour un Allemand, *dit le Cardinal du Perron*: *Et le P. Bouhours met en question*, Si un Allemand peut être bel esprit? *On ne doit juger ni bien ni mal d'une Nation par un particulier, ni d'un particulier par sa Nation. Il y a des Allemands, comme des François, qui n'ont point d'esprit; des Allemands, qui ont scû plus d'Hebreu, plus de Grec, que Scaliger & le Cardinal du Perron: J'honore fort le P. Bouhours, qui a du merite; mais j'ose dire, que la France n'a point de plus bel Esprit que* Madame la Duchesse de Hanovre d'aujourdhui, *ni de personne plus solidement savante en Philosophie que l'etoit* Madame la Princesse Elizabeth de Boheme, sa Sœur: *& je ne croi pas que l'on refuse le même titre à beaucoup d'Accademiciens d'Allemagne, dont les Ouvrages meriteroient bien d'être traduits. Il y a d'autres Princesses en Allemagne, qui ont infiniment de l'esprit. Les François disent* c'est un Allemand, *pour exprimer un homme pesant, brutal: & les Allemands, comme les Italiens,* c'est un François, *pour dire un fou & un etourdi. C'est aller trop loin: comme le Prince de* Salé *dit de* Ruyter, Il est honnête homme, c'est bien dommage qu'il soit Chrétien. *Chevræana, Tom.* I.[9]

'*Tilenus*, says *Scaliger*, speaks and writes well for a *German*. *Gretzer* has a great deal of Wit for a *German*, says Cardinal *Perron*. And Father *Bouhours* makes it a Question, Whether a *German* can be a Wit? One ought not to judge well or ill of a Nation from a particular Person, nor of a particular Person from his Nation. There are *Germans*, as there are *French*, who have no Wit; and *Germans* who are better skilled in *Greek* and *Hebrew* than either *Scaliger* or the Cardinal *du Perron*. I have a great Honour for Father *Bouhours*, who is a Man of Merit; but will be bold to say, that there is not in all *France*, a Person of more Wit than the present Dutchess of *Hanover*; nor more thoroughly knowing in Philosophy, than was the late Princess *Elizabeth* of *Bohemia* her Sister; and I believe none can refuse the same Title to many Academicians in *Germany*, whose Works very well deserve to be translated into our Tongue. There are other Princesses in *Germany* who have also an infinite deal of Wit. The *French* say of a Man, that he is a *German*, when they would signify that he is dull and heavy; and

[9] Urbain Chevreau, *Chevræana* (Amsterdam, 1700), i. 91–2. Addison omits three brief passages not relevant to his point.

the *Germans*, as well as the *Italians*, when they would call a Man a Hair-brain'd Coxcomb, say he is a *French* Man. This is going too far, and is like the Governour of *Sally's* Saying of *De Ruyter*, the *Dutch* Admiral, *He's an honest Man, 'tis great Pity he is a Christian.*'

Having already run my Paper out to its usual Length, I have not room for many Reflections on that which is the Subject of it. The last cited Author has been beforehand with me in its proper Moral. I shall only add to it, that there has been an unaccountable Disposition among the *English* of late Years, to fetch the Fashion from the *French*, not only in their Dress and Behaviour, but even in their Judgments and Opinions of Mankind. It will however be reasonable for us, if we concur with them in their Contempt of other neighbouring Nations, that we should likewise regard our selves under the same View in which they are wont to place us. The Representations they make of us, are as of a Nation the least favoured by them; and as these are agreeable to the natural Aversion they have for us, are more disadvantageous than the Pictures they have drawn of any other People in *Europe*.

Numb. XXXI — *Friday*, *April* 6, 1716

Omnes homines, P.C. qui de rebus dubiis consultant, ab odio, amicitia, ira, atque misericordia vacuos esse decet.
Cæsar ap. Sallust.

I HAVE purposely avoided, during the whole Course of this Paper, to speak any thing concerning the Treatment which is due to such Persons as have been concerned in the late Rebellion, because I would not seem to irritate Justice against those who are under the Prosecution of the Law, nor incense any of my Readers against unhappy though guilty Men. But when we find the Proceedings of our Government in this Particular traduced and mis-represented, it is the Duty of every good Subject to set them in their proper Light.

I am the more prompted to this Undertaking by a Pamphlet, intituled, *An Argument to prove the Affections of the People of* England *to be the best Security of the Government; humbly offer'd to the Consideration of the Patrons*

Motto. Sallust, *De Catilinae Coniuratione*, 51: It becomes all, most Illustrious Fathers, who have Cases before 'em for Debate and Judgment, to divest themselves of the several Passions of Love, Hatred, Compassion, and Revenge (trans. ROWE).

of Severity, and apply'd to the present Juncture of Affairs.[2] Had the whole Scope of the Author been answerable to his Title, he would have only undertaken to prove what every Man in his Wits is already convinced of. But the Drift of the Pamphlet is to stir up our Compassion towards the Rebels, and our Indignation against the Government. The Author, who knew that such a Design as this could not be carried on without a great deal of Artifice and Sophistry, has puzzled and perplexed his Cause, by throwing his Thoughts together in such a study'd Confusion, that upon this Account, if upon any, his Pamphlet is, as the Party have represented it, Unanswerable.

The famous Monsieur *Bayle* compares the answering of an immethodical Author, to the Hunting of a Duck: When you have him full in your Sight, and fancy yourself within Reach of him, he gives you the Slip, and becomes invisible. His Argument is lost in such a Variety of Matter, that you must catch it where you can, as it rises and disappears, in the several Parts of his Discourse.

The Writer of this Pamphlet could, doubtless, have ranged his Thoughts in much better Order, if he had pleased: But he knew very well, that Error is not to be advanced by Perspicuity. In order therefore to answer this Pamphlet, I must reduce the Substance of it under proper Heads; and disembroil the Thoughts of the Author, since he did not think fit to do it himself.

In the first Place I shall observe, that the Terms which the Author makes use of are loose, general, and undefined, as will be shewn in the Sequel of this Paper; and, what less becomes a fair Reasoner, he puts wrong and invidious Names on every thing to colour a false Way of Arguing. He allows that *the Rebels indisputably merit to be severely Chastised*;

[2] This pamphlet by Francis Atterbury was published on 1 Mar. 1716 (*Post Boy*, 1–3 Mar.) and it appealed to the King for clemency for the six rebel Lords who had been impeached and sentenced to execution by Parliament on 9 Feb. (*L.J.* xx. 288). The pamphlet was written after 22 Feb. because on that day the House of Lords put the rebel Lords' fate into the hands of the King by deciding that, although the Act of Settlement did not permit royal pardons for persons impeached by Parliament, the King could grant reprieves to the rebel Lords; the House also addressed the King 'to grant a Reprieve to such of the Petitioners as shall appear to His Majesty to deserve the same' (*L.J.* xx. 299). Before 22 Feb. this pamphlet's appeal to the King would have been pointless. The pamphlet was part of the anti-Court agitation which surrounded the manoeuvres in Parliament to gain clemency from the Crown on 22 Feb. and climaxed with the execution of two rebel Lords on 24 Feb. (see below, n. 4). One reason Addison is responding to a pamphlet five weeks after its publication is that the Commission for trying rebel commoners at the Court of Common Pleas in Westminster was scheduled to meet on 7 Apr., the day after his essay appeared (Tindal, p. 489). By pointing to the fallacies and intemperance of such criticism as Atterbury's, Addison is attempting to avert a recurrence of anti-Court sentiment. This *Freeholder* was reprinted in duodecimo and entitled *An Answer to a Pamphlet entituled, An Argument to prove the Affections* . . ..

that they *deserve it according to Law*; and that *if they are punished, they have none to thank but themselves*, (p. 7).[3] How can a Man after such a Concession make use sometimes of the Word *Cruelty*, but generally of *Revenge*, when he pleads against the Exercise of what,[a] according to his own Notion, is at the most but rigid Justice! Or why are such Executions, which, according to his own Opinion, are legal, so often to be called *Violences* and *Slaughter*? Not to mention the Appellations given to those who do not agree with him in his Opinion for Clemency, as the *Blood-thirsty*, the *Political Butchers*, *State-Chirurgeons*, and the like.

But I shall now speak of that Point which is the great and reigning Fallacy of the Pamphlet, and runs more or less through every Paragraph. His whole Argument turns upon this single Consideration; Whether the King should exert Mercy or Justice towards those who have openly appeared in the present Rebellion? By Mercy he means a general Pardon; by Justice, a general Punishment: So that he supposes no other Method practicable in this Juncture, than either the Forgiving All, or the Executing All.[4] Thus he puts the Question, *Whether it be the Interest of the Prince to*

[a] what,/that, which, *Fol.*

[3] All quotations are accurate and any page-references Addison omitted have been silently added to the text. Citation punctuation has been regularized.

[4] On 9 Dec. 1715 the rebel prisoners from Preston arrived in London and the seven Lords impeached by Parliament were among them: Derwentwater, Widdrington, Nithsdale, Wintoun, Carnwath, Kenmure, and Nairne (see *F.* 7, n. 7). On 9 Jan. 1716 articles of impeachment were presented and on 19 Jan. all the Lords pleaded guilty except Wintoun who requested more time to prepare his defence (*C.J.* xviii. 330–4; *L.J.* xx. 264–8). Three of the Lords—Kenmure, Nairne, and Carnwath—simply asked for mercy, but Nithsdale claimed that the King's officers at Preston had promised 'That, if they submitted, they might expect the King's Mercy' (*L.J.* xx. 266) and Derwentwater claimed that he encouraged the rebels to surrender 'and rely entirely on His Majesty's Clemency and Goodness, which he had Encouragement to expect' (*L.J.* xx. 264). On 9 Feb. Lord Cowper pronounced judgement against the six Lords and sentenced them to execution (*L.J.* xx. 286–8). During the next ten days, the wives of Nithsdale, Derwentwater, and Nairne appealed to the King for mercy but received no satisfaction; on 18 Feb. the King's Council sent orders to the Lieutenant of the Tower to proceed with the planned executions (Tindal, p. 485). Three days later, the wives, along with twenty other women of distinction, went to the lobby of the House of Lords to ask the peers to intercede, but the Lords refused to act (Tindal, p. 486). Countess Cowper wrote, 'Every body in a Consternation. 'Tis a trap . . . to undo the Ministry' (Diary, 21 Feb.). On 22 Feb. the women appealed to the House of Commons. Both houses seemed inclined toward clemency, and the ministry failed to prevent petitions for mercy from being presented (Tindal, p. 486). In the House of Commons petitions were heard, but a successful motion to adjourn until 1 Mar. thwarted any further action on them (*Parl. Hist.* vii. 291–2). In the House of Lords the Court was less successful; when the question was raised whether petitions for mercy should be received and read, Townshend opposed it, but the Earl of Nottingham supported the petitioners and a number of peers voted with him (H.M.C. *Stuart MSS.* ii. 21). Then the House debated whether the King had the power to grant a reprieve and decided that he did. Finally the House voted to address the King for clemency (*L.J.* xx. 299). Countess Cowper wrote that the King was 'more vexed by what happend' in the House of Lords than at anything that had yet happened; the King 'takes it desperately Ill of 54 [Nottingham] who

destroy the Rebels by Fire, Sword, or Gibbet? (p. 4) And, speaking of the *Zealots for the Government*, he tells us, *They think no Remedy so good, as to make clear Work; and that they declare for the utter Extirpation of All who are its Enemies in the most minute Circumstance: As if Amputation were the sole Remedy these political Butchers cou'd find out for the Distempers of a State; or that they thought the only Way to make the Top flourish, were to lop off the Under-Branches* (p. 5). He then speaks of the *Coffee-house Polititians, and the Casuists in Red-Coats; Who*, he tells us, *are for the utmost Rigour that their Laws of War or Laws of Convenience can inspire them with* (p. 5). Again, *It is represented*, says he, *that the Rebels deserve the highest Punishment the Laws can inflict* (p. 7). And afterwards tells us, *The Question is, Whether the Government shall shew Mercy, or take a Reverend Divine's Advice, to slay Man and Woman, Infant and Suckling?* (p. 8) Thus again he tells us, *The Friends to severe Counsels alledge, that the Government ought not to be moved by Compassion*; and that *the Law should have its Course* (p. 9). And in another Place puts these Words in their Mouths, *He may still retain their Affection, and yet let the Laws have their Course in punishing the Guilty* (p. 18). He goes upon the same Supposition in the following Passages; *It is impracticable in so general a Corruption, to, destroy* All *who are infected; and unless you destroy* All *you do nothing to the purpose* (p. 10). *Shall our Rightful King shew himself less the true Father of his People, and afford his Pardon to* None *of those People, who (like King* Lear *to his Daughters) had so great a Confidence in his Vertue as to give him All* (p. 25). I shall only add, that the concluding Paragraph, which is worked up with so much artificial Horrour, goes upon a Supposition answerable to the whole Tenor of the Pamphlet; and implies, that *the Impeach'd Lords* were to be Executed without Exception or Discrimination.[5]

Thus we see what is the Author's Idea of that Justice against which all his Arguments are levell'd. If, in the next Place, we consider the Nature of

enjoys £15000 ... from y[e] king's bounty' (Diary, 23 Feb.). The King met in council on 23 Feb. and decided that the most guilty Lords—Derwentwater, Kenmure, and Nithsdale—should be executed the following day and that the other condemned Lords should be granted reprieves until 7 Mar. (Tindal, p. 487). During that night Nithsdale escaped from the Tower, perhaps with the complicity of the ministry, and Derwentwater and Kenmure were executed on 24 Feb. Two days later Bernstorff visited Lord Cowper and said there would be no more executions of the rebel Lords and that the ministry was resolved to dismiss Nottingham as President of the Council (Diary, 26 Feb.).

[5] 'Just as I was entring upon the Consideration, how much it is the Interest of the whole Royal Family, to have their Name and Succession endeared to their People; and that nothing could be of that Service to the *Child that is unborn*, as Acts of Mercy, Generosity and Goodness, I was struck with Horror at the News that *in spight* of the visible and almost universal Inclination of all Ranks of People, in favour of their Countrymen, the Impeach'd Lords are to be Executed. *Obstupui, steteruntq; comae & vox faucibus haesit* [I was shocked and my hair stood on end and the voice in my throat died. *Aeneid*, ii. 774].'

that Clemency which he recommends, we find it to be no less universal and unrestrain'd.

He declares for a *General Act of Indemnity* (p. 20), and tells us, *It is the Sense of every dispassionate Man of the Kingdom, that the Rebels may, and ought to be Pardoned* (p. 19). *One popular Act*, says he, *wou'd even yet retrieve all* (p. 21). He declares himself not *over-fond of the Doctrines of making Examples of Traitors* (ibid.). And that *the Way to prevent Things from being brought to an Extremity, is to deal mildly with those unfortunate Gentlemen engaged in the Rebellion* (p. 25).

The Reader may now see in how fallacious a Manner this Writer has stated the Controversy: He supposes there are but two Methods of treating the Rebels; that is, by cutting off every one of them to a Man, or pardoning every one of them without Distinction. Now if there be a third Method between these two Extreams, which is on all Accounts more eligible than either of them, it is certain that the whole Course of his Argumentation comes to nothing. Every Man of the plainest Understanding will easily conclude, that in the Case before us, as in most others, we ought to avoid both Extreams; that to destroy every Rebel would be an excessive Severity, and to forgive every one of them an unreasonable Weakness. The proper Method of Proceeding, is that which the Author has purposely omitted: Namely, to temper Justice with Mercy; and, according to the different Circumstances that aggravate or alleviate the Guilt of the Offenders, to restrain the Force of the Laws, or to let them take their proper Course. Punishments are necessary to shew there is Justice in a Government, and Pardons to shew there is Mercy; and both together convince the People, that our Constitution under a good Administration does not only make a Difference between the Guilty and the Innocent, but even among the Guilty between such as are more or less criminal.

This middle Method which has been always practiced by wise and good Governours, has hitherto been made use of by our Soveraign. If, indeed, a Stranger, and one who is altogether unacquainted with His Majesty's Conduct, should read this Pamphlet, he would conclude, that every Person engaged in the Rebellion was to die *by the Sword, the Halter, or the Ax* (p. 8); nay, that their Friends and Abettors were involved in the same Fate. Would it be possible for him to imagine, that of the several Thousands openly taken in Arms, and liable to Death by the Laws of their Country, not above Forty have yet suffered?[6] How would he be surpriz'd to hear,

[6] About 1,500 prisoners were taken at Preston and approximately 100 of them were sent to London for trial (*Pol. State* x. 492–7). Of those remaining behind, one in twenty, selected by lot, stood trial in Lancashire; of those tried during January and February, only thirty-four were executed (C. Hardwick, *History of Preston*, Preston, 1857, p. 237). Four officers of the

that, notwithstanding His Majesty's Troops have been Victorious in every Engagement, more of His Friends have lost their Lives in this Rebellion, than of His traiterous Subjects; though we add to those who have dy'd by the Hand of Justice those of them who fell in Battle?[7] And yet we find a more popular Compassion endeavoured to be raised for the Deaths of the Guilty, who have brought such Calamities on their Country, than for the Innocent who perished in the Defence of it.

This middle Method of Proceeding, which has been pursued by His Majesty, and is wilfully overlooked by the Author, best answers the Ends of Government; which is to maintain the Safety of the Publick by Rewards and Punishments. It is also incumbent on a Governour, according to the received Dictates of Religion: Which instructs us, *That he beareth not the Sword in vain; but ought to be a Terrour to Evil-doers, and a Praise to them that do Well.*[8] It is likewise in a particular manner the Duty of a *British* King, who obliges himself by his Coronation-Oath to execute *Justice in Mercy*, that is, to mix them in his Administration, and not to exercise either of them to the total Exclusion of the other.

But if we consider the Arguments which this Author gives for Clemency, from the good Effects it would produce, we shall find, that they hold true only when apply'd to such a Mercy as serves rather to mitigate than exclude Justice. The Excellence of that unlimited Clemency which the Author contends for, is recommended by the following Arguments.

First, That it endears a Prince to his People. This he descants on in several Parts of his Book. *Clemency will endear his Person to the Nation; and then they will neither have the Power nor Will to disturb him* (p. 8). *Was there ever a cruel Prince, that was not hated by his Subjects?* (p. 24) *A merciful good-natur'd Disposition is of all others the most amiable Quality, and in Princes always attended with a popular Love* (p. 18).

It is certain, that such a popular Love will always rise towards a good Prince, who exercises such a Mercy as I have before described, which is consistent with the Safety of the Constitution, and the Good of his Kingdom. But if it be thrown away at random, it loses its Virtue, lessens the Esteem and Authority of a Prince, and cannot long recommend him, even to the weakest of his Subjects, who will find all the Effects of Cruelty

King's army who had joined the rebels were executed in early December (*Pol. State* x. 583). About 1,000 prisoners in Lancashire petitioned for transportation to the colonies (Tindal, p. 485).

[7] Contemporary estimates vary on the numbers lost. The most recent study of those sources concludes that government forces killed or wounded at Preston and Sheriffmuir totaled 806 while only 192 rebel soldiers suffered similar fates in those battles (John Baynes, *The Jacobite Rising of 1715*, 1970, pp. 126–7, 152).

[8] Romans 13:3–4.

in such an ill-grounded Compassion. It was a famous Saying of *William Rufus*, and is quoted to his Honour by Historians, 'Whosoever spares perjured Men, Robbers, Plunderers and Traitors, deprives all good Men of their Peace and Quietness, and lays a Foundation of innumerable Mischiefs to the Vertuous and Innocent.'[9]

Another Argument for unlimited Clemency, is, that it shews a couragious Temper: *Clemency is likewise an Argument of Fearlessness; whereas Cruelty not only betrays a weak, abject, depraved Spirit, but also is for the most part a certain Sign of Cowardice* (p. 19). —*He had a truly great Soul, and such will always disdain the Coward's Vertue, which is Fear; and the Consequence of it, which is Revenge* (p. 27). This Panegyrick on Clemency, when it is governed by Reason, is likewise very right; but it may so happen, that the putting of Laws in execution against Traitors to their Country may be the Argument of Fearlessness, when our Governours are told that they dare not do it; and such Methods may be made use of to extort Pardons, as would make it look like Cowardice to grant them. In this last Case the Author should have remembred his own Words, that *then only Mercy is meritorious when it is voluntary, and not extorted by the Necessity of Affairs* (p. 13). Besides, the Author should have considered, that another Argument which he makes use of for his Clemency, are the Resentments that may arise from the Execution of a Rebel: An Argument adapted to a cowardly, not a fearless Temper. This he infers from the Disposition of *the Friends, Wel-wishers or Associates of the Sufferers* (p. 4). *Resentment will inflame some; in others Compassion will, by degrees, rise into Resentment. This will naturally beget a Disposition to overturn what they dislike, and then there will want only a fair Opportunity* (p. 12). This Argument, like most of the others, pleads equally for Malefactors of all kinds, whom the Government can never bring to Justice, without disobliging their Friends, Well-wishers, or Associates. But, I believe, if the Author would Converse with any Friend, Well-wisher, or Associate of these Sufferers, he would find them rather deterr'd from their Practices by their Sufferings, than disposed to rise in a new Rebellion to revenge them. A Government must be in a very weak and melancholy Condition, that is not armed with a sufficient Power for its own Defence against the Resentment of its Enemies, and is afraid of being overturn'd if it does Justice on those who attempt it. But I am afraid the main Reason why these Friends, Well-wishers and Associates are against Punishing any of the Rebels, is that, which must be an Argument with every wise Governour for doing Justice upon some of them; namely, that it is a likely Means to come at the Bottom of this Conspiracy, and to

[9] Addison's quotation follows Laurence Echard's *History of England* (1707), i. 154.

detect those who have been the private Abettors of it, and who are still at work in the same Design; if we give Credit to the Suggestions of our Malecontents themselves, who labour to make us believe that there is still Life in this wicked Project.

I am wonderfully surprized to see another Argument made use of for a General Pardon, which might have been urged more properly for a general Execution. The Words are these; *The Generality will never be brought to believe, but that those who suffer only for Treason have very hard Measure; nor can you with all your Severity undeceive them of their Error* (p. 12). If the Generality of the *English* have such a favourable Opinion of Treason, nothing can cure them of an Error so fatal to their Country as the Punishment of those who are guilty of it. It is evident, that a General Impunity would confirm them in such an Opinion: For the Vulgar will never be brought to believe, that there is a Crime where they see no Penalty. As it is certain no Error can be more destructive to the very Being of Government than this, a proper Remedy ought to be applied to it: And I would ask this Author, Whether upon this Occasion, *The Doctrine of making Examples of Traitors* be not very seasonable; though he declares himself *not over-fond of it*: The way to awaken Men's Minds to the Sense of this Guilt, is to let them see by the Sufferings of some who have incurr'd it, how heinous a Crime it is in the Eye of the Law.

The foregoing Answer may be apply'd likewise to another Argument of the same Nature. *If the Faction be as numerous as is pretended; if the Spirit has spread itself over the whole Kingdom; if it has mixed with the Mass of the People; then certainly all bloody Measures will but whet Men the more for Revenge* (p. 10). If Justice inflicted on a few of the most flagrant Criminals, with Mercy extended to the Multitude, may be called *bloody Measures*, they are without doubt absolutely necessary, in case the Spirit of Faction be thus spread among the Mass of the People; who will readily conclude, that if open Rebellion goes unpunished, every Degree of Faction which leads to it must be altogether innocent.

I am come now to another Argument for Pardoning all the Rebels, which is, that it would inspire them all with Gratitude, and reduce them to their Allegiance. *It is truly Heroick to overcome the Hearts of one's Enemies; and when it is compassed, the Undertaking is truly Politick* (p. 8). *He has now a fair Opportunity of Conquering more Enemies by one Act of Clemency, than the most successful General will be able to do in many Campaigns* (p. 9). *Are there not infinite Numbers who would become most Dutiful upon any fair Invitation, upon the least Appearance of Grace?* (p. 13) *Which of the Rebels could be ungrateful enough to resist or abuse Goodness exemplified in Practice, as well as extoll'd in*

Theory? (p. 20) Has not His Majesty then shewn the least Appearance of Grace in that generous Forgiveness which he has already extended to such great Numbers of his Rebellious Subjects, who must have died by the Laws of their Country, had not his Mercy interpos'd in their Behalf? But if the Author means (as he doth, thro' this whole Pamphlet by the like Expressions) an[b] universal Forgiveness, no unprejudiced Man can be of his Opinion, that it wou'd have had this good Effect. We may see how little the Conversion of Rebels is to be depended on, when we observe, that several of the Leaders in this Rebellion were Men who had been pardoned for Practices of the same Nature:[10] And that most of those who have suffered, have avowed their Perseverance in their Rebellious Principles, when they spoke their Minds at the Place of Execution, notwithstanding their Professions to the contrary while they sollicited Forgiveness.[11] Besides, were Pardon extended indifferently to All, which of them would think himself under any particular Obligation? Whereas by that prudent Discrimination which His Majesty has made between the Offenders of different Degrees, He naturally obliges those whom he has considered with so much Tenderness, and distinguished as the most proper Objects of Mercy. In short, those who are pardoned would not have known the Value of Grace, if none had felt the Effects of Justice.

I must not omit another Reason which the Author makes use of against Punishment; *Because*, he says, *those very Means, or the Apprehensions of them, have brought Things to the pass in which they are, and consequently will reduce them from bad to worse* (p. 10), and afterwards, *This Growth of Disaffection is in a great Measure owing to the groundless Jealousies Men entertain'd of the present Administration, as if they were to expect nothing but Cruelty under it* (p. 10). If our Author would have spoken out, and have applied these Effects to the real Cause, he could ascribe this Change of Affections among the People to nothing else but the Change of the Ministry: For we find that

[b] an / a *Fol.*

[10] On 8 Mar. 1708 the Privy Council issued warrants for the arrests of over thirty Scots 'upon suspicion of high treason ... in the late intended invasion of Scotland' and Nithsdale, Kenmure, and Nairne were among them (H.M.C. *House of Lords MSS.* viii. 111). They were questioned and eventually released for lack of evidence although Lockhart claims that the approaching elections prompted both parties in Parliament to avoid creating resentment among so many Scots peers (*Lockhart Papers* i. 293–4). Lord Griffin was actually tried and condemned for treason, but Queen Anne pardoned him; her action prompted Sunderland to complain that her clemency was 'a declaration to the whole world ... against the Protestant succession' (B. L. Lansdowne MS. 1236, fos. 244–5).

[11] At their executions both Derwentwater and Kenmure regretted pleading guilty to the charge of treason and professed their allegiance to the Pretender (Tindal, pp. 487–8).

a great many Persons lost their Loyalty with their Places;[12] and that their Friends have ever since made use of the most base Methods to infuse those groundless Discontents into the Minds of the Common People, which have brought so many of them to the Brink of Destruction, and proved so detrimental to their Fellow-Subjects. However, this Proceeding has shewn how dangerous it would have been for His Majesty to have continued in their Places of Trust a Set of Men, some of whom have since actually joined with the Pretender to His Crown: While others may be justly suspected never to have been faithful to Him in their Hearts, or, at least, whose Principles are precarious, and visibly conducted by their Interest. In a Word, if the Removal of these Persons from their Posts has produced such popular Commotions, the Continuance of them might have produced something much more fatal to their King and Country, and have brought about that Revolution, which has now been in vain attempted. The Condition of a *British* King would be very poor indeed! should a Party of His Subjects threaten Him with a Rebellion upon his bringing Malefactors to Justice, or upon His refusing to employ those whom He dares[c] not Trust.

I shall only mention another Argument against the Punishment of Any of the Rebels, whose Executions he represents as very shocking to the People, because they are their *Countrymen* (p. 12). And again, *The Quality of the Sufferers, their Alliances, their Characters, their being* Englishmen, *with a thousand other Circumstances, will contribute to breed more ill Blood than all the State-Chirurgeons can possibly let out* (p. 12). The Impeached Lords likewise, in the last Paragraph of the Pamphlet, are recommended to our Pity, because they are our *Countrymen.* By this way of Reasoning, no Man that is a Gentleman, or born within the three Seas, should be subject to Capital Punishment. Besides, who can be guilty of Rebellion that are not our *Countrymen*? As for the endearing Name of *Englishman*, which be bestows upon every one of the Criminals,[13] he should consider, that a Man deservedly cuts himself off from the Affections as well as the Privileges of that Community which he endeavours to subvert.

These are the several Arguments which appear in different Forms and

[c] dares / dare *Fol.*

[12] In 1714 the King removed the Earl of Mar from his post as Secretary of Scotland, the Duke of Ormonde from his post as Captain General, and Viscount Bolingbroke from his as Secretary of State (Tindal, p. 404). All three entered the Pretender's service in the following year: Mar as his Commander-in-chief in Scotland, Ormonde as the same for England and Ireland, and Bolingbroke as his Secretary of State (H.M.C. *Mar and Kellie MSS.* 511; H.M.C. *Stuart MSS.* i. 353–4, 379–80).

[13] Of the seven rebel Lords only two, Derwentwater and Widdrington, were English; the rest were Scots.

Expressions thro' this whole Pamphlet, and under which everyone that is urged in it may be reduced. There is indeed another Set of them, derived from the Example and Authority of Great Persons, which the Author produces in Favour of his own Scheme. These are *William* the Conquerour, *Henry* the IVth of *France*, our late King *William*, King *Solomon*, and the *Pretender*. If a Man were disposed to draw Arguments for Severity out of History, how many Instances might one find of it among the greatest Princes of every Nation? But as different Princes may act very laudably by different Methods in different Conjunctures, I cannot think this a conclusive Way of Reasoning. However, let us examine this Set of Arguments, and we shall find them no less defective than those abovementioned.

One of the greatest of our English *Monarchs*, says our Author, *was* William the Conquerour; *and he was the greater because he put to Death only one Person of Quality that we read of, and him after repeated Treacheries; yet he was a Foreigner, had Power sufficient, and did not want Provocations to have been more bloody* (p. 27). This Person of Quality was the Earl *Waltheof*,[d] who being overtaken with Wine, engaged in a Conspiracy against this Monarch,[e] but repenting of it the next Morning, repaired to the King who was then in *Normandy*, and discovered[f] the whole Matter. Notwithstanding which, he was Beheaded upon the Defeat of the Conspiracy, for having but thus far tampered in it.[14] And as for the rest of the Conspirators, who rose in an actual Rebellion, the King used them with the utmost Rigour, he cut off the Hands of some, put out the Eyes of others, some were hanged upon Gibbets, and those who fared the best, were sent into Banishment. There are, indeed, the most dreadful Examples of Severity in this Reign: Tho' it must be confess'd, that, after the Manner of those Times, the Nobility generally escaped with their Lives, tho' Multitudes of them were punished with Banishment, perpetual Imprisonment, Forfeitures, and other great Severities: While the poor People, who had been deluded by these their Ring-leaders, were executed with the utmost Rigour. A Partiality which I

[d] Earl *Waltheof*/Earl of *Waltheof Fol.* [e] Monarch/King *Fol.* [f] repaired to the King who was then in *Normandy*, and discovered/came to him in Person, and revealed *Fol.*

[14] Addison's source is Echard's *History of England* (1707), i. 145–6. The Earl of Waltheof was the only nobleman in William's reign condemned to death and his execution was not as unjust as Addison suggests. Waltheof rebelled against William in 1069 but was pardoned and married the Conqueror's niece the following year. William pardoned him again in 1075 when he revealed the conspiracy Addison mentions, but, when the King returned from Normandy, he found his kingdom beset with rebellion and invaded by Danes; he reconsidered his pardon, then tried and executed Waltheof in May 1076. Echard claims that William 'oftentimes shew'd uncommon Generosity' in pardoning noble offenders, but he was, as Addison emphasizes, ruthless in his punishment of rebel commoners.

believe no Commoner of *England* will ever think to be either just or reasonable.

The next Instance is *Henry* the IVth of *France, who* (says our Author) *so handsomely expressed his Tenderness for his People, when, at Signing the Treaty of* Vervins, *he said, That by one Dash of his Pen he had overcome more Enemies than he cou'd ever be able to do with his Sword* (p. 9). Would not an ordinary Reader think that this Treaty of *Vervins* was a Treaty between *Henry* the IVth and a Party of his Subjects? For otherwise how can it have a Place in the present Argument? But instead of that, it was a Treaty between *France* and *Spain*; so that the Speech expressed an equal Tenderness to the *Spaniards* and *French*; as Multitudes of either Nation must have fallen in that War, had it continued longer.[15] As for this King's Treatment of Conspirators, (tho' he is quoted thrice in the Pamphlet as an Example of Clemency) you have an eminent Instance of it in his Behaviour to the Mareschal *de Biron*, who had been his old faithful Servant, and had contributed more than any one to his Advancement to the Throne. This Mareschal, upon some Discontent, was enter'd into a Conspiracy against his Master, and refusing to open the whole Secret to the King, he was sent to the *Bastile*, and there beheaded, notwithstanding he sought for Mercy with great Importunities, and in the most moving Manner:[16] There are other Instances in this King's Reign, who notwithstanding was remarkable for his Clemency, of Rebels and Conspirators who were hanged, beheaded, or broken alive on the Wheel.

The late King *William* was not disturbed by any Rebellion from those who had once submitted to him. But we know he treated the Persons concerned in the Assassination-Plot as so horrid a Conspiracy deserved. As for the Saying which this Author imputes to that Monarch, it being a Piece of Secret History, one doth not know when it was spoken, or what it alluded to, unless the Author had been more particular in the Account of it.[17]

[15] Philip II actively supported the French Holy League in civil war against Henry IV for several years before the latter declared war on Spain in January 1595. The war went badly for France, but the Treaty of Vervins, concluded in May 1598 and later signed by Henry in Paris, gave him much more than his successes in the war deserved. Henry told the Duke of Epernon, '*With this Stroke of a Pen, I have done more Exploits than I could have done in a long time with the best Swords of my Kingdom*' (Bayle, *Historical Dictionary*, article 'Henry IV', remark o).

[16] Charles de Gontaut, duc de Biron (1562–1602), a favourite of Henry IV, entered into a conspiracy with the Duke of Savoy. When an accomplice gave Henry some of Biron's correspondence, Henry attempted to persuade Biron to confess by assuring him of a full pardon, but Biron refused to do so. 'The king ... therefore resolved to abandon him to the severity of Justice, since he refused to cast himself into the arms of Mercy' (Eudes de Mézeray, *History of France*, 1683, p. 895).

[17] In 1696 several conspirators revealed to the Earl of Portland a plot to assassinate

(*continued*)

The Author proceeds in the next Place to no less an Authority than that of *Solomon*: *Among all the general Observations of the wisest Princes we know of, I think there is none holds more universally than Mercy and Truth preserve a King, and his Throne is established in Mercy* (p. 18).[18] If we compare the different Sayings of this wise King, which relate to the Conduct of Princes, we cannot question but that he means by this Mercy that kind of it which is consistent with Reason and Government, and by which we hope to see his Majesty's Throne established. But our Author shou'd consider that the same wise Man has said in another Place, that 'An evil Man seeketh Rebellion, therefore a cruel Messenger shall be sent against him.'[19] Accordingly his Practice was agreeable to his Proverb: No Prince having ever given a greater Testimony of his Abhorrence to Undertakings of this treasonable Nature. For he dispatched such a cruel Messenger as is here mentioned to those who had been engaged in a Rebellion many Years before he himself was on the Throne, and even to his elder Brother, upon the bare Suspicion that he was Projecting so wicked an Enterprize.[20]

How the Example of the Pretender came into this Argument, I am at a Loss to find out. *The Pretender declared a general Pardon to All: And shall our rightful King shew himself less the true Father of his People, and afford his Pardon to none, &c.* (p. 25). The Pretender's general Pardon was to a People who were not in his Power; and had he ever reduced them under it, it was only promised to such as immediately joined with him for the Recovery of what he called his Right. It was such a general Pardon as would have been

---

William III prior to an invasion by James II. On 23 Feb. William ordered twenty-nine conspirators to be apprehended; ten were arrested almost immediately and eight of those were tried and executed (Burnet, *History* iv. 296–316, 327–51; Kennett, *History of England* (1706), iii. 709–31). Atterbury ignores the executions and only relates that 'The late King William . . . upon the Discovery of a Plot against him . . . called a consultation of his Friends, some of whom urged him to Execute every Man concern'd in the Business: After canvassing the Whole, he dismissed his Counsellors, and said to one of his Confidants, *Those People think I have had nothing to do but to come into* England *to be their Hangman*' (p. 19). The source for this remark has not been identified, but Burnet says that William was reluctant to expose the whole conspiracy because 'the king apprehended, that so many persons would be found concerned . . .' (*History* iv. 309).

[18] Prov. 20:28.

[19] Prov. 17:11.

[20] Following instructions David made on his deathbed, Solomon sent Benaiah, the 'cruel Messenger', to execute Joab for murdering Abner and Amasa and for supporting Adonijah. Benaiah was also sent to execute Shimei who had cursed David in his flight from Absalom (1 Kgs. 2:5–9, 28–34; 2 Sam. 16:5–13). Solomon's older brother, Adonijah, had proclaimed himself king while David lay dying, although Solomon had been designated successor and had been annointed. Adonijah submitted to his brother and was pardoned; however, after David's death, he asked to be given Abishag, the woman who ministered to David in his last illness, for his wife. Solomon suspected that Adonijah was planning to reassert his claim to the throne and sent Benaiah to execute him (1 Kgs. 1:5, 32–40, 50–3; 1 Kgs. 2:13–25).

consistent with the Execution of more than nine Parts in ten of the Kingdom.[21]

There is but one more Historical Argument, which is drawn from King *Philip*'s Treatment of the *Catalans. I think it would not be unseasonable for some Men to recollect what their own Notions were of the Treatment of the* Catalans; *how many Declamations were made on the Barbarity used towards them by King* Philip, *&c.* (p. 29). If the Author remembers, these Declamations, as he calls them, were not made so much on the Barbarity used towards them by King *Philip*, as on the Barbarity used towards them by the *English* Government. King *Philip* might have some Colour for treating them as Rebels, but we ought to have regarded them as Allies; and were obliged, by all the Ties of Honour, Conscience, and publick Faith, to have sheltered them from those Sufferings, which were brought upon them by a firm and inviolable Adherence to our Interests.[22] However, none can draw into a Parallel the Cruelties which have been inflicted on that unhappy People, with those few Instances of Severity which our Government has been obliged to exert towards the *British* Rebels. I say no Man would make such a Parallel, unless his Mind be so blinded with Passion and Prejudice, as to assert, in the Language of this Pamphlet, *That no Instances can be produced of the least Lenity under the present Administration, from the first Hour it commenc'd to this Day* (p. 20), with other astonishing

[21] In the Pretender's *Declaration* (see *F.* 9), he promised to pardon all crimes of treason for persons who joined the rebels.

[22] Addison is exploiting the popular Whig complaint against the Tory ministers who negotiated the Treaty of Utrecht. With Queen Anne's guarantee that the Habsburg Archduke Charles would recognize their liberties and privileges (which were different from those elsewhere in Spain), the Catalans declared for the Archduke, rebelled against the Bourbon Philip V in 1705, fought with the British in Spain, and assisted in the capture of Madrid in 1710. In the peace negotiations two years later, Philip was adamant about revoking the Catalans' special privileges and, although the Queen felt obliged to secure those rights, her Tory ministers were unable to do so (H.M.C. *House of Lords MSS.* x. 260). The peace treaty signed with Spain in 1713 only required Philip to grant the Catalans the same rights which Castilians enjoyed (Article XIII). Prompted by Whig dissatisfaction concerning the settlement, the Lords asked for an account of 'what Endeavours have been used, that the Catalans might have . . . their Liberties and Privileges' (*Parl. Hist.* vi. 1331–32; *L.J.* xix. 638). The ministry's response, presented on 2 Apr. 1714, included some relevant diplomatic correspondence, argued that the British involvement with the Catalans was principally the 'Consequence of the Sollicitations of the Catalans', and that 'the Engagements Her Majesty was entered into, subsisted no longer than while King Charles was in Spain' (H.M.C. *House of Lords MSS.* x. 249–69; Chandler, v. 121; Boyer, *Queen Anne*, p. 682). The Lords addressed the Queen 'to continue her Interposition' on the Catalans' behalf, but nothing came of this (*L.J.* xix. 645). The Catalans continued their resistance to Philip, and Barcelona was subjected to a long siege, finally surrendering to the Bourbon forces in September 1714; London newspapers published vivid descriptions of the suffering there (e.g. *Post Boy*, 29 July to 23 Sept. *passim*). Walpole's Committee of Secrecy blamed this suffering on the Tory ministers who allowed Britain's allies to be 'given up to their enemies, contrary to faith and honour' (*Parl. Hist.* vii, appendix 1, p. lxxxiv).

Reflexions of the same Nature, which are contradicted by such innumerable Matters of Fact, that it would be an Affront to a Reader's Understanding to endeavour to confute them. But to return to the *Catalans*; *During the whole Course of the War*, says the Author, *which ever of them submitted to Discretion, were received to Mercy* (p. 29). This is so far from being truly related, that in the Beginning of the War they were executed without Mercy. But, when in Conjunction with their Allies, they became Superiour to King *Philip's* Party in Strength, and extended their Conquests up to the very Gates of *Madrid*, it cannot be supposed the *Spanish* Court would be so infatuated as to persist in their first Severities, against an Enemy that could make such terrible Reprizals. However, when this Reason of State ceased, how dreadful was the Havock made among this brave, but unhappy People! The whole Kingdom, without any Distinction to the many Thousands of its innocent Inhabitants, was stript of its Immunities, and reduced to a State of Slavery. *Barcelona* was filled with Executions; and all the Patriots of their antient Liberties either beheaded, stowed in Dungeons, or condemned to work in the Mines of *America*.

God be thanked we have a King who punishes with Reluctancy, and is averse to such Cruelties as were us'd among the *Catalans*, as much as to those practised on the Persons concern'd in *Monmouth*'s Rebellion. Our Author, indeed, condemns these *Western* Assizes in King *James*'s *Reign* (p. 26). And it would be well if all those who still adhere to the Cause of that unfortunate King, and are clamorous at the Proceedings of His present Majesty, would remember, that notwithstanding that Rebellion fell very much short of This both in the Number and Strength of the Rebels, and had no Tendency either to destroy the National Religion, to introduce an Arbitrary Government, or to subject us to a Foreign Power; not only the Chief of the Rebels was beheaded, but even a Lady, who had only harbour'd one of the Offenders in her House, was in her extreme old Age put to the same kind of Death: That about two hundred and thirty were hanged, drawn, and quartered, and their Limbs dispersed through several Parts of the Country, and set up as Spectacles of Terror to their Fellow-Subjects. It would be too tedious a Work to run thro' the numberless Fines, Imprisonments, Corporal Punishments, and Transportations, which were then likewise practised as wholesome Severities.[23]

[23] Referring to the aftermath of Monmouth's rebellion in 1685, Atterbury argued that 'the *Western Assizes* in King *James*'s Reign, disposed those Countries to receive the Prince of Orange with open Arms' (p. 26) and Addison naturally takes the opportunity to contrast George's treatment of the Jacobite rebels with James's harsher measures. In 1716 this contrast was expanded in a pamphlet entitled *An Account of the Proceedings against the Rebels . . . before the Lord Chief Justice Jeffries* which listed the hundreds of persons executed after

We have now seen how fallaciously the Author has stated the Cause he has undertaken, by supposing that nothing but unlimited Mercy, or unlimited Punishment, are the Methods that can be made use of in our present Treatment of the Rebels: That he has omitted the middle Way of Proceeding between these two Extreams: That this middle Way is the Method in which His Majesty, like all other wise and good Kings, has chosen to proceed: That it is agreeable to the Nature of Government, Religion, and our *British* Constitution: And that every Argument which the Author has produced from Reason and Example, would have been a true one, had it been urged for[9] that restrain'd Clemency which His Majesty has exercised: But is a false one, when apply'd to such a general, undistinguishing Mercy as the Author wou'd recommend.

Having thus answered that which is the main Drift and Design of this Pamphlet, I shall touch upon those other Parts of it which are interwoven with the Arguments, to put Men out of Humour with the present Government.

And here we may observe, that it is our Author's Method to suppose Matters of Fact, which are not in Being, and afterwards to descant upon them. As he is very sensible that the Cause will not bear the Test of Reason, he has indeed every where chosen rather Topicks for Declamation than Argument. Thus he entertains us with a laboured Invective against a standing Army.[24] But what has this to do in the present Case? I suppose he wou'd not advise His Majesty to disband his Forces while there is an Army of Rebels in his Dominions. I cannot imagine he would think the Affections of the People of *England* a Security of the Government in such a Juncture, were it not at the same Time defended with a sufficient Body of Troops. No Prince has ever given a greater Instance of his Inclinations to rule without a Standing-Army, if we consider, that upon the very first News of the Defeat of the Rebels, he declared to both Houses of Parliament, that he had put an immediate Stop to the Levies which he had begun to raise at their Request, and that he wou'd not make use of the Power which they had entrusted him with, unless any new Preparations of the Enemy shou'd make it necessary for our Defence.[25] This Speech was receiv'd with

[9] for / from *Fol.*

Monmouth's rebellion. At Winchester, Mrs. Alicia Lisle, widow of the regicide, John Lisle, was tried and executed for harbouring a noncomformist minister named Hickes who had been with Monmouth; she was over seventy years old and Hickes had not yet been convicted of treason when she was executed.

[24] pp. 14–18.

[25] In his speech to Parliament on 17 Feb. 1716, the King announced that the Pretender had fled from Scotland and that he would not need the 'necessary Dispositions ... made for raising additional Forces' (*C.J.* xviii. 294).

the greatest Gratitude by both Houses; and it is said, that in the House of Commons a very candid and honourable Gentleman (who generally votes with the Minority) declared, that he had not heard so gracious a Speech from the Throne for many Years last past.

In another Place, he supposes that the Government has not endeavoured to gain the Applause of the Vulgar, by doing something for the Church; and very gravely makes Excuses for this their pretended Neglect. What greater Instances could His Majesty have given of his Love to the Church of *England*, than those he has exhibited by his most solemn Declarations; by his daily Example; and by his Promotions of the most eminent among the Clergy to such Vacancies as have happened in his Reign. To which we must add, for the Honour of his Government in this Particular, that it has done more for the Advantage of the Clergy, than those, who are the most Zealous for their Interest, could have expected in so short a Time; which will farther appear, if we reflect upon the Valuable and Royal Donative to one of our Universities, and the Provision made for those who are to officiate in the Fifty New Churches.[26] His Majesty is, indeed, a Prince of too much Magnanimity and Truth, to make use of the Name of the Church for drawing his People into any thing that may be prejudicial to them; for what our Author says to this Purpose, redounds as much to the Honour of the present Administration, as to the Disgrace of others. *Nay, I wish with all my Soul they had stooped a little* ad captum vulgi, *to take in those shallow fluttering Hearts, which are to be caught by any thing baited with the Name of* Church (p. 11).

Again; The Author asks, *Whether Terror is to become the only National Principle?* With other Questions of the same Nature: And in several Parts of his Book, harangues very plentifully against such a Notion. Where he talks in Generals upon this Topick, there is no question but every *Whig* and *Tory* in the Kingdom perfectly agree with him in what he says. But if he would insinuate, as he seems to do in several Places, that there should be no Impressions of Awe upon the Mind of a Subject, and that a Government shou'd not create Terror in those who are disposed to do ill, as well as encourage those that do their Duty: In short, if he is for an entire Exclusion of that Principle of Fear which is supposed to have some Influence in every Law, he opposes himself to the Form of every Government in the World, and to the Common Sense of Mankind.

[26] In September 1715 the King gave the library of John Moore, the late Bishop of Ely, to Cambridge University. It contained about 29,000 books and 1,800 manuscripts (H.M.C. *Southampton MSS.* 133, 341). In the same month he gave his royal assent to 'An Act for making Provisions for the Ministers of the Fifty new Churches' (*L.J.* xx. 235).

The Artifice of this Author in starting Objections to the Friends of the Government, and the foolish Answers which he supposes they return to them, is so very visible, that every one sees they are designed rather to divert his Reader, than to instruct him.

I have now examined this whole Pamphlet, which, indeed, is written with a great deal of Art, and as much Argument as the Cause would bear: And after having stated the true Notion of Clemency, Mercy, Compassion, Good-nature, Humanity, or whatever else it may be called, so far as it is consistent with Wisdom, and the Good of Mankind, or, in other Words, so far as it is a moral Vertue, I shall readily concur with the Author in the highest Panegyricks that he has bestowed upon it. As, likewise, I heartily join with him in every thing he has said against Justice, if it includes, as his Pamphlet supposes, the Extirpation of every Criminal, and is not exercised with a much greater Mixture of Clemency than Rigour. Mercy, in the true Sense of the Word, is that Vertue by which a Prince approaches nearest to Him whom he represents; and whilst he is neither remiss nor extream to animadvert upon those who offend him, that Logick will hold true of him which is apply'd to the Great Judge of all the Earth; *With thee there is Mercy, therefore shalt thou be Feared.*[27]

Numb. XXXII *Monday, April* 9, 1716

Heu miseræ Cives! non hostem inimicaque castra
Argivum; vestras spes uritis — —

Virg.

I QUESTION not but the *British* Ladies are very well pleased with the Compliment I have payed them in the Course of my Papers, by regarding them, not only as the most amiable, but as a most important Part of our Community. They ought, indeed, to resent the Treatment they have met with from other Authors, who have never troubled their Heads about them, but address'd all their Arguments to the Male Half of their Fellow-Subjects; and taken it for granted, that if they could bring these into their Measures, the Females would of Course follow their political Mates. The Arguments they have made use of, are like *Hudibras*'s Spur, which he

[27] Ps. 130:4.

Motto. Virgil, *Aeneid*, v. 671–2: Alas, wretched countrywomen! It is not the foe and hostile camp of the Greeks, it is your own hopes which are burning.

apply'd to one Side of his Horse, as not doubting but the other would keep Pace with it.[2] These Writers seem to have regarded the Fair Sex but as the Garniture of a Nation; and when they consider them as Parts of the Commonwealth, it is only as they are of use to the Consumption of our Manufacture. *Could we persuade our* British *Women* (says one of our eminent Merchants in a Letter to his Friend in the Country upon the Subject of Commerce) *to cloath themselves in the comely Apparel which might be made out of the Wooll of their own Country; and instead of Coffee, Tea and Chocolate, to delight in those wholesome and palatable Liquors which may be extracted from our* British *Simples; they would be of great Advantage to Trade, and therein to the Publick Weal.*[3]

It is now, however, become necessary to treat our Women as Members of the Body Politick; since it is visible that great Numbers of them have of late eloped from their Allegiance, and that they do not believe themselves obliged to draw with us, as Yoke-Fellows in the Constitution. They will judge for themselves; look into the State of the Nation with their own Eyes; and be no longer led Blindfold by a Male Legislature. A Friend of mine was lately complaining to me, that his Wife had turned off one of the best Cook-Maids in *England*, because the Wench had said something to her Fellow-Servants, which seemed to favour the Suspension of the *Habeas-Corpus* Act.

When Errors and Prejudices are thus spread among the Sex, it is the hardest thing in the World to root them out. Arguments, which are the only proper Means for it, are of little use: They have a very short Answer to all Reasonings that turn against them, *Make us believe That, if you can*; which is in *Latin*, if I may upon this Occasion be allowed the Pedantry of a Quotation, *Non persuadebis, etiamsi persuaseris.* I could not but smile at a young University Disputant, who was complaining the other Day of the Unreasonableness of a Lady with whom he was engaged in a Point of Controversy. Being left alone with her, he took the Opportunity of pursuing an Argument which had been before started in Discourse, and put it to her in a Syllogism: Upon which, as he informed us with some Heat, she granted him both the Major and the Minor, but[a] deny'd him the Conclusion.

[a] but/and *Fol.*

[2] Samuel Butler, *Hudibras*, I. i. 447–50:

> For Hudibras wore but one Spur,
> As wisely knowing, could he stir
> To active trot one side of 's Horse
> The other would not hang an Arse.

[3] Source unidentified.

The best Method, therefore, that can be made use of with these Polemical Ladies, who are much more easy to be Refuted than Silenced, is to shew them the ridiculous Side of their Cause, and to make them laugh at their own Politicks. It is a kind of ill Manners to offer Objections to a fine Woman; and a Man would be out of Countenance that should gain the Superiority in such a Contest. A Coquette Logician may be Railly'd, but not Contradicted. Those who would make use of solid Arguments and strong Reasonings to a Reader or Hearer of so delicate a Turn, would be like that foolish People whom *Ælian* speaks of, that worshipped a Fly, and sacrificed an Ox to it.[4]

The Truth of it is, a Man must be of a very disputatious Temper, that enters into State Controversies with any of the Fair Sex. If the Malignant be not Beautiful, she cannot do much Mischief; and if she is, her Arguments will be so enforced by the Charms of her Person, that her Antagonist may be in danger of betraying his own Cause. *Milton* puts this Confession into the Mouth of our Father *Adam*; who, tho' he asserts his Superiority of Reason in his Debates with the Mother of Mankind, adds,

— — Yet when I approach
Her Loveliness, so absolute she seems,
And in herself Compleat; so well to know
Her own, that what she wills to do or say,
Seems wisest, vertuousest, discreetest, best:
All higher Knowledge in her Presence falls
Degraded, Wisdom in Discourse with her
Looses, discount'nanc'd, and like Folly shews;
Authority and Reason on her wait — —[5]

If there is such a native Loveliness in the Sex, as to make them Victorious even when they are in the wrong, how resistless is their Power when they are on the Side of Truth! And, indeed, it is a peculiar good Fortune to the Government, that our Female Malecontents are so much overmatched in Beauty, as well as Number, by those who are Loyal to their King, and Friends to their Country.

Every Paper, which I have hitherto address'd to our beautiful Incendiaries, hath been filled with Considerations of a different Kind; by which Means I have taken Care that those, who are Enemies to the Sex, or to my self, may not accuse me of Tautology, or pretend that I attack them with their own Weapon. For this Reason I shall here lay together a new Set

[4] Claudius Aelian, *On the Nature of Animals*, xi. 8.

[5] *Paradise Lost*, viii. 546–54.

of Remarks, and observe the several Artifices by which the Enemies to our Establishment do raise such unaccountable Passions and Prejudices in the Minds of our discontented Females.

In the first Place; It is usual among the most Cunning of our Adversaries, to represent all the Rebels as very handsome Men. If the Name of a Traitor be mentioned, they are very particular in describing his Person; and when they are not able to extenuate his Treason, commend his Shape. This has so good an Effect in one of these Female Audiences, that they represent to themselves a thousand poor, tall, innocent, fresh coloured young Gentlemen, who are dispers'd among the several Prisons of *Great Britain*, and extend their generous Compassion towards a Multitude of agreeable Fellows that never were in being.

Another Artifice is, to instill Jealousies into their Minds of Designs upon the Anvil to retrench the Privileges of the Sex. Some represent the *Whigs* as Enemies to *Flanders*-Lace: Others had spread a Report, that in the late Act of Parliament for four Shillings in the Pound upon Land, there would be inserted a Clause for raising a Tax upon Pin-Money. That the Ladies may be the better upon their Guard against Suggestions of this Nature, I shall beg Leave to put them in mind of the Story of *Papirius*, the Son of a *Roman* Senator. This young Gentleman, after having been present in publick Debates, was usually teazed by his Mother to inform her of what had passed. In order to deliver himself from this Importunity, he told her one Day, upon his Return from the Senate-House, that there had been a Motion made for a Decree to allow every Man Two Wives. The good Lady said nothing; but managed Matters so well among the *Roman* Matrons, that the next Day they met together in a Body before the Senate-House, and presented a Petition to the Fathers against so unreasonable a Law. This groundless Credulity raised so much Raillery upon the Petitioners, that we do not find the Ladies offer'd to direct the Law-givers of their Country ever after.[6]

There has been another Method lately made use of, which has been practised with extraordinary Success; I mean the spreading abroad Reports of Prodigies, which has wonderfully gratified the Curiosity, as well as the Hopes of our fair Malignants.[7] Their Managers turn Water into Bloud for

[6] The story appears in several Latin sources. Papirius told his mother that the Senate was debating whether it was more appropriate for each husband to be allowed two wives or each wife allowed two husbands. The Roman matrons went to the Senate to complain about the pending legislation and also to lobby for wives having two husbands if such legislation was inevitable (Aulus Gellius, *Noctes Atticae*, i. 23; Macrobius, *Saturnalia*, i. 6).

[7] The 'prodigy' which received the most attention was the aurora borealis of 6 March (see *F.* 24, n. 5). Dudley Ryder reports visiting a Mrs. Evans in Watford, 'an ignorant Tory' who 'looked upon the strange appearance in the air as a prodigy that portended great things, and

them; frighten them with Sea-Monsters; make them see Armies in the Air; and give them their Word; the more to ingratiate themselves with them, that they signify nothing less than future Slaughter and Desolation. The disloyal Part of the Sex immediately hug themselves at the News of the Bloody Fountain; look upon these Fish as their Friends; have great Expectations from the Clouds; and are very angry with you, if you think they do not all portend Ruin to their Country.

Secret History and Scandal have always had their Allurements; and I have in other Discourses shewn the great Advantage that is made of them in the present Ferment among the fair Ones.

But the Master Engine, to[b] overturn the Minds of the Female World, is the *Danger of the Church.* I am not so uncharitable as to think there is any thing in an Observation made by several of the *Whigs*, that there is scarce a Woman in *England* who is troubled with the Vapours, but is more or less affected with this Cry: Or, to remark with others, that it is not utter'd in any Part of the Nation with so much Bitterness of Tongue and Heart, as in the Districts of *Drury-Lane.*[8] On the contrary, I believe there are many devout and honourable Women who are deluded in this Point by the Artifice of designing Men. To these, therefore, I would apply my self in a more serious Manner, and desire them to consider how that laudable Piety, which is natural to the Sex, is apt to degenerate into a groundless and furious Zeal, when it is not kept within the Bounds of Charity and Reason. Female Zeal, though proceeding from so good a Principle, has been infinitely detrimental to Society, and to Religion itself. If we may believe the *French* Historians, it often put a Stop to the Proceedings of their Kings, which might have ended in a Reformation. For, upon their breaking with the Pope, the Queens frequently interposed, and by their Importunities, reconciled them to the Usurpations of the Church of *Rome.* Nay, it was this vicious Zeal which gave a remarkable Check to the first Progress of Christianity, as we find it recorded by a Sacred Historian, in the following Passage, which I shall leave to the Consideration of my Female Readers. *But the* Jews *stirred up the devout and honourable Women, and the chief Men of the City, and raised a Persecution against* Paul *and* Barnabas, *and expelled them out of their Coasts.*[9]

[b] Engine, to/Engine, which is made use of to *Fol.*

---

her sister said that the King would not have pardoned the rest of the lords as is talked of except it had been for that' (*Diary*, 4 Apr. 1716).

[8] See *F.* 3, n. 4.

[9] Acts 13:50.

Numb. XXXIII *Friday, April* 13, 1716

Nulli adversus Magistratus ac Reges gratiores sunt; nec immerito, nullis enim plus præstant quam quibus frui tranquillo otio licet. Itaque hi, quibus ad propositum bene vivendi confert Securitas publica, necesse est auctorem hujus boni ut parentem colant. Senec. Ep. 73.

WE find by our publick Papers, the University of *Dublin* have lately presented to the Prince of *Wales*, in a most humble and dutiful Manner, their Diploma for constituting His Royal Highness Chancellor of that Learned Body; and that the Prince received this their Offer with the Goodness and Condescension which is natural to his illustrious House.[2] As the College of *Dublin* have been long famous for their great Learning, they have now given us an Instance of their good Sense; and it is with Pleasure[a] that we find such a Disposition in this famous Nursery of Letters, to propagate sound Principles, and to act in its proper Sphere for the Honour and Dignity of the Royal Family. We hope that such an Example will have its Influence on other Societies of the same Nature;[3] and cannot but

[a] with Pleasure / with great Pleasure *Fol.*

Motto. Seneca, *Epistles*, lxxiii. 1–2: For contrariwise there is not any one that reverenceth and respecteth them [the Magistrates and Kings] more than they. And not without cause; for that Kings cannot doe greater good unto any man in this World, than to those that may enjoy a peaceable repose. It must then necessarily fall out, that they to whom publike assurance openeth the way to the intention they have to live well, should reverence the Author of the same good as their Lord and Father (trans. LODGE). [Addison has replaced *illos* in Seneca's text with its antecedent, *Magistratus ac Reges.*]

[2] The Prince of Wales was unanimously elected Chancellor of Trinity College, Dublin, on 16 Feb. 1716. A month earlier Charles Dering wrote that 'the University of Dublin have offer'd to chuse Lord Anglesey for their Chancellor', but Anglesey, a leader in the Irish House of Lords, was voted an 'enemy to King and Country' later in January because he refused to sign a loyalist association, and the college appointment was never made. On 10 Apr. a delegation from Trinity College attended the Prince of Wales to admit him to his new office and he gave an entertainment at Somerset House for the Irish visitors; as a former Secretary of Ireland, Addison may have been among the guests (Percival Letterbook, 14, 21 Jan.; *Pol. State* xi. 407–12). The speech of Benjamin Pratt, Provost of Trinity College, to the Prince of Wales upon delivering 'the Instrument of his election' was published in the *St. James's Evening Post*, 14–17 Apr.

[3] On 19 Sept. 1715 Percival wrote, 'The University of Oxford being obliged upon the Duke of Ormonds attainder to chuse some other Chancellor had a private intimation that it would be acceptable to the Court if they elected the prince, but they to their shame, and Eternal Mark of indiscretion Elected my Lord Aran the Duke of Ormonds brother' (Letterbook). Dudley Ryder reported that his cousin, a student at Cambridge, told him 'the great majority there are against the King, though they all, except five or six, take the oaths to

rejoice to see the Heir of *Great Britain* vouchsafing to Patronize in so peculiar a Manner that[b] Noble Seminary, which is perhaps at this Time Training up such Persons as may hereafter be Ornaments to his Reign.

When Men of Learning are acted thus by a Knowledge of the World as well as of Books, and shew that their Studies naturally inspire them with a Love to their King and Country; they give a Reputation to Literature, and convince the World of its Usefulness. But when Arts and Sciences are so perverted as to dispose Men to act in Contradiction to the rest of the Community, and to set up for a kind of separate Republick among themselves, they draw upon them the Indignation of the Wise, and the Contempt of the Ignorant.[4]

It has, indeed, been observed, that Persons, who are very much esteemed for their Knowledge and Ingenuity in their private Characters, have acted like Strangers to Mankind, and to the Dictates of right Reason, when joined together in a Body. Like several Chymical Waters, that are each of them clear and transparent when separate, but ferment into a thick troubled Liquor when they are mixed in the same Vial.

There is a Piece of Mythology which bears very hard upon Learned Men; and which I shall here relate, rather for the Delicacy of the Satyr, than for the Justness of the Moral. When the City of *Athens* was finished, we are told that *Neptune* and *Minerva* presented themselves as Candidates for the Guardianship of the Place. The *Athenians*, after a full Debate upon the Matter, came to an Election, and made choice of *Minerva*. Upon which,[c] *Neptune*, who very much resented the Indignity, upbraided them with their Stupidity and Ignorance; that a Maritime Town should reject the Patronage of him who was the God of the Seas, and could defend them against all the Attacks of their Enemies. He concluded with a Curse upon the Inhabitants, which was to stick to them and their Posterity; namely, *That they should be all Fools.* When *Minerva*, their Tutelary Goddess, who presides over Arts and Sciences, came among them to receive the Honour they had conferr'd upon her, they made heavy Complaints of the Curse which *Neptune* had laid upon the City; and begg'd her, if possible, to take it off. But she told them it was not in her Power; for that one Deity could not reverse the Act of another. *However*, said she, *I may alleviate the Curse*

[b] that/this *Fol.* [c] which,/this *Fol.*

him . . . When Dr. Sherlock was last year Vice-Chancellor of the University he was so far from discouraging the expression of disaffection and disloyalty in the students and those belonging to the University that he encouraged it . . . and checked the informers and refused to punish the criminals' (*Diary*, 24, 25 Feb.).

[4] Later in 1716 Oxford was compared to Avignon, a separate church state within the boundaries of a secular nation, in the *St. James's Post* (7–10 Dec.).

which I cannot remove: It is not possible for me to hinder you from being Fools, but I will take care that you shall be Learned.[5]

There is nothing which Bodies of Learned Men should be more careful of, than, by all due Methods, to[d] cultivate the Favour of the Great and Powerful. The Indulgence of a Prince is absolutely necessary to the Propagation, the Defence, the Honour, and Support of Learning. It naturally creates in Men's Minds an Ambition to distinguish themselves by Letters; and multiplies the Number of those who are dedicated to the Pursuits of Knowledge. It protects them against the Violence of Brutal Men; and gives them Opportunities to pursue their Studies in a State of Peace and Tranquility. It puts the Learned in[e] Countenance; and gives them a Place among the fashionable Part of Mankind. It distributes Rewards; and encourages Speculative Persons, who have neither Opportunity nor a Turn of Mind to increase their own Fortunes, with all the Incentives of Place, Profit and Preferment. On the contrary, nothing is in itself so pernicious to Communities of Learned Men, nor more apprehended by those that wish them well, then the Displeasure of their Prince, which those may justly expect to feel, who would make use of his Favour to his own Prejudice, and put in Practice all the Methods that lye within their Power to vilify his Person, and distress his Government. In both these Cases, a Learned Body is in a more particular Manner exposed to the Influence of their King, as described by the wisest of Men, *The Wrath of a King is as the Roaring of a Lion; but his Favour is as the Dew upon the Grass.*[6]

We find in our *English* Histories, that the Empress *Matilda*, (who was the great Ancestor of His present Majesty, and whose Grand-Daughter of the same Name has[f] a Place upon several of the *Hanover* Medals) was particularly favoured by the University of *Oxford*, and defended in that Place, when most parts of the Kingdom had revolted against her.[7] Nor is it to be questioned, but an University so famous for Learning, and sound Knowledge, will shew the same Zeal for her illustrious Descendent, as they

[d] than, by all due Methods, to / than to *Fol.* [e] puts the Learned in / puts Learned Men in *Fol.* [f] and whose Grand-Daughter of the same Name has / and for that Reason has *Fol.*

[5] Various versions of this story appear in classical literature. A Latin version close to Addison's is repeated by St. Augustine in *De Civitate Dei*, xviii. 9.

[6] Prov. 19:12.

[7] The Empress Matilda (1102–67), daughter of Henry I, married a German king, Henry V, in 1114 and learned the language and customs of her husband's country. After her father's death in 1135, she returned to Normandy and England to claim her right to his crown. During the struggle with King Stephen which ensued, she was defended at Oxford Castle in 1142. Although there were scholars like Robert Pullen lecturing in Oxford as early as 1133, the University was not officially established until the next century.

will every Day discern His Majesty's Royal Vertues, through those Prejudices which have been raised in their Minds by artful and designing Men. It is with much Pleasure we see this great Fountain of Learning already beginning to run clear, and recovering its Natural Purity and Brightness.[8] None can imagine that a Community, which is taxed by the worst of its Enemies, only for overstraining the Notions of Loyalty even to bad Princes, will fall short of a due Allegiance to the best.

When this happy Temper of Mind is fully established among them, we may justly hope to see the largest Share of His Majesty's Favours fall upon that University, which is the Greatest, and upon all Accounts the most Considerable not[g] only in His Dominions, but in all *Europe*.

I shall conclude this Paper with a Quotation out of *Cambden*'s History of Queen *Elizabeth*, who, after having described that Queen's Reception at *Oxford*, gives an Account of the Speech which she made to them at her Departure; concluding with a Piece of Advice to that University. Her Counsel was, *That they would first serve God, not after the Curiosity of some, but according to the Laws of God and the Land; that they would not go before the Laws, but follow them; nor*[h] *dispute whether better might be prescribed, but keep those prescribed already; obey their Superiors; and lastly, embrace one another in Brotherly Piety and Concord.*[9]

Numb. XXXIV *Monday*, *April* 16, 1716

— — sævus apertam
In rabiem cœpit verti jocus — —

Hor.

It is very justly, as well as frequently observed, that if our Nation be ever ruined, it must be by itself. The Parties and Divisions which reign among

g Considerable not / Considerable University, not *Fol.* h nor / not *Fol.*

[8] On 27 Nov. 1715 John Russell wrote 'You cannot be ignorant of the deplorable condition of the University of Oxford ... Rebellion is avowedly own'd & encouraged ... Some Tutors read Lectures to their Pupils on Hereditary Right, &c. And there are several Houses in which there's not so much as One (what they please to call a) Whig. There are but three Houses viz Wadham, Jesus, & Merton, whose Heads are not violent Tories & Jacobites. Merton stands fairest for a Cure, as having as yet several sound Members left among them' (Christ Church MS. Arch. W. Epis. 15). The recovery Addison mentions was the election of six loyalist fellows to Merton in March 1716 (*Flying Post*, 13–15 Mar.).

[9] Addison's folio text follows the 1630 edition of William Camden's *Elizabeth* (Bk. IV, p. 42) exactly. Elizabeth made the speech in 1592.

Motto. Horace, *Epistles*, II. i. 148–9: The fierce raillery began to turn into open rage.

us may several Ways bring Destruction upon our Country, at the same Time that our united Force would be sufficient to secure us against all the Attempts of a foreign Enemy. Whatever Expedients therefore can be found to allay those Heats and Animosities, which break us into different Factions and Interests, cannot but be useful to the Publick, and highly tend to its Safety, Strength, and Reputation.

This dangerous Dissention among us, discovers itself in all the most indifferent Circumstances of Life. We keep it up, and cherish it with as much Pains, as if it were a kind of National Blessing. It insinuates itself into all our Discourses, mixes in our Parties of Pleasure, has a Share in our Diversions, and is an Ingredient in most of our publick Entertainments.

I was not long ago at the Play call'd Sir *Courtly Nice*, where, to the eternal Reproach of good Sense, I found the whole Audience had very gravely ranged themselves into two Parties, under *Hot-head* and *Testimony*.[2] *Hot-head* was the applauded Hero of the *Tories*, and *Testimony* no less the Favourite of the *Whigs*.[3] Each Party followed their Champion. It was wonderful to see so polite an Assembly distinguishing themselves by such extraordinary Representatives, and avowing their Principles as conformable either to the Zeal of *Hot-head*, or the Moderation of *Testimony*. Thus the two Parts which were designed to expose the Faults of both Sides, and were accordingly received by our Ancestors in King *Charles* the Second's Reign, meet with a kind of Sanction from the Applauses which are respectively bestowed on them by their wise Posterity. We seem to imagine that they were written as Patterns for Imitation, not as Objects of Ridicule.

This Humour runs so far, that most of our late Comedies owe their Success to it. The Audience listens after nothing else. I have seen little *Dicky* place himself with great Approbation at the Head of the *Tories* for

[2] *Sir Courtly Nice*, a comedy by John Crowne, was first produced in 1685. During the 1715–16 season before this essay was published, it had been produced three times at the Theatre Royal, Drury Lane (*London Stage*, Pt. II, pp. 371, 385, 397) and Addison probably saw it on 11 Apr. (see below, n. 5). The two characters he mentions are described in the play's first act: 'The one is a poor Kinsman of ours, so fierce an Enemy to Fanaticks, that he cou'd eat no other meat; and he needs no other Fire than himself to roast 'em, for he's always in a flame when he comes near 'em, his Name is *Hot-head* ... The other is a Fanatick ... a most Zealous Scrupulous one; with a conscience swadled as hard in its Infancy by strict Education, and now Thump'd and Cudgel'd so sore with daily Sermons and Lectures, that the weak ricketty thing can endure nothing ... The Fanatick's Name's *Testimony*.'

[3] By 1705 Hothead and Testimony were common political caricatures: during the debate over 'the Church in danger', Lord Dartmouth claims, 'I happen to sit by lord Godolphin, when lord Rochester accepted lord Halifax's challenge, and said to him, (not thinking it would have gone further,) that I believed a scene between Hothead and Testimony would be very diverting. He was pleased with the conceit, and told it to all about him, knowing nothing damps a debate more than turning it into ridicule; and it had such an effect, that every body was ready to laugh, when either of them spoke' (Burnet, *History* v. 242n).

five Acts together, and *Pinky* espouse the Interest of the *Whigs* with no less Success.[4] I do not find that either Party has yet thrown themselves under the Patronage of Scaramouch, or that Harlequin has violated[a] that Neutrality, which, upon his late Arrival[b] in *Great Britain*, he professed to both Parties, and which it is thought he will punctually observe, being allowed on all Sides to be a Man of Honour.[5] It is true, that upon his first Appearance, a violent *Whig* Tradesman in the Pit begun to compliment him with a Clap, as overjoyed to see him mount a Ladder, and fancying him to be drest in a Highland Plad.

I question not but my Readers will be surprised to find me animadverting on a Practice that has been always favourable to the Cause which now prevails. The *British* Theatre was *Whig* even in the worst of Times; and in the last Reign did not scruple to testify its Zeal for the Good of our Country, by many magnanimous Claps in its lower Regions, answered with loud Huzzas from the upper Gallery.[6] This good Disposition is so much heightned of late, that the whole Neighbourhood of the *Drury-Lane* Theater very often shakes with the Loyalty of the Audience. It is said, that a young Author, who very much relies on this prevailing Humour, is now writing a Farce to be called *A Match out of Newgate*, in Allusion to the Title of a Comedy called *A Match in Newgate*;[7] and that his chief Person is a round Shoulder'd Man, with a pretty large Nose and a wide Mouth, making his Addresses to a lovely black Woman that passes for a Peeress of *Great Britain*. In short, the whole Play is built upon the late Escape of General *Forster*,[8] who is supposed upon the Road to fall in Love with my

[a] has violated/has yet violated *Fol.* [b] his late Arrival/his Arrival *Fol.*

[4] A reference to two actors, Henry Norris (Dicky) and William Penkethman (Pinky). Norris was known as 'Jubilee Dicky' after a performance in George Farquhar's *Constant Couple* (*Spectator*, i. 191n).

[5] On 11 Apr. the afterpiece which played with *Sir Courtly Nice* was a farce called *La Guinquette*; *or, Harlequin Turned Tapster*. It was played by 'Mons Sorin and Mr. Baxter' who were advertised a week earlier as 'lately arriv'd from Paris' (*London Stage*, Pt. II, pp. 395, 397).

[6] The predominantly Whig bias of plays produced during Anne's reign was partly due to the extensive Whig patronage of the theatre, particularly by the Kit Cat Club. After 1710, however, the Tory ministry exerted sufficient pressure to lessen Whig sentiment in plays. If Addison means the period before 1688 when he refers to 'the worst of Times', his statement is inaccurate; the dominant political themes of Dryden and Otway were Tory (Loftis, *Politics of Drama*, pp. 7–22, 40–56).

[7] Christopher Bullock's *A Woman's Revenge*; *or*, *A Match in Newgate* was first published in November 1715. Its most recent performance before this essay was published would have been on 14 Apr. 1716 (*London Stage*, Pt. II, p. 397).

[8] Thomas Forster (1675–1738) was the Pretender's general at Preston. After surrendering there he was brought to Newgate to await trial on 13 Apr. and he escaped, probably with the complicity of the authorities, in the early hours of 11 Apr. (Cowper Diary, December 1715; Ryder, *Diary*, 11 Apr.).

Lord *Nithisdale*, whom the ingenious Author imagines to be still in his Riding-Hood.[9]

But notwithstanding the good Principles of a *British* Audience in this one Particular, it were to be wished that every thing should be banished the Stage which has a Tendency to exasperate Men's Minds, and enflame[c] that Party-Rage which makes such a miserable and divided People. And that in the first Place, because such a Proceeding as this disappoints the very Design of all publick Diversions and Entertainments. The Institution of Sports and Shows was intended, by all Governments, to turn off the[d] Thoughts of the People from busying themselves in Matters of State, which did not belong to them; to reconcile them to one another by the common Participations of Mirth and Pleasure; and to wear out of their Minds that Rancour which they might have contracted by the interfering Views of Interest and Ambition. It would therefore be for the Benefit of every Society, that is disturbed by contending Factions, to encourage such innocent Amusements as may thus disembitter the Minds of Men, and make them mutually rejoyce in the same agreeable Satisfactions. When People are accustomed to sit together with Pleasure, it is a Step towards Reconciliation: But as we manage Matters, our politest Assemblies are like boisterous Clubs, that meet over a Glass of Wine, and before they have done, throw Bottles at one anothers Heads. Instead of multiplying those desirable Opportunities where we may agree in Points that are indifferent, we let the Spirit of Contention into those very Methods that are not only foreign to it, but should in their Nature dispose us to be Friends. This our Anger in our Mirth is like Poison in a Perfume, which taints the Spirits instead of chearing and refreshing them.

Another manifest Inconvenience which arises from this Abuse of Publick Entertainments, is, that it naturally destroys the Taste of an Audience. I do not deny, but that several Performances have been justly applauded for their Wit, which have been written with an Eye to this predominant Humour of the Town: But it is visible even in these, that it is not the Excellence, but the Application of the Sentiment that has raised Applause. An Author is very much disappointed to find the best Parts of his Productions received with Indifference, and to see the Audience discovering Beauties which he never intended.[10] The Actors, in the midst

[c] enflame/foment *Fol.*　　[d] turn off the/turn the *Fol.*

[9] A reference to William Maxwell, Lord Nithsdale who escaped from the Tower in February (see *F.* 26, n. 5).

[10] Addison is drawing upon his own experience with London audiences. Pope described the reception of *Cato*, Addison's play which both parties claimed expressed their sentiments,

of an innocent old Play, are often startled with unexpected Claps or Hisses; and do not know whether they have been talking like good Subjects, or have spoken Treason. In short, we seem to have such a Relish for Faction, as to have lost that of Wit; and are so used to the Bitterness of Party-Rage, that we cannot be gratified with the highest Entertainment that has not this kind of Seasoning in it. But as no Work must expect to live long, which draws all its Beauty from the Colour of the Times; so neither can that Pleasure be of greater Continuance, which arises from the Prejudice or Malice of its Hearers.

To conclude; Since the present Hatred and Violence of Parties is so unspeakably Pernicious to the Community, and none can do a better Service to their Country than those who use their utmost Endeavours to extinguish it, we may reasonably hope, that the more elegant Part of the Nation will give a good Example to the rest; and put an end to so absurd and foolish a Practice, which makes our most refined Diversions detrimental to the Publick, and, in a particular Manner destructive of all Politeness.

Numb. XXXV *Friday, April* 20, 1716

Atheniensium res gestæ, sicut ego existumo, satis amplæ magnificæque fuere, verum aliquanto minores tamen quam fama feruntur: Sed, quia provenere ibi magna Scriptorum ingenia, per terrarum orbem Atheniensium facta pro maxumis celebrantur. Ita eorum, qui ea fecere, virtus tanta habetur, quantum verbis ea potuere extollere præclara ingenia.

Sallust.

GRATIAN, among his Maxims for raising a Man to the most consummate Character of Greatness, advises first to perform extraordinary Actions,

in a letter to John Caryll: 'The numerous and violent claps of the Whig party on the one side the theatre, were echoed back by the Tories on the other' (*Correspondence* i. 175). Contemporary remarks on the political bias of *Cato* are discussed by Loftis (pp. 57–61) and Smithers (*Addison*, pp. 259–67). Addison may have experienced something similar with his less successful play, *The Drummer*, which was first produced in March 1716 (Ryder, *Diary*, 13 Mar.).

Motto. Sallust, *De Catilinæ Coniuratione*, 8: The deeds of the Athenians were, in my judgement, quite distinguished and glorious but less impressive than tradition represents them. Because great genius emerged among writers there, the exploits of Athenians are praised throughout the world as the most outstanding.

and in the next Place to secure a good Historian.[2] Without the last, he considers the first as thrown away; as indeed they are in a great Measure by such illustrious Persons, as make Fame and Reputation the end of their Undertakings. The most shining Merit goes down to Posterity with Disadvantage, when it is not placed by Writers in its proper Light.

The Misfortune is, that there are more Instances of Men who deserve this kind of Immortality, than of Authors who are able to bestow it. Our Country, which has produced Writers of the first Figure in every other kind of Work, has been very barren in good Historians. We have had several who have been able to compile Matters of Fact, but very few who have been able to digest them with that Purity and Elegance of Stile, that Nicety and Strength of Reflection, that Subtilty and Discernment in the Unravelling of a Character, and that Choice of Circumstances for enlivening the whole Narration, which we so justly admire in the antient Historians of *Greece* and *Rome*, and in some Authors of our neighbouring Nations.

Those who have succeeded best in[a] Works of this kind, are such, who, beside their natural Good Sense and Learning, have themselves been versed in publick Business, and thereby acquired a thorough Knowledge of Men and Things. It was the Advice of the great Duke of *Schomberg*, to an eminent Historian of his Acquaintance, who was an *Ecclesiastick*, That he should avoid being too particular in the drawing up of an Army, and other Circumstances of the Day of Battle; for that he had always observed most notorious Blunders and Absurdities committed on that Occasion, by such writers as were not conversant in the Art of War.[3] We may reasonably expect the like Mistakes in every other kind of Publick Matters, recorded by those who have only a distant Theory of such Affairs. Besides; it is not very probable, that Men, who have passed all their Time in low and vulgar Life, should have a suitable Idea of the several Beauties and Blemishes in the Actions or Characters of Great Men. For this Reason I find an old Law quoted by the famous Monsieur *Bayle*, that no Person below the Dignity of a *Roman* Knight should presume to write an History.[4]

In *England* there is scarce any one, who has had a Tincture of Reading

[a] succeeded best in / succeeded in *Fol.*

[2] *The Heroe*: 'There is also the favour of Historians to be had in ambition as much as Immortality; because their pennes are the wings of renown: They set not out so much the favours of Nature, as of the Soul ... the greatness of an *Heroe* consisted in two things, by inuring his hand to Glorious Actions, and to the Pen, because Characters of Gold bind up Eternity' (trans. Skeffington), pp. 102–3.

[3] Frederick, Duke of Schomberg (1615–90), distinguished military leader and adviser to William III, gave the advice to Gilbert Burnet who recorded the warning in his *History* (i. 90).

[4] 'Dissertation concerning Defamatory Libels', *Historical Dictionary*, IV. xvii.

or Study, that is not apt to fancy himself equal to so great a Task; tho' it is plain, that many of our Countrymen, who have tampered in History, frequently shew, that they do not understand the very Nature of those Transactions which they recount. Nay, nothing is more usual than to see every Man, who is versed in any particular Way of Business, finding fault with several of these Authors, so far as they treat of Matters within his Sphere.

There is a race of Men lately sprung up among this sort of Writers, whom one cannot reflect upon without Indignation as well as Contempt. These are our *Grub-Street* Biographers, who watch for the Death of a Great Man, like so many Undertakers, on purpose to make a Penny of him.[5] He is no sooner laid in his Grave, but he falls into the Hands of an Historian; who, to swell a Volume, ascribes to him Works which he never wrote, and Actions which he never performed; celebrates Vertues which he was never famous for, and excuses Faults which he was never guilty of. They fetch their only authentick Records out of *Doctors Commons*; and when they have got a Copy of his last Will and Testament, they fancy themselves furnished with sufficient Materials for his History. This might indeed enable them in some Measure to write the History of his Death; but what can we expect from an Author that undertakes to write the Life of a Great Man, who is furnished with no other Matters of Fact, besides Legacies; and instead of being able to tell us what he did, can only tell us what he bequeathed. This manner of exposing the private Concerns of Families, and sacrificing the Secrets of the Dead to the curiosity of the Living, is one of those licentious Practices which might well deserve the Animadversion of our Government, when it has Time to contrive Expedients for remedying the many crying Abuses of the Press.[6] In the

[5] Shortly after the death of Lord Wharton an anonymous *Memoirs of Lord Wharton* was published in May 1715 (*Post Boy*, 21–4 May) and, although flattering, it was inaccurate and was padded with previously published materials such as the dedication to Wharton which had appeared in Hughes's edition of Fontenelle's *Dialogues of the Dead*. The *Memoirs* also included the dedication to Wharton which was published in the fifth volume of the *Spectator* and the title-page of the *Memoirs* advertised itself as including a character of Wharton written by Richard Steele. Anticipating the death of his patron, Lord Somers, who died six days after this *Freeholder* was published, Addison is trying to avert a similar fate for Somers. He was unsuccessful, however, and the same author published the *Memoirs of Lord Somers* in July 1716 (*Post Man*, 10–12 July) which included an eight-page 'Vindication ... Occasion'd by some General Reflections... in the Free-Holder'. Both memoirs have been attributed to John Oldmixon by Pat Rogers in 'The Memoirs of Wharton and Somers', *Bulletin of the New York Public Library*, lxxvii (1974), pp. 224–35.

[6] Edward and Lillian Bloom suggest that Addison is recommending 'governmental censorship to silence those who were critical of the ministry' (*Sociable Animal*, p. 111n) but the biographies of the Junto leaders which Addison has in mind here were not particularly critical of the government. Addison also clearly disavows censorship in *S.* 451 because 'it

(*continued*)

mean while, what a poor Idea must Strangers conceive of those Persons, who have been famous among us in their Generation, should they form their Notions of them from the Writings of these our Historiographers![b] What would our posterity think of their illustrious Forefathers, should they only see them in such weak and disadvantageous Lights! But, to our Comfort, Works of this Nature are so short-lived, that they cannot possibly diminish the Memory of those Patriots, which they are not able to preserve.

The Truth of it is, as the Lives of Great Men cannot be written with any tolerable Degree of Elegance or Exactness, within a short Space after their Decease; so neither is it fit that the History of a Person, who has acted among us in a publick Character, should appear till Envy and Friendship are laid asleep, and the Prejudice both of his Antagonists and Adherents be, in some Degree, softned and subdued.[7] There is no question but there are several eminent Persons in each Party, however they may represent one another at present, who will have the same Admirers among Posterity, and be equally celebrated by those, whose Minds will not be distempered by Interest, Passion, or Partiality. It were happy for us, could we prevail upon our selves to imagine, that one, who differs from us in Opinion, may possibly be an honest Man; and that we might do the same Justice to one another, which will be done us hereafter by those who shall make their Appearance in the World, when this Generation is no more. But in our present miserable and divided Condition, how just soever a Man's Pretensions may be to a great or blameless Reputation, he must expect his Share of Obloquy and Reproach; and, even with regard to his Posthumous Character, content himself with such a kind of Consideration, as induced the famous Sir *Francis Bacon*, after having bequeathed his Soul to God, and his Body to the Earth, to leave his Fame to Foreign Nations; and, after some Years, to his own Country.[8]

[b] our Historiographers / our profound Historiographers *Fol.*

---

would operate promiscuously, and root up the Corn and Tares, together' (*Spectator*, iv. 87). Invasion of privacy is one obvious licentious practice Addison has in mind in this essay.

[7] Somers's biographer counters these arguments by claiming that 'it is much more difficult to collect the *Memoirs* of a Man's *Life*, several years after he is dead, than to do it while the Remembrance of him is yet fresh in Mens Minds, and his Friends are desirous to have it preserv'd' (p. 2). He goes on to attack critics like Addison who assume 'they are *Sovereigns* in all parts of *Literature*, and no Body must dare to write without their *Permission* ... no Man must pretend to a Talent, that has not their Stamp upon it, that is not of their *Cabal*...' (p. 3).

[8] 'First, I bequeath my Soul and Body, into the Hand of God ... For my Name and Memory, I leave it to Foreign Nations, and to mine own Country-Men, after some Time be passed over' *Baconiana* (1679), p. 203.

Numb. XXXVI *Monday, April* 23, 1716

— — *Illa se jactet in Aula.*

Virg.

AMONG all the Paradoxes in Politicks which have been advanced by some among us, there is none so absurd and shocking to the most ordinary Understanding, as that it is possible for *Great Britain* to be quietly governed by a *Popish* Sovereign.[2] King *Henry* the Fourth found it impracticable for a *Protestant* to Reign even in *France*, notwithstanding the Reformed Religion does not engage a Prince to the Persecution of any other; and notwithstanding the Authority of the Sovereign in that Country is more able to support itself, and command the Obedience of the People, than in any other *European* Monarchy.[3] We are convinced by the Experience of our own Times, that our Constitution is not able to bear a *Popish* Prince at the Head of it. King *James* the Second was endowed with many Royal Vertues, and might have made a nation of *Roman Catholicks* happy under his Administration. The Grievances we suffered in his Reign proceeded purely from his Religion: But they were such as made the whole Body of the Nobility, Clergy, and Commonalty, rise up as one Man against him, and oblige him to quit the Throne of his Ancestors.[4] The Truth of it is, we have only the Vices of a *Protestant* Prince to fear, and may be made happy by his Vertues: But in a *Popish* Prince we have no Chance for our Prosperity; his very Piety obliges him to our Destruction; and in Proportion as he is more Religious, he becomes more Insupportable. One would wonder, therefore, to find many, who call themselves *Protestants*, favouring the Pretensions of a Person who has been bred up in the utmost Bitterness and Bigotry of the Church of *Rome*; and who, in all Probability, within[a] less than a Twelvemonth, would be opposed by those very Men

[a] within / in *Fol.*

Motto. Virgil, *Aeneid*, i. 140: Let him throw his weight about in that court.

[2] Addison's point was so common during the Exclusion debates that one member of the Commons complained in 1679 that 'it cannot be new to any man here' (Grey's *Debates* vii. 245). However, it was repeated frequently and eventually was passed as a resolution by the Convention Parliament in 1689 (*C.J.* x. 15).

[3] Henry IV, another popular topic in Exclusion arguments, was used as an example by both sides (Grey's *Debates* vii. 419; *Somers Tracts* viii. 214–15).

[4] Burnet also argued that James's failure 'ought to be chiefly charged on his religion' (*History* iii. 2–3).

that are industrious to set him upon the Throne, were it possible for so wicked and unnatural an Attempt to succeed.[5]

I was some Months ago in a Company, that diverted themselves with the Declaration which he had then published, and particularly with the Date of it, *In the Fourteenth Year of Our Reign.*[6] The Company was surprized to find there was a King in *Europe* who had Reigned so long, and made such a Secret of it. This gave occasion to one of them, who is now in *France*, to enquire into the history of this remarkable Reign, which he has digested into Annals, and lately transmitted hither for the Perusal of his Friends. I have suppressed such Personal Reflexions as are mixed in this short Chronicle, as not being to the purpose; and find that the whole History of his Regal Conduct and Exploits may be comprized in the remaining part of this Half-Sheet.

The History of the Pretender's *Fourteen Years Reign digested into Annals.*

Anno Regni 1°. He made Choice of his Ministry, the First of whom was his Confessor. This was a Person recommended by the Society of Jesuits, who represented him as one very proper to guide the Conscience of a King that hoped to rule over an Island which is not within the Pale of the Church. He then proceeded to name the President of his Council, his Secretaries of State, and gave away a very honourable Sine-Cure to his principal Favourite, by constituting him his Lord-High-Treasurer. He likewise signed a dormant Commission for another to be his High-Admiral, with orders to produce it whenever he had Sea-Room for his Employment.

Anno Regni 2°. He perfected himself in the Minuet-Step.

Anno Regni 3°. He grew half a Foot.

Anno Regni 4°. He wrote a Letter to the Pope, desiring him to be as kind to him as his Predecessor had been, who was his God-father.[7] In the same Year he ordered the Lord-High-Treasurer to pay off the Debts of the Crown, which had been contracted since his Accession to the Throne; particularly, a Milk-Score of three Years standing.

[5] James II enjoyed the support of many Tory Churchmen when he ascended the throne, but they withdrew their allegiance in less than two years (*Somers Tracts* xii. 684–5). Bolingbroke claims that in 1715 the Pretender himself wondered 'why the tories were so desirous to have him, if they expected those things from him which his religion did not allow?' (*Letter to Windham*, pp. 226–7).

[6] Addison is referring to the Pretender's Declaration dated at Plombières 'le 29 jour d'Aout 1714, & de notre Regne le 14' (Lamberty, *Mémoires* viii. 689).

[7] The Pretender's godfather was Innocent XI. The Pope addressed here would have been Clement XI.

Anno Regni 5°. He very much improved himself in all Princely Learning, having read over the Legends of the Saints, with the History of those several Martyrs in *England*, who had attempted to blow up a whole Parliament of Hereticks.

Anno Regni 6°. He apply'd himself to the Arts of Government with more than ordinary Diligence; took a Plan of the Bastile with his own hand; visited the Galleys; and studied the Edicts of his great Patron *Louis* XIV.

Anno Regni 7°. Being now grown up to Years of Maturity, he resolved to seek Adventures; but was very much divided in his Mind, whether he should make an Expedition to *Scotland*, or a Pilgrimage to *Loretto*; being taught to look upon the latter in a religious Sense, as the Place of his Nativity.[8] At length he resolved upon his *Scotch* Expedition; and, as the first Exertion of that Royal Authority which he was going to assume, he Knighted himself. After a short Piece of Errantry upon the Seas, he got safe back to *Dunkirk*, where he paid his Devotions to St. *Antony*, for having delivered him from the Dangers of the Sea, and Sir *George Byng*.[9]

Anno Regni 8°. He made a Campaign in *Flanders*, where, by the Help of a Telescope, he saw the Battle of *Oudenarde*, and the Prince of *Hanover*'s Horse shot under him; being posted on a high Tower, with two *French* Princes of the Blood.[10]

Anno Regni 9°. He made a second Campaign in *Flanders*;[11] and, upon his Return to the *French* Court, gained a great Reputation by his Performance in a Rigadoon.

Anno Regni 10°. The Pope, having heard the Fame of these his Military Atchievements, made him the Offer of a Cardinal's Cap; which he was advised not to accept, by some of his Friends in *England*.

Anno Regni 11°. He retir'd to *Lorrain*, where every Morning he made great Havock among the Wild-Fowl, by the Advice and with the Assistance

[8] Catholic legends claimed that the Virgin's house at Nazareth, the scene of the Annunciation, was moved by angels to Loreto where it has been visited by pilgrims since the middle ages. Addison is suggesting that the Pretender's conception was also miraculous (see *F.* 9, n. 5).

[9] Before embarking on his first Scottish expedition in 1708, the Pretender assumed the title, Chevalier de St. George. His ships were turned back by Admiral George Byng at the Firth of Forth and the Pretender returned safely to France (Tindal, pp. 56–8). St. Antony of Padua (d. 1231), while travelling from Africa to Portugal, was driven by strong winds to Italy where he became a famous religious leader; his diversion at sea was considered providential.

[10] After returning from Scotland the Pretender joined the French army in Flanders and fought his first battle at Oudenard in July 1708. Dutch reports of the battle claimed that he watched it from a steeple in a village nearby, but at least one British observer attests to the bravery of both the Prince of Hanover, later George II, and the Pretender (Tindal, p. 75; *P.O.A.S.* vii. 338–44; 'The Remembrance', *Publ. Scot. Hist. Soc.* xxxviii (1901), p. 412).

[11] The Pretender fought bravely at the battle of Malplaquet in 1709 (Saint-Simon, *Mémoires*, ed. A. de Boislisle, Paris, 1915, xviii. 185).

of his Privy-Council.[12] He is said, this Summer, to have shot with his own Hands fifty Brace of Pheasants, and one wild Pig; to have set thirty Coveys of Partridges; and to have hunted down forty Brace of Hares; to which he might have added as many Foxes, had not most of them made their Escape, by running out of his Friend's Dominions, before his Dogs could finish the Chace. He was particularly animated to these Diversions by his Ministry, who thought they would not a little recommend him to the good Opinion and kind Offices of several *British* Fox-Hunters.

Anno Regni 12°. He made a Visit to the Duke *d'Aumont*, and passed for a *French* Marquis in a Masquerade.[13]

Anno Regni 13°. He visited several Convents, and gathered Subscriptions from all the well-disposed Monks and Nuns, to whom he communicated his Design of an Attempt upon *Great Britain.*

Anno Regni 14°. He now made great Preparations for the Invasion of *England*, and got together vast Stores of Ammunition, consisting of Reliques, Gun-Powder and Cannon-Ball. He received from the Pope a very large Contribution, one Moiety in Money, and the other in Indulgences.[14] An *Irish* Priest brought him an authentick Tooth of St. *Thomas a Becket*, and, it is thought, was to have for his Reward, the Archbishoprick of *Canterbury.* Every Monastery contributed something: One gave him a thousand Pound; and another as many Masses.

This Year containing farther the[b] Battles which he fought in *Scotland*, and the Towns which he took, is so fresh in every one's Memory, that we shall say no more of it.

[b] This Year containing farther the | *Anno Regni* 15°. This Year containing the *Fol.*

[12] Article IV of the Treaty of Utrecht obliged Louis XIV to discontinue the asylum he had given the Pretender in France. In 1713 the Jacobite Court was moved to Bar-le-Duc in the Duchy of Lorraine.

[13] Louis, duc d'Aumont (1666–1723) was Louis XIV's ambassador extraordinary in London during treaty negotiations in 1713. The flamboyant d'Aumont entertained lavishly and it was rumoured that the Pretender, who had come to England incognito, was using the Duke's masquerades as opportunities for meeting with his British sympathizers (Boyer, *Queen Anne*, p. 645; *Wentworth Papers*, p. 333).

[14] In 1708 Pope Clement XI furnished Louis XIV with a 'million of crowns for the expedition of the pretended Prince of Wales' (H.M.C. *House of Lords MSS.* viii. 105) and Tindal claims that the Pope also gave some support in 1715 (p. 56 n). The *St. James's Evening Post* reported that the Irish Commons 'was informed that several Papers in the Nature of indulgences from the Pope to several Papists who had taken the oath of abjuration etc. had been seiz'd' (25–8 Feb. 1716).

Numb. XXXVII *Friday, April* 27, 1716

—quod si
Frigida curarum fomenta relinquere posses;
Quo te cœlestis sapientia duceret, ires.
Hoc opus hoc studium parvi properemus et ampli,
Si patriæ volumus, si nobis vivere cari.
Hor.

It is a melancholy Reflection, that our Country, which in Times of Popery was called the Nation of Saints, should now have less Appearance of Religion in it, than any other neighbouring State or Kingdom; whether they be such as continue still immersed in the Errours of the Church of *Rome*, or such as are recovered out of them. This is a Truth that is obvious to every one, who has been conversant in foreign Parts. It was formerly thought dangerous for a young Man to Travel, lest he should return an *Atheist* to his native Country: But at present it is certain, that an *Englishman*, who has any tolerable Degree of Reflection, cannot be better awakened to a Sense of Religion in general, than by observing how the Minds of all Mankind are set upon this important Point; how every Nation is serious and attentive to the great Business of their Being; and that in other Countries a Man is not out of the Fashion, who is bold and open in the Profession and Practice of all Christian Duties.

This Decay of Piety is by no Means to be imputed to the *Reformation*, which in its first Establishment produced its proper Fruits, and distinguished the whole Age with shining Instances of Vertue and Morality.[2] If we would trace out the Original of that flagrant and avowed

Motto. Horace, *Epistles*, I. iii. 25–29: And if you could abandon the cold-water poultices which your anxieties administer, you would go where heaven-born philosophy would lead you. If we want to live dear to our country and ourselves, we, both great and small, should press forward in this work, this pursuit.

[2] The decay of piety in England was a popular theme for both parties in the reign of William III. The Legion Memorial (1701) accused the Commons of 'neglecting the great work of the Reformation of manners' (*Parl. Hist.* v. 1255); Francis Atterbury complained similarly about the nation's morals in 1697 (see below, n. 3). Societies for reforming manners, groups which pressed for the enforcement of laws concerning vice and profanity, were begun in various parts of the country with the assistance of such publications as *A Help to a National Reformation* (1700), a compendium of such laws, and Josiah Woodward's *Account of the Societies for Reformation of Manners* (1698); see G. V. Portus, *Caritas Anglicana* (1912), pp. 50–82. Both parties complained that elections were an occasion for 'detestable Abuses' which led to bribery, 'vice, debauchery, and decay of trade' (Swift, *Prose Works* ii. 45–6; *Parl. Hist.* vii.
(*continued*)

Impiety, which has prevailed among us for some Years, we should find that it owes its Rise to that opposite Extream of *Cant* and *Hypocrisie*, which had taken Possession of the People's Minds in the Times of the Great Rebellion, and of the Usurpation that succeeded it. The Practices of these Men, under the Covert of a feigned Zeal, made even the Appearances of sincere Devotion ridiculous and unpopular. The Raillery of the Wits and Courtiers, in King *Charles* the Second's Reign, upon every thing which they then called Precise, was carried to so great an Extravagance, that it almost put Christianity out of Countenance. The Ridicule grew so strong and licentious, that from this Time we may date that remarkable Turn in the Behaviour of our fashionable *Englishmen*, that makes them Shame-faced in the Exercise of those Duties which they were sent into the World to perform.[3]

The late Cry of the *Church* has been an Artifice of the same Kind with that made use of by the Hypocrites of the last Age, and has had as fatal an Influence upon Religion.[4] If a Man would but seriously consider how much greater Comfort he would receive in the last Moments of his Life from a Reflection that he has made one vertuous Man, than that he has made a thousand *Tories*, we should not see the Zeal of so many Good Men turned off from its proper End, and employed in making such a Kind of Converts. What Satisfaction will it be to an Immoral Man, at such a Time, to think he is a good *Whig*! Or to one that is conscious of Sedition, Perjury, or Rebellion, that he dies with the Reputation of a *High-Churchman*!

But to consider how this Cry of the *Church* has corrupted the Morals of both Parties. Those, who are the loudest in it, regard themselves rather as a political, than a religious Communion; and are held together rather by State-Notions than by Articles of Faith. This fills the Minds of weak Men, who fall into the Snare, with groundless Fears and Apprehensions,

---

302, 323–4). In this essay Addison presents the Whigs' moral arguments for less frequent elections, probably to offset the anticipated unpopularity of the Septennial Bill which had already passed its second reading in the Commons on 24 Apr. (H.M.C. *Stuart MSS.* ii. 123; *C.J.* xviii. 429). In this paragraph he echoes the opening rhetoric of Atterbury's *Representation of the Present State of Religion* (1711), p. 4; Atterbury had attacked the Bill on 16 Apr. and lashed at the ministry which supported it (*Parl. Hist.* vii. 307; H.M.C. *Stuart MSS.* ii. 131).

[3] In his history of the decay of piety Addison ignores the lapsing of the Licensing Act (1695), a popular topic for High Church writers complaining about the state of morality. Atterbury's *Letter to a Convocation Man* (1697) and *Present State of Religion* (1711) both blame this 'general Liberty of the Press' for the 'Deluge of Impiety' (*Somers Tracts* ix. 414; *Representation*, pp. 13–14, 4).

[4] John Dennis defined the hypocrisy this way: 'Why do . . . they who while they speak of the Danger of the Church, declaim so very warmly? Is it not shrewdly to be suspected, that by the Church they mean themselves, mean their own Interests and their own Power?' (*Priestcraft Distinguish'd from Christianity*, 1715, p. 46).

unspeakable Rage towards their Fellow Subjects, wrong Ideas of Persons whom they are not acquainted with, and uncharitable Interpretations of those Actions of which they are not competent Judges. It instills into their Minds the utmost Virulence and Bitterness, instead of that Charity, which is the Perfection and Ornament of Religion, and the most indispensable and necessary Means for attaining the End of it. In a Word, among these mistaken Zealots, it sanctifies Cruelty and Injustice, Riots and Treason.[5]

The Effects which this Cry of the *Church* has had on the other Party, are no less manifest and deplorable. They see themselves unjustly aspersed by it, and vindicate themselves in Terms no less opprobrious, than those by which they are attacked. Their Indignation and Resentment rises in proportion to the Malice of their Adversaries. The unthinking Part of them are apt to contract an unreasonable Aversion even to that Ecclesiastical Constitution to which they are represented as Enemies; and not only to particular Persons, but to that Order of Men in general, which will be always held Sacred and Honourable so long as there is Reason and Religion in the World.[6]

I might mention many other Corruptions common to both Parties, which naturally flow from this Source; and might easily shew, upon a full Display of them, that this Clamour, which pretends to be raised for the Safety of Religion, has almost worn out the very Appearance of it; and rendered us not only the most divided, but the most immoral People upon the Face of the Earth.

When our Nation is overflowed with such a Deluge of Impiety, it must be a great Pleasure to find any Expedient take Place, that has a Tendency to recover it out of so dismal a Condition. This is one great Reason why an honest Man may rejoyce to see an Act so near taking Effect, for making Elections of Members to serve in Parliament, less frequent. I find my self prevented by other Writings (which have considered the Act now

[5] In his harangue against dissenters and latitudinarian Anglicans, Sacheverell argued that the doctrines of the Church and the state were 'so nicely *Correspondent*, and so happily *Intermixt* ... that whosoever *Presumes* to *Innovate*, *Alter*, or *Misrepresent* any *Point* in the *Articles* of the *Faith* of our *Church*, ought to be *Arraign'd* as a *Traytor* to our *State*' (*Perils of False Brethren*, p. 12). At Sacheverell's trial Sir Thomas Parker argued that the clergyman had 'with *Rancour* and *Uncharitableness*' branded 'all that differ from him, though through *Ignorance*' (*Tryal of Sacheverell*, p. 167).

[6] In response to Sacheverell's *Political Union* (Oxford, 1702), John Dennis argued that a political clergyman 'makes more Atheists than any thing in the world besides: For many People are apt to imagine that there can be nothing in Religion, when they see that the Priests ... make it a mere Pretext' (*The Danger of Priestcraft*, 1702, p. 7). In the Commons' debate on the Septennial Bill, Richard Hampden claimed that less frequent elections would 'procure to the clergy an interval from being politicians, that they may be the better able to take care of their flocks, in the manner the Scripture has prescribed' (*Parl. Hist.* vii. 325).

depending, in this particular Light) from expatiating upon this Subject. I shall only mention two short Pieces which I have been just now reading, under the following Titles, *Arguments about the Alteration of the Triennial Elections of Parliament*: And, *The Alteration in the Triennial Act considered.*[7]

The Reasons for this Law, as it is necessary for settling His Majesty in his Throne; for extinguishing the Spirit of Rebellion; for procuring foreign Alliances; and other Advantages of the like Nature; carry a great Weight with them. But I am particularly pleased with it, as it may compose our unnatural Feuds and Animosities; revive an honest Spirit of Industry in the Nation, and cut off all Occasions of brutal Rage and Intemperance. In short, as it will make us not only a more safe, a more flourishing, and a more happy, but also a more Vertuous People.

Numb. XXXVIII *Monday, April* 30, 1716

— — *Longum, formosa, Vale* —
Virg.

It is the Ambition of the Male-Part of the World to make themselves Esteemed, and of the Female to make themselves Beloved. As this is the last Paper which I shall address to my Fair Readers,[2] I cannot perhaps oblige them more, than by leaving them as a kind of Legacy, a certain

[7] *Arguments about the Alteration* ... was published in April and reprinted in Boyer's *Political State* (xi. 485–501) where it was described as 'father'd' by Addison (i.e. probably written by another Whig under Addison's supervision). It presents fuller moral arguments for septennial elections than those included in the recorded Parliamentary debates or in this essay. The opposition to the Whigs' moral arguments had been varied: Nottingham argued that longer terms would diminish the frequency of bribery but increase the amount of bribes; Lord Trevor admitted there were widespread election abuses, but 'that laws might be made to rectify the same'; Buckingham exclaimed, 'Why, to prevent robbing on the high-way, you forbid travelling' (*Parl. Hist.* vii. 304, 298, 299). *Arguments about the Alteration* ... admits that septennial elections will not eliminate bribery but claims that by reducing the frequency of abuses the nation might recover its moral sense better (*Pol. State* xi. 488). *The Alteration of the Triennial Act Considered*, published after 18 Apr. (see p. 8) and attributed to Defoe, presents a better case for the Whigs: it argues that local magistrates, the persons who usually heard cases involving such abuses of manners as vice and profanity, were remiss and partial in their justice because they were often involved in managing the local electorate and therefore had to be careful not to disoblige persons eligible to vote (p. 12).

Motto. Virgil, *Eclogues*, iii. 79: For a long while, fair one, adieu. [Addison has changed the masculine *formose* to the feminine *formosa.*]

[2] Addison's farewell to his women readers may have been prompted by rumours that Parliament would soon be prorogued when the Septennial Bill received royal assent (H.M.C. *Portland MSS.* v. 522).

Secret which seldom fails of procuring this Affection, which they are naturally formed both to Desire and to Obtain. This *Nostrum* is comprized in the following Sentence of *Seneca*, which I shall translate for the Service of my Countrywomen. *Ego tibi monstrabo Amatorium sine medicamento, sine herbâ, sine ullius Veneficæ carmine; si vis Amari, Ama.*[3] *I will discover to you a Philter that has neither Drug nor Simple, nor Enchantment in it. Love, if you would raise Love.* If there be any Truth in this Discovery, and this be such a Specifick as the Author pretends, there is nothing which makes the Sex more Unamiable than Party-Rage. The finest Woman, in a Transport of Fury, loses the Use of her Face. Instead of charming her Beholders, she frights both Friend and Foe. The latter can never be smitten by so bitter an Enemy, nor the former captivated by a Nymph, who, upon Occasion, can be so very Angry. The most endearing of our beautiful Fellow Subjects, are those whose Minds are the least imbittered with the Passions and Prejudices of either Side; and who discover the native Sweetness of the Sex in every part of their Conversation and Behaviour. A lovely Woman, who thus flourishes in her Innocence and Good-Humour, amidst that mutual Spite and Rancour which prevails among her exasperated Sisterhood, appears more amiable by the Singularity of her Character; and may be compared with *Solomon*'s Bride, to *a Lilly among Thorns.*

A States-woman is as ridiculous a Creature as a Cott-Quean.[4] Each of the Sexes should keep within its particular Bounds, and content themselves to excel within their respective Districts. When *Venus* complain'd to *Jupiter* of the Wound which she had received in Battle, the Father of the Gods smiled upon her, and put her in mind, that instead of mixing in a War, which was not her Business, she should have been officiating in her proper Ministry, and carrying on the Delights of Marriage.[5] The Delicacy of several modern Criticks has been offended with *Homer*'s *Billingsgate* Warriours;[6] but a scolding Heroe is, at the worst, a more tolerable Character than a Bully in Petticoats. To which we may add, that the keenest Satyrist among the Ancients, looked upon nothing as a more proper Subject of Raillery and Invective, than a Female Gladiator.[7]

[3] *Epistles*, ix. 6.

[4] Cotquean: a man who acts the housewife, who busies himself unduly with a housewife's duties (*O.E.D.*).

[5] *Iliad*, v. 427–30.

[6] Homer's warriors presented some problems for eighteenth-century literary critics because their occasionally foul language violated literary decorum for the epic. Problems in translating their speeches are discussed seriously in E. Fourmont's *Examen pacifique de la querelle de Madame Dacier et Monsieur de la Motte* (Paris, 1716), vol. II, chap. ix, and comically in *Homerides* by Sir Iliad Doggrel [Thomas Burnet], 1715, pp. 20–21.

[7] Juvenal, *Satires*, vi. 246–67.

I am the more disposed to take into Consideration these Ladies of Fire and Politicks, because it would be very monstrous to see Feuds and Animosities kept up among the soft Sex, when they are in so hopeful a Way of being composed among the Men, by the Septennial Bill, which is now ready for the Royal Assent. As this is likely to produce a Cessation of Arms, till the Expiration of the present Parliament, among one half of our Island, it is very reasonable that the more beautiful Moiety of His Majesty's Subjects should establish a Truce among themselves for the same Term of Years. Or rather it were to be wished, that they would summon together a kind of Senate, or Parliament of the fairest and wisest of our Sister-Subjects, in order to enact a perpetual Neutrality among the Sex. They might at least appoint something like a Committee, chosen from among the Ladies residing in *London* and *Westminster*, in order to prepare a Bill to be laid before the Assembly upon the first Opportunity of their Meeting. The Regulation might be as follows:

'That a Committee of Toasts be forthwith appointed to consider the present State of the Sex in the *British* Nation.

'That this Committee do meet at the House of every respective Member of it on her Visiting-Day; and that every one who comes to it shall have a Vote, and a Dish of Tea.

'That the Committee be empowered to send for Billets-doux, Libels, Lampoons, Lists of Toasts, or any other the like Papers and Records.

'That it be an Instruction to the said Committee, to consider of proper Ways and methods to reclaim the obstinately Opprobrious and Virulent; and how to make the Ducking-Stool more useful.'

Being always willing to contribute my Assistance to my Countrywomen, I would propose a Preamble, setting forth, 'That the late Civil War among the Sex has tended very much to the Lessening of that ancient and undoubted Authority, which they have[a] claimed over the Male Part of the Island; to the Ruin of good Huswifery, and to the Betraying of many important Secrets: That it has produced much Bitterness of Speech, many sharp and violent Contests, and a great Effusion of Citron-Water: That it has raised Animosities in their Hearts, and Heats in their Faces: That it has broke out in their Ribbons, and caused unspeakable Confusions in their Dress: And above all, That it has introduced a certain Frown into the Features, and a Soureness into the Air of our *British* Ladies, to the great Damage of their Charms, and visible Decay of the National Beauty.'

As for the Enacting Part of the Bill, it may consist of many Particulars,

[a] have/had *Fol.*

which will naturally arise from the Debates of the Tea-Table; and must, therefore, be left to the Discretion and Experience of the Committee. Perhaps it might not be amiss to enact, among other Things,

'That the Discoursing on Politicks shall be looked upon as dull as Talking on the Weather.

'That if any Man troubles a Female Assembly with Parliament-News, he shall be marked out as a Blockhead, or an Incendiary.

'That no Woman shall henceforth presume to stick a Patch upon her Forehead, unless it be in the very middle, that is, in the neutral Part of it.

'That all Fans and Snuff Boxes, of what Principles soever, shall be called in: And that Orders be given to *Motteux* and *Mathers*,[8] to deliver out in exchange for them such as have no Tincture of Party in them.

'That when any Lady bespeaks a Play, she shall take effectual Care, that the Audience be pretty Equally checquer'd with *Whigs* and *Tories*.

'That no Woman of any Party presume to influence the Legislature.

'That there be a general Amnesty and Oblivion of all former Hostilities and Distinctions, all publick and private Failings on either Side: And that every one who comes into this Neutrality within the Space of Weeks, shall be allowed an Ell extraordinary, above the present Standard, in the Circumference of her Petticoat.

'Provided always nevertheless, That nothing herein contained shall extend, or be construed to extend, to any Person or Persons, Inhabiting and Practising within the Hundreds of *Drury*, or to any other of that Society in what Part soever of the Nation in like manner Practising and Residing; who are still at liberty to Rail, Calumniate, Scold, Frown and Pout, as in afore times, any thing in this Act to the contrary notwithstanding.'

Numb. XXXIX *Friday, May* 4, 1716

Prodesse quam Conspici.

IT often happens, that extirpating the Love of Glory, which is observed to take the deepest Root in noble Minds, tears up several Vertues with it; and

[8] Peter Motteux's fashionable India shop in Leadenhall Street and Charles Mather's toyshop in Fleet Street. According to *T.* 142, Mather's shop was 'the first that brought Toys in Fashion, and Bawbles to Perfection'.

Motto. To be useful rather than conspicuous.

that suppressing the Desire of Fame, is apt to reduce Man to a State of Indolence and Supineness. But when, without any Incentive of Vanity, a Person of great Abilities is zealous for the Good of Mankind; and as solicitous for the Concealment, as the Performance of illustrious Actions; we may be sure that he has something more than ordinary in his Composition, and has a Heart filled with Goodness and Magnanimity.

There is not perhaps in all History, a greater Instance of this Temper of Mind, than what appeared in that excellent Person, whose Motto I have placed at the Head of this Paper.[2] He had worn himself out in his Application to such Studies as made him useful or ornamental to the World, in concerting Schemes for the Welfare of his Country, and in prosecuting such Measures as were necessary for making those Schemes effectual: But all this was done with a View to the Publick Good that should rise out of these generous Endeavours, and not to the Fame which should accrue to himself. Let the Reputation of the Action fall where it would; so his Country reaped the Benefit of it, he was satisfied. As this Turn of Mind threw off in a great Measure the Oppositions of Envy and Competition, it enabled him to gain the most Vain and Impracticable into his Designs, and to bring about several great Events for the Safety and Advantage of the Publick, which must have died in their Birth, had he been as desirous of appearing Beneficial to Mankind, as of being so.

As he was admitted into the secret and most retired Thoughts and Counsels of his Royal Master King *William*, a great Share in the Plan of the

[2] This essay is Addison's eulogy for John, Lord Somers, his friend and patron since 1695, who died on 26 Apr. 1716. Somers was born near Worcester in 1651, studied at Trinity College, Oxford, was admitted to the Middle Temple in 1669, and was called to the Bar seven years later. He entered public life at the Exclusion Crisis as a friend of Whig leaders and he is reputed to have written three pamphlets supporting them: *A Brief History of the Succession* (1680), *A Just and Modest Vindication of the Proceedings of the Two Last Parliaments* (1681) and *The Security of Englishmen's Lives* (1681). In 1688 he defended the seven bishops (see below, n. 7) and after the Revolution he represented Worcester at the Convention Parliament; there he defended the legality of that Parliament, helped to frame the Bill of Rights, and helped manage the resolution that James had abdicated rather than simply deserted the throne (*Parl. Hist.* v. 583–4; Chandler, ii. 209–11, 238–9; *C.J.* x. 23). The Earl of Sunderland described Somers as 'the life, the soul, and the spirit' of the Whig party during William's reign (*Misc. State Papers* ii. 446). A favourite adviser to the monarch, he was raised to the peerage in 1697 as Baron Somers of Evesham. Addison's affiliation with Somers began in 1695 when Addison wrote an elegant verse epistle to him, claiming that the recent peace had been obtained '*By* Somer's *Counsels, and by* Nassau's *Sword*'. Somers supported allocating government money to help to pay for Addison's travels on the continent. Their friendship continued after Addison returned to England in 1703 and, when the Whigs were in power during Anne's reign, Somers and the other Junto Lords assisted Addison in his political career. The most recent biography of Somers is William Sachse's *Lord Somers* (Manchester, 1975); for Addison's relations with Somers, see Sachse, pp. 198–9 and Smithers, *Addison*, pp. 30–4 and *passim*.

Protestant Succession is universally ascribed to him:[3] And if he did not entirely project the Union of the Two Kingdoms, and the Bill of Regency, which seem to have been the only Methods in Humane Policy, for securing to us so inestimable a Blessing, there is none who will deny him to have been the chief Conductor in both these glorious Works:[4] For Posterity are obliged to allow him that Praise after his Death, which he industriously declined while he was Living. His Life indeed seems to have been prolonged beyond its Natural Term, under those Indispositions which hung upon the latter Part of it, that he might have the Satisfaction of seeing the[a] happy Settlement take Place, which he had proposed to himself as the principal End of all his publick Labours. Nor was it a small Addition to his Happiness, that by this Means he saw those who had been always his most intimate Friends, and who had concerted with him such Measures for the Guaranty of the Protestant Succession, as drew upon them the Displeasure of Men who were averse to it, advanced to the highest Posts of Trust and Honour under His present Majesty.[5] I believe there are none of these Patriots, who will think it a Derogation from their Merit to have it said, that they received many Lights and Advantages from their Intimacy with my Lord *Somers*: Who had such a general Knowledge of Affairs, and so

[a] the/that *Fol.*

[3] As William's Lord Keeper and later Lord Chancellor (1693–1700), Somers was naturally an important adviser although, as in the negotiations for the first Partition Treaty, the King did not always heed Somers's advice (see below, n. 13). Even after leaving office Somers continued to play an influential role in William's policies and the King's last speech to Parliament on 31 Dec. 1701 has been attributed to Somers (Burnet, *History* iv. 546n). Contemporaries confirm that Somers influenced William's policies as much as anyone, and it was William's support for the Act of Settlement which, according to Lord Cowper, ensured its passage (*Vernon Letters* i. 450; Burnet, *History* iv. 397; Cowper, 'Impartial History', p. 342).

[4] The Regency Act (1706) was designed to provide for a caretaker government between the Queen's death and the arrival of the Hanoverian successor; the Act of Union (1707) united the kingdoms of England and Scotland. Somers figured prominently in both acts which he considered important for securing the Protestant succession (B. L. Add. MS. 34521, fo. 43). The Earl of Hardwicke, who inherited Somers's papers, claimed that the Regency Bill was 'drawn by Lord Somers' and Arthur Onslow, using other evidence, concluded the same (Burnet, *History* v. 235n). The Duchess of Marlborough attended several conferences Somers held with the Queen concerning the Union and wrote, 'he was the chief man in promoting the union ... One argument was, that it would shut up the door to ... the Pretender' (*Private Correspondence* ii. 143). The Earl of Marchmont, a leading Scots peer who negotiated the Union, wrote to Somers: 'I am convinced, that more depends upon you than upon any other man' (*Marchmont Papers* iii. 290). When the Union was debated in the House of Lords, Burnet claims that it was defended 'above all by the lord Somers' (*History* v. 287).

[5] All the Junto Lords except Somers were appointed to high office by George I: Halifax became First Lord of the Treasury; Wharton, Lord Privy Seal; Orford, First Lord of the Admiralty; Sunderland, Lord Lieutenant of Ireland. Cowper, a Junto associate, became Lord Chancellor. Because of Somers's failing health, he was appointed to no office but was given a pension and was made a member of the King's Cabinet.

tender a Concern for his Friends, that whatever Station they were in, they usually applied to him for his Advice in every Perplexity of Business, and in Affairs of the greatest Difficulty.

His Life was in every Part of it set off with that graceful Modesty and Reserve, which made his Vertues more beautiful, the more they were cast in such agreeable Shades.

His Religion was sincere, not ostentatious; and such as inspired him with an universal Benevolence towards all his Fellow-Subjects, not with Bitterness against any Part of them.[6] He shewed his firm Adherence to it as model'd by our national Constitution, and was constant to its Offices of Devotion, both in Publick and in his Family. He appeared a Champion for it with great Reputation in the Cause of the Seven Bishops, at a Time when the Church was Really in Danger.[7] To which we may add, that he held a strict Friendship and Correspondence with the Great Archbishop *Tillotson*, being acted by the same Spirit of Candour and Moderation; and moved rather with Pity than Indignation towards the Persons of those, who differed from him in the unessential Parts of Christianity.

His great Humanity appeared in the minutest Circumstances of his Conversation. You found it in the Benevolence of his Aspect, the Complacency of his Behaviour, and the Tone of his Voice. His great Application to the severer Studies of the Law, had not infected his Temper with any thing positive or litigious. He did not know what it was to wrangle on indifferent Points, to triumph in the Superiority of his Understanding, or to be Supercilious on the Side of Truth. He joined the greatest Delicacy of Good Breeding to the greatest Strength of Reason. By approving the

[6] Somers was a latitudinarian. In 1689 he was a member of the committee which recommended to the Convention Parliament that provision should be made 'for uniting all Protestants in the Matter of publick Worship, as far as may be' (*C.J.* x. 15, 17). During the debates over the coronation oath in March 1689, he supported one member who argued, 'I would have the Church-doors made wider, and I think it might easily be done' (*Parl. Hist.* v. 200, 204); in the following month he was a member of the committee which expressed to the King the Commons' willingness to grant some 'Ease to Protestant Dissenters' (*C.J.* x. 84, 86). During Anne's reign Somers was one of the managers in the conference with the Commons over the first Occasional Conformity Bill (January 1703); there he described dissenters as differing from Anglicans only 'in some little forms' (*Parl. Hist.* vi. 59–92). Later he was one of the peers who protested the Schism Bill (*L.J.* xix. 716–17). His enemies accused him of deism, socinianism, and Hobbism (Swift, *Prose Works* iii. 79; *Vernon Letters* iii. 13).

[7] After James II issued his second Declaration of Indulgence in April 1688, Archbishop Sancroft and six of his suffragens presented the King with a petition which questioned its legality. James prosecuted the bishops for seditious libel, and Somers, although not well known as a lawyer, was retained for the defendants because he was considered a good legal scholar. As junior counsel Somers spoke last, briefly but ably summarizing the bishops' case, and the jury brought in a verdict of not guilty (Kennett, *History of England*, 1706, iii. 481–6; *State Trials* xii. 396–7).

Sentiments of a Person, with whom he conversed, in such Particulars as were just, he won him over from those Points in which he was mistaken; and had so agreeable a Way of conveying Knowledge, that whoever conferr'd with him grew the wiser, without perceiving that he had been instructed. We may probably ascribe to this masterly and engaging Manner of Conversation, the great Esteem which he had gained with the late Queen, while she pursued those Measures which had carry'd the *British* Nation to the highest Pitch of Glory; notwithstanding she had entertained many unreasonable Prejudices against him, before she was acquainted with his personal Worth and Behaviour.[8]

As in his political Capacity we have before seen how much he contributed to the Establishment of the Protestant Interest, and the Good of his Native Country, he was always true to these great Ends. His Character was uniform and consistent with itself, and his whole Conduct of a Piece. His Principles were founded in Reason, and supported by Vertue; and therefore did not lie at the Mercy of Ambition, Avarice, or Resentment. His Notions were no less steady and unshaken, than just and upright. In a Word, he concluded his Course among the same well-chosen Friendships and Alliances, with which he began it.[9]

This Great Man was not more Conspicuous as a Patriot and a Statesman, than as a Person of universal Knowledge and Learning. As by dividing his Time between the publick Scenes of Business, and the private Retirements of Life, he took care to keep up both the Great and Good Man; so by the same Means he accomplished himself not only in the Knowledge of Men

[8] During Anne's reign Somers was not appointed to any significant post until the end of 1708, partly because the Queen held an 'aversion ... that was personal to that Lord' (Marlborough, *Private Correspondence* i. 156). Her disfavour may have originated as early as 1690 when Somers argued against giving her a separate revenue from King William's, but it became more intense in November 1707 when he was one of the leaders in Parliament's attack on the Admiralty which her husband nominally presided over (*Parl. Hist.* v. 495–6; Marlborough, *Private Correspondence* i. 156). The Queen wrote to Marlborough in the following spring that it would 'be utter destruction to me to bring Lord Somers into my service' (Coxe, *Marlborough* iv. 73). Later that year the Whigs successfully pressured Godolphin to have the Queen appoint Somers Lord President of the Council, and while in that office he gained the Queen's confidence; the Earl of Dartmouth wrote that, when he was ordered to inform Somers in 1710 that he was being replaced, the Queen asked him to assure Somers 'that she ... should be glad if he came often to her ... She often told me ... that he was a man that never deceived her' (Burnet, *History* iv. 12n). The Duchess of Marlborough was informed that Somers did visit the Queen often after 1710 (*Private Correspondence* ii. 143–4).

[9] The Junto Lords were noted for their solidarity as a political group, but their alliances with others were not always consistent. After successfully opposing the three Occasional Conformity Bills during 1703–4, they were willing to negotiate support for the Occasional Conformity Bill of 1711, presumably in return for Tory concessions concerning the peace negotiations (H.M.C. *Portland MSS.* v. 120).

and Things, but in the Skill of the most refined Arts and Sciences.[10] That unwearied Diligence which followed him through all the Stages of his Life, gave him such a thorough Insight into the Laws of the Land, that he passed for one of the greatest Masters of his Profession, at his first Appearance in it. Tho' he made a regular Progress through the several Honours of the Long Robe, he was always looked upon as one who[b] deserved a Superior Station to that he was possess'd of; 'till he arrived at the highest Dignity to which those Studies could advance him.[11]

He enjoyed in the highest Perfection two Talents, which do not often meet in the same Person, the greatest Strength of good Sense, and the most exquisite Taste of Politeness. Without the first, Learning is but an Incumbrance; and without the last, is ungraceful. My Lord *Somers* was Master of these two Qualifications in so eminent a Degree, that all the Parts of Knowledge appeared in him with such an additional Strength and Beauty, as they want in the Possession of others. If he delivered his Opinion of a Piece of Poetry, a Statue, or a Picture, there was something so just and delicate in his Observations, as naturally produced Pleasure and Assent in those who heard him.

His Solidity and Elegance, improved by the reading of the finest Authors both of the Learned and Modern Languages, discovered itself in all his Productions. His Oratory was masculine and persuasive, free from every thing trivial and affected. His Stile in Writing was chaste and pure, but at the same time full of Spirit and Politeness; and fit to convey the most intricate Business to the Understanding of the Reader, with the utmost clearness and Perspicuity. And here it is to be lamented, that this extraordinary Person, out of his natural Aversion to Vain glory, wrote

[b] who / that *Fol.*

[10] Somers's library of over 9,000 books is testimony for Burnet's claim that he 'was very learned in his own profession, with a great deal more learning in other professions, in divinity, philosophy and history' (*History* iv. 193). His library catalogue includes works as varied as Greek poetry and contemporary medical treatises; the library contained over 600 books on British history and law, and well over 1,000 books on theology. Motteux's sale catalogue for the 1717 auction of Somers's collection of prints and drawings includes about 4,000 drawings, many by Italian masters, and 'a much greater Number of Prints'. He offered to assist Pierre Bayle with the costs of producing his *Dictionnaire historique* (1697) and he was a friend of John Locke and the third Earl of Shaftesbury, both of whom dedicated works to him. Other works dedicated to Somers include Swift's *A Tale of a Tub*, Tonson's 1688 edition of *Paradise Lost*, and Addison and Steele's first collected volume of the *Spectator*. In 1698 Somers was elected President of the Royal Society. William Sachse describes Somers' intellectual interests in detail (*Lord Somers*, pp. 189–210).

[11] Somers was appointed Solicitor-General in 1689 and Attorney-General three years later. He became Lord Keeper in 1693 and served as Lord Chancellor from 1697 to 1700. His judgement in the Bankers' case of 1696 (Williamson *v.* Regem) is evidence of his thoroughness in legal research (*State Trials* xiv. 39–105).

several Pieces, as well as performed several Actions, which he did not assume the Honour of: Tho' at the same time so many Works of this Nature have appeared, which every one has ascribed to him, that I believe no Author of the greatest Eminence would deny my Lord *Somers* to have been the best Writer of the Age in which he lived.[12]

This noble Lord, for the great Extent of his Knowledge and Capacity, has been often compared with the Lord *Verulam*, who had also been Chancellor of *England*. But the Conduct of these two extraordinary Persons, under the same Circumstances, was vastly different. They were both Impeach'd by a House of Commons. One of them, as he had given just Occasion for it, sunk under it; and was reduced to such an abject Submission, as very much diminished the Lustre of so exalted a Character: But my Lord *Somers* was too well fortified in his Integrity to fear the Impotence of an Attempt upon his Reputation; and tho' his Accusers would gladly have drop'd their Impeachment, he was instant with them for the Prosecution of it, and would not let that Matter rest till it was brought to an Issue. For the same Vertue and Greatness of Mind which gave him a Disregard of Fame, made him impatient of an undeserved Reproach.[13]

There is no question but this wonderful Man will make one of the most distinguish'd Figures in the History of the present Age; but we cannot expect that his Merit will shine out in its proper Light, since he wrote many things which are not publish'd in his Name; was at the Bottom of

[12] In addition to works written at the time of the Exclusion Crisis (see above, n. 2), the following political tracts have also been attributed to Somers: *A Vindication of the Proceedings of the Late Parliament of England* (1690), *A Letter Balancing the Necessity of Keeping a Land Force in Times of Peace* (1697), *Jus Regium* (1701), and *Jura Populi Anglicani* (1701). Somers also translated the Life of Alcibiades for *Plutarch's Lives* (1683–86) and two epistles for the 1680 translation of Ovid's *Epistles*. Other works which some scholars have attributed to him include *A Just and Modest Vindication of the Proceedings of the Two Last Parliaments* (1681), *Anguis in Herba* (1701), and *Vox Populi, Vox Dei* (1709); these attributions have been questioned or qualified by Somers's biographer (Sachse, *Lord Somers*, pp. 16, 206–7n, 295n).

[13] In its struggle with James I in 1621, the House of Commons accused Bacon, the King's minister, of 'great Bribery and Corruption', although he was not guilty of more than the common practices of the time; Bacon renounced defence and confessed to the charges brought against him (*L.J.* iii. 53, 98–101). Eighty years later Somers was the victim of 'the animosity of a party' when, in 1701, the Tory Commons impeached the Whig ministers who had been privy to the Partition Treaties (1698, 1700); they did not impeach the Tory Earl of Jersey who had signed the second treaty (Burnet, *History* iv. 509, 487). On 14 Apr. 1701 the Commons resolved that Somers, Orford, and Halifax, 'by advising his Majesty . . . to the Treaty for Partition of the *Spanish* Monarchy; whereby large Territories of the King of *Spaine*'s Dominions were to be delivered up to France, is guilty of high Crime and Misdemeanor.' Somers responded by presenting his correspondence with the King concerning the first treaty which showed that he had been informed of the negotiations only in their last stages and that he cautioned William against the French. Other articles accused Somers of corruption and illegal judicial practices which he also answered, but the Commons did not proceed with a replication and the impeachment died in the quarrelling between the Tory Commons and the Whig House of Lords (*C.J.* xiii. 489–91, 546–51, 574–8).

many excellent Counsels, in which he did not appear; did Offices of Friendship to many Persons, who knew not from whom they were derived; and performed great Services to his Country, the Glory of which was transfer'd to others: In short, since he made it his Endeavour rather to do worthy Actions, than to gain an illustrious Character.

Numb. XL *Monday, May* 7, 1716

Urit enim fulgore suo qui prægravat artes
Infra se positas: extinctus amabitur idem.
Hor.

IT requires no small Degree of Resolution, to be an Author in a Country so Facetious and Satyrical as this of *Great Britain*. Such a one raises a kind of Alarm among his Fellow-Subjects, and by pretending to distinguish himself from the Herd, becomes a Mark of publick Censure, and sometimes a standing Object of Raillery and Ridicule. Writing is indeed a Provocation to the Envious, and an Affront to the Ignorant. How often do we see a Person, whose Intentions are visibly to do Good by the Works which he publishes, treated in as scurrilous a Manner, as if he were an Enemy to Mankind. All the little Scramblers after Fame fall upon him, publish every Blot in his Life, depend upon Hear-say to defame him, and have recourse to their own Invention, rather than suffer him to erect himself into an Author with Impunity. Even those who write on the most indifferent Subjects, and are conversant only in Works of Taste, are looked upon as Men that make a kind of Insult upon Society, and ought to be humbled as Disturbers of the publick Tranquillity. Not only the Dull and the Malicious, which make a formidable Party in our Island, but the whole Fraternity of Writers rise up in Arms against every new Intruder into the World of Fame; and a thousand to one, before they have done, prove him not only to be a Fool, but a Knave. Successful Authors do what they can to exclude a Competitor, while the Unsuccessful with as much Eagerness lay in their Claim to him as a Brother. This natural Antipathy to a Man who breaks his Ranks, and endeavours to signalize his Parts in the World, has very probably hindered many Persons from making their Appearance

Motto. Horace, *Epistles*, II. i. 13–14: For he who oppresses abilities inferior to his own scorches with his brilliance: when his fire is extinguished, the same man will be admired.

in Print, who might have enriched our Country with better Productions in all kinds than any that are now extant. The Truth of it is, the active Part of Mankind, as they do most for the Good of their Contemporaries, very deservedly gain the greatest Share in their Applauses; whilst Men of speculative Endowments, who employ their Talents in Writing, as they may equally benefit or amuse succeeding Ages, have generally the greatest Share in the Admiration of Posterity. Both good and bad Writers may receive great Satisfaction from the Prospects of Futurity; as in After-ages the former will be remember'd, and the latter forgotten.

Among all Sets of Authors,[a] there are none who draw upon themselves more Displeasure, than those who deal in political Matters, which indeed is very often too justly incurred; considering that Spirit of Rancour and Virulence, with which Works of this Nature generally abound. These are not only regarded as Authors, but as Partisans, and are sure to exasperate at least one half of their Readers. Other Writers offend only the Stupid or Jealous among their Countrymen; but these, let their Cause be never so Just, must expect to irritate a supernumerary Party of the self-interested, prejudiced, and ambitious. They may however comfort themselves with considering, that if they gain any unjust Reproach from one Side, they generally acquire more Praise than they deserve from the other; and that Writings of this kind, if conducted with Candour and Impartiality, have a more particular Tendency to the Good of their Country, and of the present Age, than any other Compositions whatsoever.

To consider an Author further,[b] as the Subject of Obloquy and Detraction. We may observe with what Pleasure a Work is received by the invidious Part of Mankind, in which a Writer falls short of himself, and does not answer the Character which he has acquired by his former Productions. It is a fine Simile in one of Mr. *Congreve*'s Prologues, which compares a Writer to a Buttering-Gamester, that stakes all his Winnings upon every Cast: So that if he loses the last Throw, he is sure to be undone.[2] It would be well for all Authors, if, like that Gentleman, they knew when to give over, and to desist from any further[c] Pursuits after Fame, whilst they are in the full Possession of it. On the other Hand, there is not a more melancholly Object in the Learned World, than a Man who has written himself down. As the Publick is more disposed to Censure than

[a] Authors/Writers *Fol.* [b] further/*Fol.*; farther *8vo, 12mo.* [c] further/*Fol.*; farther *8vo, 12mo.*

[2] In the Prologue to *The Way of the World* (1700), Congreve claimed that for poets 'Each time they write, they venture all they've won:/ The Squire that's butter'd still, is sure to be undone.' *Buttering* meant 'to double or treble the Bet ... to recover all Losses' (*Dictionary of the Canting Crew*, 1699).

to Praise, his Readers will ridicule him for his last Works, when they have forgot to applaud those which preceeded them. In this Case, where a Man has lost his Spirit by old Age and Infirmity, one could wish that his Friends and Relations would keep him from the use of Pen, Ink and Paper, if he is not to be reclaimed by any other Methods.

The Author indeed often grows old before the Man, especially if he treats on Subjects of Invention, or such as arise from Reflections upon Humane Nature: For in this Case, neither his own Strength of Mind, nor those Parts of Life which are commonly unobserved, will furnish him with sufficient Materials to be at the same Time both pleasing and voluminous. We find even in the outward Dress of Poetry, that Men, who write much without taking Breath, very often return to the same Phrases and Forms of Expression, as well as to the same Manner of Thinking. Authors, who have thus drawn off the Spirit of their Thoughts, should lie still for some Time, till their Minds have gathered fresh Strength, and by Reading, Reflection, and Conversation, laid in a new Stock of Elegancies, Sentiments, and Images of Nature. The Soil, that is worn with too frequent Culture, must lie fallow for a While, till it has recruited its exhausted Salts, and again enriched itself by the Ventilations of the Air, the Dews of Heaven, and the kindly Influences of the Sun.

For my own Part, notwithstanding this general Malevolence towards those who communicate their Thoughts in Print, I cannot but look with a friendly Regard on such as do it, provided there is no Tendency in their Writings to Vice and Prophaneness. If the Thoughts of such Authors have nothing in them, they at least do no harm, and shew an honest Industry and a good Intention in the Composer. If they teach me any thing I did not know before, I cannot but look upon my self as obliged to the Writer, and consider him as my particular Benefactor, if he conveys to me one of the greatest Gifts that is in the Power of Man to bestow, an Improvement of my Understanding, an innocent Amusement, or an Incentive to some moral Vertue. Were not Men of Abilities thus communicative, their Wisdom would be in a great Measure useless, and their Experience uninstructive. There would be no Business in Solitude, nor proper Relaxations in Business. By these Assistances, the retired Man lives in the World, if not above it; Passion is composed; Thought hindred from being barren; and the Mind from preying upon itself. That Esteem, indeed, which is payed to good Writers by their Posterity, sufficiently shews the Merit of Persons who are thus employed. Who does not now more admire *Cicero* as an Author, than as a Consul of *Rome*! And does not oftner talk of the celebrated Writers of our own Country, who lived in former Ages, than of any other particular Persons among their Contemporaries and Fellow Subjects!

When I consider myself as a *British* Free-holder, I am in a particular Manner pleased with the Labours of those who have improved our Language with the Translation of old *Latin* and *Greek* Authors; and by that Means let us into the Knowledge of what passed in the famous Governments of *Greece* and *Rome*. We have already most of their Historians in our own Tongue: And what is still more for the Honour of our Language, it has been taught to express with Elegance, the greatest of their Poets in each Nation. The illiterate among our Countrymen, may learn to judge from *Dryden*'s *Virgil*, of the most perfect Epic Performance: And those Parts of *Homer*, which have already been published by Mr. *Pope*, give us reason to think that the *Iliad* will appear in *English* with as little Disadvantage to that immortal Poem.[3]

There is another Author, whom I have long wished to see well translated into *English*, as his Work is filled with a Spirit of Liberty, and more directly tends to raise Sentiments of Honour and Vertue in his Reader, than any of the Poetical Writings of Antiquity. I mean the *Pharsalia* of *Lucan*. This is the only Author of Consideration among the *Latin* Poets, who was not explained for the Use of the *Dauphin*, for a very obvious Reason; because the whole *Pharsalia* would have been no less than a Satyr upon the *French* Form of Government. The Translation of this Author is now in the Hands of Mr. *Rowe*, who has already given the World some admirable Specimens of it; and not only kept up the Fire of the Original, but delivered the Sentiments with greater Perspicuity, and in a finer Turn of Phrase and Verse.[4]

As Undertakings of so difficult a Nature required the greatest Encouragements, one cannot but rejoyce to see those general Subscriptions which have been made to them; especially since if the two Works last

[3] There is general agreement that this essay was Addison's attempt to bring about a truce in the literary battle between his circle and Pope's (Smithers, *Addison*, pp. 359–62; Norman Ault, *New Light on Pope*, 1949, pp. 101–19). Addison's criticism of Pope's *Essay on Criticism* (*S.* 253) has been cited as one cause for the feud (Ault, p. 109), but Addison's association with the literary excursions of his protégés—Thomas Tickell, Thomas Burnet, and Charles Gildon—was more likely to require an apology. Of all their works, Gildon's *New Rehearsal* (1714) is probably foremost in Addison's mind here. In that play both Pope and Rowe, the two contemporaries commended in this essay, were attacked, and Pope's limited knowledge of Greek was ridiculed at some length (pp. 41–2). The second volume of Pope's *Iliad* was advertised as published on 3 Apr. in the *Post Man* (3–5 Apr. 1716) and Addison's closing remarks make it clear that he did not intend to encourage or assist in any further competition or criticism of Pope's translation.

[4] Nicholas Rowe's complete translation of Lucan's *Pharsalia* was not published until 1718, but parts of it had been published in Tonson's *Poetical Miscellanies* in 1704 and 1709.

mentioned are not finished by those masterly Hands, which are now employed in them, we may despair of seeing them attempted by others.

Numb. XLI *Friday, May* 11, 1716

Dissentientis conditionibus
Fœdis, et exemplo trahenti
Perniciem veniens in ævum.
Hor.

As the Care of our National Commerce redounds more to the Riches and Prosperity of the Publick, than any other Act of Government, it is pity that we do not see the State of it marked out in every particular Reign with greater Distinction and Accuracy, than what is usual among our *English* Historians. We may however observe in general, that the best and wisest of our Monarchs have not been less industrious to extend their Trade, than their Dominions; as it manifestly turns in a much higher Degree to the Welfare of the People, if not to the Glory of the Soveraign.

The first of our Kings who carried our Commerce, and consequently our Navigation to a very great Height, was *Edward* the Third. This victorious Prince, by his many excellent Laws for the Encouragement of Trade, enabled his Subjects to support him in his many glorious Wars upon the Continent, and turned the Scale so much in Favour of our *English* merchandise, that, by a Balance of Trade taken in his Time, the Exported Commodities amounted to Two Hundred Ninety Four Thousand Pounds, and the Imported but to Thirty Eight Thousand.[2]

Those of his Successors, under whose Regulations our Trade flourish'd most, were *Henry* the Seventh, and Queen *Elizabeth.* As the first of these was for his great Wisdom very often stiled the *English Solomon*, he followed the Example of that wise King in nothing more, than by advancing the Traffick of his People. By this Means he reconciled to him the Minds of his Subjects, strengthened[a] himself in their Affections, improved very much

[a] strengthened / established *Fol.*

Motto. Horace, *Odes,* III. v. 14–16: He scorned the detestable terms and the precedent destined to bring ruin for future ages.

[2] Addison's source is *Britannia Languens* (1680), pp. 220–1, which cites these figures for the year 1354.

the Navigation of the Kingdom, and repelled the frequent Attempts of his Enemies.

As for Queen *Elizabeth*, she had always the Trade of Her Kingdom very much at Heart, and we may observe the Effects of it through the whole Course of her Reign, in the Love and Obedience of her People, as well as in the Defeats and Disappointments of her Enemies.

It is with great Pleasure that we see our present Soveraign applying his thoughts so successfully to the Advancement of our Traffick, and considering himself as the King of a Trading Island.[3] His Majesty has already gained very considerable Advantages for his People, and is still employed in concerting Schemes, and forming Treaties, for retrieving and enlarging our Privileges in the World of Commerce.

I shall only in this Paper take Notice of the Treaty concluded at *Madrid* on the 14th of *December* last, 1715; and, by comparing it with that concluded at *Utrecht* on the 9th of *December*, 1713, shew several Particulars in which the Treaty made with his present Majesty is more advantageous to *Great Britain*, than that which was made in the last Reign; after this general Observation, that it is equally surprizing how so bad a Treaty came to be made at the End of a glorious and successful War; and how so good a One has been obtained in the Beginning of a Reign disturbed by such intestine[b] Commotions. But we may learn from hence, that the Wisdom of a Soveraign, and the Integrity of his Ministers, are more necessary for bringing about Works of such Consequence for the publick Good, than any Juncture of Time, or any other the most favourable Circumstance.[4]

[b] by such intestine / by intestine *Fol.*

---

[3] In his opening speech to the 1716 Parliament the King emphasized the issue of trade and its improvement since his accession (*C.J.* xviii. 330).

[4] Here and in the next essay Addison is advertising the successful commercial agreements with foreign powers which the King and Whig ministers had negotiated. The Treaty of Madrid (14 Dec. 1715 N.S.) was especially important because it was the Hanoverian's first treaty with a nation which had not been an ally during the war and, since it was negotiated during the rebellion, it assumed that the Spanish government expected George I to remain on the British throne. The Treaty was also important because the Whigs obtained trade concessions which the Tories, in their eagerness to obtain the *Asiento* slave trade, had overlooked in negotiating the Treaty of Utrecht. The principal shortcomings of the 1713 Treaty were that the third article increased tariffs on British goods brought into Spain and the fifteenth article weakened the legal rights of British merchants in Spain by eliminating *Jueces Conservadores* (lawyers who represented their interests) everywhere except in the Canary Islands. The Treaty of 1715 reduced tariffs to the rates set by the 1667 Treaty of Madrid and re-established the *Jueces Conservadores.* The texts of the three treaties Addison refers to are published in *Complete Collection of Commercial Treaties*, ed. Lewis Hertslet, 1827, ii. 140–57, 204–19, 220–3. The articles of the Treaty of 1715 were published in the *St. James's Evening Post*, 27–9 Dec. 1715.

We must here premise, that by the Treaty concluded at *Madrid* in 1667, the Duties of Importation payable upon the Manufactures and Products of *Great Britain*, amounted upon the established Valuation in the *Spanish* Book of Rates, (after the Deduction of the Gratia's). In *Andalusia*, to $11\frac{1}{3}$ *per Cent.* In *Valentia*, to 5 *per Cent.*[c] and in *Catalonia* to about 7 *per Cent.* or less; and consequently upon the whole aforesaid Trade, those Duties could not exceed 10 *per Cent.* in a Medium.[5]

After this short Account of the State of our Trade with *Spain*, before the Treaty of *Utrecht* under the late Queen, we must observe, that by the explanatory Articles of this last mentioned Treaty, the Duties of Importation upon the Products and Manufactures of *Great Britain* were augmented in *Andalusia* to $27\frac{1}{5}$ *per Cent.* at a Medium.[6]

But by the late Treaty made with His present Majesty at *Madrid*, the said Duties are again reduced according to the aforesaid Treaty of 1667: And the Deduction of the Gratia's is established as an inviolable Law, whereas before the Gratia's of the Farmers particularly were altogether precarious, and depended entirely upon Courtesy.[7]

That the common Reader may understand the Nature of these Gratia's, he must know that when the King of *Spain* had laid higher Duties upon our *English* Goods, than what the Merchants were able or willing to comply with, he used to abate a certain Part, which Indulgence, or Abatement went under the Name of a Gratia. But when he had Farmed out these his Customs to several of his Subjects, the Farmers, in order to draw more Merchandise to their respective Ports, and thereby to increase their own particular Profits, used to make new Abatements, or Gratia's to the *British* Merchants, endeavouring sometimes to outvy one another in such Indulgences, and by that Means to get a greater Proportion of Custom into their own Hands.

But to proceed: The Duties on Exportation may be computed to be raised by the *Utrecht*-Treaty, near as much as the foresaid Duties of

[c] to 5 *per Cent.*/to $7\frac{5}{6}$ *per Cent.* *Fol.*

[5] The *gratias* were abatements in tariffs granted by the Spanish King or his tax collectors. The King's abatement was 25 per cent and the tax collectors' varied from place to place. The rates Addison cites are approximately the same as those cited in a report to the Commissioners of Trade made before the Treaty of 1713 (*Journal of the Commissioners for Trade and Plantations*, 1925, ii. 473).

[6] Andalusia was not a typical example. The average duties paid by British merchants rose about 7 per cent after the Treaty of 1713 (Tindal, p. 408).

[7] The fifth article of the Treaty of 1715 regulated the *gratias* (Hertslet, *Commercial Treaties* ii. 221).

Importation: Whereas, by the Treaty made with His present Majesty, they are reduced to their ancient Standard.[8]

Complaint having been made, that the *Spaniards* after the Suspension of Arms had taken several *New-England* and other *British* Ships gathering Salt at the Island of *Tertuga*, a very full and just Report concerning that Affair was laid before Her late Majesty, of which I shall give the Reader the following Extract:[9]

'Your Majesty's Subjects have, from the first Settlement of the Continent of *America*, had a free Access to this Island; and have without Interruptions, unless in Time of War, used to take what Salt they pleased there: And we have Proofs of that Usage for above 50 Years, as appears by Certificates of Persons who have been employed in that Trade.

'It doth not appear, upon the strictest Enquiry, that the *Spaniards* ever inhabited or settled on the said Island; nor is it probable they ever did, it being all either barren Rock, or dry Sand, and having no fresh Water or Provisions in it.

'We take Leave to lay before Your Majesty, the Consequence of Your Majesty's Subjects being prohibited to fetch Salt at *Tertuga*; which will in part appear from the Number of Ships using that Trade, being, as we are inform'd, one Year with another about 100 Sail.

'The Salt carried from thence to *New-England* is used chiefly for Curing of Fish, which is either *Cod, Scale-Fish*, or *Mackrel*: The former of which is the principal Branch of the Returns made from the Continent to *Great Britain* by Way of *Spain, Portugal*, and the *Straits*, for the Woollen and other Goods sent from this Kingdom thither. Besides which, the *Scale-Fish* and *Mackrel* are of such Consequence, that the Sugar Islands cannot subsist without them, their Negroes being chiefly supported by this Fish: So that if they were not supplied therewith from *New-England* (which they cannot be, if Your Majesty's Subjects are prohibited from getting Salt at *Tertuga*), they would not be able to carry on their Sugar-Works. This hath

[8] Because both treaties included reciprocal 'most favoured nation' agreements, the lowering of Spanish tariffs in 1715 resulted in some lower British tariffs also (Hertslet, *Commercial Treaties* ii. 205, 223). The new tariffs, however, covered goods which usually were not exported from Spain to Britain, so the reciprocity meant less profit for the Spanish than for the British.

[9] Addison is referring to the complaint registered with the Commissioners for Trade and Plantations on 25 Sept. 1713. Bolingbroke sent a letter to the Commissioners concerning a memorial from Jeremiah Dummer, agent for the Massachusetts Bay Colony, who complained about the loss of salt-gathering privileges on Tortuga, an island off the coast of Venezuela. Dummer appeared before the Commissioners in October and December 1713, and he presented letters and testimony from New England traders (*Journal* ii. 471–94 *passim*). As a Commissioner Addison would have had access to the records from which this memorial was drawn.

been confirmed to us by several considerable Planters concerned in those Parts.

'Upon the Whole, Your Majesty's Subjects having enjoyed an uninterrupted Usage of gathering Salt at *Tertuga* ever since the first Settlement of the Continent as aforesaid, we humbly submit to Your Majesty the Consequence of preserving that Usage and Right upon which the Trade of Your Majesty's Plantations so much depends.'

Notwithstanding that it appears from what is above-written,[d] that our Sugar-Islands were like to suffer considerably for want of Fish from *New-England*, no Care was taken to have this Matter remedied by the Explanatory Articles, which were posterior to the above mentioned Report.

However, in the third Article of the Treaty made with His present Majesty, this Business is fully settled to our Advantage.[10]

The *British* Merchants having had several Hardships put upon them at *Bilboa*, which occasioned the Decay of our Trade at that Place, the said Merchants did make and execute in the Year 1700, a Treaty of Privileges with the Magistrates and Inhabitants of St. *Ander*, very much to the Advantage of this Kingdom, in order to their removing and settling there: The Effect of which was prevented by the Death of King *Charles* the Second of *Spain*, and the War which soon after ensued. This Matter, it seems, was slighted or neglected by the Managers of the *Utrecht*-Treaty: For, by the 14th Article of that Treaty, there is only *a Liberty given to the* British *Subjects to settle and dwell at St.* Ander, *upon the Terms of the 9th and 30th Articles of the Treaty of* 1667, which are general. But no regard was had to the forementioned Treaty of Privileges in 1700; whereas by the Second Article of the Treaty now made with His present Majesty, the forementioned Treaty of Privileges with St. *Ander* is confirmed and ratified.[11]

Another considerable Advantage is, that the *French*, by the Treaty made with His present Majesty, are to pay the same Duties at the *Dry-Ports*, through which they pass by Land-Carriage, as we pay upon Importation

[d] above-written / aforesaid *Fol.*

[10] The inclusion of this article in the Treaty of 1715, the only point not directly pertaining to Anglo-Spanish trade, was important enough for George Bubb, the British envoy at Madrid, to complain to Secretary Stanhope, 'I am sure I have had as many Disputes about it, as if I had ask'd a Province of Spain' (P.R.O. State Papers 94/84, 15 Dec. 1715 N.S.).

[11] The magistrates of Santander signed a treaty with British merchants on 12 Sept. 1700 N.S. in which they made generous concessions to the merchants in order to attract trade away from Bilboa, the port from which about half of Spanish wool exports were sent (Hertslet, *Commercial Treaties* ii. 397–407; *Hispania Illustrata*, 1703, p. 108).

or Exportation by Sea:[12] Which was not provided for by the *Utrecht*-Treaty.

By the Cedula's annexed to the Treaty of 1667, the valuable Privilege of having Judge-Conservators (appointed to make a more speedy and less expensive Determination of all Controversies arising in Trade) was fully established. But by the 15th Article of *Utrecht*,[e] that Privilege was in effect given up. For it is therein only stipulated, *That in case any other Nation have that Privilege, we shall in like Manner enjoy it.* But by the 5th Article of the Treaty now made with his present Majesty it is stipulated, that *We shall enjoy all the Rights, Privileges, Franchises, Exemptions, and Immunities whatsoever, which we enjoyed by virtue of the Royal Cedula's or Ordinances by the Treaty of* 1667. So that hereby the Privilege of Judge-Conservators is again confirmed to us.[13]

As nothing but the Reputation of His Majesty in foreign Countries, and of His fixed Purposes to pursue the real Good of His Kingdoms, could bring about Treaties of this Nature: So it is impossible to reflect with Patience on the Folly and Ingratitude of those Men, who labour to disturb Him in the midst of these His royal Cares, and to misrepresent His generous Endeavours for the Good of His People.

Numb. XLII *Monday, May* 14, 1716.

O Fortunatos Mercatores!

Hor.

SEVERAL Authors have written on the Advantage of Trade in general; which is indeed so copious a Subject, that as it is impossible to exhaust it in a short Discourse, so it is very difficult to observe any thing New upon

[e] Article of *Utrecht* | Article of the Treaty of *Utrecht* *Fol.*

[12] Article 5 (Hertslet, *Commercial Treaties* ii. 223).

[13] 'The Office of this Judge-Conservator was to enforce the Execution of the Treaties between the two Crowns, to take Cognizance of all Causes in which *English* Merchants were Defendants, and to represent the same to the Council of *Madrid* for the Determination of that Court; to inhibit all other Judges or Officers that presumed to intermeddle in any of the said Causes; but above all to take care that no other Officers should at any time enter or search the Houses, or seize the Books of our said Merchants upon any Pretense whatsoever without his Conusance...' (*British Merchant*, 2–6 July 1714). The *cedulas* Addison mentions are reprinted in Hertslet, *Commercial Treaties* ii. 165–85.

Motto. Horace, *Satires*, I. i. 4: O happy traders!

it. I shall, therefore, only consider Trade in this Paper, as it is absolutely necessary and essential to the Safety, Strength, and Prosperity of our own Nation.

In the first Place, as we are an Island accommodated on all Sides with convenient Ports, and encompassed with navigable Seas, we should be inexcusable, if we did not make these Blessings of Providence and Advantages of Nature turn to their proper Account. The most celebrated Merchants in the World, and those who make the greatest Figure in Antiquity, were situated in the little Island of *Tyre*, which, by the prodigious Increase of its Wealth and Strength at Sea, did very much influence the most considerable Kingdoms and Empires on the neighbouring Continent, and gave birth to the *Carthaginians*, who afterwards exceeded all other Nations in Naval Power. The old *Tyre* was indeed seated on the Continent, from whence the Inhabitants, after having been besieged by the Great King of *Assyria* for the Space of thirteen Years, withdrew themselves and their Effects into the Island of *Tyre*;[2] where, by the Benefit of such a Situation, a Trading People were enabled to hold out for many Ages against the Attempts of their Enemies, and became the Merchants of the World.

Further; as an Island, we are accessible on every Side, and exposed to perpetual Invasions; against which it is impossible to fortify ourselves sufficiently without such a Power at Sea, as is not to be kept up, but by a People who flourish in Commerce. To which we must add, that our inland Towns being destitute of Fortifications, it is our indispensable Concern to preserve this our Naval Strength, which is as a general Bulwark to the *British* Nation.[3]

Besides; as an Island, it has not been thought agreeable to the true *British* Policy to make Acquisitions upon the Continent. In lieu, therefore, of such an Increase of Dominion, it is our Business to extend to the utmost our Trade and Navigation. By this Means we reap the Advantages of Conquest, without Violence or Injustice; we not only strengthen ourselves, but gain the Wealth of our Neighbours in an honest Way; and, without any Act of Hostility, lay the several Nations, of the World under a kind of Contribution.

Secondly, Trade is fitted to the Nature of our Country, as it abounds with a great Profusion of Commodities of its own Growth very convenient for other Countries, and is naturally destitute of many Things suited to the

[2] Nebuchadnezzar besieged Tyre from 586 to 573 B.C.

[3] Addison is repeating the popular Tory notion that Britain's navy was its 'Wooden walls' (see *F.* 22, n. 14).

Exigences, Ornaments and Pleasures of Life, which may be fetched from foreign Parts. But that which is more particularly to be remarked, our *British* Products are of such Kinds and Quantities, as can turn the Balance of Trade to our Advantage, and enable us to sell more to Foreigners than we have occasion to buy from them.

To this we must add, that by extending a well-regulated Trade, we are as great Gainers by the Commodities of many other Countries, as by those of our own Nation; and by supplying foreign Markets with the Growth[a] and Manufactures of the most distant Regions, we receive the same Profit from them, as if they were the Produce of our own Island.

Thirdly, We are not a little obliged to Trade, as it has been a great Means of civilizing our Nation, and banishing out of it all the Remains of its antient Barbarity. There are many bitter Sayings against Islanders in general, representing them as fierce, treacherous and inhospitable. Those who live on the Continent have such Opportunities of a frequent Intercourse with Men of different Religions and Languages, and who live under different Laws and Governments, that they become more kind, benevolent, and open-hearted to their Fellow-Creatures, than those who are the Inhabitants of an Island, that hath not such Conversations with the rest of the Species. *Cæsar*'s Observation upon our Fore-fathers is very much to our present Purpose; who remarks, That those of them who lived upon the Coast, or in Sea-Port Towns, were much more Civilized, than those who had their Dwellings in the Inland Country, by reason of frequent Communications with their Neighbours on the Continent.[4]

In the last Place. Trade is absolutely necessary for us, as our Country is very populous. It employs Multitudes of Hands both by Sea and Land, and furnishes the poorest of our Fellow-Subjects with the Opportunities of gaining an honest Livelihood. The Skilful or Industrious find their Account in it: And many, who have no fixed Property in the Soil of our Country, can make themselves Masters of as considerable Estates, as those who have the greatest Portions of the Land descending to them by Inheritance.[5]

If what has been often charged upon us by our Neighbours has any

[a] Growth / Growths *Fol.*

[4] *De Bello Gallico*, v. 14: Of all the Britons the inhabitants of Kent, an entirely maritime region, are by far the most civilized; their way of life differs only a little from Gallic custom.

[5] Addison is countering a common Tory complaint against those whom Swift called 'the Mony'd Interest', those traders, merchants, and bankers whose wealth was not in land and was therefore 'transient or imaginary' property. As a consequence, these people paid less tax than large property owners, could invest in tax-free annuities, profit from war expenses, and were able to divert their wealth into foreign banks or investments (*Prose Works* iii. 119, 169–70; vi. 59).

Truth in it, That we are prone to Sedition and delight in Change, there is no cure more proper for this Evil than Trade, which thus supplies Business to the Active, and Wealth to the Indigent. When Men are easy in their Circumstances, they are naturally Enemies to Innovations: And indeed we see in the Course of our *English* Histories, many of our popular Commotions have taken their Rise from the Decay of some Branch of Commerce, which created Discontents among Persons concerned in the Manufactures of the Kingdom. When Men are sower'd with Poverty, and unemploy'd, they easily give into any Prospect of Change which may better their Condition, and cannot make it much worse.

Since therefore it is manifest, that the promoting of our Trade and Commerce is necessary and essential to our Security and Strength, our Peace and Prosperity, it is our particular Happiness to see a Monarch on the Throne, who is sensible[b] of the true Interest of his Kingdoms, and applies himself with so much Success to the Advancement of our National Commerce.

The Reader may see, in my last Paper, the Advantages which His Majesty has gained for us in our *Spanish* Trade. In this I shall give a short Account of those procured for us from the *Austrian* Low-Countries, by Virtue of the 26th Article of the Barrier-Treaty made at *Antwerp* the 15th of *November* last.[6]

This Branch of our Trade was regulated by a *Tariff*, or Declaration of the Duties of Import and Export in the year 1670, which was superseded by another made in 1680, that continued till this last *Tariff* settled in 1715 with His present Majesty. As for the two former, those who are at the Pains of perusing them will find, the *Tariff* of 1670 laid higher Duties on several considerable Branches of our Trade, than that of 1680, but in many Particulars, was more favourable to us than the latter. Now, by the present *Tariff* of 1715, these Duties are fixed and regulated for the future by those which were most favourable in either of the former *Tariffs*: And all our

[b] is sensible / is so sensible *Fol.*

[6] Commercial agreements negotiated by Cadogan at Brussels on 6 Nov. 1715 N.S. were incorporated into the third Barrier Treaty which Addison refers to here. These agreements repaired disadvantages British merchants suffered as a result of the commercial agreements in the previous Barrier Treaty (1709). The 1709 treaty gave the Dutch a considerable advantage over the British for trading in the Austrian Netherlands, and these concessions became a vulnerable target in Whig foreign policy during Godolphin's ministry which the Tories attacked vigorously in the Commons during February and March 1712 (*C.J.* xvii. 92, 122). Swift brought the issue to the public in his *Remarks on the Barrier Treaty* (1712) where he claimed that the Dutch '*our good Friends and Allies* are wholly shutting us out from Trading in those Towns we have Conquered for them with so much Blood and Treasure' (*Prose Works* vi. 91–2).

Products and Manufactures (one only excepted, which I shall name by and by) settled upon rather an easier foot than ever.

Our Woollen Cloths, being the most profitable Branch of our Trade into these Countries, have by this means gained a very considerable Advantage. For the *Tariff* of 1680 having laid higher Duties upon the finer sorts, and lower Duties on ordinary Cloth, than what were settled in the *Tariff* of 1670, His Majesty has, by the present Treaty, reduced the Duties on the finer sorts to the *Tariff* of 1670 and confirmed the Duties on ordinary Cloth according to the *Tariff* of 1680. Insomuch that this present *Tariff* of 1715 considered, with relation to this valuable part of our Trade, reduces the Duties at least one sixth Part, supposing the Exportation of all sorts to be equal. But as there is always a much greater Exportation of the ordinary Cloth, than of the finer sorts, the Reduction of these Duties becomes still much more considerable.[7]

We must further[c] observe, that there had been several Innovations made to the Detriment of the *English* Merchant since the *Tariff* of 1680, all which Innovations are now entirely set aside upon every Species of Goods, except Butter; which is here particularly mentioned, because we cannot be too minute and circumstantial in Accounts of this nature. This Article however is moderated, and is rated in proportion to what has been, and is still to be, payed by the *Dutch.*[8]

As our Commerce with the *Netherlands* is thus settled to the Advantage of our *British* Merchants, so is it much to their Satisfaction: And if His Majesty, in the several succeeding Parts of his Reign (which we hope may be many Years prolonged) should advance our Commerce in the same Proportion as he has already done, we may expect to see it in a more flourishing Condition, than under any of His Royal Ancestors. He seems to place his Greatness in the Riches and Prosperity of his People; and what may we not hope from him in a Time of Quiet and Tranquillity? Since, during the late Distractions, he has done so much for the Advantage of our

[c] further / *Fol.*; farther *8vo, 12mo.*

---

[7] The schedule of duties for British woollens negotiated in 1715 is published in Charles Jenkinson's *Collection of Treaties* (1785), ii. 144–6. The terms of the agreement were as favourable as Addison claims, both for the British and the Dutch, but the economy of the Austrian Netherlands suffered considerably (J. P. de Mérode-Westerloo, *Mémoires*, Brussels, 1840, ii. 121).

[8] No reference to butter was published with the Treaty although the subject was discussed by the Commissioners for Trade and Plantations which advised the ministry (*Journal of the Commissioners for Trade and Plantations*, 1924, iii. 37, 119, 127, and *passim*). Addison's source for this information was probably the Commission's records.

Trade, when we could not reasonably expect he should have been able to do any thing.

Numb. XLIII *Friday, May* 18, 1716

Hoc fonte derivata clades
In patriam populumque fluxit.
Hor.

ONE would wonder how any Person endow'd with the ordinary Principles of Prudence and Humanity, should desire to be King of a Country, in which the Establish'd Religion is directly opposite to that which he himself professes. Were it possible for such a one to accomplish his Designs, his own Reason must tell him, there could not be a more uneasy Prince, nor a more unhappy People. But how it can enter into the Wishes of any private Persons to be the Subjects of a Man, whose Faith obliges him to use the most effectual means for extirpating their Religion, is altogether incomprehensible, but upon the Supposition that whatever Principles they seem to adhere to, their Interest, Ambition, or Revenge, is much more active and predominant in their Minds, than the Love of their Country, or of its National Worship.

I have never heard of any one particular Benefit, which either the *Pretender* himself, or the Favourers of his Cause, could promise to the *British* Nation from the Success of his Pretensions; though the Evils which would arise from it, are numberless and evident. These Men content themselves with one general Assertion, which often appears in their Writings, and in their Discourse; That the Kingdom will never be Quiet till He is upon the Throne. If by this Position is meant, that those will never be quiet who would endeavour to place him there, it may possibly have some Truth in it; though we hope even these will be reduced to their Obedience by the Care of their Safety, if not by the Sense of their Duty. But on the other side, how ineffectual would this strange Expedient be, for establishing the publick Quiet and Tranquillity, should it ever take place! for, by way of Argument, we may suppose Impossibilities. Would that Party of Men which comprehends the most wealthy, and the most valiant,

Motto. Horace, *Odes*, III. vi. 19–20: Drawn from this source, disaster's stream has overflowed the country and the People.

of the Kingdom, and which, were the Cause put to a Trial, would undoubtedly appear the most numerous (for I am far from thinking all those who are distinguished by the Name of *Tories*, to be Favourers of the *Pretender*), can we, I say, suppose these Men would live Quiet under a Reign which they have hitherto opposed, and from which they apprehend such a manifest Destruction to their Country?[2] Can we suppose our present Royal Family, who are[a] so powerful in foreign Dominions, so strong in their Relations and Alliances, and so universally supported by the Protestant Interest of *Europe*, would continue Quiet, and not make vigorous and repeated Attempts for the Recovery of their Right, should it ever be wrested out of their Hands? Can we imagine that our *British* Clergy would be quiet under a Prince, who is zealous for his Religion, and obliged by it to subvert those Doctrines, which it is their Duty to defend and propagate? Nay, would any of those Men themselves, who are the Champions of this desperate Cause, unless such of them as are professed Roman-Catholicks, or disposed to be so, live quiet under a Government, which at the best would make use of all indirect Methods in favour of a Religion, which is inconsistent with our Laws and Liberties, and would impose on us such a Yoke, as neither We nor our Fathers were able to bear? All the Quiet that could be expected from such a Reign, must be the Result of absolute Power on the one hand, and a despicable Slavery on the other: And I believe every reasonable Man will be of the *Roman* Historian's Opinion, That a disturbed Liberty is better than a quiet Servitude.[3]

There is not indeed a greater Absurdity than to imagine the Quiet of a Nation can arise from an Establishment, in which the King would be of one Communion, and the People of another; especially when the Religion of the Soveraign carries in it the utmost Malignity to that of the Subject. If any of our *English* Monarchs might have hop'd to Reign quietly under such Circumstances, it would have been King *Charles* II, who was receiv'd with all the Joy and Good-will that are natural to a People, newly rescu'd from a Tyranny which had long oppress'd them in several Shapes. But this Monarch was too wise to own himself a *Roman* Catholick, even in that Juncture of Time; or to imagine it practicable for an avow'd Popish Prince to govern a Protestant People. His Brother try'd the Experiment, and every one knows the Success of it.

[a] who are / which is *Fol.*

---

[2] Addison appears to be conceding that the Whigs were the minority party, since they would require Hanoverian Tories to become 'the most numerous' party of men in the kingdom.

[3] Sallust, *Fragmenta*, i. 26.

As Speculations are best supported by Facts, I shall add to these domestick Examples one or two parallel Instances out of the *Swedish* History, which may be sufficient to shew us, that a Scheme of Government is impracticable in which the Head does not agree with the Body, in that Point which is of the greatest Concern to reasonable Creatures. *Sweden* is the only Protestant Kingdom in *Europe* besides this of *Great Britain*, which has had the Misfortune to see Popish Princes upon the Throne; and we find that they behaved themselves as we did, and as it is natural for Men to do, upon the same Occasion. Their King *Sigismond* having, contrary to the Inclinations of his People, endeavour'd by several clandestine Methods, to promote the *Roman* Catholick Religion among his Subjects, and shown several Marks of Favour to their Priests and Jesuits, was, after a very short Reign, depos'd by the States of that Kingdom, being represented as one who could neither be held by Oaths nor Promises, and over-rul'd by the Influence of his Religion, which dispenses with the Violation of the most sacred Engagements that are opposite to its Interests. The States to shew farther their Apprehensions of Popery, and how incompatible they thought the Principles of the Church of *Rome* in a Sovereign were with those of the Reform'd Religion in his Subjects, agreed that his Son should succeed to the Throne, provided he were brought up a Protestant. This the Father seemingly comply'd with; but afterwards refusing to give him such an Education, the Son was likewise set aside, and for ever excluded from that Succession.[4] The famous Queen *Christina*, Daughter to the Great *Gustavus*, was so sensible of those Troubles which would accrue both to her self and her People, should she avow the *Roman* Catholick Religion while she was upon the Throne of *Sweden*, that she did not make an open Profession of that Faith, 'till she had resigned her Crown, and was actually upon her Journey to *Rome*.[5]

In short, if there be any political Maxim, which may be depended upon as sure and infallible, this is one; that it is impossible for a Nation to be happy, where a People of the Reform'd Religion are govern'd by a King

[4] Sigismund III (1566–1623) was crowned King of Sweden in 1594. In 1598 his Protestant uncle, Duke Charles, usurped the throne with assistance from other Protestant nobles. Sigismund's inability to gain support among his Protestant subjects was used as an example in criticisms of James II at the Convention Parliament (Grey's *Debates* ix. 16) and later in pamphlet attacks on the Pretender (*State Tracts*, 1705, i. 229–30).

[5] Christina was crowned Queen of Sweden in December 1644, abdicated the throne in July 1654, and was converted to Catholicism in the following year. Contemporaries assumed that her conversion was the principal motive for abdicating (Urbain Chevreau, *The Life of Christina, Queen of Sweden*, 1656, pp. 23–5). During the Exclusion debate in 1679 Sir Thomas Player reversed the sequence to argue, 'When Queen *Christina* of *Sweden* changed her Religion, she parted with her Crown' (Grey's *Debates* vii. 240).

that is a Papist. Were he indeed only a nominal *Roman* Catholick, there might be a possibility of Peace and Quiet under such a Reign; but if he is sincere in the Principles of his Church, he must treat Heretical Subjects as that Church directs him, and knows very well, that he ceases to be Religious, when he ceases to be a Persecutor.

Numb. XLIV *Monday, May* 21, 1716

Multaque præterea variarum monstra ferarum
Centauri in foribus stabulant, Scyllæque biformes,
Et centum-geminus Briareus, ac bellua Lernæ
Horrendum stridens, flammisque armata Chimæra,
Gorgones, Harpyiæque, & forma tricorporis umbræ.
Corripit hic subita trepidus formidine ferrum
Æneas, strictamque aciem venientibus offert.
Et, ni docta comes tenues sine corpore vitas
Admoneat volitare cava sub imagine formæ,
Irruat, & frustra ferro diverberet umbras.

Virg.

As I was last Friday taking a Walk in the Park, I saw a County Gentleman at the side of *Rosamond's* Pond,[2] pulling a Handful of Oats out of his Pocket, and with a great deal of Pleasure gathering the Ducks about him. Upon my coming up to him, who should it be but my Friend the Fox-hunter, whom I gave some Account of in my 22d Paper! I immediately joined him, and partook of his Diversion, till he had not an Oat left in his

Motto. Virgil, *Aeneid*, vi. 285–94:

Of various Forms unnumber'd Specters more;
Centaurs, and double Shapes, besiege the Door:
Before the Passage horrid *Hydra* stands,
And *Briareus* with all his hundred Hands:
Gorgons, *Geryon* with his triple Frame;
And vain *Chimaera* vomits empty Flame.
The chief unsheath'd his shining Steel, prepar'd,
Tho seiz'd with sudden Fear, to force the Guard.
Off'ring his brandish'd Weapon at their Face;
Had not the Sibyl stop'd his eager Pace,
And told him what those empty Fantomes were;
Forms without Bodies, and impassive Air.

(trans. DRYDEN)

[2] In St. James's Park.

Pocket. We then made the Tour of the Park together, when, after having entertained me with the Description of a Decoy-Pond that lay near his Seat in the Country, and of a Meeting-House that was going to be re-built in a neighbouring Market-Town, he gave me an Account of some very odd Adventures which he had met with that Morning; and which I shall lay together in a short and faithful History, as well as my Memory will give me Leave.

My Friend, who has a natural Aversion to *London*, would never have come up, had not he been subpæna'd to it, as he told me, in order to give his Testimony for one of the Rebels, whom he knew to be a very fair Sports man.[3] Having travelled all Night to avoid the Inconveniencies of Dust and Heat, he arrived with his Guide, a little after Break of Day, at *Charing Cross*; where, to his great Surprize, he saw a Running Footman carried in a Chair, followed by a Water-man in the same kind of Vehicle. He was wondering at the Extravagance of their Masters that furnished them with such Dresses and Accommodations, when on a sudden he beheld a Chimney-Sweeper, convey'd after the same manner, with three Footmen running before him. During his Progress through the *Strand*, he met with several other Figures no less wonderful and surprizing. Seeing a great many in rich Morning-Gowns, he was amazed to find that Persons of Quality were up so early: And was no less astonished to see many Lawyers in their Bar-Gowns, when he knew by his Almanack the Term was ended. As he was extremely puzzled and confounded in himself what all this should mean, a Hackney-Coach chancing to pass by him, Four *Batts*[4] popp'd out their Heads all at once, which very much frighted both him and his Horse. My Friend, who always takes Care to cure his Horse of such starting Fits, spurred him up to the very side of the Coach, to the no small Diversion of the *Batts*; who, seeing him with his long Whip, Horse-hair Perriwig, Jockey Belt, and Coat without Sleeves, fancied him to be one of the Masqueraders on Horseback, and received him with a loud Peal of Laughter.[5] His Mind being full of idle Stories which are spread up and

[3] By the provisions of an Act passed on 6 Mar. 1716, some rebel prisoners from Lancashire were tried in Westminster and Southwark. Between 7 and 18 May fifteen rebels were tried, and others were arraigned (*Pol. State* xi. 521–54).

[4] In his edition of Addison's *Works* Bishop Richard Hurd explains that Batts were 'a sort of *maskers*', so called because they were night revellers. The *O.E.D.* does not include such a definition however.

[5] On the previous Thursday night (17 May) 'his Excellancy Count de Volkra, his Imperial Majesty's Minister at this Court, made a splendid Entertainment, together with a Ball and Masquerade at Somerset-House, in honour of the young Arch-Duke, his Imperial Majesty's first son, lately born. At which was present his Majesty, the prince in a rich suit of Masquerade, and the Princess, who danc'd two French Dances . . . and it was not over till 4 in the Morning, at which Time their Royal Highnesses departed, his Majesty having gone two hours before.

down the Nation by the Disaffected, he immediately concluded that all the Persons he saw in these strange Habits were Foreigners, and conceived a great Indignation against them, for pretending to laugh at an *English* Country Gentleman. But he soon recovered out of his Errour, by hearing the Voices of several of them, and particularly of a Shepherdess quarrelling with her Coach-man and threatning to break his Bones in very intelligible *English*, though with a masculine Tone. His Astonishment still increased upon him, to see a continued Procession of Harlequins, Scaramouches, Punchinello's and a thousand other merry Dresses, by which People of Quality distinguish their Wit from that of the Vulgar.

Being now advanced as far as *Somerset-House*, and observing it to be the great Hive whence this Swarm of Chimeras issued forth from Time to Time, my Friend took his Station among a Cluster of Mob, who were making themselves merry with their Betters. The first that came out was a very venerable Matron, with a Nose and Chin that were within a very little of touching one another. My Friend, at the first View fancying her to be an old Woman of Quality, out of his good breeding put off his Hat to her, when the Person pulling off her Masque, to his great Surprize appear'd a Smock faced young Fellow. His Attention was soon taken off from this Object, and turned to another that had very hollow Eyes and a wrinkled Face, which flourished in all the Bloom of Fifteen. The Whiteness of the Lilly was blended in it with the Blush of the Rose. He mistook it for a very whimsical kind of Masque; but upon a nearer View he found that she held her Vizard in her Hand, and that what he saw was only her natural Countenance, touched up with the usual Improvements of an aged Coquette.

The next who[a] shew'd her self was a Female Quaker, so very pretty that he could not forbear licking his Lips, and saying to the Mob about him, *'Tis ten thousand Pities she is not a Church-Woman.* The Quaker was followed by half a dozen Nuns, who filed off one after another up *Catharine-street*, to their respective Convents in *Drury-lane.*

The 'Squire observing the Preciseness of their Dress, began now to imagine after all, that this was a Nest of Sectaries; for he had often heard that the Town was full of them. He was confirmed in this Opinion upon seeing a Conjurer, whom he guess'd to be the Holder-forth. However, to satisfie himself he asked a Porter, who stood next him, What Religion these

[a] who/that *Fol.*

None enter'd without Tickets, the Motto of which was, Exhilarat Orbem' (*London Post*, 12–19 May).

People were of? The Porter reply'd, *They are of no Religion; 'tis a Masquerade.* Upon that, says my Friend, I began to smoak that they were a Parcel of Mummers; and being himself one of the Quorum in his own County, could not but wonder that none of the *Middlesex* Justices took Care to lay some of them by the Heels. He was the more provoked in the Spirit of Magistracy, upon discovering two very unseemly Objects: The first was a Judge, who rapp'd out a great Oath at his Footman; and the other a big-belly'd Woman, who upon taking a Leap into the Coach miscarry'd of a Cushion. What still gave him greater Offence was a drunken Bishop, who reeled from one side of the Court to the other, and was very sweet upon an *Indian* Queen. But his Worship, in the midst of his Austerity, was mollify'd at the Sight of a very lovely Milk-maid, whom he began to regard with an Eye of Mercy, and conceived a particular Affection for her, 'till he found, to his great Amazement, that the Standers by suspected her to be a Dutchess.

I must not conclude this Narrative without mentioning one Disaster which happened to my Friend on this Occasion. Having for his better Convenience dismounted, and mixed among the Crowd, he found upon his Arrival at the Inn, that he had lost his Purse and his Almanack. And though 'tis no Wonder such a Trick should be played him by some of the curious Spectators, he cannot beat it out of his Head, but that it was a Cardinal who picked his Pocket, and that this Cardinal was a Presbyterian in disguise.

Numb. XLV — *Friday, May* 25, 1716

Nimium Risus pretium est si Probitatis impendio constat.
Quintil.

I HAVE lately read, with much Pleasure, the Essays upon several Subjects published by Sir *Richard Blackmore*; and though I agree with him in many of his excellent Observations, I cannot but take that reasonable Freedom, which he himself makes use of, with regard to other Writers, to dissent from him in some few particulars.[2] In his Reflections upon Works of Wit

Motto. Quintilian, *Institutio Oratoria*, VI. iii. 35: Laughter costs too much if it is tallied with a loss of honesty.

[2] Sir Richard Blackmore (1655–1729), Court physician and author, published his *Essays upon Several Subjects* in March 1716 (*Post Man*, 8–10 Mar.). His 'Essay on Wit' and this *Freeholder* essay have been published by the Augustan Reprint Society (ser. 1, no. 1).

and Humour, he observes how unequal they are to combat Vice and Folly; and seems to think, that the finest Raillery and Satyr, though directed by these generous Views, never reclaimed one vicious Man, or made one Fool depart from his Folly.[3]

This is a Position very hard to be contradicted, because no Author knows the Number or Names of his Converts. As for the *Tatlers* and *Spectators* in particular, which are obliged to this ingenious and useful Author for the Character he has given of them,[4] they were so generally dispersed in single Sheets, and have since been printed in so great Numbers, that it is to be hoped they have made some Proselytes to the Interests, if not to the Practice, of Wisdom and Virtue, among such a Multitude of Readers.

I need not remind this learned Gentleman, that *Socrates*, who was the greatest Propagator of Morality in the heathen World,[a] and a Martyr for the Unity of the Godhead, was so famous for the Exercise of this Talent among the politest People of Antiquity, that he gained the Name of (ὁ Ἔιρων) *the Drole*.[5]

There are very good Effects which visibly arose from the above-mentioned Performances and others of the like Nature; as, in the first Place, They diverted Raillery from improper Objects, and gave a new Turn to Ridicule, which for many Years had been exerted on Persons and Things of a sacred and serious Nature. They endeavoured to make Mirth Instructive, and if they failed in this great End, they must be allowed at least to have made it Innocent. If Wit and Humour begin again to relapse into their former Licentiousness, they can never hope for Approbation from those who know that Raillery is Useless when it has no Moral under it, and Pernicious when it attacks any thing that is either unblameable or praise-worthy. To this we may add, what has been commonly observed, that it is not difficult to be merry on the side of Vice, as serious Objects are the most capable of Ridicule; as the Party, which naturally favour such a

[a] in the heathen World/among the Heathens *Fol.*

[3] 'Let the famous Author of the *Tatlers* and *Spectators* declare his Experience, who, if Wit could have made Men wiser, must certainly have succeeded; that Gentleman says, in one of his Discourses, *I have many Readers, but few Converts*; I believe he might have said none: for it is my Opinion, that all his fine Raillery and Satire, tho admirable in their kind, never reclaim'd one vicious Man, or made one Fool depart from his Folly' *Essays*, p. xlviii.

[4] Blackmore praised the *Tatler* and *Spectator* for 'the just and generous Sentiments, the fertile Invention, the Variety of Subjects, the surprizing Turns of Wit ... the genteel Satire' but concluded that 'it must chiefly be owing to the great Depravity of Manners ... that such worthy Performances have produc'd no better Effects' *Essays*, p. 203.

[5] Aristotle, *Nichomachean Ethics*, IV. vii. 14.

Mirth, is the most numerous; and as there are the most standing Jests, and Patterns for Imitation in this kind of Writing.

In the next Place: Such Productions of Wit and Humour, as have a Tendency to expose Vice and Folly, furnish useful Diversions to all kinds of Readers. The good, or prudent Man may, by these Means, be diverted, without Prejudice to his Discretion, or Morality. Raillery, under such Regulations, unbends the Mind from serious Studies and severer Contemplations, without throwing it off from its proper Byass. It carries on the same Design that is promoted by Authors of a graver Turn, and only does it in another manner. It also awakens Reflection in those who are the most Indifferent in the Cause of Virtue or Knowledge, by setting before them the Absurdity of such Practices as are generally unobserved, by Reason of their being Common or Fashionable: Nay, it sometimes catches the Dissolute and Abandoned before they are aware of it; who are often betrayed to laugh at themselves, and upon Reflection find, that they are merry at their own Expence. I might further[b] take Notice, that by Entertainments of this Kind, a Man may be cheerful in Solitude, and not be forced to seek for Company every Time he has a Mind to be merry.

The last Advantage I shall mention from Compositions of this Nature, when thus restrained, is, that they shew Wisdom and Virtue are far from being inconsistent with Politeness and good Humour. They make Morality appear amiable to People of gay Dispositions, and refute the common Objection against Religion, which represents it as only fit for gloomy and melancholy Tempers. It was the Motto of a Bishop, very eminent for his Piety and good Works in King *Charles* the Second's Reign, *Inservi Deo & Lætare, Serve God and be chearful.*[6] Those therefore who supply the World with such Entertainments of Mirth as are instructive, or at least harmless, may be thought to deserve well of Mankind; to which I shall only add, that they retrieve the Honour of polite Learning, and answer those sowr Enthusiasts who affect to stigmatize the finest and most elegant Authors, both ancient and modern, (which they have never read,) as dangerous to Religion, and destructive of all sound and saving Knowledge.

Our Nation are such Lovers of Mirth and Humour, that it is impossible for detached Papers, which come out on stated Days, either to have a general Run, or long Continuance, if they are not diversify'd, and enlivened from Time to Time, with Subjects and Thoughts, accommodated to this

[b] further / *Fol.*; farther *8vo, 12mo.*

---

[6] Person unidentified. Mottos were not part of formal heraldry in the seventeenth century, and anyone could choose or change a motto at whim.

Taste, which so prevails among our Countrymen. No Periodical Author who always maintains his Gravity, and does not sometimes sacrifice to the Graces, must expect to keep in vogue for any considerable Time. Political Speculations in particular, however Just and Important, are of so dry and austere a Nature, that they will not go down with the Publick without frequent Seasonings of this Kind. The Work may be well performed, but will never take, if it is not set off with proper Scenes and Decorations. A mere Politician is but a dull Companion, and, if he is always wise, is in great Danger of being tiresome or ridiculous.

Besides, Papers of Entertainment are necessary to increase the Number of Readers, especially among those of different Notions and Principles; who, by this Means, may be betray'd to give you a fair Hearing, and to know what you have to say for your self. I might likewise observe, that in all political Writings there is something that grates upon the Mind of the most candid Reader, in Opinions which are not conformable to his own Way of thinking; and that the Harshness of Reasoning is not a little softened and smoothed by the Infusions of Mirth and Pleasantry.

Political Speculations do likewise furnish us with several Objects that may very innocently be ridiculed, and which are regarded as such by Men of Sense in all Parties; of this Kind are the Passions of our States-women, and the Reasonings of[c] our Fox-hunters.

A Writer who makes Fame the chief End of his Endeavours, and would be more desirous of pleasing than of improving his Readers, might find an inexhaustible Fund of Mirth in Politicks. Scandal and Satyr are never-failing Gratifications to the Publick. Detraction and Obloquy are received with as much Eagerness as Wit and Humour. Should a Writer single out particular Persons, or point his Raillery at any Order of Men, who by their Profession ought to be exempt from it; should he slander the Innocent, or satyrize the Miserable; or should he, even on the proper Subjects of Derision, give the full Play to his Mirth, without regard to Decency and good Manners: he might be sure of pleasing a great Part of his Readers, but must be a very ill Man, if by such a Proceeding he could please himself.

[c] Passions of our States-women, and the Reasonings of/Reasonings of our States-women in general, and of many of *Fol.*

Numb. XLVI *Monday, May* 28, 1716.

— — — *Male nominatis*
Parcite verbis.
Hic dies, vere mihi festus, atras
Eximet curas; ego per tumultum
Nec mori per vim metuam, tenente
Cæsare terras.
Hor.

THE usual Salutation to a Man upon his Birth-day among the ancient *Romans* was *Multos & fœlices*; in which they wished him many happy Returns of it. When *Augustus* celebrated the Secular Year, which was[a] kept but once in a Century, and received the Congratulations of his People on that Account, an eminent Court-Wit saluted him in the Birth-day Form (*Multos & fœlices*) which is recorded as a beautiful Turn of Compliment, expressing a Desire that he might enjoy a happy Life of many Hundreds of Years.[2] This Salutation cannot be taxed with Flattery, since it was directed to a Prince, of whom it is said by a great Historian, *It had been happy for* Rome *if he had never been born, or if he had never died.*[3] Had he never been born, *Rome* would, in all Probability, have recovered its former Liberty: Had he never died, it would have been more happy under his Government, than it could have been in the Possession of its ancient Freedom.

It is our good Fortune that our Sovereign, whose Nativity is celebrated on this Day, gives us a Prospect, which the *Romans* wanted under the Reign of their *Augustus*, of his being succeeded by an Heir, both to his Virtues and his Dominions. In the mean Time it happens very luckily, for the Establishment of a new Race of Kings upon the *British* Throne, that

[a] Year, which was / Games, which were *Fol.*

Motto. Horace, *Odes*, III. xiv. 11–16: Refrain from inauspicious words. This day for me will be truly festive and will take away dark cares. Neither civil strife nor violent death shall I fear while Caesar reigns.

[2] Addison may be thinking of a similar remark made to Claudius at the Secular Games in A.D. 47 and reported by Suetonius (*De Vita Caesarum*, Vitellius, ii. 5). Augustus celebrated the Secular Games in 17 B.C.

[3] Francis Bacon wrote, 'It was said of Augustus, and afterwards the like was said of Septimius Severus, both which did infinite mischief in their beginnings, and infinite good towards their ends; *That they should either have never been born or never died*' (*Works* vii. 139).

the first of this Royal Line has all those high Qualifications which are necessary to fix the Crown upon his own Head, and to transmit it to his Posterity. We may indeed observe, that every Series of Kings who have kept up the Succession in their respective Families, in spite of all Pretensions and Oppositions formed against them, has been headed by Princes famous for Valour and Wisdom. I need only mention the Names of *William the Conqueror*, *Henry* II, *Henry* IV, *Edward* IV, and *Henry* VII. As for King *James* I, the Founder of the *Stuart* Race, had he been as well turned for the Camp, as the Cabinet, and not confined all his Views to the Peace and Tranquillity of his own Reign, his Son had not been involved in such fatal Troubles and Confusions.

Were an honest *Briton* to wish for a Sovereign, who in the present Situation of Affairs would be most capable of advancing our national Happiness, what could he desire more than a Prince mature in Wisdom and Experience, renowned for his Valour and Resolution, successful and fortunate in his Undertakings, zealous for the Reformed Religion, related or allied to all the most considerable Protestant Powers of *Europe*, and blest with a numerous Issue! A Failure in any one of these Particulars has been the cause of infinite Calamities to the *British* Nation; but when they all thus happily concur in the same Person, they are as much as can be suggested, even by our Wishes, for making us a happy People, so far as the Qualifications of a Monarch can contribute to it.

I shall not attempt a Character of His present Majesty, having already given an imperfect Sketch of it in my second Paper; but shall chuse rather to observe that cruel Treatment which this excellent Prince has met with from the Tongues and Pens of some of his disaffected Subjects. The Baseness, Ingratitude and Injustice of which Practice will appear to us, if we consider,

First, That it reflects highly upon the good Sense of the *British* Nation, who do not know how to set a just Value upon a Prince, whose Virtues have gained him the universal Esteem of foreign Countries. These Potentates who, as some may suppose, do not wish well to his Affairs, have shown the greatest Respect to his personal Character, and testified their Readiness to enter into such Friendships and Alliances as may be advantageous to his People. The Northern Kings solicite him with Impatience to come among them, as the only Person capable of settling the several Claims and Pretensions which have produced such unspeakable Calamities in that Part of the World.[4] Two of the most remote and formidable Powers of *Europe*

[4] In February the *Post Man* reported from The Hague that 'his Czarish Majesty was ready to enter into a Negotiation with Sweden, with the joint Mediation of the Emperor, Great (*continued*)

have entertained Thoughts of submitting their Disputes to his Arbitration.[5] Every one knows His ancient Subjects had such a long Experience of his Sovereign Virtues, that at his Departure from them his whole People were in Tears; which were answered with all those Sentiments of Humanity, that arise in the Heart of a good Prince on so moving an Occasion. What a Figure therefore must we make among Mankind, if we are the only People of *Europe* who derogate from his Merit, that may be made happy by it! and if in a Kingdom which is grown Glorious by the Reputation of such a Sovereign, there are Multitudes who would endeavour to lessen and undervalue it!

In the next Place; Such a Treatment from any part of our Fellow-Subjects, is by no means answerable to what we receive from His Majesty. His Love and Regard for our Constitution is so remarkable, that as we are told by those whose Office it is to lay the Business of the Nation before him, it is his first Question, upon any Matter of the least Doubt or Difficulty, Whether it be in every Point according to the Laws of the Land? He is easy of Access to those who desire it, and is so gracious in his Behaviour and Condescension on such Occasions, that none of his Subjects retire from his Presence without the greatest Idea of his Wisdom and Goodness. His continued Application to such publick Affairs as may conduce to the Benefit of his Kingdoms, diverts him from those Pleasures and Entertainments which may be indulged by Persons in a lower Station, and are pursued with Eagerness by Princes who have not the Care of the Publick so much at Heart. The least Return which we can make to such a Sovereign, is that Tribute which is always payed by honest Men, and is always acceptable to Great Minds, the Praise and Approbation that are due to a virtuous and noble Character. Common Decency forbids opprobrious Language, even to a bad Prince; and common Justice will exact from us, towards a good Prince, the same Benevolence and Humanity with which he treats his Subjects. Those who are influenced by Duty and Gratitude, will rise much higher in all the Expressions of Affection and Respect, and

Britain, and this Republick, or either of them, but could not admit the Mediation of France, because that Crown had all along acted in favour of his Enemies' (14–16 Feb.). On 25 May Admiral Norris led twenty-one British warships to the Baltic, ostensibly to guard British shipping which had been severely damaged there during the Northern War. Swedish sympathies for the Pretender and Hanoverian interest in expelling Sweden from German dominions were additional reasons for this show of force (J. Murray, *George I, the Baltic and the Whig Split of 1717*, 1969, pp. 234–6; Michael, p. 301).

[5] The *Flying Post* (24–6 May) reported that 'so renown'd is *his Majesty Abroad*, that even the *Grand Seignior* . . . had offer'd him a Mediation between *himself* and the *Venetians*, which he refused to the *Emperor of Germany*.' The Turk's refusal of the Emperor as mediator for the conflict which began in December 1714 was understandable since Austria was, by the terms of the Treaty of Carlovitz, an ally of Venice (Michael, pp. 359–70).

think they can never do too much to advance the Glory of a Sovereign, who takes so much Pains to advance their Happiness.

When we have a King who has gain'd the Reputation of the most unblemish'd Probity and Honour, and has been fam'd through the whole Course of his Life, for an inviolable Adherence to his Promises, we may acquiesce (after his many solemn Declarations) in all those Measures which it is impossible for us to judge rightly of, unless we were let into such Schemes of Council and Intelligence as produce them; and therefore we should rather turn our Thoughts upon the Reasonableness of his Proceedings, than busy our selves to form Objections against them. The Consideration of His Majesty's Character, should at all times suppress our Censure of his Conduct: And since we have never yet seen, or heard of any false Steps in his Behaviour, we ought in Justice to think, that he governs himself by his usual Rules of Wisdom and Honour, 'till we discover something to the contrary.

These Considerations ought to reconcile to His Majesty the Hearts and Tongues of all His People: But as for those who are the obstinate irreclaimable professed Enemies to our present Establishment, we must expect their Calumnies will not only continue, but rise against him, in proportion as he pursues such Measures as are likely to prove successful, and ought to recommend him to his People.

Numb. XLVII *Friday, June* 1, 1716

— — cessit furor, et rabida ora quierunt.

Virg.

I QUESTION not but most of my Readers will be very well pleased to hear, that my Friend the Fox-hunter, of whose Arrival in Town I gave Notice in my 44th Paper, is become a Convert to the present Establishment, and a good Subject to King *George*. The Motives to his Conversion shall be the Subject of this Paper, as they may be of use to other Persons who labour under those Prejudices and Prepossessions, which hung so long upon the Mind of my worthy Friend. These I had an Opportunity of learning the other Day, when, at his Request, we took a Ramble together to see the Curiosities of this great Town.

The first Circumstance, as he ingenuously confessed to me (while we were in the Coach together) which helped to disabuse him, was seeing

Motto. Virgil, *Aeneid*, vi. 102: The fury subsided and the raving lips fell silent.

King *Charles* I on Horseback at *Charing-Cross*;[2] for he was sure that Prince could never have kept his Seat there, had the Stories been true he had heard in the Country, that *Forty One* was come about again.

He owned to me that he looked with Horror on the new Church that is half built in the *Strand*, as taking it at first Sight to be half demolished: But upon enquiring of the Workmen, was agreeably surprized to find, that instead of pulling it down, they were building it up; and that Fifty more were raising in other Parts of the Town.[3]

To these I must add a Third Circumstance, which I find had no small Share in my Friend's Conversion. Since his coming to Town, he chanced to look into the Church of St. *Paul*, about the middle of Sermon-time, where having first examined the Dome, to see if it stood safe, (for the Screw Plot still ran in his Head)[4] he observed, that the Lord-Mayor, Aldermen, and City-Sword were a part of the Congregation. This Sight had the more Weight with him, as by good Luck not above two of that Venerable Body were fallen a sleep.

This Discourse held us till we came to the Tower; for our first Visit was to the Lions.[5] My Friend, who had a great deal of Talk with their Keeper, enquired very much after their Health, and whether none of them had fallen sick upon the taking of *Perth*, and the Flight of the *Pretender*? and hearing they were never better in their Lives, I found he was extreamly startled: For he had learned from his Cradle, that the Lions in the Tower were the best Judges of the Title of our *British* Kings, and always sympathized with our Sovereigns.

After having here satiated our Curiosity, we repaired to the *Monument*, where my Fellow-Traveller, being a well-breathed Man, mounted the Ascent with much Speed and Activity. I was forced to halt so often in this perpendicular March, that, upon my joining him on the Top of the Pillar, I found he had counted all the Steeples and Towers which were discernible

[2] 'As to the *Royal Statues*, that of King Charles I at *Charing-cross* is the best. This is a *Statue* in Brass on Horseback, raised on a high Pedestal of Marble, adorned with Trophies of War, and compassed about with Iron-Rails' (Guy Miege, *Present State of Great Britain*, 1707, pp. 111–12).

[3] St. Mary-le-Strand, designed by James Gibbs and located near Somerset House, was one of the new churches being built in London; its foundation had been laid in February 1714.

[4] The *London Gazette* published an advertisement on 9 Nov. 1710 which offered a pardon and reward of £50 to anyone involved in unscrewing iron bolts from the west roof of St. Paul's. The advertisement, signed by Henry St. John, prompted rumours of a thwarted attempt to assassinate Queen Anne by having the roof of the cathedral collapse during the Thanksgiving service which was to be held there on 7 Nov. The service was held elsewhere, and the investigation revealed only that workers' negligence was responsible for the missing bolts (Boyer, *Queen Anne*, p. 480).

[5] In *T.* 30 Isaac Bickerstaff described visiting the Tower lions and Bedlam as 'Entertainments for raw Minds'.

from this advantageous Situation; and was endeavouring to compute the Number of Acres they stood upon. We were both of us very well pleased with this Part of the Prospect; but I found he cast an evil Eye upon several Warehouses, and other Buildings, that looked like Barns, and seemed capable of receiving great Multitudes of People. His Heart misgave him that these were so many Meeting Houses, but upon communicating his Suspicions to me, I soon made him easy in this particular.

We then turned our Eyes upon the River, which gave me an Occasion to inspire him with some favourable Thoughts of Trade and Merchandize, that had fill'd the *Thames* with such Crowds of Ships, and covered the Shore with such Swarms of People.

We descended very leisurely, my Friend being careful to count the Steps, which he register'd in a blank Leaf of his new Almanack. Upon our coming to the bottom, observing an *English* Inscription upon the Basis, he read it over several Times, and told me he could scarce believe his own Eyes, for that he had often heard from an old Attorney, who lived near him in the Country, that it was the Presbyterians who burned down the City; whereas, says he, this Pillar positively affirms in so many Words, that *the burning of this ancient City was begun and carried on by the Treachery and Malice of the Popish Faction, in order to the carrying on their horrid Plot for extirpating the Protestant Religion, and old* English *Liberty, and introducing Popery and Slavery.* This Account, which he looked upon to be more authentick, than if it had been in print, I found, made a very great Impression upon him.

We now took Coach again, and made the best of our Way for the *Royal Exchange*, though I found that he did not much care to venture himself into the Throng of that Place; for he told me he had heard they were, generally speaking, Republicans, and was afraid of having his Pocket pick'd amongst them. But he soon conceived a better Opinion of them, when he spied the Statue of King *Charles* II, standing up in the middle of the Crowd, and most of the Kings in *Baker*'s Chronicle ranged in order over their Heads;[6] from whence he very justly concluded, that an Antimonarchical Assembly could never chuse such a Place to meet in once a Day.

To continue this good Disposition in my Friend, after a short stay at *Stocks Market*,[7] we drove away directly for the *Meuse*, where he was not a

[6] Miege described the Royal Exchange as a quadrangular structure with a paved court surrounded by arched galleries and niches in which statues of English monarchs were placed. In the centre of the court was a statue of Charles II in Roman dress (*Present State*, pp. 157–8).

[7] The market, originally named for the stocks set up there for punishing offenders, sold 'Herbs, Flowers, Roots and other Commodities of Gardiners' (W. Stow, *Remarks on London*, 1722, p. 76).

little edified with the Sight of those fine Sets of Horses which have been brought over from *Hanover*, and with the Care that is taken of them.[8] He made many good Remarks upon this Occasion, and was so pleased with his Company, that I had much ado to get him out of the Stable.

In our Progress to St. *James's* *Park* (for that was the end of our Journey) he took Notice, with great Satisfaction, that contrary to his Intelligence in the Country, the Shops were all open and full of Business; that the Soldiers walked civilly in the Streets; that Clergymen, instead of being affronted, had generally the Wall given them;[9] and that he had heard the Bells ring to Prayers from Morning to Night, in some Part of the Town or another.

As he was full of these honest Reflections, it happened very luckily for us that one of the King's Coaches passed by with the three young Princesses in it, whom by an accidental Stop we had an opportunity of surveying for some Time: my Friend was ravished with the Beauty, Innocence, and Sweetness, that appeared in all their Faces.[10] He declared several Times that they were the finest Children he had ever seen in all his Life; and assured me that before this Sight, if any one had told him it had been possible for three such pretty Children to have been born out of *England*, he should never have believed them.

We were now walking together in the Park, and as it is usual for Men who are naturally warm and heady, to be transported with the greatest Flush of Good-nature, when they are once sweetened; he owned to me very frankly, he[a] had been much imposed upon by those false Accounts of Things he had heard in the Country; and that he would make it his Business, upon his Return thither, to set his Neighbours right, and give them a more just Notion of the present State of Affairs.

What confirm'd my Friend in this excellent Temper of Mind, and gave him an inexpressible Satisfaction, was a Message he received, as we were walking together, from the Prisoner, for whom he had given his Testimony in his late Tryal. This Person having been condemned for his Part in the late Rebellion, sent him word that His Majesty had been graciously pleased to Reprieve him, with several of his Friends, in order, as it was thought, to give them their Lives;[11] and that he hoped before he went out of Town

[a] frankly, he / frankly, that he *Fol.*

[8] The King's stables were located near Charing Cross.

[9] In 1714 David Diverson wrote, 'I am weary of London, & will be in y[e] country as soon as I can, for I am assured by good friends y[t] a clergy man can scarce walk 2 paces in y[e] great streets but he will be spit-on' (Bodl. Ballard MS. 38, fo. 29–30, 23 Sept.).

[10] The Princesses were Anne, Amelia, and Caroline.

[11] When the courts trying rebel prisoners recessed for Whitsun holidays (20 May), 'the Prisoners condemn'd were all repriev'd except Mr. *Gascoigne*, and the Grand Jury of *Middlesex*

they should have a cheerful Meeting, and drink Health and Prosperity to King *George.*

Numb. XLVIII *Monday, June* 4, 1716

> *Tu tamen, si habes aliquam spem de Republica sive desperas; ea para, meditare, cogita, quæ esse in eo cive ac viro debent, qui sit Rempublicam afflictam et oppressam miseris temporibus ac perditis moribus in veterem dignitatem ac libertatem vindicaturus.* Cicer.

THE Condition of a Minister of State is only suited to Persons, who, out of a Love to their King and Country, desire rather to be useful to the Publick, than easy to themselves. When a Man is posted in such a Station, whatever his Behaviour may be, he is sure, beside the natural Fatigue and Trouble of it, to incur the Envy of some, and the Displeasure of others; as he will have many Rivals, whose Ambition he cannot satisfy, and many Dependents whose Wants he cannot provide for.[2] These are Misfortunes inseparable from such publick Employments in all Countries; but there are several others which hang upon this Condition of Life in our *British* Government, more than any other Sovereignty in *Europe*: As, in the first Place, There is no other Nation which is so equally divided into two opposite Parties, whom it is impossible to please at the same Time. Our Notions of the Publick Good, with relation both to our selves and

... was told there was no farther Business for them for the present, which gave Ground for a Report ... That the King was resolved no more Blood should be shed' (*Mercurius Politicus*, May 1716, p. 57). However, the trials were resumed after the holiday recess (*Pol. State* xi. 580).

Motto. Cicero, *Epistulae ad Familiares*, ii. 5: Whether you have any hope for the nation or not, nevertheless prepare, reflect upon, and consider those things which a citizen or hero should who would restore the nation, which has been ruined and oppressed by the miseries of the times and the degeneration of morals, to its old dignity and freedom.

[2] While the theme of this essay is the burdens of public office, a theme discussed by Cicero and Algernon Sidney, Addison's principal criticism is directed towards those Country Members of Parliament who opposed government ministers (*Paradoxa Stoicorum I; Discourses Concerning Government*, 1698, p. 70). One contemporary described such Country Members as persons 'who, if they are not employed, will always be of a different opinion from that which they would have held had they been in office, and though on the whole they may follow their party will hurt the Court in important debates by taking some popular pretext for differing from it or even by abstaining' (Worsley MS., *History of Parliament*, i. 23–4).

Foreigners, are of so different a Nature, that those Measures which are extolled by one half of the Kingdom, are naturally decryed by the other. Besides, that in a *British* Administration, many Acts of Government are absolutely necessary, in which one of the Parties must be favoured and obliged, in opposition to their Antagonists. So that the most perfect Administration, conducted by the most consummate Wisdom and Probity, must unavoidably produce Opposition, Enmity, and Defamation, from Multitudes who are made happy by it.

Further,[a] It is peculiarly observed of our Nation, That almost every Man in it is a Politician, and hath a Scheme of his own, which he thinks preferable to that of any other Person. Whether this may proceed from that Spirit of Liberty which reigns among us, or from those great Numbers of all Ranks and Conditions, who from Time to Time are concerned in the *British* Legislature, and by that means are let into the Business of the Nation, I shall not take upon me to determine. But for this reason it is certain, that a *British* Ministry must expect to meet with many Censurers, even in their own Party, and ought to be satisfied, if, allowing to every particular Man that his private Scheme is wisest, they can perswade him that next to his own Plan that of the Government is the most eligible.

Besides, we have a Set of very honest and well-meaning Gentlemen in *England*, not to be met with in other Countries, who take it for granted, they can never be in the wrong, so long as they oppose Ministers of State. Those whom they have admired through the whole Course of their Lives for their Honour and Integrity, though they still persist to act in their former Character, and change nothing but their Stations, appear to them in a disadvantageous Light, as soon as they are placed upon State-Eminences. Many of these Gentlemen have been used to think there is a kind of Slavery in concurring with the Measures of Great Men, and that the Good of the Country is inconsistent with the Inclinations of the Court: By the Strength of these Prejudices, they are apt to fancy a Man loses his Honesty, from the very Moment that it is made the most capable of being useful to the Publick; and will not consider that it is every whit as honourable to assist a good Minister, as to oppose a bad one.[3]

[a] Further / *Fol.*; Farther *8vo*, *12mo*.

---

[3] Opposition to ministers and placemen was the most distinguishing characteristic of Country Members. Here Addison includes Country Whigs in his criticism when he says the ministry 'must expect . . . many Censurers, even in their own Party.' The most recent Whig critics of Court policies were Members like Richard Steele who originally opposed the Septennial Act (see *F.* 25, n. 9). A better example was Nicholas Lechmere, 'a good lawyer, a quick and distinguished orator . . . but of a temper violent, proud and impracticable', who was

In the last Place, We may observe, that there are greater Numbers of Persons who solicit for Places, and perhaps are fit for them in our own Country, than in any other. To which we must add, That, by the Nature of our Constitution, it is in the Power of more particular Persons in this Kingdom, than in any other, to distress the Government when they are disobliged. A *British* Minister must therefore expect to see many of those Friends and Dependents fall off from him, whom he cannot gratify in their Demands upon him; since, to use the Phrase of a late Statesman, who knew very well how to form a Party, *The Pasture is not large enough.*

Upon the Whole: The Condition of a *British* Minister labours under so many Difficulties, that we find in almost every Reign since the Conquest, the chief Ministers have been New Men, or such as have raised themselves to the greatest Posts in the Government, from the State of private Gentlemen. Several of them neither rose from any conspicuous Family, nor left any behind them, being of that Class of eminent Persons whom Sir *Francis Bacon* speaks of, who, like Comets or blazing Stars, draw upon them the whole Attention of the Age in which they appear, though no Body knows whence they came, nor where they are lost. Persons of Hereditary Wealth and Title have not been over forward to engage in so great a Scene of Cares and Perplexities, nor to run all the Risques of so dangerous a Situation. Nay, many whose Greatness and Fortune were not made to their Hands, and had sufficient Qualifications and Opportunities of rising to these high Posts of Trust and Honour, have been deterred from such Pursuits by the Difficulties that attend them, and chose rather to be Easie than Powerful; or, if I may use the Expression; to be Carried in the Chariot than to Drive it.

As the Condition of a Minister of State in general is subject to many Burdens and Vexations; and as that of a *British* Minister in particular is involved in several Hazards and Difficulties peculiar to our own Country; so is this high Station exposed more than ordinary to such Inconveniencies in the present Juncture of Affairs; first, as it is the beginning of a new Establishment among us; and secondly, as this Establishment hath been disturbed by a dangerous Rebellion.

If we look back into our *English* History, we shall always find the first Monarch of a new Line received with the greatest Opposition, and reconciling to himself by Degrees the Duty and Affection of his People.

forced to resign his post as Solicitor-General in December 1715; during the spring he attempted to obstruct such measures as the Land Tax Act, the punishment of captured rebels, and the Septennial Act (T. Nash, *Worcestershire*, 1781, i. 561; Cowper Diary, 11 Feb. 1716; *Parl. Hist.* vii. 374).

The Government, on such Occasions, is always shaken before it settles. The Inveteracy of the Peoples Prejudices, and the Artifices of domestick Enemies, compelled their rulers to make use of all Means for reducing them to their Allegiance, which perhaps, after all, was brought about rather by Time than by Policy. When Commotions and Disturbances are of an extraordinary and unusual Nature, the Proceedings of the Government must be so too. The Remedy must be suited to the Evil, and I know no Juncture more difficult to a Minister of State, than such as requires uncommon Methods to be made use of; when at the same Time no others can be made use of, than what are prescribed by the known Laws of our Constitution. Several Measures may be absolutely necessary in such a Juncture, which may be represented as hard and severe, and would not be proper in a Time of publick Peace and Tranquility. In this Case *Virgil*'s Excuse, which he puts in the Mouth of a fictitious Sovereign upon a Complaint of this Nature, hath the utmost force of Reason and Justice on its Side.

Res dura et regni Novitas me talia cogunt.
The Difficulties I meet with in the beginning of my
Reign make such a Proceeding necessary.[4]

In the next Place: As this Establishment has been disturbed by a dangerous Rebellion, the Ministry has been involved in many additional and supernumerary Difficulties. It is a common Remark, that *English* Ministers never fare so well as in a Time of War with a foreign Power, which diverts the private Feuds and Animosities of the Nation, and turns their Efforts upon the common Enemy. As a foreign War is favourable to a Ministry, a Rebellion is no less dangerous; if it succeeds, they are the first Persons who must fall a Sacrifice to it; if it is defeated, they naturally become odious to all the secret Favourers and Abettors of it. Every Method they make use of for preventing or suppressing it, and for deterring others from the like Practices for the future, must be unacceptable and displeasing to the Friends, Relations and Accomplices of the Guilty. In Cases where it is thought necessary to make Examples, it is the Humour of the Multitude to forget the Crime and remember the Punishment. However, we have already seen, and still hope to see, so many Instances of Mercy in His Majesty's Government, that our chief Ministers have more to fear from the Murmures of their too violent Friends, than from the Reproaches of their Enemies.

[4] *Aeneid*, i. 563.

Numb. XLIX *Friday, June* 8, 1716

— — jam nunc sollennes ducere pompas
Ad delubra juvat — —

Virg.

YESTERDAY was set apart as a Day of Publick Thanksgiving for the late extraordinary Successes, which have secured to us every Thing that can be esteemed, and delivered us from every Thing that can be apprehended, by a Protestant and a Free People. I cannot but observe, upon this Occasion, the natural Tendency in such a National Devotion, to inspire Men with Sentiments of religious Gratitude, and to swell their Hearts with inward Transports of Joy and Exultation.[2]

When Instances of Divine Favour are great in themselves, when they are fresh upon the Memory, when they are peculiar to a certain Country, and commemorated by them in large and solemn Assemblies; a Man must be of a very cold or degenerate Temper, whose Heart doth not burn within him in the midst of that Praise and Adoration, which arises at the same Hour in all the different Parts of the Nation, and from the many Thousands of the People.

It is impossible to read of Extraordinary and National Acts of Worship, without being warmed with the Description, and feeling some Degree of that Divine Enthusiasm, which spreads[a] it self among a joyful and religious Multitude. A Part of that exuberant Devotion, with which the whole

[a] spreads / spread *Fol.*

Motto. Virgil, *Georgics*, iii. 22–3: At this moment it is pleasing to lead the solemn procession to the temple.

[2] The King had proclaimed 7 June a 'Day of Publick Thanksgiving' on 8 May 1716, charging the Bishops 'to compose a Form of Prayer suitable to this Occasion, to be used in all Churches' and generally commanding that the day 'be Religiously Observed by all Our Loving Subjects'; those who ignored the command were threatened with punishments (*Pol. State* xi. 630–1). The King and his family attended services at St. James's Chapel and heard a sermon on the abhorrence of rebellion by William Talbot, Bishop of Salisbury. Thomas Sherlock preached to the Commons, and Edmund Gibson, in his sermon to the Lords, emphasized the ingratitude of the Israelites after Moses had delivered them from their oppressors. The religious observation of the day did not exclude such public show as firing the Tower cannons, displaying the standards, and bell ringing. In the evening Sir Joseph Hodges gave a ball for some nobility and gentry; before it began 'Sir Joseph threw Handfuls of Silver among the numerous Crowd, who with one Voice . . . cry'd Long Live King *George*' (*St. James's Evening Post*, 7–9 June). Some Jacobites hoped that the ministry might support 'an Act for a General Pardon . . . that the Tories may rejoice with them,' but this never occurred (H.M.C. *Stuart MSS.* ii. 200).

Assembly raised and animated one another, catches a Reader at the greatest Distance of Time, and makes him a kind of Sharer in it.

Among all the publick Solemnities of this Nature, there is none in History so glorious as that under the Reign of King *Solomon*, at the Dedication of the Temple.[3] Besides the great Officers of State, and the Inhabitants of *Jerusalem*, all the Elders and Heads of Tribes, with the whole Body of the People ranged under them, from one End of the Kingdom to the other, were summoned to assist in it. We may guess at the prodigious Number of this Assembly from the Sacrifice on which they feasted, consisting of a Hundred and Twenty Thousand Sheep, and Two Hundred and Twenty Hecatombs of Oxen. When this vast Congregation was formed into a regular Procession to attend the Ark of the Covenant, the King marched at the Head of his People, with Hymns and Dances to the new Temple, which he had erected for its Reception. *Josephus* tells us, that the *Levites* sprinkled the Way as they passed with the Blood of Sacrifices, and burned the holy Incense in such Quantities as refreshed the whole Multitude with its Odours, and filled all the Region about them with Perfume.[4] When the Ark was deposited under the Wings of the Cherubims in the holy Place, the great Consort of Praise began. It was enlivened with a Hundred and Twenty Trumpets, assisted with a proportionable Number of other kinds of musical Instruments, and accompanied with innumerable Voices of all the Singers of *Israel*, who were instructed and set apart to religious Performances of this kind. As this mighty Chorus was extolling their Maker, and exciting the whole Nation thus assembled to the Praise of his never-ceasing Goodness and Mercy, the *Shekinah* descended. Or to tell it in the more emphatical Words of holy Writ, *It came to pass, as the Trumpets and Singers were as one, to make one sound to be heard in praising and thanking the Lord, and when they lift up their Voice with the Trumpets and Cymbals, and Instruments of Musick, and praised the Lcrd, saying,* For he is good, for his Mercy endureth for ever; *that then the House was filled with a Cloud.*[5] The Priests themselves, not able to bear the Awfulness of the

[3] Addison's choice of religious examples of public thanksgiving was prompted no doubt by the King's proclamation as well as his eagerness to advertise the Hanoverians' religious devotions. His choice of Solomon's dedication of the Temple is interesting for various reasons: both Solomon and David gained their thrones through divine intervention rather than primogeniture (Addison assumes in various essays that Providence brought George I to England); God commanded David to have a temple built in Jerusalem to preserve the sacred Ark of the Covenant (the preservation of Protestantism in England by the Hanoverian succession is another common theme in Addison's essays). John Asgill had also used the examples of Solomon and David to argue that George I was monarch by divine right (*The Title of Hannover to the Succession*, 1715, p. 20).

[4] Addison's sources are 2 Chr. 5–7 and Flavius Josephus, *Antiquities of the Jews*, viii. 99–125.

[5] 2 Chr. 5:13.

Appearance, retired into the Court of the Temple, where the King being placed upon a brazen Scaffold, so as to be seen by the whole Multitude, blessed the Congregation of *Israel*, and afterwards, spreading forth his Hands to Heaven, offered up that divine Prayer which is twice recorded at length in Scripture, and has always been looked upon as a Composition fit to have proceeded from the wisest of Men.[6] He had no sooner finished his Prayer, when a Flash of Fire fell from Heaven, and burned up the Sacrifice which lay ready upon the Altar. The People whose Hearts were gradually moved by the Solemnity of the whole Proceeding, having been exalted by the religious Strains of Musick, and aw'd by the Appearance of that Glory which filled the Temple, seeing now the miraculous Consumption of the Sacrifice, and observing the Piety of their King, who lay prostrate before his Maker, *bowed themselves with their Faces to the Ground upon the Pavement, and worshipped and praised the Lord, saying,* For he is good, for his Mercy endureth for ever.

What Happiness might not such a Kingdom promise to itself, where the same elevated Spirit of Religion ran through the Prince, the Priests, and the People! But I shall quit this Head, to observe that such an uncommon Fervour of Devotion shewed itself among our own Countrymen, and in the Persons of three Princes, who were the greatest Conquerours in our *English* History. These are *Edward* the Third, his Son the *Black Prince*, and *Henry* the Fifth. As for the first, we are told that, before the famous Battle of *Cressy*, he spent the greatest Part of the Night in Prayer, and in the Morning received the Sacrament with his Son, the chief of his Officers, and Nobility. The Night of that glorious Day was no less piously distinguished by the Orders, which he gave out to his Army, that they should forbear all insulting of their Enemies, or Boasting of their own Valour, and employ their Time in returning Thanks to the great Giver of the Victory. The *Black Prince*, before the Battle of *Poictiers*, declared, that his whole Confidence was in the Divine Assistance; and after that great Victory, behaved himself in all Particulars like a truly Christian Conquerour. Eight Days successively were appointed by his Father in *England*, for a Solemn and Publick Thanksgiving; and when the young Prince returned in Triumph with a King of *France* as his Prisoner, the Pomp of the Day consisted chiefly in extraordinary Processions, and Acts of Devotion. The Behaviour of the *Black Prince*, after a Battle in *Spain*, whereby he restored the King of *Castile* to his Dominions, was no less remarkable. When that King, transported with his Success, flung himself upon his Knees to thank him, the generous Prince ran to him, and, taking

[6] 1 Kgs. 8:23–53; 2 Chr. 6:14–42.

him by the Hand, told him it was not He who could lay any Claim to his Gratitude, but desired they might go to the Altar together, and jointly return their Thanks to whom only it was due.[7]

Henry V (who at the Beginning of his Reign, made a publick Prayer in the Presence of his Lords and Commons, that he might be Cut off by an immediate Death, if Providence foresaw he would not prove a just and good Governour, and promote the Welfare of his People) manifestly derived his Courage from his Piety, and was scrupulously careful not to ascribe the Success of it to himself. When he came within Sight of that prodigious Army, which offered him Battel at *Agincourt*, he ordered all his Cavalry to dismount, and with the rest of his Forces, to implore upon their Knees a Blessing on their Undertaking. In a noble Speech, which he made to his Soldiers immediately before the first Onset, he took Notice of a very remarkable Circumstance, namely, that this very Day of Battle was the Day appointed in his own Kingdom, to offer up publick Devotions for the Prosperity of his Arms, and therefore bid them not doubt of Victory, since at the same Time that they were fighting in the Field, all the People of *England* were lifting up their Hands to Heaven for their Success. Upon the Close of that memorable Day, in which the King had performed Wonders with his own Hand, he ordered the CXVth Psalm to be repeated in the midst of his victorious Army, and at the Words, *Not unto us, not unto us, but unto thy Name be the Praise*, He himself, with his whole Host, fell to the Earth upon their Faces, ascribing to Omnipotence the whole Glory of so great an Action.[8]

I shall conclude this Paper with a Reflection, which naturally rises out of it. As there is nothing more beautiful in the Sight of God and Man, than a King and his People concurring in such extraordinary Acts of Devotion, one cannot suppose a greater Contradiction and Absurdity in a Government, than where the King is of one Religion and the People of another. What Harmony or Correspondence can be expected between a Soveraign and his Subjects, when they cannot join together in the most joyful, the most solemn, and most laudable Action of reasonable Creatures; in a word, where the Prince considers his People as Hereticks, and the People look upon their Prince as an Idolater!

[7] Addison's source is Joshua Barnes, *Edward III* (1688), pp. 354, 503, 517, 526, 711.

[8] Addison's source is Laurence Echard, *History of England* (1707), i. 435, 445, 448.

Numb. L *Monday, June* 11, 1716

O quisquis volet impias
Cædes, et rabiem tollere civicam:
Si quæret pater urbium
Subscribi statuis; indomitam audeat
Refrœnare licentiam
Clarus postgenitis —— Hor.

WHEN *Mahomet* had for many Years endeavoured to propagate his Imposture among his Fellow-Citizens, and, instead of gaining any Number of Proselytes, found his Ambition frustrated, and his Notions ridiculed; he forbad his Followers the Use of Argument and Disputation in the advancing of his Doctrines, and to rely only upon the Scimeter for their Success. Christianity, he observed, had made its way by Reason and Miracles, but he profess'd it was his Design to save Men by the Sword. From that Time he began to knock down his Fellow-Citizens with a great deal of Zeal, to plunder Caravans with a most exemplary Sanctity, and to fill all *Arabia* with an unnatural Medly of Religion and Bloodshed.[2]

The Enemies of our happy Establishment seem at present to copy out the Piety of this seditious Prophet, and to have Recourse to his laudable Method of Club Law, when they find all other Means for enforcing the Absurdity of their Opinions to be ineffectual. It was usual among the antient *Romans*, for those, who had saved the Life of a Citizen, to be drest in an Oaken Garland; but among Us, This has been a Mark of such well-intentioned Persons, as would betray their Country, if they were able, and beat out the Brains of their Fellow-Subjects.[3] Nay, the Leaders of this poor unthinking Rabble, to shew their Wit, have lately decked them out of their

Motto. Horace, *Odes*, III. xxiv. 25–30: O whoever would be willing to stop ungodly slaughter and the frenzy of civil strife: if he would have 'Father of Cities' inscribed beneath his statues, let him dare to bridle unrestrained boldness; among later generations he will win fame.

[2] In 622 Mohammed told his followers in Medina that 'the way that his *Religion* was to be propagated ... was not by Disputing, but by Fighting; and therefore commands them all to ... slay with the Sword all those that would not embrace it' (Humphrey Prideaux, *Life of Mahomet*, 1716, p. 77).

[3] Oaken boughs were worn by Jacobite sympathizers on 29 May, the anniversary of Charles II's restoration (Tindal, p. 500; Cowper Diary, 29 May 1716). The boughs symbolized Stuart sympathies because Charles II hid in an oak tree when fleeing from England in 1651 (Clarendon, *History* v. 194–5).

Kitchen Gardens in a most insipid Pun, very well suited to the Capacity of such Followers.[4]

This manner of proceeding has had an Effect quite contrary to the Intention of these ingenious Demagogues: For by setting such an unfortunate Mark on their Followers, they have exposed them to innumerable Drubs and Contusions. They have been cudgell'd most unmercifully in every part of *London* and *Westminster*; and over all the Nation have avowed their Principles, to the unspeakable Damage of their Bones. In short, if we may believe our Accounts both from Town and Country, the Noses and Ears of the Party are very much diminished, since they have appeared under this unhappy Distinction.[5]

The Truth of it is, there is such an unaccountable Frenzy and Licentiousness spread through the basest of the People, of all Parties and Denominations, that if their Skirmishes did not proceed to too great an Extremity, one would not be sorry to see them bestowing so liberally, upon one another, a Chastisement which they so richly deserve. Their Thumps and Bruises might turn to account, and save the Government a great deal of Trouble, if they could beat each other into good Manners.

Were not Advice thrown away on such a thoughtless Rabble, one would recommend to their serious Consideration what is suspected, and indeed known, to be the Cause of these popular Tumults and Commotions in this great City. They are the *Popish* Missionaries, that lie concealed under many Disguises in all Quarters of the Town, who mix themselves in these dark Scuffles, and animate the Mob to such mutual Outrages and Insults.[6] This profligate Species of Modern Apostles divert themselves at the Expence of a Government, which is opposite to their Interests, and are pleased to see the broken Heads of Hereticks, in what Party soever they have listed themselves. Their Treatment of our silly Countrymen, puts me in mind of an Account in *Tavernier*'s Travels through the *East Indies*. This Author tells us, there is a great Wood in those Parts very plentifully stocked with Monkies; that a large High-way runs through the middle of this Wood; and that the Monkies who live on the one Side of this High-

[4] On 7 June 1716, the Day of Thanksgiving, some Jacobites in London wore badges made of rue and thyme (*Flying Post*, 9–12 June).

[5] On 7 June some Jacobites roamed London attacking small groups of loyalists who celebrated the day by wearing hats with orange cockades on which were written 'With Heart and Hand, by *George* we'll stand' (*Flying Post*, 9–12 June). A detailed description of the confrontations between Jacobites and loyalists on 29 May was published in the *Flying Post*, 29–31 May. Jacobite activities outside London are described in the *Flying Post*, 23–6 and 28–30 June.

[6] There is no evidence in the Jacobite correspondence from London at this time that any provocateurs were employed (H.M.C. *Stuart MSS.* ii. 227–9).

way, are declared Enemies to those who live on the other. When the Inhabitants of that Country have a Mind to give themselves a Diversion, it is usual for them to set these poor Animals together by the Ears; which they do after this Manner. They place several Pots of Rice in the middle of the Road, with great Heaps of Cudgels in the Neighbourhood of every Pot. The Monkies, on the first Discovery of these Provisions, descend from the Trees on either Side in prodigious Numbers, take up the Arms, with which their good Friends have furnished them, and belabour one another with a Storm of Thwacks, to the no small Mirth and Entertainment of the Beholders.[7] This Mob of Monkies act however so far reasonably in this Point, as the victorious Side of the Wood find, upon the Repulse of their Enemies, a considerable Booty on the Field of Battle; whereas our Party-Mobs are betrayed into the Fray without any Prospect of the Feast.

If our common People have not Virtue enough left among them to lay aside this wicked and unnatural Hatred which is crept into their Hearts against one another, nor Sense enough to resist the Artifice of those Incendiaries, who would animate them to the Destruction of their Country; it is high Time for the Government to exert itself in the repressing of such seditious Tumults and Commotions. If that extraordinary Lenity and Forbearance which has been hitherto shown on those Occasions, proves ineffectual to that Purpose, these Miscreants of the Community ought to be made sensible, that our Constitution is armed with a sufficient Force for the Reformation of such Disorders, and the Settlement of the publick Peace.[8]

There cannot be a greater Affront to Religion, than such a tumultuous Rising of the People, who distinguish the Times set apart for the National Devotions by the most brutal Scenes of Violence, Clamour, and Intemperance. The Day begins with a Thanksgiving, and ends in a Riot. Instead of the Voice of mutual Joy and Gladness, there is nothing heard in our Streets but opprobrious Language, Ribaldry and Contention.

As such a Practice is scandalous to our Religion, so is it no less a Reproach to our Government. We are become a By-word among the Nations for our ridiculous Feuds and Animosities, and fill all the publick

[7] 'Mr. Tavernier's Travels into India', *Compleat Collection of Voyages and Travels*, ed. John Harris, 1705, ii. 362.

[8] According to Jacobite sources, the government did so the day before this essay was published. Menzies wrote on 10 June, the Pretender's birthday, that horse and foot guards patrolled London and Westminister 'with their swords drawn'; Hugh Thomas wrote that thousands of soldiers guarded the city, that they killed three people and sent a multitude to prison (H.M.C. *Stuart MSS.* ii. 227–9). Dudley Ryder also describes the military patrols (*Diary*, 10 June).

Prints of *Europe* with the Accounts of our Mid-night Brawls and Confusions.

The Mischiefs arising to private Persons from these vile Disturbers of the Commonwealth are too many to be enumerated. The Great and Innocent are insulted by the Scum and Refuse of the People. Several poor Wretches, who have engaged in these Commotions, have been disabled, for their Lives, from doing any Good to their Families and Dependents; nay, several of them have fallen a Sacrifice to their own inexcusable Folly and Madness. Should the Government be wearied out of its present Patience and Forbearance, and forced to execute all those Powers with which it is invested for the Preservation of the publick Peace; what is to be expected by such Heaps of turbulent and seditious Men?

These and the like Considerations, though they may have no Influence on the headstrong unruly Multitude, ought to sink into the Minds of those who are their Abettors, and who, if they escape the Punishment here due to them, must very well know that these several Mischiefs will be one Day laid to their Charge.

Numb. LI *Friday, June* 15, 1716

Quod si in hoc erro, libenter erro; nec mihi hunc errorem, quo delector, dum vivo, extorqueri volo.

Cicer.

As there is nothing which more improves the Mind of Man, than the Reading of antient Authors, when it is done with Judgment and Discretion; so there is nothing which gives a more unlucky Turn to the Thoughts of a Reader, when he wants Discernment, and loves and admires the Characters and Actions of Men in a wrong Place. *Alexander* the Great was so inflamed with false Notions of Glory, by reading the Story of *Achilles* in the Iliad, that after having taken a Town, he ordered the Governor, who had made a gallant Defence, to be bound by the Feet to his Chariot, and afterwards dragg'd the brave Man round the City, because *Hector* had been treated in the same barbarous manner by his admired Hero.[2]

Motto. Cicero, *De Senectute*, 85: If I am wrong in this ... I err gladly and, while I am alive, I am unwilling to have this pleasing error wrested from me.

[2] After the siege of Gaza in 332 B.C., Alexander was angered by the arrogance of Betis, the governor of the conquered city, and ordered Betis 'to be dragg'd alive round the City, valuing

Many *Englishmen* have proved very pernicious to their own Country, by following blindly the Examples of Persons to be met with in *Greek* and *Roman* History, who acted in Conformity with their own Governments, after a quite different manner than they would have acted in a Constitution like that of ours. Such a Method of proceeding is as unreasonable in a Politician, as it would be in a Husbandman to make use of *Virgil*'s Precepts of Agriculture, in managing the Soil of our Country, that lies in a quite different Climate, and under the Influence of almost another Sun.

Our Regicides in the Commission of the most execrable Murder used to justify themselves from the Conduct of *Brutus*, not considering that *Cæsar*, from the Condition of a Fellow-Citizen, had risen by the most indirect Methods, and broken through all the Laws of the Community, to place himself at the Head of the Government, and enslave his Country.[3] On the other side, several of our *English* Readers, having observed that a Passive and Unlimited Obedience was payed to *Roman* Emperors, who were possessed of the whole Legislative, as well as Executive Power, have formerly endeavoured to inculcate the same kind of Obedience, where there is not the same kind of Authority.[4]

Instructions therefore to be learned from Histories of this Nature, are only such as arise from Particulars agreeable to all Communities, or from such as are common to our own Constitution, and to that of which we read. A tenacious Adherence to the Rights and Liberties transmitted from a wise and virtuous Ancestry, Publick Spirit and a Love of one's Country, Submission to established Laws, impartial Administrations of Justice, a strict Regard to National Faith, with several other Duties, which are the Supports and Ornaments of Government in general, cannot be too much admired among the States of *Greece* and *Rome*, nor too much imitated by our own Community.

But there is nothing more absurd, than for Men, who are conversant in these antient Authors, to contract such a Prejudice in favour of *Greeks* and *Romans*, as to fancy we are in the wrong in every Circumstance whereby

himself *for having imitated* Achilles (*from whom he descended*) *in punishing his Enemy*' (Quintus Curtius, *History of the Wars of Alexander*, trans. Digby, 1714, p. 214).

[3] Milton used the assassination of Caesar as a historical precedent for executing tyrants in his *Defence of the People of England* (1651), *Complete Prose Works*, ed. D. Wolfe *et al.*, New Haven, 1966, IV. i. 446.

[4] Robert Filmer used Rome as an example in his argument for obedience to unlimited monarchs: 'But, you will say, yet the Roman Empire grew all up under this kind of popular government, and became mistress of the world. It is not so. For Rome began her empire under Kings, and did perfect it under Emperors. . . . Her greatest exultation was under Trajan, as her longest peace had been under Augustus . . .' (*Patriarcha*, ed. P. Laslett, Oxford, 1949, p. 87).

we deviate from their Moral or Political Conduct.[5] Yet nothing hath been more usual, than for Men of warm heads to refine themselves up into this kind of State-Pedantry: Like the Country School-master, who, being used for many Years to admire *Jupiter, Mars, Bacchus* and *Apollo,* that appear with so much Advantage in Classick Authors, made an Attempt to revive the Worship of the Heathen Gods. In short, we find many worthy Gentlemen, whose Brains have been as much turned by this kind of Reading, as the grave Knight's of *Mancha* were by his unwearied Application to Books of Knight-Errantry.

To prevent such Mischiefs from arising out of Studies, which, when rightly conducted, may turn very much to our Advantage, I shall venture to assert, That in our Perusal of *Greek* or *Roman* Authors, it is impossible to find a Religious or Civil Constitution, any way comparable to that which we enjoy in our own Country. Had not our Religion been infinitely preferable to that of the antient Heathens, it would never have made its way through Paganism, with that amazing Progress and Activity. Its Victories were the Victories of Reason unassisted by the Force of Humane Power, and as gentle as the Triumphs of Light over Darkness. The sudden Reformation which it made among Mankind, and which was so justly and frequently boasted of by the first Apologists for Christianity, shew how infinitely preferable it was to any System of Religion, that prevailed in the World before its Appearance. This Pre-eminence of Christianity to any other general Religious Scheme, which preceded it, appears likewise from this Particular, that the most eminent and the most enlightened among the Pagan Philosophers disclaimed many of those superstitious Follies, which are condemned by Revealed Religion, and preached up several of those Doctrines which are some of the most essential Parts of it.

And here I cannot but take Notice of that strange Motive which is made use of in the History of Free-thinking, to incline us to depart from the Revealed Doctrines of Christianity, as adher'd to by the People of *Great Britain*, because *Socrates*, with several other eminent *Greeks*, and *Cicero*, with many other learned *Romans*, did in the like Manner depart from the religious Notions of their own Country-men.[6] Now this Author should

[5] Parallel histories were popular during the early eighteenth century and Addison uses the device in *F.* 12; Swift's *Contests and Dissentions in Athens and Rome* (*Prose Works* i. 191–236) and several *Examiner* essays (e.g. *Prose Works* iii. 27–9) are the best examples of the device in this period. A more recent use of parallel history, and one which Addison probably has in mind, was the *Freeholder Extraordinary* (6 Mar. 1716) which was printed in a format similar to Addison's periodical. It criticized George I's treatment of the rebel Lords by comparing it with the clemency Marcus Aurelius showed towards the accomplices of the rebellious Avidius Cassius.

[6] Addison is referring to Anthony Collins's *Discourse of Freethinking*, 1713, pp. 123–41.

have consider'd, that those very Points, in which these wise Men disagreed from the Bulk of the People, are Points in which they agreed with the received Doctrines of our Nation. Their Free-thinking consisted in asserting the Unity and Immateriality of the Godhead, the Immortality of the Soul, a State of future Rewards and Punishments, and the necessity of Virtue, exclusive of all silly and superstitious Practices, to procure the Happiness of this separate State. They were therefore only Free-thinkers, so far forth as they approach'd to the Doctrines of Christianity, that is, to those very Doctrines which this kind of Authors would perswade us, as Free-thinkers, to doubt the Truth of. Now I would appeal to any reasonable Person, whether these great Men should not have been proposed to our Imitation, rather as they embraced these divine Truths, than only upon the Account of their breaking loose from the common Notions of their Fellow Citizens. But this would disappoint the general Tendency of such Writings.

I shall only add under this Head, that as Christianity recovered the Law of Nature out of all those Errors and Corruptions, with which it was overgrown in the Times of Paganism, our National Religion has restored Christianity it self to that Purity and Simplicity in which it appeared, before it was gradually disguised and lost among the Vanities and Superstitions of the *Romish* Church.

That our Civil Constitution is preferable to any among the *Greeks* or *Romans*, may appear from this single Consideration; that the greatest Theorists in Matters of this Nature, among those very People, have given the Preference to such a Form of Government, as that which obtains in this Kingdom, above any other Form whatsoever. I shall mention *Aristotle, Polybius* and *Cicero*, that is, the greatest Philosopher, the most impartial Historian, and the most consummate Statesman of all Antiquity. These famous Authors give the Pre-eminence to a mixt Government consisting of three Branches, the Regal, the Noble, and the Popular.[7] It would be very easie to prove, not only the Reasonableness of this Position, but to shew, that there was never any Constitution among the *Greeks* or *Romans*, in which these three Branches were so well distinguished from each other, invested with such suitable Proportions of Power, and concurred together in the Legislature, that is, in the most sovereign Acts of Government, with such a necessary Consent and Harmony, as are to be met with in the Constitution of this Kingdom. But I have observed, in a foregoing Paper, how defective the *Roman* Commonwealth was in this Particular, when

[7] Aristotle, *Politics*, iii, iv; Polybius, *Histories*, vi. 2; Cicero, *De Republica*, i. 25–9.

compared with our own Form of Government,[8] and it will not be difficult for the Reader, upon singling out any other ancient State, to find how far it will suffer in the Parallel.

Numb. LII *Monday, June* 18, 1716

> *An tu Populum Romanum esse illum putas, qui constat ex iis, qui mercede conducuntur? qui impelluntur, ut vim afferant magistratibus? ut obsideant senatum? optent quotidie cædem, incendia, rapinas? quem tu tamen populum, nisi tabernis clausis, frequentare non poteras: Cui populo Duces Lentidios, Lollios, Sergios, præfeceras. O speciem, dignitatemque Populi Romani, quam Reges, quam Nationes exteræ, quam Gentes ultimæ pertimescunt; Multitudinem hominum ex servis conductis, ex facinorosis, ex egentibus congregatam!*
>
> Cicer.

THERE is in all Governments a certain Temper of Mind, natural to the Patriots and Lovers of their Constitution, which may be called State-Jealousy. It is this which makes them apprehensive of every Tendency in the People, or in any particular Member of the Community, to endanger or disturb that Form of Rule, which is established by the Laws and Customs of their Country. This Political Jealousy is absolutely requisite in some degree for the Preservation of a Government, and very reasonable in Persons, who are perswaded of the Excellency of their Constitution, and believe that they derive from it the most valuable Blessings of Society.

This publick spirited Passion is more strong and active under some Governments, than others. The Commonwealth of *Venice*, which hath subsisted by it for near fourteen hundred Years is so jealous of all its Members, that it keeps continual Spies upon their Actions; and if any one of them presume to censure the established Plan of that Republick, or

[8] *F.* 16.

Motto. Cicero, *Oratio de Domo Sua*, 89: Do you consider that group which is composed of persons bribed with money to be the Roman people? Those who are driven to use violence against magistrates and who besiege the Senate? Those who daily seek slaughter, conflagration and plundering? Without closing the taverns you would be unable to assemble such a mob as you have placed under leaders like Lentidius, Lollius, and Sergius. The image and dignity of the Roman people, which kings, foreign nations, and remote tribes consider formidable, here represented by a mob gathered together from the ranks of hired slaves, criminals, and the destitute!

touch upon any of its Fundamentals, he is brought before a Secret Council of State, tried in a most rigorous manner, and put to Death without Mercy. The usual way of proceeding with Persons, who discover themselves unsatisfied with the Title of their Sovereign in Despotick Governments, is to confine the Malecontent, if his Crimes are not Capital, to some Castle or Dungeon for Life. There is indeed no Constitution so tame and careless of their own Defence, where any Person dares to give the least Sign or Intimation of being a Traitour in his Heart. Our *English* History furnishes us with many Examples of great Severities during the Disputes between the Houses of *York* and *Lancaster*, inflicted on such Persons as shew'd their Disaffection to the Prince who was on the Throne. Every one knows, that a factious Inn-keeper, in the Reign of *Henry* the Seventh, was hanged, drawn and quartered, for a saucy Pun, which reflected, in a very dark and distant manner, upon the Title of that Prince to the Crown. I do not mention the Practice of other Governments, as what should be imitated in ours, which, God be thanked, affords us all the reasonable Liberty of Speech and Action, suited to a Free People; nor do I take Notice of this last Instance of Severity in our own Country, to justify such a Proceeding, but only to display the Mildness and Forbearance made use of under the Reign of His present Majesty. It may, however, turn to the Advantage of those, who have been instrumental in stirring up the late Tumults and Seditions among the People, to consider the Treatment which such a lawless, ungoverned Rabble would have met with in any other Country, and under any other Sovereign.

These Incendiaries have had the Art to work up, into the most unnatural Ferments, the most heavy and stupid part of the Community; and, if I may use a fine Saying of *Terence* upon another Occasion, *to convert Fools into Mad men.*[2] This Frenzy hath been raised among them to such a degree, that it has lately discovered it self in a Sedition which is without a Parallel. They have had the Fool-hardiness to set a Mark upon themselves on the *Pretender*'s Birthday, as the declared Friends to his Cause, and profest Enemies to their King and Country.[3] How fatal would such a Distinction,

[2] *Eunuchus*, 254.

[3] Jacobites wore white roses on 10 June, the Pretender's birthday, to display their sympathies for the abdicated Stuarts because the roses were 'the old Badge of the Family of York' (*Flying Post*, 9–12 June 1716). One Jacobite reported that troops patrolled London that day 'in jealousy and imagination of white roses' and that men were killed by them without being questioned (H.M.C. *Stuart MSS.* ii. 228). Dudley Ryder confirms that soldiers and constables were ordered to remove 'any white roses they saw... and many quarrels happened' (*Diary*, 10 June). Hugh Thomas described London as 'become like a garrison; 3000 foot guard it day and night ... Three people were killed ... for wearing white roses, and a multitude sent to prison' (H.M.C. *Stuart MSS.* ii. 227).

of which every one knew the Meaning, have proved in former Reigns, when many a Circumstance of less Significancy has been construed into an Overt Act of High Treason! This unexampled Piece of Insolence will appear under its just Aggravations, if we consider in the first place, that it was aimed personally at the King.

I do not remember among any of our popular Commotions, when Marks of this Nature have been in Fashion, that either Side were so void of common Sense, as to intimate by them an Aversion to their Sovereign. His Person was still held as sacred by both Parties. The Contention was not who should be the Monarch over them, but whose Scheme of Policy should take Place in his Administration. This was the Conduct of Whigs and Tories, under King *Charles* the Second's Reign, when Men hung out their Principles in different-coloured Ribbons.[4] Nay, in the Times of the great Rebellion the avowed Disaffection of the people always terminated in evil Counsellors. Such an open Outrage upon Majesty, such an Ostentation of Disloyalty, was reserved for that infamous Rabble of *Englishmen*, who may be justly looked upon as the Scandal of the present Age, and the most shameless and abandoned Race of Men that our Nation has yet produced.

In the next Place. It is very peculiar to this Mob of Malecontents, that they did not only distinguish themselves against their King, but against a King possessed of all the Power of the Nation, and one who had so very lately crushed all those of the same Principles, that had Bravery enough to avow them in the Field of Battle. When ever was there an Instance of a King who was not contemptible for his Weakness, and want of Power to resent, insulted by a few of his unarmed dastard Subjects?

It is plain from this single Consideration, that such a base ungenerous Race of Men could rely upon nothing for their Safety in this Affront to His Majesty, but the known Gentleness and Lenity of His Government. Instead of being deterred by knowing that he had in his Hands the Power to punish them, they were encouraged by knowing that he had not the Inclination. In a word, they presumed upon that Mercy, which in all their Conversations they endeavour to depreciate and misrepresent.

It is a very sensible Concern to every one, who has a true and unfeigned Respect for our National Religion, to hear these vile Miscreants calling themselves Sons of the Church of *England*, amidst these impious Tumults and Disorders; and joining in the Cry of High-Church at the same Time that they wear a Badge, which implies their Inclination to destroy the Reformed Religion. Their Concern for the Church always rises highest,

[4] Narcissus Luttrell reports that the Tories wore blue ribbons and the Whigs red ones (*Brief Relations*, 3 July 1687).

when they are acting in direct Opposition to its Doctrines. Our Streets are filled at the same Time with Zeal and Drunkenness, Riots and Religion. We must confess, if Noise and Clamour, Slander and Calumny, Treason and Perjury, were Articles of their Communion, there would be none living more punctual in the Performance of their Duties; but if a peaceable Behaviour, a love of Truth, and a Submission to Superiors, are the genuine Marks of our Profession, we ought to be very heartily ashamed of such a profligate Brotherhood. Or if we will still think, and own, these Men to be true Sons of the Church of *England*, I dare say there is no Church in *Europe* who will envy her the Glory of such Disciples. But[a] it is to be hoped we are not so fond of Party, as to look upon a Man, because he is a bad Christian, to be a good Church of *England* Man.

Numb. LIII *Friday, June* 22, 1716

—— *Bellua Centiceps.*

Hor.

THERE is scarce any Man in *England*, of what Denomination soever, that is not a Free-thinker in Politicks, and hath not some particular Notions of his own, by which he distinguishes himself from the rest of the Community. Our Island, which was formerly called a Nation of Saints, may now be called a Nation of Statesmen. Almost every[a] Age, Profession, and Sex among us, has its Favourite Set of Ministers, and Scheme of Government.

Our Children are initiated into Factions, before they know their Right Hand from their Left. They no sooner begin to speak, but Whig and Tory are the first Words they learn. They are taught in their Infancy to hate one half of the Nation; and contract all the Virulence and Passion of a Party, before they come to the Use of their Reason.[2]

As for our Nobility, they are Politicians by Birth; and though the Commons of the Nation delegate their Power in the Community to certain

[a] But / In a word, *Fol.* [a] Statesmen. Almost every / Statesmen. Every *Fol.*

Motto. Horace, *Odes*, II. xiii. 34: The hundred-headed monster.

[2] In 1710 Ann Clavering reported that 'Att Eaton the school is devided Whig and Tory. Jacky was one day ingaged fighting a Tory boy and Lady Oglethorp came and bid him give over . . . This, you may believe, fired Johny, who turned and gave her a severe blow on the face and bid her a Popish hussy' (*Clavering Correspondence*, p. 106).

Representatives, every one reserves to himself a private Jurisdiction, or Privilege, of censuring their Conduct, and rectifying the Legislature. There is scarce a Fresh-man in either University, who is not able to mend the Constitution in several Particulars. We see 'Squires and Yeomen coming up to Town every Day, so full of Politicks, that, to use the Thought of an ingenious Gentleman, we are frequently put in mind of *Roman* Dictators, who were called from the Plough. I have often heard of a Senior Alderman in *Buckinghamshire*, who, at all publick Meetings, grows drunk in Praise of Aristocracy, and is as often encountered by an old Justice of Peace who lives in the Neighbourhood, and will talk you from Morning till Night on the *Gothick* Balance.[3] Who hath not observed several Parish Clerks, that have ransacked *Hopkins* and *Sternhold* for Staves in favour of the Race of *Jacob*; after the Example of their Politick Predecessors in *Oliver*'s Days, who on every Sabbath were for binding Kings in Chains, and Nobles in Links of Iron! You can scarce see a Bench of Porters without two or three Casuists in it, that will settle you the Right of Princes, and state the Bounds of the Civil and Ecclesiastical Power, in the drinking of a Pot of Ale. What is more usual, than on a Rejoicing Night to meet with a drunken Cobler bawling out for the Church, and perhaps knocked down a little after, by an Enemy in his own Profession, who is a Lover of Moderation!

We have taken notice in former Papers of this Political Ferment being got into the Female Sex, and of the wild Work it makes among them. We have had a late most remarkable Instance of it in a Contest between a Sister of the *White Rose*, and a beautiful and loyal young Lady, who, to shew her Zeal for Revolution-Principles, had adorned her pretty Bosom with a *Sweet William*. The Rabble of the Sex have not been ashamed very lately to gather about Bonfires, and to scream out their Principles in the Publick Streets. In short, there is hardly a Female in this our Metropolis, who is not a competent Judge of our highest Controversies in Church and State. We have several Oister-women that hold the Unlawfulness of Episcopacy; and Cinder wenches that are great Sticklers for indefaisable Right.

Of all the Ways and Means by which this Political Humour hath been propagated among the People of *Great Britain*, I cannot single out any so prevalent and universal, as the late constant Application of the Press to the publishing of State-Matters. We hear of several that are newly erected in

[3] The balance of power between the monarch and Parliament. According to Swift, 'great councils were convoked . . . for time immemorial by the *Saxon* princes, who first introduced them into this island, from the same original with other *Gothick* forms of government in most parts of Europe' (*Prose Works* v. 35).

the Country, and set apart for this particular Use.[4] For, it seems, the People of *Exeter, Salisbury*, and other large Towns, are resolved to be as great Politicians as the Inhabitants of *London* and *Westminster*; and deal out such News of their own Printing, as is best suited to the Genius of the Market-People, and the Taste of the County.[5]

One cannot but be sorry, for the sake of these Places, that such a pernicious Machine is erected among them; for it is very well known here, that the making of the Politician is the breaking of the Tradesman. When a Citizen turns a *Machiavel*, he grows too cunning to mind his own Business; and I have heard a curious Observation, that the Woollen Manufacture has of late Years decayed in Proportion as the Paper Manufacture has encreased. Whether the one may not properly be looked upon as the Occasion of the other, I shall leave to the Judgment of Persons more profound in political Enquiries.

As our News-Writers record many Facts which, to use their own Phrase, *afford great Matter of Speculation*, their Readers speculate accordingly, and by their variety of Conjectures in a few Years, become consummate Statesmen; besides, as their Papers are filled with a different Party-Spirit, they naturally divide the People into different Sentiments, who generally consider rather the Principles, than the Truth of the News-Writer. This Humour prevails to such a Degree, that there are several Well-meaning Persons in the Nation, who have been so misled by their favourite Authors of this kind, that in the present Contention between the *Turk* and the Emperor, they are gone over insensibly from the Interests of Christianity, and become Well-wishers to the *Mahometan* Cause. In a word, almost every News-Writer has his Sect, which (considering the natural Genius of our Country-men to mix, vary or refine in Notions of State) furnishes

[4] The earliest extant provincial English newspaper is an issue of the *Bristol Post-Boy* (12 Aug. 1704), but evidence suggests that an earlier provincial newspaper, the *Norwich Post*, began publishing in September 1701. War news and domestic crises like the Sacheverell trial increased the appetite for news in the provinces, and by 1710 thirteen newspapers were publishing in nine provincial towns. The Stamp Act (1712), combined with the end of war news, resulted in seven provincial newspapers expiring. Eventually a loop-hole in that Act was found and concern about the Queen's successor helped three new papers to become established during 1714–15. The Jacobite uprising also bolstered provincial newspapers: between September 1715 and June 1716 the number of provincial newspapers increased about 50 per cent. The papers Addison describes as 'newly erected' would have included the *Bristol Weekly Mercury*, the *Exeter Mercury*, the *Exeter Protestant Mercury*, the *Salisbury Post-Man*, the *Nottingham Mercury*, and the *St. Edmund's Bury Post* (G. A. Cranfield, *The Development of the Provincial Newspaper 1700–1760*, Oxford, 1962, pp. 13–19; *A Hand-List of English Provincial Newspapers*, Cambridge Bibliographical Society, 1961, items 11, 35, 36, 106, 90, 18).

[5] Those provincial newspapers with Tory or Jacobite prejudices included the *Newcastle Courant*, the *Worcester Post-Man*, and the *Exeter Mercury* (Cranfield, *Development*, pp. 118–21).

every Man, by Degrees, with a particular System of Policy. For, however any one may concur in the general Scheme of his Party, it is still with certain Reserves and Deviations, and with a Salvo to his own private Judgment.

Among this innumerable Herd of Politicians, I cannot but take Notice of one Sett, who do not seem to play fair with the rest of the Fraternity, and make a very considerable Class of Men. These are such as we may call the *Afterwise*, who, when any Project fails, or hath not had its desired Effect, foresaw all the Inconveniencies that would arise from it, though they kept their Thoughts to themselves till they discovered the Issue. Nay, there is nothing more usual than for some of these wise Men, who applauded publick Measures before they were put in Execution, to condemn them upon their proving unsuccessful. The Dictators in Coffee-Houses are generally of this Rank, who often give shrewd Intimations that Things would have taken another Turn, had They been Members of the Cabinet.

How difficult must it be for any Form of Government to continue undisturbed, or any Ruler to live uncensured, where every one of the Community is thus qualified for modelling the Constitution, and is so good a Judge in Matters of State! A famous *French* Wit; to show how the Monarch of that Nation, who has no Partners in his Soveraignty, is better able to make his Way through all the Difficulties of Government, than an Emperor of *Germany*, who acts in concert with many inferior Fellow-Soveraigns; compares the first to a Serpent with many Tails to one Head; and the other to a Serpent with one Tail to many Heads; and puts the Question, which of them is like to glide with most Ease and Activity through a Thicket?[6] The same Comparison will hold in the Business of a Nation, conducted by a Ministry, or a whole Kingdom of Politicians.

[6] Source unidentified.

Numb. LIV *Monday, June* 25, 1716

— — Tu, nisi ventis
Debes ludibrium, cave.
Nuper solicitum quæ mihi tædium,
Nunc desiderium, curaque non levis.
Hor.

THE general Division of the *British* Nation is into Whigs and Tories, there being very few, if any, who stand Neuters in the Dispute, without ranging themselves under one of these Denominations. One would therefore be apt to think, that every Member of the Community, who embraces with Vehemence the Principles of either of these Parties, had thoroughly sifted and examined them, and was secretly convinced of their Preference to those of that Party which he rejects. And yet it is certain, that most of our Fellow-Subjects are guided in this particular, either by the Prejudice of Education, private Interest, personal Friendships, or a Deference to the Judgment of those, who, perhaps in their own Hearts disapprove the Opinions which they industriously spread among the Multitude. Nay, there is nothing more undoubtedly true, than that great Numbers of one side concur in reality with the Notions of those whom they oppose, were they able to explain their implicit Sentiments, and to tell their own Meaning.[2]

However, as it becomes every reasonable Man to examine those Principles by which he acts, I shall in this Paper select some Considerations, out of many, that might be insisted on, to shew the Preference of what is generally called the Whig-Scheme, to that which is espoused by the Tories.

This will appear in the First place, if we reflect upon the Tendency of their respective Principles, supposing them carried to their utmost Extremity. For if, in this Case, the worst Consequences of the one are more eligible, than the worst Consequences of the other, it is a plain Argument, that those Principles are the most eligible of the two, whose Effects are the least pernicious.[3] Now the Tendency of these two different Sets of

Motto. Horace, *Odes*, I. xiv. 15–18: Be careful that you do not become the plaything of the winds. Not long ago you were a source of worry and weariness for me, but now you are my beloved and deep concern.

[2] During Anne's reign this conciliatory theme was usually used when political leaders wanted support for coalition ministries or measures. See, e.g., *Faults on Both Sides* (1710) in which these same arguments are used (*Somers Tracts* xii. 702).

[3] Offering readers a choice between oversimplified and extreme party policies was a common rhetorical device in propaganda; see, e.g., *Chuse which you Please* (1710) and Atterbury's concluding remarks in *English Advice* (p. 30).

Principles, as they are charged upon each Party by its Antagonists, is as follows. The Tories tell us, that the Whig-Scheme would end in Presbyterianism and a Common-wealth. The Whigs tell us on the other side, that the Tory-Scheme would terminate in Popery and Arbitrary Government. Were these Reproaches mutually true; which would be most preferable to any Man of Common Sense, Presbyterianism and a Republican Form of Government, or Popery and Tyranny? Both Extremes are indeed dreadful, but not equally so; both to be regarded with the utmost Aversion by the Friends of our Constitution, and Lovers of our Country: But if one of them were inevitable, who would not rather chuse to live under a State of excessive Liberty, than of Slavery, and not prefer a Religion that differs from our own in the Circumstantials, before one that differs from it in the Essentials of Christianity!

Secondly, Let us look into the History of *England*, and see under which of these two Schemes the Nation hath enjoyed most Honour and Prosperity. If we observe the Reigns of Queen *Elizabeth* and King *James* I (which an impudent *Frenchman* calls the Reigns of King *Elizabeth* and Queen *James*)[4] we find the Whig Scheme took place under the first, and the Tory Scheme under the latter. The first, in whom the Whigs have always gloried, opposed and humbled the most powerful among the *Roman* Catholick Princes; raised and supported the *Dutch*; assisted the *French* Protestants; and made the Reformed Religion an Over-balance for Popery through all *Europe*. On the contrary, her Successor aggrandized the Catholick King; alienated himself from the *Dutch*; suffered the *French* Power to increase, till it was too late to remedy it; and abandoned the Interests of the King of *Bohemia*, Grand-father to His present Majesty, which might have spread the Reformed Religion through all *Germany*. I need not describe to the reader the different State of the Kingdom, as to its Reputation, Trade, and Wealth, under these two Reigns. We might after this compare the Figure in which these Kingdoms, and the whole Protestant Interest of *Europe*, were placed by the Conduct of King *Charles* the Second, and that of King *William*; and every one knows which of the Schemes prevailed in each of those Reigns. I shall not impute to any Tory Scheme the Administration of King *James* the Second, on Condition that they do not reproach the Whigs with the Usurpation of *Oliver*; as being satisfied that the Principles of those Governments are respectively disclaimed and abhorred by all the Men of Sense and Virtue in both Parties, as they now stand.[5] But we have

[4] Urbain Chevreau, *Chevræana* (Amsterdam, 1700) i. 74.

[5] In this survey of seventeenth-century history Addison purposely omits any reference to Charles I who was considered a Tory martyr (Bolingbroke, *Letter to Windham*, p. 282).

a fresh Instance which will be remembered with Grief by the present Age and all our Posterity, of the Influence both of Whig and Tory Principles in the late Reign. Was *England* ever so glorious in the Eyes of *Europe*, as in that Part of it when the first prevailed? Or was it ever more contemptible than when the last took Place?

I shall add, under this Head, the Preference of the Whig-Scheme, with regard to Foreigners. All the Protestant States of *Europe*, who may be considered as Neutral Judges between both Parties, and are Well-wishers to us in general, as to a Protestant People, rejoice upon the Success of a Whig-Scheme; whilst all of the Church of *Rome*, who contemn, hate and detest us as the great Bulwark of Heresy, are as much pleased when the opposite party triumphs in its Turn. And here let any impartial Man put this Question to his own Heart, whether that Party doth not act reasonably, who look upon the *Dutch* as their genuine Friends and Allies, considering that they are of the Reformed Religion, that they have assisted us in the greatest Times of Necessity, and that they can never entertain a Thought of reducing us under their Power. Or, on the other Hand, let him consider whether that Party acts with more Reason, who are the avowed Friends of a Nation, that are of the *Roman* Catholick Religion, that have cruelly persecuted our Brethren of the Reformation, that have made Attempts in all Ages to conquer this Island, and supported the Interest of that Prince, who abdicated the Throne, and had endeavoured to subvert our Civil and Religious Liberties.[6]

Thirdly, Let us compare these two Schemes from the Effects they produce among our selves within our own Island; and these we may consider, first with regard to the King, and secondly with regard to the People.

1st. With regard to the King. The Whigs have always professed and practised an Obedience which they conceive agreeable to the Constitution; whereas the Tories have concurr'd with the Whigs in their Practice, though they differ from them in their Professions; and have avowed a Principle of Passive Obedience to the Temptation, and afterwards to the Destruction, of those who have relied upon it. Nor must I here omit to take Notice of that firm and zealous Adherence which the Whig-Party have shown to the Protestant Succession, and to the Cause of His present Majesty. I have never heard of any in this Principle, who was either guilty or suspected of Measures to defeat this Establishment, or to overturn it, since it has taken effect. A Consideration, which, it is hoped, may put to

[6] As in *F.* 5 Addison ignores Britain's Catholic allies, Portugal and Austria.

silence those who upbraid the Whig-Schemes of Government, with an Inclination to a Common-wealth, or a Disaffection to Kings.

2dly. With regard to the People. Every one must own, that those Laws which have most conduced to the Ease and Happiness of the Subject, have always passed in those Parliaments, which their Enemies branded with the Name of Whig, and during the Time of a Whig-Ministry. And what is very remarkable, the Tories are now forced to have Recourse to those Laws for Shelter and Protection, by which they tacitly do Honour to the Whig-Scheme, and own it more accommodated to the Happiness of the People, than that which they espouse.[7]

I hope I need not qualify these Remarks with a Supposition which I have gone upon through the whole Course of my Papers, that I am far from considering a great Part of those who call themselves Tories, as Enemies to the present Establishment; and that by the Whigs I always mean those who are Friends to our Constitution, both in Church and State. As we may look upon these to be, in the main, true Lovers of their Religion and Country, they seem rather to be divided by accidental Friendships and Circumstances, than by any essential Distinction.

Numb. LV *Friday, June* 29, 1716

— — *cæstus artemque repono.*

Virg.

A RISING of Parliament being a kind of Cessation from Politicks, the *Freeholder* cannot let his Paper drop at a more proper Juncture. I would not be accessary to the continuing of our Political Ferment, when Occasions of Dispute are not administer'd to us by Matters depending before the Legislature; and when Debates without Doors naturally fall with those in the two Houses of Parliament. At the same Time, a *British* Free-holder would very ill discharge his Part, if he did not acknowledge, with becoming Duty and Gratitude, the Excellency and Seasonableness of those Laws, by which the Representatives of Men in his Rank have recover'd their Country in a great measure out of its Confusions, and provided for its future peace and Happiness, under the present Establishment. Their unanimous and regular Proceeding, under the Conduct of a Person who

[7] Addison is referring to habeas corpus which had been suspended in January (see *F.* 16). The suspension recently expired, and rebel prisoners who had not yet been indicted were using habeas corpus to obtain their release from prison (*Annals*, ii. 322).

Motto. Virgil, *Aeneid* v. 484: I lay down my gauntlets and my art.

fills their Chair with the most consummate Abilities, and hath justly gained the Esteem of all sides by the Impartiality of his Behaviour;[2] the absolute Necessity of some Acts which they have[a] Passed, and their Disinclination to extend them any longer, than that Necessity required; Their manifest Aversion to enter upon Schemes, which the Enemies of our Peace had insinuated to have been their Design;[3] together with that Temper so suitable to the Dignity of such an Assembly, at a Juncture when it might have been expected that very unusual Heats would have arisen in a House of Commons, so zealous for their King and Country;[4] will be sufficient to quiet those groundless Jealousies and Suspicions, which have been industriously propagated by the Ill wishers to our Constitution.

The Undertaking, which I am now laying down, was entered upon in the very Crisis of the late Rebellion, when it was the Duty of every *Briton* to contribute his utmost Assistance to the Government, in a manner suitable to his Station and Abilities. All Services, which had a Tendency to this End, had a Degree of Merit in them, in proportion as the Event of that Cause which they espoused was then doubtful. But at present they might be regarded, not as Duties of private Men to their endanger'd Country, but as Insults of the successful over their defeated Enemies.

Our Nation indeed continues to be agitated with Confusions and Tumults; but, God be thanked, these are only the impotent Remains of an unnatural Rebellion, and are no more than the After-tossings of a Sea when the Storm is laid. The Enemies of His present Majesty, instead of seeing him driven from his Throne, as they vainly hoped, find him in a Condition to visit his Dominions in *Germany*, without any Danger to himself or to the Publick; whilst his dutiful Subjects would be in no ordinary Concern upon this Occasion, had they not the Consolation to find themselves left under the Protection of a Prince who makes it his Ambition to copy out his Royal Father's Example; and who, by his Duty to His Majesty, and Affection to His People, is so well qualified to be the Guardian of the Realm.[5]

[a]which they have / which have *Fol.*

---

[2] Spencer Compton, elected Speaker of the House on 17 Mar. 1715, remained in that post until 1727 (*C.J.* xviii. 16–17).

[3] Atterbury claimed that the Whigs would need and use a large standing army 'to overcome . . . the Liberties of the People' (*English Advice*, p. 27).

[4] The lack of heated debates during the 1716 session had less to do with the calm temper of the House than with the absence of many of the Court's most outspoken critics (Percival Letterbook, 28 Jan. 1716).

[5] The King's intended visit to Germany caused some concern among Whigs like Townshend who wrote to Bernstorff that he thought the country still needed 'the invigorating influence of his majesty's presence'. However, Parliament supported the intended visit and (*continued*)

It would not be difficult to continue a Paper of this kind, if one were disposed to resume the same Subjects, and weary out the Reader with the same Thoughts in a different Phrase, or to ramble through the Cause of Whig and Tory, without any certain Aim or Method, in every particular Discourse. Such a Practice in Political Writers, is like that of some Preachers taken Notice of by Dr. *South*, who being prepared only upon two or three Points of Doctrine, run the same Round with their Audience, from one end of the Year to the other, and are always forced to tell them, by way of Preface, These[b] are Particulars of so great Importance, that they cannot be sufficiently *inculcated*.[6] To avoid this Method of Tautology, I have endeavoured to make every Paper a distinct Essay upon some particular Subject, without deviating into Points foreign to the Tenor of each Discourse. They are indeed most of them Essays upon Government, but with a View to the present Situation of Affairs in *Great Britain*; so that if they have the good Fortune to live longer than Works of this Nature generally do, future Readers may see, in them, the Complexion of the Times in which they were written. However, as there is no Employment so irksome, as that of transcribing out of one's self, next to that of transcribing out of others, I shall let drop the Work, since there do not occur to me any material Points arising from our present Situation, which I have not already touched upon.

As to the Reasonings in these several Papers, I must leave them to the Judgment of others. I have taken particular Care that they should be conformable to our Constitution, and free from that Mixture of Violence and Passion, which so often creeps into the Works of Political Writers. A good Cause doth not want any Bitterness to support it, as a bad one cannot subsist without it. It is indeed observable, that an Author is scurrilous in Proportion as he is dull; and seems rather to be in a Passion, because he cannot find out what to say for his own Opinion, than because he has discovered any pernicious Absurdities in that of his Antagonists. A Man, satirized by Writers of this Class, is like one burnt in the Hand with a cold Iron: There may be ignominious Terms and Words of Infamy in the Stamp, but they leave no Impression behind them.

[b] These / they *Fol.*

the clause in the Act of Settlement forbidding the monarch to leave the country without the consent of Parliament was repealed. As for the Prince of Wales, the King did not share Addison's enthusiasm: he named him Guardian of the Realm rather than Prince Regent. The Guardian of the Realm, an office which had not been used since the middle ages, had considerably more limited powers (Coxe, *Walpole* ii. 51–4; *C.J.* xviii. 467; Cowper Diary, 26–28 June 1716).

[6] Robert South criticized Puritan preachers this way in a sermon given at the University Church, Oxford, on 29 July 1660 (*Sermons*, 1715, iv. 23).

It would indeed have been an unpardonable Insolence for a Fellow-Subject to treat, in a vindictive and cruel Style, those Persons whom His Majesty has endeavoured to reduce to Obedience by *Gentle Methods*, which he has declared from the Throne to be *most agreeable to his Inclinations.*[7] May we not hope that all of this Kind, who have the least Sentiments of Honour or Gratitude, will be won over to their Duty by so many Instances of Royal Clemency, in the midst of so many repeated Provocations! May we not expect that *Cicero*'s Words to *Cæsar*, in which he speaks of those who were *Cæsar*'s Enemies, and of his Conduct towards them, may be applied to His Majesty; *Omnes enim qui fuerunt, aut suâ pertinaciâ vitam amiserunt, aut tuâ misericordiâ retinuerunt; ut aut nulli supersint de inimicis, aut qui superfuerunt, amicissimi sint. —— Quare gaude tuo isto tam excellenti bono, et fruere cùm fortunâ, et gloriâ, tum etiam naturâ, et moribus tuis. Ex quo quidem maximus est fructus, jucunditasque sapienti —— Nihil habet nec fortuna tua majus, quàm ut possis, nec natura tua melius, quàm ut velis quamplurimos conservare.*[8]

As for those Papers of a gayer Turn, which may be met with in this Collection, my Reader will, of himself, consider, how requisite they are to gain and keep up an Audience to Matters of this Nature; and will perhaps be the more Indulgent to them, if he observes, that they are none of them without a Moral, nor contain any Thing, but what is consistent with Decency and Good Manners.

It is obvious, that the Design of the whole Work, has been to free the People's Minds from those Prejudices conveyed into them by the Enemies to the present Establishment, against the King and Royal Family, by opening and explaining their real Characters; to set forth His Majesty's Proceedings, which have been very grossly mis-represented, in a fair and impartial Light; to shew the Reasonableness and Necessity of our opposing the Pretender to his Dominions, if we have any Regard to our Religion and Liberties: And, in a word, to incline the Minds of the People to the Desire and Enjoyment of their own Happiness. There is no Question, humanly speaking, but these great Ends will be brought about insensibly, as Men will grow weary of a fruitless Opposition; and be convinced, by Experience, of a Necessity to acquiesce under a Government which daily gathers

[7] The King's speech to Parliament, 26 June 1716 (*C.J.* xviii. 471).

[8] 'For all who were your enemies have either lost their lives by their own obstinacy or have saved them through your mercy, so that none are left who are your enemies, and those who were so are now your warmest friends . . . Therefore rejoice in your impressive goodness and enjoy the fortune and fame as well as the nature and character which are yours. From this indeed the philosopher derives a rich reward and pleasure' (*Oratio pro Marcello*, 21, 19). 'Your fate contains nothing greater than that you are capable, your nature contains nothing better than that you are willing to save as many people as possible' (*Oratio pro Ligario*, 38).

Strength, and is able to disappoint the utmost Efforts of its Enemies. In the mean while, I would recommend to our Malecontents, the Advice given by a great Moralist to his Friend upon another Occasion; that he would shew, it was in the Power of Wisdom to compose his Passions; and let that be the Work of Reason which would certainly be the Effect of Time.[9]

I shall only add, that if any Writer shall do this Paper so much Honour, as to inscribe the Title of it to others, which may be published upon the laying down of this Work; the whole Praise, or Dispraise, of such a Performance will belong to some other Author; this LVth being the last Paper that will come from the Hand of the *Free-holder*.[10]

[9] Cicero, *Disputationes Tusculanae*, iii. 58.

[10] Addison's concern about imitators was not unfounded: in January 1715 an imitation of the *Spectator* appeared and continued publishing until the following August (Smithers, *Addison*, p. 330); in December 1715 an imitation of the *St. James's Evening Post* was published which contained treasonable remarks (the 20–2 Dec. issue contains a disclaimer); in March 1716 the *Freeholder Extraordinary* was published (see *F.* 51, n. 5).

APPENDIX

The Raree-Show, or an Explication of the O——d A——c, for the Year 1716. *By* Jeremiah Van Husen, *a German Artist.*

1. Masters, behold that pretty little *Boy*,
Whom early Prayers for his Friends employ,
He, who is plac'd over against those *Scales,*
Is *James* the Third; *alias* the Prince of *Wales.*
For say whate're you will about that Youth,
Believe me, Sirs, this is the *naked* Truth.
2. That Figure there, which leers on Master's Face,
And points to *O——d*, Learn'd and Loyal Place!
Has puzzl'd much the wife to know if she,
His Cozen, Nurse, or else his Mother be.
But in this Search, I think they all have miss'd her,
Depend upon't, that's put there for his *Sister.*
3. That smiling Parson next, in Camisado,
Is one, about whom Men have made much ado;
Some call him '*Chev—el*, and some call him *Tr—p*:
But I can tell you (howe're that may hap)
Who those three Persons are which stand behind him.
4. The first is Doctor *Phipps.* Gentlemen mind him.
5. The next is,—or may my End be a Rope;
That little High-Church Rhimer, Poet *Po*——;
Or, that I may guess yet a little nigher,
Hang me, but it may happen to be *Pr*——.
6. The hindmost! You may know him by his Air,
It is the thirsty, dry Vice-Cha——llor.
See! How they all do promise, that the Rules,
7. Taught in *That* Theatre, and in *Those* Schools,
Shall tend to strengthen *His*, their Sov'reign's Right,
For which, as they have *studied*, so they'l fight.
    The *Right* and *Centre* past. The left beware on;
9. That first is *Ormond*; tho' some call him *Ar—n.*
See how he points! As tho'f that he would say,
This self same Loyal University,

10. Shall place This Crown (in *Alma Mater*'s Hand)
Upon that Infant's Head; if I command.
11. Dos'nt the Scale by Justice held, incline
Towards Him, to shew that he has Right Divine?
12. And what else means this circl'd Serpents Tail?
But that His Kingly Race shall never fail?
Thus *Ormond* spoke. But you must know they jest on,
This Prophecy; since *Wills* appear'd at *Preston*,
And curse in loudest Terms (since they've been crost here)
Their Bully *Butler*, and their Gen'ral *Forster*.

(*Flying Post*, 3–5 Jan. 1716)

INDEX

Index

KING ALFRED'S COLLEGE
LIBRARY